# Essentials of Development Economics

—

 Problems, programs, and data sets are available
at rebeltext.org/development.

# Essentials of Development Economics

Second Edition

J. Edward Taylor and
Travis J. Lybbert

UNIVERSITY OF CALIFORNIA PRESS

*To Peri, Sebastian, and Julian*

· · ·

*To Heather, Hannah, and Rockwell*

University of California Press, one of the most distinguished university presses in the United States, enriches lives around the world by advancing scholarship in the humanities, social sciences, and natural sciences. Its activities are supported by the UC Press Foundation and by philanthropic contributions from individuals and institutions. For more information, visit www.ucpress.edu.

University of California Press
Oakland, California

First edition published 2012 by Arc Light Books/RebelText, Berkeley, California. © 2012, 2013 by J. Edward Taylor. RebelText logo by Peri Fletcher.

REBELTEXT
www.rebeltext.org

Library of Congress Cataloging-in-Publication Data

Taylor, J. Edward, author.
    Essentials of development economics / J. Edward Taylor and Travis J. Lybbert. — Second edition.
        pages   cm
    Includes bibliographical references and index.
    ISBN 978-0-520-28316-9 (cloth) — ISBN 978-0-520-28317-6 (pbk.) — ISBN 978-0-520-95905-7 (ebook)
    1. Development economics.   2. Economic development.   3. Developing countries—Economic policy.   I. Lybbert, Travis J., author.   II. Title.
    HD75.T39   2015
    338.9—dc23                                                      2014044821

24   23   22   21   20   19   18   17   16   15
10   9   8   7   6   5   4   3   2   1

# Contents

# Sidebars

# Figures and Tables

## TABLES

# Preface

The RebelText alternative textbook project was launched at the Taylor dinner table one night in fall 2012. Ed had just told the campus bookstore to order up 125 copies of an undergraduate econometrics textbook at $150 a shot. (That's a gross of $18,750 just from one class.) Over dinner that night, Ed's twenty-year-old son, Sebastian, announced that he had spent $180 (of his parents' money) on a new edition calculus text required for his course. Sebastian's little brother, Julian, exclaimed, "That's obscene!" Sebastian responded, "You're right. Basic calculus hasn't changed in decades. You don't need new editions to learn calculus."

Before dinner was over, Ed's two kids had ambushed him and made him promise never, ever, to assign an expensive textbook to his students again.

"So, what do you want me to do then, write one?" Ed asked them.

"Exactly," they answered in unison.

"And get a good title for it," Ed's wife, Peri, added.

The first RebelText creation was *Essentials of Econometrics,* with Aaron Smith and Abbie Turiansky. That seemed like a big enough project, but then Ed was assigned to teach a 350-student undergraduate development economics course. Naturally, he felt he had to write a book for that one, too. Travis climbed on board. That's how *Essentials of Development Economics* became the second member of the RebelText line.

What's RebelText? It's a textbook series designed to be affordable, compact, and concisely written for a new generation that is more at ease "Googling" than wading through big textbooks. Being both more affordable and compact, it's easier to carry around. Write in it. Don't worry about keeping the pages clean or whether there will be a market for your edition later, because at this price there's no need to resell it after the class is through. RebelText will naturally evolve as needed to keep pace with the field, but there will never, ever, be a new edition just for profits' sake.

In 2014, RebelText and UC Press struck an alliance. This UC Press edition offers readers a more complete coverage of what we see as the essentials of development economics than the original print-on-demand edition, while keeping the book affordable and compact. Through our new partnership with UC Press, we hope to turn RebelText into a better and higher impact alternative textbook initiative in a world that we all believe is in desperate need of textbook reform.

There is particularly a need for a new undergraduate development economics textbook. The books out there seem more interested in summarizing a bunch of topics than in teaching people what they really need to know in order to do development economics. This book is different.

## WHO SHOULD USE THIS BOOK AND HOW

When we sat down to write *Essentials of Development Economics,* we wanted a compact book for an upper-division undergraduate development economics class. That is primarily what this is. The knowledge in this book should poise any undergraduate to engage in further study or to venture out into the real world with an appreciation for the essential concepts and tools of economic development. More than a textbook, this can be a helpful basic reference for any graduate student, researcher, or development practitioner.

There's a striking disconnect between development textbooks and journal articles. Specialized journal articles really are what shape the way we think about development economics problems and research. Sadly, they are not written for undergraduate courses. Nevertheless, the topics they cover, research approaches they use, and critical findings they present are essential to understanding development economics, and they *can* be made accessible. Journal article synopses are highlighted in sidebars throughout this book.

RebelText is intended to be used interactively with online content. QR (Quick Reference) codes at the end of each chapter link readers with online materials, including images, animations, video clips, and interviews with some influential development economists. You can access all of the URLs behind the QR codes on the website rebeltext .org, or by clicking on links in the e-version of this book. We encourage you to explore the multimedia material as a way to make the concepts come to life. On the website you'll also find the data sets included in this book, homework problems, study questions, and supplementary appendixes. When we use RebelText, the website becomes a center of class activity.

RebelText was created to make learning and teaching as efficient as possible. Students need to learn the essentials of the subject. They do not want to wade through thick textbooks in order to locate what they need, constantly wondering what will and won't be on the next test. Because it is concise, there is no reason *not* to read and study every word of *Essentials of Development Economics*. All of it could be on the test. Master it, and you will be conversant enough to strike up a conversation with any development economist and may even be able to get directly involved with development economics projects. You can think of this book as presenting the "best practices" and state-of-the-art methods for doing development economics. By mastering it, you'll also have the conceptual and intuitive grounding you need in order to move on to higher level development economics courses. You'll probably find yourself referring back to it from time to time, so keep it on your shelf!

If you are teaching or learning with RebelText, consider contributing your ideas about novel uses of the book and website, interesting data sets, programs, and projects. To find out how, visit rebeltext.org and click on "contributing to RebelText." Some of our best links have come from our students!

## ABOUT THE AUTHORS

Ed loves teaching economics, especially microeconomics, econometrics, and economic development. He's been doing it for about twenty-five years now at UC Davis, where he is a professor in the Department of Agricultural and Resource Economics. He's also done a lot of economics research; he has published more than one hundred articles, book chapters, and books on topics ranging from international trade reforms to ecotourism, immigration, and rural poverty. He's in *Who's Who in*

*Economics,* the list of the world's most cited economists, and he has been editor of the *American Journal of Agricultural Economics.* He has worked on projects with the United Nations, the World Bank, the Organization for Economic Cooperation and Development, and the Inter-American Development Bank, as well as with foreign governments, including those of Mexico, Honduras, Canada, and China. His new book, *Beyond Experiments in Development Economics: Local Economy-Wide Impact Evaluation* (Oxford University Press, 2014), presents a new approach to doing impact evaluation and cost-benefit analysis. You can learn more about Ed at his website: jetaylor.ucdavis.edu.

Travis Lybbert was initially torn between environmental studies and landscape architecture as an undergraduate major at Utah State University. A class on environmental and resource economics demonstrated the power of economics as a way to size up social problems and evaluate potential solutions. After graduating with an economics major (and French and environmental studies minors), he and his wife, Heather, lived in Morocco for a year on a Fulbright fellowship. The experience prompted him to pursue graduate work in economic development at Cornell University. After teaching for two years at the Honors College at Florida Atlantic University, he arrived at UC Davis, where he is currently Associate Professor in the Department of Agricultural and Resource Economics. Travis has worked in North Africa (Morocco, Tunisia, Syria), sub-Saharan Africa (Burkina Faso, Niger, Ghana, Ethiopia, Kenya), India, and Haiti. As a visiting researcher, he has spent time at the World Trade Organization and the World Intellectual Property Organization in Geneva, the University of Cape Coast in Ghana, and the Max Planck Institute in Munich. His current projects cover a range of topics, including drought risk and vulnerability, asset and poverty dynamics, technology adoption and markets, childhood and maternal nutrition, and intellectual property and international technology transfer. Travis teaches graduate and undergraduate courses in economic development, applied economics, and econometrics. To learn more about him, visit his faculty website: tlybbert.ucdavis.edu.

## ACKNOWLEDGMENTS

RebelText would not exist if it weren't for our families and students. Special thanks go to Sebastian and Julian, who shamed Ed into launching RebelText; to Peri, who has supported this project from the start; to Heather, Hannah, and Rockwell, who fully embraced the adventurous sabbatical year in Ghana that gave Travis the professional breathing room to work on this book; to colleagues at the Economics Department of the University of Cape Coast who made Travis's sabbatical year possible; to Steve Boucher and Michael Carter for providing many thoughts, inputs, and field tests of our book in the classroom; and to our cutting-edge team of graduate student assistants, including Anil Barghava, Isabel Call, Michael Castelhano, Diane Charlton, Mateusz Filipski, Justin Kagin, Dale Manning, Karen Thome, and Abbie Turiansky, all of whom provided valuable research assistance and advice at various stages of this project. Finally, we thank the many undergraduate students who kept us going by repeatedly telling us how "awesome" RebelText was and for catching errors and typos. They, too, are part of this project.

*J. Edward Taylor and Travis J. Lybbert*
*Davis and Berkeley, California*

# What Development Economics Is All About

Suppose you were blindfolded and airlifted abroad. After you arrive in a small town and remove the blindfold, your job is to determine the income level of the place based only on sixty seconds of observation. What would you look for? If you have traveled or lived in a developing country, you might have a head start on this assignment: Is it hot and humid? What are people wearing? Eating? How are people getting around? What do the streets and buildings look like? Do the animals look pampered? Do you see trash or trash cans? And the smells! Most people, when exposed to living standards far below their own, want to help in some way. Economists (yes, even economists!) feel this impulse and wonder: Why are some places rich and others poor? What can be done to reduce poverty and encourage economic growth? In this chapter, we introduce development economics and describe the emergence and evolution of this field.

### ESSENTIALS

- Description of development economics
- Evolution of development economics
- Import substitution and export promotion
- Market failures
- Inseparability of efficiency and equity
- Millennium Development Goals

Malawi is one of the poorest countries in the world. The average person living there had an annual income of $330 in 2010. That is not even a dollar a day. Even when we adjust for a low cost of living, the average Malawian lived off what in the United States would be the equivalent of around $850 per year.[1]

What is the solution to Malawi's pervasive poverty?

Like other least-developed countries (LDCs),[2] Malawi has tried a number of different strategies to stimulate development and raise the welfare of its people. It made the growth of smallholder production a cornerstone of its development and poverty-alleviation strategy by focusing on improving smallholders' access to agricultural input and output markets. Eighty-one percent of Malawi's population is rural, and smallholders make up about 90% of the poor. Food production is a major source of livelihood for most rural households. Productivity and, in particular, fertilizer use are low. Only 67% of agricultural households used fertilizer in 2004.[3]

Before 1998, Malawi relied on market price supports to transfer income to farm households. (Next door in Zambia, where per capita income was $1,400 in 2010, the government continues to pay farmers prices well above market levels for their maize.)[4] In recent years, fertilizer subsidies were the primary method of transferring income to rural Malawi households. Paying for farmers' inputs is expensive and controversial. More than 50% of the Ministry of Agriculture's budget has gone toward paying for input subsidies.[5]

Most recently, the country has taken a new line of attack by introducing a social cash transfer (SCT) scheme that targets ultra-poor households (those living on less than $0.10 per day) whose members are unable to work due to disability, age, illness, or a high dependency ratio (too many people to take care of at home). Rather than specifically targeting agricultural production, like the price supports or fertilizer subsidies, cash transfers raise incomes directly, allowing households to increase consumption or to invest in production activities. The government and researchers hope these transfers will stimulate production in other ways while creating positive spillovers that benefit other households in the economy.

Field research to test the effectiveness of SCT programs is ongoing. SCT programs are being implemented throughout the continent, in Ethiopia, Ghana, Kenya, Zambia, Zimbabwe, Lesotho, and other poor countries. The United Nations Children's Fund (UNICEF) and the UN's Food and Agricultural Organization (FAO), in conjunction with several universities and agencies, have launched an ambitious project to document the impacts of these transfer programs on a range of outcomes, from crop production to HIV/AIDS prevention.[6]

Development economists are on the front line of this effort, helping to design and evaluate SCT programs. On a micro level, this is a good example of the sorts of things development economists do. A whole chapter in this book (chapter 2, "What Works and What Doesn't?") is dedicated to project impact evaluation.

Development economics involves much more than this, though.

## WHAT IS DEVELOPMENT ECONOMICS?

Usually, a development economics class is a potpourri of special topics. It's hard for it not to be, because economic development involves so many different things:

- It's income growth (how can we have development without growth in countries whose per capita incomes now hover around $1–$2 per day?).
- It's welfare economics, including the study of poverty and inequality.
- It's agricultural economics. How to make agriculture more productive is a big question in countries where most of the population—particularly the *poor* population—is rural and agricultural.
- It's economic demography, the study of population growth in a world with more than 7 billion people, and population distribution in a world with more than a quarter of a billion international migrants and many more internal ones. (China will have about that many internal migrants in the near future, if it doesn't already.)
- It's labor economics: education, health, conditions in the workplace.
- It's the study of markets for goods, services, inputs, outputs, credit, and insurance, without which whole economies can grind to a standstill.
- It's public economics, including the provision of public goods from roads and communications to utilities and waste treatment, and it's about managing the macroeconomy, too.
- It's about natural resources and the environment: energy, water, deforestation, pollution, climate change, sustainability.

What is development economics *not* about, you might ask?

Lurking behind this question is another one, which lies at the heart of why we wrote this book: Why is there even a field of development economics? After all, most economics departments have courses in each one of the above areas—and more.

Development economics seeks to understand the economic aspects of the development process in low-income countries. This implies that there must be something different about studying economics in low-income countries.

Clearly there is. Economic development entails far-reaching changes in the structure of economies, technologies, societies, and political systems. Development economics is the study of economies that do not fit many of the basic assumptions underpinning economic analysis in high-income countries, including well-functioning markets, perfect information, and low transaction costs. When these assumptions break down, so do the most basic welfare and policy conclusions of economics.

This book, like other development economics texts, touches on many different topics. However, its focus is on the fundamental things that distinguish rich and poor countries and the methods we use to analyze critical development economics issues. After reading and studying it, you'll be familiar with the basic tool kit development economists use to do research, begin to understand what makes rich and poor countries different, and have an appreciation for the theory and practice of development economics.

## THE EVOLUTION OF DEVELOPMENT ECONOMICS

Economics classes rarely spend much time on history. But the brief history of development economics is instructive. Appreciating how economists have come to understand economic development helps *us* understand the various development approaches people have taken over time and how we got to the ideas that are popular now. What economists *thought* development meant at the beginnings of our field's history is quite different from the way we see it today.

The origins of modern development economics are not found in low-income countries, but rather in relatively developed countries devastated by war.[7] In the aftermath of World War II, there was a need for economic theories and policies to support the rebuilding of war-torn Europe and Japan. The United States adopted the Marshall Plan to help rebuild European economies. This was a massive program: $13 billion over four years was a lot of money back then!

In the wake of the success of the Marshall Plan, economists shifted their attention in the 1950s and 1960s from Europe to the economic problems of Africa, Asia, and Latin America. Lessons learned in Europe did not transfer easily to those settings; it quickly became clear that poor countries faced fundamentally different challenges.

Early development economists focused on income growth, often blurring the lines between growth and development. In poor countries, major structural transformations were needed to achieve growth. By comparing different countries' growth experiences (including the past experiences of the more developed countries), economists tried to uncover the conditions that determine successful development and economic growth.

*Taking Off*

Seminal work during this early period of development economics includes Walter Rostow's treatise on the stages of economic growth: the traditional society, the preconditions for takeoff, the takeoff, the drive to maturity, and the age of high mass consumption.[8] Nobel laureate Simon Kuznets (whom we shall revisit later in this chapter) countered this simplistic view that all countries go through a similar linear set of stages in their economic history. He argued instead that key characteristics of today's poor countries are fundamentally different from those of high-income countries before they developed.

*The Anatomy of Growth*

Economists recognized the need to understand how the growth process works. Growth is important enough to get its own chapter in this book (chapter 7). There, we'll focus on modern growth theory, but growth models have played an important role since the start of development economics.

A simple aggregate growth model developed by Sir Roy F. Harrod and Evsey Domar became part of the basic creed of development economists in the 1950s and 1960s.[9] The Harrod-Domar model's main implication was that investment is the key driver of economic growth. It focused economists' and policy makers' attention on generating the savings required to support higher growth rates in poor countries. Although simplistic, this was a precursor to models used to analyze economic growth in developing countries today.

Nobel laureate W. Arthur Lewis viewed growth through a higher resolution lens. His famed work, "Economic Development with Unlimited

Supplies of Labor," shifted attention from aggregate growth to structural transformation.[10] Lewis introduced the dual-sector model, demonstrating that the expansion of the modern (industrial or capitalist) sector depends on drawing labor from the traditional (agricultural or subsistence) sector. He focused on poor, labor-rich countries, in which a labor surplus in the subsistence sector could be a valuable resource for industrial growth: industry could expand without putting upward pressure on wages. Implicit in the Lewis model is a simple, demand-driven model of migration: as urban industry expands, people move off the farm to fill the new jobs. Whether or not workers really can be moved out of agriculture without losing crop production is an empirical question that some economists still try to answer today.

Lewis was criticized for largely ignoring agriculture. His work was extended and formalized by Gustav Ranis and John Fei, who demonstrated that industrial growth depends on agricultural growth as well as industrial profits.[11] If agricultural production does not keep up, food prices rise, and this forces urban wages up, squeezing profits and investment in industry. The growth of industry, then, depends on agriculture in a way that is easy to miss. Recognition that different sectors of the economy are linked in critical ways was an important contribution of dual-economy models and is a basis for more sophisticated economy-wide models today. We look at these models in chapter 10 ("Structural Transformation").

The assumption that there is surplus labor in the traditional sector (i.e., that the marginal product of labor there is zero) was questioned by another Nobel laureate, Theodore Schultz.[12] He pointed out evidence of labor shortages during peak harvest periods even in economies like India and China, where a labor surplus existed at other times of the year. Thus, he argued, one cannot assume that countries can move labor out of agriculture without suffering a drop in crop production—unless they adopt new agricultural technologies. Schultz emphasized the importance of technological innovation and revolutionized economists' thinking by putting forth the thesis that farmers in LDCs are "efficient but poor." That is, while they might appear to be inefficient (compared, say, to commercial farmers in rich countries), poor farmers actually optimize given the severe resource constraints they face, including traditional technologies and limited human capital. The efficient-but-poor hypothesis continues to shape the way development economists think about and model poor rural economies, as we see in chapter 9 ("Agriculture"). Nevertheless, recent work questions whether production, land tenancy (e.g., sharecropping), and other institutions in poor countries really are efficient in an economic sense.

The burgeoning early development economics literature produced far too many works to catalogue here, but two others deserve special mention because of the far-reaching impact they had on economic thinking and, more importantly, policies.

### Import-Substitution Industrialization

In 1950, Raúl Prebisch and Hans Singer independently observed that the terms of trade, or the ratio of prices, between primary (agricultural, resource extraction) and manufactured products erodes over time.[13] As people's income increases, the share of income they spend on manufactures increases, while the share spent on primary goods falls. This happens globally as well as locally. Prebisch and Singer argued that this drives up the prices of manufactured goods relative to primary goods. Poor countries that continue to specialize in primary-goods production lose out compared to countries that protect and promote their industries. The way Prebisch and Singer saw it, sticking with primary-goods production is like investing in a waning industry—the opposite of what good investors do.

Prebisch and Singer's work was enormously influential in promoting protectionist trade policies, shielding infant industries in poor countries from international competition. Its policy prescriptions ran soundly against the doctrine that countries should follow their comparative advantage in trade. In retrospect, countries that followed this advice did not fare as well as countries like the "Asian Tigers" (Hong Kong, Singapore, South Korea, and Taiwan), which followed more outward (trade)-oriented development models, as we shall see in chapter 13 ("International Trade and Globalization").

### Linkages

Albert Hirschman, another early pioneer in development economics, put forth the interesting and influential argument that imbalances between demand and supply in LDC economies can be good: they create pressures that stimulate economic growth.[14] Hirschman was instrumental in creating a focus on economic linkages, which pervade economy-wide modeling, a staple of development policy analysis today (chapter 10, "Structural Transformation") as well as of some recent project impact evaluation models (chapter 2, "What Works and What Doesn't?"). By promoting investments in industries with many linkages to other firms, governments can have a multiplier effect on economic growth; the effects of a policy spread to industries linked to the targeted industry. Backward linkages transmit growth effects from an input-demanding activity (e.g., textiles) to input suppliers (cotton mills or wool producers). Forward linkages stimulate the growth of activities ahead of firms, as when investment in an electricity generator facilitates the growth of electricity-using industries.

Hirschman argued that agriculture generated few linkages with the rest of the economy. This, particularly when combined with the Prebisch-Singer hypothesis, contributed to the sense among policy makers that agriculture is unimportant and countries ought to use their scarce resources to promote industrial, not agricultural, growth. John Mellor countered this argument in his seminal work, *The New Economics of Growth*, which documented the importance of consumption linkages between rural households and urban industries.[15] If most of a country's population is rural, where will the demand for new industrial production be if not in rural households? Rising agricultural incomes, then, provide a critical market for manufactures, thereby stimulating industrial growth.

Development economists had begun to take more of a systems view of poor economies, recognizing the linkages among production sectors and between firms and households that are important in shaping economic growth. They would soon rethink their emphasis on growth, though.

### Rethinking Growth: Inequality and Poverty

The United Nations declared the 1960s to be the decade of development. In 1961, it "called on all member states to intensify their efforts to mobilize support for measures required to accelerate progress toward self-sustaining economic growth and social advancement in the developing countries." Each developing country set its own target, but the overall goal was to achieve a minimum annual growth rate of 5% in aggregate national income by the end of the decade.[16] The world came close to realizing the UN's goal. LDCs achieved an average annual growth rate of 4.6% from 1960 to 1967. However, their population also increased. As a result, their per capita gross domestic product (income divided by population) rose only about 2%.

When the UN Development Decade ended in 1970, the gap between rich and poor countries had widened: two-thirds of the world's population had less than one-sixth of the world's income. This raised new questions about the meaning of development. Evidently, a tide of rising world income did not lift all—or even most—boats. The UN General Assembly concluded that one of the reasons for the slow progress was the absence of a clear international development strategy.

The problem of rising inequality made development economists rethink their focus on growth. Before then, the key work linking growth and inequality was Simon Kuznets's "inverted U" hypothesis. It stated that economic growth decreases inequality in rich countries but increases it in poor countries.[17] It tended to create a sense of complacency about inequality: sure, inequality increases for a while as poor countries grow, but eventually countries "outgrow" it and become more equal. At least, that's what Kuznets saw when he used cross-section data to compare rich and poor countries. (Cross-section data are data on different countries at the same point in time. It would have been nice to track the same countries over time to see if inequality first increases then decreases as economies grow, but we didn't have the data to do that back when Kuznets put forth his novel theory.)

As panel data have became available to track individual countries' growth and inequality, the inverted-U theory has been challenged repeatedly in the development economics literature, though it seems to fit some countries well. (Panel data provide information on the same units [here, countries] over time.) Today, China is growing fast, and inequality there is increasing. Brazil and Mexico have much higher per capita incomes than China, and inequality there is going down. Then there's the United States, where inequality fell through the 1970s but is rising again now.

Development economics shifted its attention from income growth to income inequality (chapter 5, "Inequality"). In 1974, Hollis Chenery, head of the World Bank's economic research department, and colleagues published an influential book called *Redistribution with Growth*.[18] It demonstrated that when assets (such as land) are distributed unequally, economic growth creates an unequal distribution of benefits. Around the same time (1973), Irma Adelman and Cynthia Taft Morris published a book called *Economic Growth and Social Equity in Developing Countries*.[19] They found that as incomes grew, not only did inequality increase, but the *absolute* position of the poor *worsened*. At the early stages of a country's economic growth, the poorest segment of society may be harmed, as traditional economic relationships in subsistence economies are displaced by emerging commercial ones. Growth was more equitable in countries that redistributed assets, like land and human capital (education), *before* the growth happened.

Robert McNamara, the World Bank's president, put the world spotlight on inequality at a 1972 UN conference in Santiago, Chile.[20] This staked out a new position for the World Bank and the development economics profession more broadly that growth alone is not enough. McNamara and many development economists recommended redistribution before growth; for example, land reforms and other measures to raise the productivity of small farmers and widespread rural education programs. The development economics mantra had shifted from income growth (chapters 3 and 7) to poverty (chapter 4) and inequality (chapter 5). The work of Amartya Sen expanded the scope of economic development yet further to include dimensions of human development such as health, nutrition, education, and even freedom (chapter 6).

National planning offices cropped up around the world, often with "five-year plans" inspired by the Soviet Union's planning models but not necessarily socialistic in nature. (While Ed was an undergraduate student he worked for a year with the National Planning Office in Costa Rica, which had five-year plans but was hardly a communist state!) This period saw the advent of economy-wide models as a tool for development planning and policy. These models were designed to simulate the complex impacts that policies have on whole economies as well as on particular social groups. They continue to be a staple of development economics research and policy design and are often at the crossfire of a lively debate about the role of planning and markets in economic development.

The 1970s marked the beginning of what has become an ongoing friction between direct government involvement in the development process and market-led development—a tension we will address throughout this book because it stems from essential ideas in development economics. The traditional neoclassical economic view, inspired by Adam Smith's "invisible hand," is that individuals and firms, in the pursuit of their self-interest, are led as if by an invisible hand to economic efficiency. For example, competition among profit-maximizing firms drives down prices for selfish, utility-maximizing consumers. However, the invisible hand does not typically lead to fair outcomes, so government intervention can often play a role in promoting social objectives other than efficiency, such as equality or protection of domestic industries.

The 1960s and 1970s witnessed increasing government involvement in markets: setting prices, controlling trade, and creating "parastatal" enterprises that did everything from buying and selling crops to drilling for oil.

Much of the focus of these efforts was on stimulating industrial growth; however, most of the population in poor countries—especially the very poor—depended heavily on agriculture. In many countries, import-substitution industrialization policies created severe biases against agriculture, in three ways:

1. "Cheap food policies" directly harmed agriculture while helping to keep urban wages low.

2. Steep tariffs and quotas on imported industrial goods and direct subsidies were used to promote industrialization. This increased the profitability of industrial compared to agricultural production.

3. Macroeconomic policies like overvalued exchange rates made imported industrial inputs and technologies (as well as food) cheaper. This created yet another bias against agriculture by making traded goods (food) less profitable than nontraded goods (manufactures, which were protected from trade competition).

### Trusting Markets

The 1980s saw the beginning of a backlash against too much state involvement in the economy. This was the era of Ronald Reagan and Margaret Thatcher, in which we recognized the inefficiencies of state-planned economic systems such as those in the Soviet Union and China compared with the more laissez-faire political systems in the west. Meanwhile, it became clear that the countries that were experiencing the most rapid and broad-based growth were *not* the inward-oriented countries following import-substitution industrialization, like Kenya, Mexico, and Brazil. Instead, they were the outward export-oriented economies, particularly the Asian Tigers. In those countries, governments were involved, sometimes heavily, in the economy, but opening up to market competition made it possible to become competitive on a world scale.

Another part of the impetus for shifting away from state involvement and toward markets came in the 1970s and 1980s as the world economy went into recession with soaring oil prices. This sparked debt crises in many LDCs (particularly in Latin America), forcing them to rethink their development policies—often as part of "structural adjustment" programs required by the International Monetary Fund (IMF) as a condition for restructuring their debt. These adjustments invariably reduced the direct involvement of the state in the troubled economies.

The World Bank's 1984 World Development Report endorsed many of these dominant promarket positions. It called for removing distortions created by governments' overinvolvement in agricultural markets. Almost overnight, governments began to withdraw from markets, dismantling import-substitution industrialization policies and opening up to trade. Less-developed countries around the world entered into free-trade agreements (see chapter 13).

### Not (Quite) Trusting Markets

The market liberalization movement continued into the 1990s; however, the enthusiasm for free trade became tempered by a realization that market liberalization does not necessarily improve people's economic welfare if markets do not work properly. This produced a surge of research documenting market failures in LDCs as well as their underlying causes. (Market failures are a focus of chapter 11.)

Broadly speaking, a free market fails if it does not work efficiently— that is, if there is another scenario in which a market participant could be made better off without making others worse off. Often, markets fail so miserably that they do not exist at all for many people. Most poor people do not have access to credit, most farmers in Africa do not sell their crops, and almost nobody in poor countries has access to formal insurance.

Joseph Stiglitz, who received the 2001 Nobel Prize in economics, along with other economists, demonstrated that markets are rarely efficient. He attributed this largely to imperfect information, which creates high transaction costs that lead to widespread market failures, particularly in poor countries. Since understanding market failures is fundamental to development economics, we will learn about several sources of market failures in this book.

When markets do not work well, government involvement in the economy can often improve welfare. Development economists have been careful to warn that market failures do not necessarily warrant broad state intervention in the economy: government failures can be worse than market failures. However, the scope for the state to improve welfare by intervening in markets, it seems, is much larger than previously thought.

### The Experimental Revolution

Today, much of the focus of development economics has shifted to the micro-level and to project evaluation. Increasingly, development economics research involves using experiments to learn about people's economic behavior and evaluate the impacts of policy interventions on welfare outcomes. When experiments are not possible, economists use other methods, including econometrics and simulation modeling, to try to identify the impacts of policies and programs. The social cash transfer programs mentioned at the start of this chapter are an example. Today, if you work for a nongovernmental organization (NGO), an international development agency, or even an LDC government, there is a good chance you'll be dealing with experimental economics. Experiments have become such an important part of development economics that we devote an entire chapter to them in this book (chapter 2).

## WHAT IS ECONOMIC DEVELOPMENT, THEN?

Economic development has different meanings in different contexts. In rich countries, it is pretty much equated with growth. Picture the urban developer who makes skyscrapers sprout from vacant lots in a blighted city core. Politically, development projects in high-income countries often are motivated by some of the same goals that inspire development projects in poor countries, particularly the creation of new jobs, incomes, and tax revenues. Their ultimate aim, however, is likely to be growth.

Most development economists today would say that economic development is not equivalent to growth, although it is difficult to achieve development goals without growth. Development projects around the world focus on concrete outcomes related to poverty, malnutrition, inequality, and health. Development is about satisfying basic physical needs like nutrition, shelter, and clothing, and about the development of the mind (and of course people's earnings potential) through education. Projects also focus on the environment, conservation, and sustainable resource use; on human rights, gender and ethnic equity, and even government corruption (a topic we take up in chapter 8, "Institutions").

All of these questions can be vital not only to determining who reaps the benefits of economic growth, but also to understanding growth itself. Herein lies a fundamental difference in the way we tend to look at economics and politics in rich and poor countries. In high-income countries (not to mention our microeconomics courses), economic efficiency and equity tend to be viewed as separate questions. The efficient allocation of resources is critical to ensure that economies produce the biggest possible economic pie, given the constraints they face (i.e., limited resources and technologies). Efficiency is the primary focus of the vast majority of our economics classes.

What about equity? How the pie gets distributed is usually an afterthought in economics—something more in the domain of politics than economics. Think about the economics courses you've taken. The textbook view is that efficiency and equity are sequential, or recursive, problems: first grow the pie, then, once that's done, think about how it gets distributed (or step back and let the market decide).

Clearly, there's an important separability assumption here: that efficiency can be achieved regardless of how income is distributed. Is this a reasonable assumption? In a competitive market equilibrium, there will be different outcomes depending upon what the initial distribution of wealth looks like. But provided the basic assumptions of the competitive model (which you learned in your introductory economics courses) hold, all will be efficient in the Pareto sense: you cannot make anyone better off without making someone else worse off. If you ever studied an Edgeworth box, you've seen how economists show this.

The separability of equity and efficiency was reinforced by the Nobel laureate Ronald Coase, who argued that bargaining will lead to an efficient outcome regardless of the initial allocation of property rights, even in the case of externalities (a cost or benefit not reflected in prices, like pollution). According to Coase, as long as we can costlessly negotiate it doesn't matter whether you have the right to smoke or I have the right to breathe clean air. Once we have finished bargaining with each other, the amount of smoke in the air will be the same. This view has achieved the status of a theorem: Coase's Theorem.

If efficiency and equity are truly separate issues, then there is not much room for economic policy, nor much reason for efficiency-minded economists to worry about equity. (Of course, even economists might worry about equity for other [i.e., humanitarian] reasons.)

If only things were that simple! Alas, negotiation is never costless (and often prohibitively expensive). For this and many other reasons, a great deal of development economists' effort goes into discovering how equity and efficiency are intertwined, especially in poor countries. How assets are distributed clearly affects efficiency if the following conditions hold:

- Banks are unwilling to loan money to small farmers.
- Poor people cannot get insurance to protect themselves against crop loss or sickness.

- Poverty and malnutrition prevent kids from growing up to become productive adults.
- Access to markets for the stuff people produce, the inputs they use, and the goods they demand is different for the poor and rich.
- The ability to get a job depends on who you are, not on how productive you are.

In these and many other cases, the separability of equity and efficiency breaks down. A person's capacity to produce (or even consume) efficiently depends upon how wealth is distributed to start out with because the basic assumptions of competitive markets often don't hold for the poorest members of society. A rich farmer can produce where the market price equals the marginal cost of producing a crop, the basic requirement for profit maximization and efficiency. But if a poor farmer lacks the cash to buy fertilizer, and no bank will lend to her, she will not be able to produce as efficiently as the large farmer. This implies that efficiency depends on how income is distributed to begin with, which is an important departure from standard assumptions in economics.

The conditions under which equity affects efficiency are many, and they permeate the economies and societies of poor countries. Development economics, more than anything else perhaps, is the study of economies in which equity and efficiency are closely interrelated. This opens up a whole realm of possibilities for policy and project interventions to increase economic efficiency as well as equity. More often than not, equity and efficiency are not only complementary; they are inseparable.

## THE MILLENNIUM DEVELOPMENT GOALS (MDGS)

Eradicating extreme poverty continues to be one of the main challenges of our time, and is a major concern of the international community. Ending this scourge will require the combined efforts of all—governments, civil society organizations and the private sector—in the context of a stronger and more effective global partnership for development. The Millennium Development Goals set timebound targets, by which progress in reducing income poverty, hunger, disease, lack of adequate shelter and exclusion—while promoting gender equality, health, education and environmental sustainability—can be measured. They also embody basic human rights—the rights of each person on the planet to health, education, shelter and security. The Goals are ambitious but feasible and, together with the comprehensive United Nations development agenda, set the course for the world's efforts to alleviate extreme poverty by 2015. (United Nations Secretary-General Ban Ki-moon)

In September 2000, 189 nations came together at United Nations Headquarters in New York and adopted the United Nations Millennium Declaration. In it, they committed to creating a new global partnership to reduce extreme poverty and achieve a set of specific development targets by 2015. These targets (see appendix at the end of this chapter), which range from health to environment to gender equality, have become known as the Millennium Development Goals (MDGs).[21] Setting goals like these and monitoring our progress toward achieving them requires tremendous amounts of data, measurement methods, and above all, commitment.

If you attend almost any international development meeting, you almost certainly will hear the MDGs come up. The MDGs are often used by governments and international development agencies to motivate and justify specific development projects. They have galvanized efforts to meet the needs of people in the world's poorest countries, but they are not without their detractors. There is ongoing debate among economists about whether this kind of formal, "technocratic" approach, in which scientists and experts are in control, is beneficial or harmful. It may help the poor by funneling funds and expertise to areas of urgent need. However, it could do the opposite by imposing external power and plans that do not reflect local context.[22]

### THE ORGANIZATION OF THIS BOOK

This book was written to provide students with the essential tools and concepts of development economics. Most development texts are written around topics: money, labor, population, and so on. The chapters in this book are less about topics than about providing a window into how developing economies are different and how this shapes the way we study them. Most of the cutting-edge research by economists is found in journal articles that are beyond the reach of most undergraduate students. Sidebars scattered throughout the book try to make this research accessible, summarizing the questions it asks, the methods it uses, key findings, and why they are important. Our hope is that by the end of this book, students will have a new understanding of what economists bring to development research and policy and be conversant in many of the approaches they employ.

The rest of this book is all about seeking answers to big questions. As households and individuals seek out livelihoods in increasingly complex and global economies, governments, international development agencies, and development banks carry out a wide diversity of development projects. Evaluating the impacts of these programs is the focus of a new generation of development economists, inspired largely by experimental methods. Chapter 2 ("What Works and What Doesn't?") looks at why economists do experiments, what the limitations of experiments are, how to evaluate impacts when there is no experiment, cost-benefit analysis of development projects, and how projects and policies may affect non-beneficiaries as well as beneficiaries.

Chapters 3 through 6 are about understanding, measuring, and analyzing the four key elements of economic development: income (chapter 3), poverty (chapter 4), inequality (chapter 5), and human development (chapter 6).

A theme that emerges from the first six chapters is that income growth is an important, though by no means sufficient, condition for achieving economic development. How can countries, regions, and households make their incomes grow? Chapter 7 ("Growth") gives an introduction to aggregate (national) growth theory and concludes by asking whether poor countries, regions, and households are "catching up," and whether income growth alone will enable countries to reach the Millennium Development Goals.

Institutions are like the operating systems for economies and societies. When they don't work well, even the best-designed development policies and projects can fail to meet their objectives. We dedicate a whole chapter (chapter 8) to institutions, what they mean to a development economist, and how they shape economic development outcomes.

Agriculture still dominates the economies of many countries in terms of income and employment. Chapter 9 ("Agriculture") presents the key tools economists have come up with to analyze agricultural economies, with an eye toward understanding a wide array of impacts, from agricultural policies to trade and climate change. This chapter begins with the agricultural household model, the staple of microeconomic analysis of agricultural and rural economies. It concludes with village and rural economy-wide models, which let us see how households are connected with each other and transmit impacts of policy, market, and environmental shocks.

Most of the world's poverty is in rural areas. Rural economies, though, are becoming less agricultural over time, as households get an increasing share of their income from non-agricultural activities. For a growing number of people, getting out of poverty means moving off the farm. Chapter 10 ("Structural Transformation") looks at the far-reaching transformations of rural and national economies that accompany economic growth and what this means for how we do economic analysis and design development policies.

Markets and trade are vital for countries to grow and spread the benefits of this growth across a broad population. However, markets fail for many people, and others find themselves unable to compete in an increasingly global economy. In chapters 11 ("Information and Markets"), 12 ("Credit and Insurance"), and 13 ("International Trade and Globalization"), we see why economists think markets are so important to economic development, why markets fail for many people, how globalization creates both winners and losers, and what this all means for development policies. Two markets, those for credit and insurance, are particularly important—and more often than not conspicuously missing—for poor people in LDCs. Chapter 12 looks at how credit and insurance markets are important, why they fail, and what development researchers and practitioners are doing about it.

The epilogue (chapter 14) is about where you will go from here and how the tools and skills in this book prepare you for new adventures in development—and life.

At the end of each chapter you will find a link to multimedia resources that you can explore to enrich your learning, meet experts, and bring the real world into the textbook and classroom.

www.rebeltext.org/development/qr1.html
Enrich your appreciation of what development economics is about by exploring multimedia resources while you read.

### APPENDIX
*The Eight Millennium Development Goals (MDGs)*

*MDG 1:* Eradicate Extreme Poverty and Hunger
   *Target 1.A:* Halve, between 1990 and 2015, the proportion of people whose income is less than $1.25 a day

*Target 1.B:* Achieve full and productive employment and decent work for all, including women and young people

*Target 1.C:* Halve, between 1990 and 2015, the proportion of people who suffer from hunger

*MDG 2:* Achieve Universal Primary Education

Ensure that, by 2015, children everywhere, boys and girls alike, will be able to complete a full course of primary schooling

*MDG 3:* Gender Equity

Eliminate gender disparity in primary and secondary education, preferably by 2005, and in all levels of education no later than 2015

*MDG 4:* Reduce Child Mortality

Reduce by two-thirds, between 1990 and 2015, the under-five mortality rate

*MDG 5:* Improve Maternal Health

*Target 5.A:* Reduce by three-quarters, between 1990 and 2015, the maternal mortality ratio

*Target 5.B:* Achieve, by 2015, universal access to reproductive health

*MDG 6:* Combat HIV/AIDS, Malaria, and Other Diseases

*Target 6.A:* Halt by 2015 and begin to reverse the spread of HIV/AIDS

*Target 6.B:* Achieve by 2010 universal access to treatment for HIV/AIDS for all those who need it

*Target 6.C:* Halt by 2015 and begin to reverse the incidence of malaria and other major diseases

*MGD 7:* Ensure Environmental Sustainability

*Target 7.A:* Integrate the principles of sustainable development into country policies and programmes and reverse the loss of environmental resources

*Target 7.B:* Reduce biodiversity loss, achieving, by 2010, a significant reduction in the rate of loss

*Target 7.C:* Halve, by 2015, the proportion of the population without sustainable access to safe drinking water and basic sanitation

*Target 7.D:* Achieve, by 2020, a significant improvement in the lives of at least 100 million slum dwellers

*MDG 8:* Develop a Global Partnership for Development

*Target 8.A:* Develop further an open, rule-based, predictable, non-discriminatory trading and financial system

*Target 8.B:* Address the special needs of least-developed countries

*Target 8.C:* Address the special needs of landlocked developing countries and small island developing states

*Target 8.D:* Deal comprehensively with the debt problems of developing countries

*Target 8.E:* In cooperation with pharmaceutical companies, provide access to affordable essential drugs in developing countries

*Target 8.F:* In cooperation with the private sector, make available benefits of new technologies, especially information and communications

Learn more about the Millennium Development Goals at www.un.org /millenniumgoals/global.shtml.

## ADDITIONAL READING

Each year, the World Bank publishes its World Development Report with its own special topic (not to mention a lot of data on an array of development indicators). As you can see, they cover an enormous array of topics. These reports are available online at http://go.worldbank.org/LOTTGBE9I0. The following are summaries taken from the World Bank website.

### World Development Reports, 2000–(Upcoming) 2016

*Upcoming WDR 2016: The Internet and Development.* Will assemble the best available evidence on the Internet's potential impact on economic growth, on equity, and on the efficiency of public service provision. Will analyze what factors have allowed some governments, firms, and households to benefit from the Internet, and identify the barriers that limit gains elsewhere.

*Upcoming WDR 2015: Mind and Society.* Will be based on three main ideas: *bounds on rationality*, which limit individuals' ability to process information and lead them to rely on rules of thumb; *social interdependence*, which leads people to care about other people as well as the social norms of their communities; and *culture*, which provides mental models that influence what individuals pay attention to, perceive, and understand (or misunderstand).

*WDR 2014: Risk and Opportunity: Managing Risk for Development.* Examines how improving risk management can lead to larger gains in development and poverty reduction. This report argues that improving risk management is crucial to reduce the negative impacts of shocks and hazards, but also to enable people to pursue new opportunities for growth.

*WDR 2013: Jobs.* Stresses the role of strong, private-sector-led growth in creating jobs and outlines how jobs that do the most for development can spur a virtuous cycle. The report finds that poverty falls as people work their way out of hardship and as jobs empower women to invest more in their children. Efficiency increases as workers get better at what they do, as more productive jobs appear, and as less productive ones disappear. Societies flourish as jobs foster diversity and provide alternatives to conflict.

*WDR 2012: Gender Equality and Development.* Finds that women's lives around the world have improved dramatically, but gaps remain in many areas. The authors use a conceptual framework to examine progress to date, and then recommend policy actions.

*WDR 2011: Conflict, Security, and Development.* Conflict causes human misery, destroys communities and infrastructure, and can cripple economic prospects. The goal of this World Development Report is to contribute concrete, practical suggestions to the debate on how to address and overcome violent conflict and fragility.

*WDR 2010: Development and Climate Change.* The main message of this report is that a "climate-smart" world is possible if we act now, act together, and act differently.

*WDR 2009: Reshaping Economic Geography.* Places do well when they promote transformations along the dimensions of economic geography: higher densities as cities grow; shorter distances as workers and businesses migrate closer to density; and fewer divisions as nations lower their economic borders and enter world markets to take advantage of scale and trade in specialized products. WDR 2009 concludes that the transformations along these three dimensions of density, distance, and division are essential for development and should be encouraged.

*WDR 2008: Agriculture for Development.* In the twenty-first century, agriculture continues to be a fundamental instrument for sustainable development and poverty reduction. WDR 2008 concludes that agriculture alone will not be enough to massively reduce poverty, but it is an essential component of effective development strategies for most developing countries.

*WDR 2007: Development and the Next Generation.* Developing countries that invest in better education, health care, and job training for their record numbers of young people between the ages of twelve and twenty-four years of age could produce surging economic growth and sharply reduced poverty, according to this report.

*WDR 2006: Equity and Development.* Inequality of opportunity, both within and among nations, sustains extreme deprivation, results in wasted human potential, and often weakens prospects for overall prosperity and economic growth, concludes this report.

*WDR 2005: A Better Investment Climate for Everyone.* Accelerating growth and poverty reduction requires governments to reduce the policy risks, costs, and barriers to competition facing firms of all types—from farmers and microentrepreneurs to local manufacturing companies and multinationals—concludes this report.

*WDR 2004: Making Services Work for Poor People.* This report warns that broad improvements in human welfare will not occur unless poor people receive wider access to affordable, better quality services in health, education, water, sanitation, and electricity. Without such improvements, freedom from illness and from illiteracy—two of the most important ways poor people can escape poverty—will remain elusive to many.

*WDR 2003: Sustainable Development in a Dynamic World.* Without better policies and institutions, social and environmental strains may derail develop-ment progress, leading to higher poverty levels and a decline in the quality of life for everybody, according to this report.

*WDR 2002: Building Institutions for Markets.* Weak institutions—tangled laws, corrupt courts, deeply biased credit systems, and elaborate business registration requirements—hurt poor people and hinder development, according to this report.

*WDR 2000–2001: Attacking Poverty.* This report focuses on the dimensions of poverty, and how to create a better world, free of poverty. The analysis explores the nature and evolution of poverty, and its causes, to present a framework for action.

# What Works and What Doesn't?

Beginning with Adam Smith, economists have long tried to understand why some people and countries are rich while others are desperately poor—typically in the hopes of alleviating poverty. Historically, this work was mostly heavy on theory and light on data. Much of the work introduced in chapter 1, for example, was focused on abstract growth and trade models. By contrast, in recent decades development economists have become decidedly more empirical and more reliant on data to understand what works in practice and what doesn't—typically with a strong microeconomic focus. Today, experiments of different forms are a basic tool in the development economist's kit. Taking a development economics class without learning about experiments and the selection problems they solve is like graduating from medical school without knowing CPR. This chapter will introduce you to randomized control trials (RCTs) and other experimental methods we use to understand the impacts of projects and policies on development outcomes.

### ESSENTIALS

- Randomized control trials (RCTs)
- The selection problem
- The reflection problem
- Cost-benefit analysis
- Lab and natural experiments
- Market interlinkages

Ed has allergies. Not the dangerous kind some people get from peanuts or bee stings, but the hay fever kind: sneezing, itchy eyes, congestion, and on bad pollen days, a grueling sinus headache. Fortunately, there is a spray he can shoot up his nose that really helps. He's sure of it. Well, he thinks so. Maybe. Alright, there are days when he uses it and still feels pretty messed up, and other days when he doesn't use it but feels just fine.

The problem is, on spring days when puffballs of pollen float through the air like in a Fellini film, Ed doesn't know what *would* have happened if he *hadn't* sniffed the stuff. Those are the days he almost always uses it. When he forgets to, he can't be sure what would have happened if he *had* taken it.

To complicate matters, once he uses that spray, he acts differently. He feels like he can take on any allergen out there! Students observe Ed bicycling through the Davis countryside with the crops in full bloom. He sneezes from time to time, but that's because he's really putting the sniffer to the test and it isn't supposed to work all the time. Right?

In 2011, international development agencies spent an estimated $US147.74 billion to solve problems far more serious than Ed's allergies.[1] Trying to evaluate whether or not development programs work is a lot like figuring out whether allergy medication works. Development programs are a treatment, and the problems they try to solve are like an allergic reaction to pollen.

Donors must have better ways of knowing whether their programs work than Ed has for nose spray, right?

Sadly, until fairly recently they did not. Development agencies' shelves and hard disks are filled with final reports concluding that the projects they funded were successful (usually) at achieving their stated goals. But it can be extremely difficult to show whether a treatment is successful or unsuccessful. That is, unless you've got an experiment.

The people who make nose spray know all about experiments. That's what drug trials are all about. Before they can market a new drug, they have to perform a *randomized control trial,* or RCT. The formula to do an RCT is simple: (1) devise a treatment; (2) identify your target population and from it randomly select a sample of people to run your experiment on; (3) split the sample randomly into two groups, a treatment group and a control group; (4) give the treatment group the treatment and the control group a "placebo" that looks like the treatment but isn't; (5) after enough time has elapsed for the treatment to take effect, gather new information on your treatment and control groups; and (6) compare outcomes of interest between the treatment and control groups.

In 1997, Mexico did something similar to a drug experiment, but it was to test an entirely different sort of treatment: a new welfare program. PROGRESA (Programa de Educación, Salud, y Alimentación) was designed to combat rural poverty from two angles. First, it gave cash to poor people. A number of studies have shown that women are more likely than men to spend income on food and other goods that benefit their families, so women were the target of the program. Second, in order to get the cash, a poor woman had to follow some rules to improve her family's nutrition, health, and education. Kids had to be enrolled in school and in the local medical clinic. These behavioral requirements made PROGRESA what is called a "conditional cash-transfer program," or "CCT."

The theory behind this CCT was simple. In the short run, cash is what poor people need most in order to feed and clothe their families and satisfy their basic needs and wants. In the long run, the best way to break the intergenerational transfer of poverty is to give kids the human capital they need to lead productive lives; hence the two C's.

So far, we've got most of the first two elements of an RCT: the treatment (the CCT) and a target population (poor rural women). Mexico had to find out who was in this target population, so it carried out a nationwide survey. It identified 2.6 million families in fifty thousand rural communities who were eligible to receive PROGRESA benefits. That's about 40% of all rural families. The plan was to give the PROGRESA treatment to all eligible women.

If all eligible women get the treatment, how can we test whether the treatment works? We could compare everyone before and after the program starts. But if we saw differences, say, in school attendance or family nutrition, could we be sure it was because of PROGRESA? Many other things were happening in Mexico at the same time as PROGRESA. NAFTA (the North American Free Trade Agreement) had just gone into effect. In Mexico, as in many other countries, the mid-1990s saw far-reaching agricultural reforms that included eliminating subsidies for small farmers, with big impacts on rural incomes. New rural schools were being built. People were migrating. The weather was changing. There was lots of pollen in the air.

If you give everyone an allergy spray, they might still sneeze if the pollen count rises—or they might not sneeze at all if it doesn't. When you can't control for everything else, you can't figure out whether your treatment worked. Something else might have changed. This has been the curse of development-program evaluations over the years. We need a control group of similar, randomly chosen people who did *not* get the treatment but experienced, on average, the same changes in all those other variables that the treated people did. If treatment and control groups go into the pollen together, we should be able to determine whether the drug works.

Fortunately, the way PROGRESA was rolled out created a random control group for evaluating the program's impacts. There was no way to roll out the program to all eligible families in rural Mexico at the same time, so the government had to choose which poor villages to "treat" first. It could have gone for the villages closest to Mexico City, near where powerful politicians lived, or where poverty was highest, but it didn't. Instead, it rolled out the program randomly. All eligible women in randomly chosen villages got PROGRESA payments the first year of the program. They were the treatment group. In the rest of the villages, none of the eligible women got PROGRESA right away. They were the control group.

Randomization ensured that the treatment and control villages, households, and women, on average, were identical except for the treatment, just like the treatment and control groups in a drug trial. Researchers could compare any outcome they wanted—school attendance, nutrition, whatever—between the eligible households in these two groups of villages. All you had to do was compare averages. The difference could be attributed to PROGRESA.

Within three years, all 2.6 million eligible families were getting PROGRESA, so the experiment vanished. But for a short period of time, Mexico had given the world the gift of a randomized "social experiment" in the form of an RCT (see sidebar 2.1). PROGRESA became the model for both designing and evaluating anti-poverty programs in many other developing countries and even in New York City.[2]

### RANDOMIZATION AND THE SELECTION PROBLEM

Over the years we've noticed that people who use nose sprays sneeze more than people who don't. Could it be that nose spray *makes* you sneeze?

That's a silly question, you say. People who use nose spray sneeze more because they had more allergies to begin with; that's why they chose the nose spray treatment. That's probably true, but you can see the problem here. We cannot determine whether the nose spray is effective by comparing people who use it with people who don't. If we do that, we might well conclude that the drug makes people sneeze! This is what experimentalists call *selection bias*. Selection bias confounds all sorts of studies. Here are three illustrations:

The economists Joshua Angrist and Jörn-Steffen Pischke took people who were hospitalized (the treatment group) and people who were not

## Sidebar 2.1 Progressing with PROGRESA

Mexico's PROGRESA data have spawned more development economics research (not to mention PhD student theses) than almost any other micro data set in the world. Here are some key findings on PROGRESA's impacts, all made possible by the way in which the program was randomly implemented across rural Mexico.

*Nutrition:* PROGRESA improved both calorie consumption and the quality of beneficiaries' diets. Eligible households in treatment localities consumed 6.4% more calories than comparable households in the control localities. When it comes to nutrition, the quality of calories also matters. The study found that PROGRESA's biggest impact was on calories from vegetable and animal products. PROGRESA made people eat not only more, but better.

J. Hoddinott and E. Skoufias, "The Impact of PROGRESA on Food Consumption," *Economic Development and Cultural Change* (October 2004):37–61.

*Schooling:* PROGRESA had a significant positive effect on school enrollment. Many kids drop out of school after grade 6, when often they must leave their village to continue on in school. The largest difference between PROGRESA and control households was for kids who had already completed grade 6; the PROGRESA kids' enrollment rate was 11.1% higher, reaching 69%, and the program's impact was disproportionately concentrated among girls. Exposure to PROGRESA for 8 years, starting at age 6, increases children's educational attainment by an average of 0.7 years, and 21% more children attend secondary school.

T. Paul Schultz, "School Subsidies for the Poor: Evaluating the Mexican Progresa Poverty Program," *Journal of Development Economics* 74, no. 2 (2004):199–250.

Jere R. Behrman, Piyali Sengupta, and Petra Todd, "Progressing through PROGRESA: An Impact Assessment of a School Subsidy Experiment," *Economic Development and Cultural Change* 54, no. 1 (2005):237–75.

*Health:* PROGRESA significantly increased preventive care, including prenatal care, child nutrition monitoring, and adult checkups. It reduced inpatient hospitalizations, suggesting a positive effect on major illness. PROGRESA children age 0–5 had a 12% lower incidence of illness, and prime age adults (18–50) had 19% fewer days of difficulty due to illness than did non-PROGRESA individuals.

Paul Guertler, "Final Report: The Impact of PROGRESA on Health" (Washington, DC: International Food Policy Research Institute, 2002 (www.ifpri.org/sites/default/files/publications/gertler_health.pdf)

(the control group) and compared their health status a year later.[3] The people who had been hospitalized were less healthy. Do hospitals make people sick?

Governments around the world offer job training programs. Many studies find that a year or two later the people who chose to be in these programs are more likely to be employed than the people who chose not to do the job training. Are job training programs successful, or is it the kind of person who chooses to go for job training?

Economic studies consistently show that people with more education have higher earnings. Is this because schools make people more productive, or do higher ability people go to school?

In these (and countless other) cases, the outcomes we see after the treatment reflect two things: first, who chooses to get the treatment (the selection effect), and second, the effect of the treatment, itself. Because of this, simply comparing outcomes for people who did and did not get a treatment may tell us nothing at all about whether the treatment was effective. We've got to untangle the two.

What we'd really like to do is compare the same person's outcome with and without the treatment. We can't do that, though, because once a person gets treated, we can't see what would have happened to her without the treatment. And if the person does not get the treatment, we'll never know what would have happened if she had been treated.

The selection problem arises when things that determine whether or not someone gets treated are correlated with the outcome we want to measure. Sick people (whether they go to hospital or not) are likely to be less healthy in the future. Motivated people choose to participate in a training program, but they are more likely to get a job with or without the program. High-ability people are more likely to have higher earnings, regardless of how much more productive schools make them.

Randomization solves the selection problem. By randomly choosing who gets the treatment and who does not, RCTs create treatment and control groups that on average are the same except for the treatment. Any differences we observe between the two, then, must be the result of the treatment. You can find a formal presentation of the selection problem and how randomization solves it in the appendix to this chapter, "The Math of Selection."

Theoretically, in a perfectly designed experiment, we could test whether or not the treatment is successful simply by comparing outcomes between treatment and control groups. Randomization would ensure that everything but the treatment is identical, on average, between the two groups. Real life rarely gives us something approaching perfect randomization, though. Thus, we usually need baseline (pretreatment) information to make sure the treatment and control groups really are the same except for the treatment. Baseline surveys are costly, but tests showing there are no significant differences between the treatment and control group prior to the treatment are important to validate RCTs.

Baseline surveys are important for other reasons. We saw previously that Mexico's PROGRESA had to carry out a baseline survey in order to find out who would be in its target population, that is, which women met the criteria for receiving PROGRESA payments.

Baseline information can help researchers control for other variables that affect the outcome of interest. For example, while treatments are carried out, other things in the economy are changing, like the weather, macroeconomic policies, and recessions. With good baseline data, we can compare *changes* in outcomes for the treated and control groups before and after the treatment. For example, we might hope that cash transfers raise crop production in poor households. Meanwhile, if the economy is growing, poor households might increase their crop production with or without the program. If the transfers really do increase crop production, though, *the change in crop production should be larger in the households that got transfers.* Instead of comparing crop production between treated and nontreated households, then, we can learn more about the program's impacts if we compare *differences* in crop production between the two groups. This is called the "difference in difference" method. We first calculate the difference in the outcome variable (crop production) before and after the treatment for both the treatment and control groups. Then we calculate the difference between these differences. If it's positive, we conclude that the treatment had a positive effect on the outcome. This useful method requires having data on the treated and control groups before as well as after the treatment.

## THE EXPERIMENTAL REVOLUTION IN DEVELOPMENT ECONOMICS

The chief architect behind PROGRESA was an economist named Santiago Levy who got his PhD from Boston University in 1980. By the time Mexican president Ernesto Zedillo (an economist with a PhD from Yale in 1974) asked him to lead a team to address extreme poverty in Mexico, Santiago had done enough data analysis to appreciate how selection bias can make it tough to know whether any program actually works in practice.

The program he and his team launched was the first large-scale randomized policy experiment in a developing country. The RCT approach to evaluating its impact was inspired by the work of economists studying policies in developed countries (especially related to labor markets). This, in turn, set the stage for a revolution in how development economists try to learn what works and what doesn't. The essence of this methodological revolution is quite simple: the less choice people have about whether to be "treated," the easier it is to test what works and what doesn't.

Many development economists see RCTs as the impact-evaluation gold standard, because in their purest form RCTs do not permit people to have any choice about whether or not they are treated. In 2003, Esther Duflo cofounded the Poverty Action Lab, which is dedicated to the use of RCTs.[4] She writes: "Creating a culture in which rigorous randomized evaluations are promoted, encouraged, and financed has the potential to revolutionize social policy during the 21st century, just as randomized trials revolutionized medicine during the 20th."[5] The J-PAL website states: "Randomized evaluations are often deemed the gold standard of impact evaluation, because they consistently produce the most accurate results . . . to determine whether a program has an impact, and more specifically, to quantify how large that impact is."[6]

Today, RCTs are being used to evaluate a wide array of development programs, from a new generation of social cash transfer (SCT) programs in sub-Saharan Africa to microcredit, HIV/AIDS prevention, immunization, and even "hope." Here are a few examples of the kinds of questions RCTs address.

### RCTs for African SCTs

African countries are different from Mexico in ways that could shape the outcome of cash transfer programs. They are poorer and characterized by a greater level of risk and vulnerability. African SCT programs typically target households that are labor-poor as well as being in extreme poverty and containing vulnerable children. HIV/AIDS has its global epicenter in Southern Africa. The region has less developed markets and greater political instability. People's livelihoods and ability to escape from poverty are more linked to small-holder agriculture and the informal economy than to the formal wage economy. Public institutions tend to be weaker, and governments have fewer resources to invest in poverty programs; thus international donors play a much more significant role in financing social programs in sub-Saharan Africa. Competing donors often have conflicting ideas as to the types of social protection interventions to pursue. There is a lack of consensus among governments, too, along with a weaker capacity to implement and evaluate programs, and fewer complementary services like health, education, and nutrition. All these considerations make sub-Saharan Africa both an important laboratory for impact evaluation and a challenging place to do it.[7]

Another fundamental difference between the African and Mexican programs is that, for the most part, the African programs are not conditional. Often, behavioral changes like better nutritional practices and keeping kids in school are encouraged, but with few exceptions they are not required as a condition of getting the transfer. That is why these programs are often referred to as SCT instead of CCT programs. Is conditionality really needed, or, given the cash and information, will people choose to do the right thing? These questions loom in the debate and evaluation of SCTs in sub-Saharan Africa. There are exceptions that involve some sort of conditionality. Ethiopia's Productive Safety Net Program (PSNP) pays people from eligible households in chronically food-insecure *woredas* (districts) to work on labor-intensive projects. It is conditional in the sense that people have to work in order to get benefits. The idea behind this project is to give cash and food to the poor while building up the country's infrastructure, particularly irrigation, via work projects in which the beneficiaries participate.

A number of evaluations have come out of pilot programs designed to test the effectiveness of SCTs before the programs are "scaled up" to the larger population. Sidebar 2.2 summarizes what some of the key African SCT evaluations have been finding. Randomizing the "SCT treatment" is the key to being able to make statements like these about causality.

*Credit*

Access to credit is vital to people in poor as well as rich countries, as we shall see in chapter 12. There is strong theoretical reason to think that people will invest in new activities and technologies when they get access to credit. But how big is the impact? Do microcredit projects really make people more productive, and if so, how much?

### Sidebar 2.2  Impacts of SCTs in Sub-Saharan Africa

An evaluation of a pilot SCT program in Malawi showed a significant reduction in child morbidity, gains in school enrollment, and increases in food consumption and diet diversity. Agricultural investments increased. The SCT also reduced child labor outside the home.

C. Miller, M. Tsoka, and K. Reichert, "Impacts on Children of Cash Transfers in Malawi," in *Social Protection for Africa's Children*, edited by S. Handa, S. Devereux, and D. Webb (London: Routledge, 2011), 96–116.

Katia Covarrubias, Benjamin Davis, and Paul Winters, "From Protection to Production: Productive Impacts of the Malawi Social Cash Transfer Scheme," *Journal of Development Effectiveness* 4, no. 1 (2012):50–77.

Ethiopia's Productive Safety Net Program caused an increase in school attendance for some groups, particularly younger children, and a reduction in child labor for some activities among boys, but an increase in girls' labor time.

J. Hoddinott, D. O. Gilligan, and A. S. Taffesse, "The Impact of Ethiopia's Productive Safety Net Program on Schooling and Child Labor," *Social Protection for Africa's Children*, edited by S. Handa, S. Devereux, and D. Webb (London: Routledge, 2011), 71–95.

South Africa's Child Support Grant decreased school absences, illnesses, and hunger and increased height-for-age scores among children receiving the grant. It increased access to cell phone use and supported the sustainability of agricultural activities in households with children receiving the grant. It also significantly reduced risky behaviors among adolescents, including sexual activity, pregnancy, alcohol use, drug use, criminal activity, and gang membership.

DSD, SASSA, and UNICEF, *The South African Child Support Grant Impact Assessment: Evidence from a Survey of Children, Adolescents and Their Households* (Pretoria: UNICEF South Africa, 2012; www.unicef.org /evaldatabase/files/CSG_QUANTITATIVE_STUDY_FULL_REPORT_2012 .pdf).

Kenya's Cash Transfers for Orphans and Vulnerable Children (CT-OVC) increased children's secondary enrollment on par with what has been found from *conditional* cash transfer programs in other parts of the world. Participating households had significantly higher expenditures than control households in food, health, and clothing and significantly less spending on alcohol and tobacco. They shifted from tubers to cereals, meat and fish, and dairy.

The Kenya CT-OVC Evaluation Team, "The Impact of Kenya's Cash Transfer for Orphans and Vulnerable Children on Human Capital," *Journal of Development Effectiveness* 4, no. 1 (2012):38–49.

Testing the effect of credit on investments and other outcomes is difficult, because the kinds of people who get loans (i.e., who apply and are accepted) are different from the kinds that do not, so we cannot simply compare the two. How can you make an experiment out of credit?

Dean Karlan and Jonathan Zinman figured out a way.[8] They convinced a lender in South Africa to grant loans to a random sample of applicants with low credit scores. These were people who applied for credit but had been deemed not credit worthy. Giving credit to people who do not qualify for it might raise some ethical concerns (see "The Ethics of Experiments" later on in this chapter), but by randomly giving credit to some people in this group, Karlan and Zinman avoided the problem that more credit-worthy people get loans and might do well with or without credit. It was an RCT because only some randomly chosen people with low credit scores were given loans, while others were not.

The researchers compared those who got credit to those who did not in terms of "economic self-sufficiency" (employment and income), food consumption, and other outcomes six to twelve months after the treatment. They found that economic self-sufficiency and food consumption were higher for the treated group. They also found that depression and stress were higher for the people who won this loan lottery, perhaps due to anxiety from being in debt.

People didn't randomly incur debt in the RCT that Suresh de Mel, David McKenzie, and Christopher Woodruff did in Sri Lanka—they just got money or machines.[9] The entrepreneurs who got chosen for this "Santa Claus treatment" ended up with a significantly larger capital stock, which is not so surprising for the ones that got the machines but not predictable for the ones that got the cash. However, the effect of this treatment on the profitability of enterprises was small or insignificant. These results suggest that some businesses are constrained by a lack of capital while others are not.

*Insurance*

Evaluating how insurance affects poor households is challenging because almost no rural households have access to insurance, and those that do have insurance tend to be very different from those that do not. Characteristics of households that are correlated with whether or not they have insurance are also likely to explain outcomes like crop production, income, or nutrition. Because of this selection problem, comparing outcomes between households that get insurance and those that do not generally tells us little.

We know from past research (see chapter 12) that poor households diversify their activities more than rich households to protect themselves against uncertainty. By not "putting all their eggs in one basket," though, they forfeit the potential income gains from specializing in what they do best. Access to insurance could bring substantial economic benefits to rural households, because if harvests are insured, banks might be more willing to lend to farmers, and farmers might be better able to specialize. To test this, though, we need a treatment group of households that have access to insurance and a control group that does not. We also need to avoid the problems of *adverse selection* and *moral hazard,* which we'll learn about in chapter 12; otherwise, insurance companies will not be willing to offer insurance to small farmers. Where can we find all of this?

Sarah Janzen and Michael Carter came up with a way.[10] They offered a new kind of insurance to a random group of pastoralists in the Marsabit District of northern Kenya: index-based livestock insurance (IBLI). Satellite measures of vegetative cover are used to predict average livestock mortality from drought in local communities. The payout households get from this insurance has nothing to do with their behavior; this insurance pays if the average livestock mortality predicted from satellite images reaches 15%. This avoids the problem of moral hazard (people changing their behavior once they have insurance). Janzen and Carter convinced an insurance company in Kenya to make this insurance randomly available to some small farmers but not others. This helped solve the problem of adverse selection (higher risk people taking out insurance).

A drought hit in 2011, after the insurance was made available. Insured households got an average payout of $150. It is too soon to assess the impact of this insurance, but we can ask what people *think* it will be. Janzen and Carter asked both the insured and uninsured households how they plan to deal with the drought. Many responded that they'll eat fewer meals, but a significantly smaller percentage of those with insurance said this. The number who anticipated selling additional livestock to cope with the drought was 50% lower for the insured households. The insured households also said they will rely less on food aid and assistance from others.

If what households end up doing is anything like what they say they'll do, this project will have succeeded in helping pastoralists deal with drought risk and avoid some of the worst impacts of the drought, while demonstrating the importance of insurance in risky environments.

*Hope and Optimism*

Most people care about their future. But what if, when they look there, what they see are dim economic prospects? Psychologists call the uncomfortable tension people feel from simultaneously holding conflicting thoughts "cognitive dissonance." Could it be that the poor, by closing their eyes on the future, reduce their psychological distress at the cost of worsening their future economic well-being? If poor people close their eyes on the future, they will have no reason to save and invest for it. This can create a "psychological poverty trap."

In November–December 2010, a team of researchers in Mozambique ran a lottery in which the winners got a free input subsidy for 70% of the cost of a seed and fertilizer package.[11] Winners of this lottery could expect to get a larger harvest. In April–May 2011 both the winners and losers of the lottery were asked the question, "How much time ahead do you plan your future expenditures?" On average, winning the lottery increased an individual's time horizon by more than a month, from 198 days to 235 days. It seems that the farmers who won the lottery became more forward looking.

Another RCT, in India, found evidence that helping desperately poor people invest gave far better results than expected, consistent with breaking out of a psychological poverty trap (see sidebar 2.3).

You will find many other RCTs scattered throughout this book. They test the impacts of a wide variety of programs, from immunizations to HIV/AIDS and government corruption.

## RCTS AND THE PRACTICE OF DEVELOPMENT

The introduction to this chapter alluded to a methodological progression in development economics. The core questions about why some people and societies are poor and what might help alleviate this poverty have stayed essentially the same, but the methods economists use to try to address these questions have changed markedly. The approach of Adam Smith and his contemporaries was largely qualitative and even

## Sidebar 2.3 Hope

In the Indian state of West Bengal, a microfinance institution, Bandhan, tried something different. Instead of giving loans to extremely poor people, who they thought would be unlikely to repay, they gave out assets: a few chickens, a cow, a pair of goats. They also taught people in this treatment group how to take care of their animals and manage their households. Just to make sure they wouldn't eat the animals right away, they also gave them a little cash to spend.

The theory behind this RCT was that people would learn how to manage their finances better and make a little income selling the products their farm animals would provide. To test the results of this project, researchers compared these treated households with a random control group of poor households, which did not get any of these things.

The results? The treatment worked better than anyone had hoped for. Long after the treatment had ended, the treated households ate 15% more, earned 20% more, and skipped meals less often than households in the control group. They were saving more, too. The improvements were far too big to be explained by the direct effects of the grants. That is, the treated households could not have sold enough eggs, milk, or meat to explain these big outcomes.

The project gave the treated households more than it had expected. The research team, headed by economist Esther Duflo, called it hope. The project gave people a reason to work harder—28% more hours, to be precise. The incidence of depression fell. In addition to a few animals and a bit of advice, it seemed, Bandhan had succeeded in administering a healthy dose of optimism. Could it be that the hope for escaping from poverty traps is hope, itself?

"Hope Springs a Trap: An Absence of Optimism Plays a Large Role in Keeping People Trapped in Poverty," *Economist* (May 12, 2012; www.economist.com/node/21554506).

philosophical. As economics became more formalized and mathematical, development economists focused mostly on theoretical models to shed light on these questions. When international development assistance expanded rapidly after World War II, there was a substantial rift between the abstract modeling of ivory tower economists and the emerging ranks of "boots on the ground" development practitioners who designed and managed development projects. These were two different worlds that, at best, shared only poverty questions as a raison d'être.

The availability of data and computing power in the 1970s and 1980s shifted many development economists away from purely theoretical models toward serious empirical analysis—and enticed them to spend more time in the field collecting data. The 1990s brought additional empirical advances to development economics. During these decades development economists tended to interact more and more with development practitioners, but there remained a persistent gap between applied development research and the practice of development.

The experimental revolution of the 2000s has shrunk this gap noticeably and increasingly brought practitioners and economists together as collaborators. In a typical collaboration, an implementing practitioner organization (e.g., an NGO, agency, or company) that intends to launch or expand a project relies on a team of research economists to design an RCT to rigorously evaluate the intervention and conduct the analysis. Success demands careful coordination and close interaction between practitioners and development economists.

These new models of collaboration have shaped both development economics and the practice of development. Greater integration of the two has brought development economists into earlier stages of project design and evaluation. Aligning research and programmatic objectives often also leads economists to analyze more directly the costs and benefits of specific development programs and interventions. (We will learn about how to do a cost-benefit analysis later on in this chapter.) Cost-benefit analysis can build directly on RCTs, which can help quantify impacts and associated benefits.[12] Close collaboration with the implementing partner makes it easier to incorporate program costs into this analysis and determine whether the carefully measured benefits justify the costs required to reap these benefits. Ideally, more rigorous cost-benefit analysis of this sort improves development policy and programs by distinguishing good projects from bad ones.

RCT-based research has also shaped the practice of development in important ways. Development organizations of all sorts now feel pressure to rigorously evaluate their projects. While this presents new opportunities to learn what works and what doesn't, it also brings new risks. The prospect of establishing very clearly and cleanly that something works sounds great, but establishing with equal clarity the opposite looks and feels like failure. This can be a threat, perceived or real, to both reputation and future funding. In contrast, less rigorous impact evaluation methods can be more forgiving, allow organizations to use selection bias to their advantage, and leave plenty of room for casting evidence in a more favorable light (glossy annual reports often do exactly this).[13]

## WHEN EXPERIMENTS CAN GO AWRY

For all their promise, RCTs have many potential pitfalls. We have high-lighted a collection of well-executed experiments, but in practice, the ideal experiment is exceedingly hard to find. In general, the best experiments are those in which the question asked lends itself neatly to experimental methods, and the researchers have control over how the experiment is designed and executed. This usually is not the case with large-scale government programs, in which many things can go wrong, from politics to poor administration of treatments and research. Anyone reading about or designing RCTs had better be aware of these pitfalls.

There are two types of pitfalls that are worth noting: technical pitfalls that may undermine what we are able to learn from an RCT, and ethical pitfalls that arise in experimenting with people. We focus initially on the technical pitfalls of RCTs and discuss the ethical considerations, of RCTs in particular and experiments more broadly, later in the chapter.

The following subsections describe a few of the technical pitfalls that may beset an RCT.

### Creating Treatment and Control Groups

An RCT requires treating one randomly selected group and denying treatment to another. Before we can conduct an experiment, we need to have valid treatment and control groups. Creating treatment groups is not as easy as it may at first seem. Why not? Because it is often difficult to ensure that the people who are randomly assigned to treatment are actually treated. For example, if you wanted to test the impact of a new crop variety on household income, you could offer incentives to adopt the new variety to the farmers in the treatment group, but you cannot ensure complete compliance. That is, farmers still must choose to plant the new variety—and this choice threatens to introduce the selection bias described above. As we will discuss later in this chapter, economists have devised ways for careful experimental design and data analysis to remedy this potential pitfall.

There are yet deeper potential problems surrounding the creation of control groups, which sometimes simply may not be possible. Take tourism, for example. Ecotourism development projects are among the fastest-growing parts of development bank loan portfolios. Many countries see tourism as a way to stimulate economic growth and fight poverty. Suppose we are interested in quantifying the impacts of a tourism-development project. The treatment is the project. The treatment group is effectively the entire population at the tourist destination, and the control group is the same population without the project. It is not possible to make this project happen for one group of people but not for others at the tourist destination. One might argue that the project could be implemented at some randomly chosen tourist sites but not others. However, almost by definition tourist destinations are unique (hence the reasons tourists want to go there). This makes it difficult to come up with reasonable alternative locations as a control, that is, sites identical to the "treated" site except without the treatment. They simply do not represent the region without the project. There is no counterfactual for the Galápagos Islands.

There are many other cases in which problems arise in the construction of treatment and control groups. Irrigation and other infrastructure projects create public goods that potentially affect everyone in the zone in which the projects are carried out. Staple price supports frequently have been used as a mechanism to transfer income to farmers (with dubious welfare benefits). However, it is generally not feasible to offer a high price to some randomly selected farmers but not others.

It may be politically infeasible to randomly create a treatment group, or it may be considered unethical to deny benefits to a control group (see "The Ethics of Experiments," below). In theory, input subsidies could be implemented randomly through targeted vouchers. In practice, though, it may not be politically feasible to deny benefits to a control group while offering them to a treatment group.[14] Even in a country like Malawi, where fertilizer vouchers targeted poor farmers, they were not given out randomly. If subsidies are given to all qualifying farmers, there is no control group.[15] It is not uncommon for researchers to be called upon to conduct impact evaluations after a project has already been implemented. In this case, we can see who got the treatment and who did not, but we might not have the pretreatment data we need to do a clean RCT, and there might be concerns over whether the creation of the treatment and control groups was truly random.

*Control Group Contamination*

Measuring a project's impact on the treated requires isolating the control group from the project's effects. This is often not so easy to do in practice. Even in a medical experiment it may be difficult to isolate the control group from the treatment group, for example, if the treatment involves curing a communicable disease. The effects of treatments on control groups frequently confound experimental research in the social sciences.

A well-known RCT in Kenya illustrates this point. It was designed to treat school children with worms in an effort to keep them in school. But treating kids in some schools caused the incidence of worms among kids in *control* schools to go down (see sidebar 2.4). When the treatment affects the control group as well as the treatment group, it can be difficult or impossible to reliably estimate the impact of the treatment, because both groups change. We call this problem "control group contamination."

Economic linkages can transmit impacts from treatment groups to others inside and outside the local economy. Take a cash transfer program. The household that gets the cash spends it. In the process, it transmits the impacts of the program to others inside and outside the village. Ed spoke with a shopkeeper in an Ethiopian village who loved the cash transfer program there. "You get transfers?" Ed asked. "No, but the people who get money come here to spend it!" he answered.

This shopkeeper was not eligible for the treatment, but he benefited from it just the same. If treated households buy more food, local farmers can benefit. If they fix up their house, so can the local bricklayer. These people, in turn, may hire more workers and buy more inputs. This can lead to a village version of Keynesian economics, in which the infusion of new cash into the economy has a multiplier effect on village income.[16] If we only look at the treated households, we are likely to underestimate the overall effects of the treatment.

Economic spillovers do not necessarily result in control group contamination, but they may. If the control households are in another village, economic linkages from the treated villages might not reach them. However, all around Africa, periodic markets bring people together from many different villages to buy and sell. If households from treated and control villages interact in these markets, the result can be control group contamination.

Treatment spillover effects raise challenges for RCTs, and they can be good or bad for people. If the treatment positively affects the control

## Sidebar 2.4  Worms

Worms are bad (unless they're the garden variety). Hookworm and roundworm each infect approximately 1.3 billion people around the world; whipworm affects 900 million, and 200 million are infected with schistosomiasi. Intense worm infections keep kids from going to school and reduce their educational achievement. Could it be that a key to literacy is (getting rid of) worms?

Edward Miguel and Michael Kremer analyzed an RCT experiment to raise school attendance in Kenya by treating children for worms. A clearly defined treatment for worms was administered to children in a randomly selected sample of schools (the treatment group) but not in other schools (the control group). This project had a simple and easily measured outcome: school attendance. The ex-post research question was whether or not children in the treated schools were more likely to attend school after the treatment.

It seemed to be a squeaky clean experimental design. What could go wrong with it?

Actually, something went too right, from an analytical point of view. The treated schools treated the control schools. Maybe treated kids played with control kids after school or had contact with others who, in turn, had contact with control kids. The study could not tell us why, but for whatever reason, kids in the control schools got better, too.

Miguel and Kremer call this an *externality* of the treatment. (We'll learn about externalities in chapters 6 and 11.) In experimental jargon, it is called control group contamination. Really, it is a linkage—in this case, an epidemiological one—that transmitted the benefits of the project from those directly affected (the kids in the treatment school) to others in the project's zone of influence. Not surprisingly, the authors found that the farther a treated school was from a control school, the bigger the measured impact of the treatment.

Since kids in control schools got better, it was hard to find a positive effect on school attendance by comparing the treatment and control groups. It is ironic that a treatment potentially can be so successful that you cannot show it has any effect at all.

Edward Miguel and Michael Kremer, "Worms: Identifying Impacts on Education and Health in the Presence of Treatment Externalities," *Econometrica* 72, no. 1 (January 2004):159–217.

group, we might conclude that the treatment was not effective when in fact it was—both the treatment and control group benefit from it. It is also possible that the spillover is negative. For example, some villagers complain that cash transfers push up food prices. Giving cash to people might lead them to work less, in which case wages could go up. This in turn creates a cost for those who hire workers. If a project negatively affects the control group, we run the risk of concluding that the treatment was effective when really it was not: the treatment appears to make the treated better off when really it makes the control group worse off.

Under ideal circumstances, randomization can ensure that the expected outcome for the control households equals the expected outcome of the treated households had they not gotten the treatment. This ideal randomization relies in fact on two conditions. The first is having a "clean" control group that is isolated from the treatment. That is, it must be absolutely unaffected by the presence or absence of the treatment. The second is that the control group needs to be so similar to the treatment group on average that, had there been no treatment, the two groups would have displayed the same outcome.

### Can Development Be Studied Like a Pill?

There is no question that the widespread use of RCTs in international development that started with PROGRESA has profoundly changed the way economists, NGOs, aid agencies, and governments approach development problems. RCTs are a major—perhaps the major—focus of development economics today. It is hard to find a development student PhD thesis that does not include some kind of randomized treatment. The strongest proponents of RCTs argue that randomized evaluations are "the gold standard of impact evaluation."[17] A big lesson from RCTs is that there is no single solution or explanation for underdevelopment. Different kinds of action are needed in different settings.

Others, we have seen, question whether RCTs are the end-all tool they claim to be and whether the most pressing development questions can be answered using a randomized experiment. For example, one of the most ambitious development interventions of recent decades—the Millennium Village Project—is a grand social experiment, but it was not designed as an RCT. In the minds of many development economists, this limits our ability to evaluate the project's impact. Jeffrey

Sachs—the architect of this project—dismisses these concerns, saying, "Millennium Villages don't advance the way that one tests a new pill."[18] His view, which is shared by some other researchers, is that restricting ourselves to a single methodological approach will severely hamper our ability to understand the complexities of the development process. What do you think?

## IF NOT RCTS, THEN WHAT?

Although RCTs have become its poster child, the experimental revolution in development economics extends beyond this method. Recall that the essence of this methodological revolution is that the less choice people have to opt in or out of a treatment, the easier it is to test the treatment effect. RCTs offer a clean and direct way to introduce random treatment (albeit not as cleanly and simply as it might seem, as discussed above), but there are experimental alternatives, specifically (1) laboratory experiments and (2) natural experiments. Let's look at each of these in turn.

### Laboratory Experiments

In a laboratory experiment, subjects make economic decisions in a contrived setting that is designed by researchers to elicit a specific kind of response from them. Travis has designed and conducted economic experiments like this in India, Morocco, Bolivia, and in several sub-Saharan African countries to learn how people make decisions. Individuals' responses in these controlled settings help us measure things that are otherwise difficult to measure: aversion to risk, patience, trust, concerns about fairness, and willingness to cooperate, to name just a few.

These "laboratory experiments" rarely take place in a laboratory when development economists do them. Instead, trained teams (often consisting of local university students or recent graduates) conduct these experiments in places where people tend to gather: under trees, in health clinics, near village schools, and so on. The structure of the experiments is carefully crafted to ensure that participants fully understand their tasks and to get a very specific kind of response from them. To encourage participants to formulate their decisions thoughtfully and to do the best they can, they are rewarded (typically paid in cash) according to their performance in the experiment.

The earliest experiments in development economics sought to understand how farmers in India make risky decisions in order to know whether risk aversion among poor farmers might prevent them from trying new seeds. As we'll describe in chapter 12, World Bank economist Hans Binswanger[19] implemented simple risk "games" in which farmers were given money and had to decide how much they were comfortable risking on defined gambles. By presenting all farmers with the same series of gambles and putting real money on the table, economists can measure each farmer's degree of risk aversion, which can influence many real-world decisions and thereby inform the design of development policy and interventions.

### Natural Experiments

The international migration of labor is an important component of globalization and economic development in many LDCs. The number of international migrants, or people residing in a country other than their country of birth, has increased at an increasing rate over the past forty years, from an estimated 76 million in 1965 to 215 million in 2010. According to the World Bank, migrants sent US$325 billion home to LDCs in 2010, far more than official development assistance programs did: for each dollar of aid rich countries give poor countries, migrants send home more than $2.50. The flow of international migrant remittances to LDCs is increasing—faster than the number of migrants, in fact.

How do these remittances affect migrant-sending economies? This is an important question in development economics. Unfortunately, the selection problem makes it very hard to answer. Migration is not like a random treatment; households and individuals decide whether or not to migrate. There is a huge selection problem. The households that send family members off as migrants are different from the households that do not, in ways that are likely to affect almost any outcome we want to study.

We could imagine a hypothetical thought experiment in which we randomly plucked some people out of some households and made them migrate (the "migration-treatment" group), while keeping everyone else at home (the control group). Then we could go back at some future date and compare outcomes of interest, like remittance income, kids' schooling attendance, and productive investments, between the two groups.

With a randomized "migration treatment," households with and without migrants would be the same, on average, except for migration. There would be no selection problem.

Such an experiment, of course, is unrealistic, and even if it weren't, it would be unethical to make some people migrate (even if they didn't want to) while preventing others from migrating (even if they wanted to). It would violate the "do no harm" axiom, which we'll learn about later in this chapter. There is no RCT to study the impacts of migration on migrant-sending economies.

Is evaluating migration's impacts hopeless, then? Dean Yang, an economist at the University of Michigan, found a way (see sidebar 2.5).

### Sidebar 2.5   A Remittance "Natural Experiment" from the Philippines

It's hard to imagine designing a randomized control trial to evaluate the impacts of migrant remittances, but Dean Yang came up with what might be the next best thing. He noticed that, at the moment of the Asian financial crisis of 1997, Philippine households had migrants in many different Asian countries. In some cases, the same household had migrants in more than one country. When the crisis hit, the Philippine peso devaluated more against some Asian countries than others. When the peso devalues, the value of remittances in pesos increases. For example, each Hong Kong dollar a migrant sent home turned into more Philippine pesos than before the crisis.

Nobody expected the crisis to happen. The impact on each household's remittances depended on where its migrants happened to be at the time of the crisis. That, Dean argued, makes the changes in remittances almost as good as random.

He found that a 1% peso devaluation increased remittances by 0.6%. These positive remittance shocks caused households to invest more time and money in human capital as well as in local businesses. Child schooling rose, while child labor decreased.

This study was important because of its "natural-experiment" approach to measure remittance impacts and its finding that remittances have a positive impact on investments in migrant-sending households.

Dean Yang, "International Migration, Remittances and Household Investment: Evidence from Philippine Migrants' Exchange Rate Shocks," *Economic Journal* 118 (April 2008):591–630.

Whereas with laboratory experiments researchers have direct control over the experiment and with RCTs researchers typically have indirect control over the experiment (because a partner NGO or agency typically administers the "treatment"), with natural experiments researchers have no control whatsoever. Instead, they take what history, legislation, or nature serves up and try to uncover circumstances in which people had little choice about being "treated" with something of interest. Used in the right way, such circumstances can remedy what is known as a "reflection problem." Often, we want to know how some "treatment" $X$ (like remittances, in the example we just saw) affects some outcome $Y$ (like poverty), but $Y$ may also affect $X$. Poor households might be more likely to migrate in search of higher incomes, or they might be less likely to migrate if migration involves high costs and risks. If $X$ reflects $Y$ in this way, it becomes very difficult to disentangle the effect of $X$ on $Y$ from the effect of $Y$ on $X$. The selection problem is related to this reflection problem.

Hollywood gives us a nice illustration of the reflection problem. Some famous movie scenes with villains have a hall of mirrors. Every time the villain moves, so does his reflection in a bunch of different mirrors. That's what happened to James Bond in *The Man with the Golden Gun*. This is a classic identification problem. You see the outcome (all those reflections of the bad guy raising his gun), but you don't know the cause (how can you identify the *real* bad guy who makes all the reflections move?).

That's how it often is with identifying cause and effect in economics. We see the outcome, but usually we don't have a neat RCT, so we need more information to figure out the cause. For example, if the villain coughs or steps on a twig, James can isolate him from the reflections and take him down. The sound is associated with the real bad guy but not his reflections, so it lets Bond figure out which is which. Basically, that's the strategy we have to follow in order to establish cause and effect in economics when we don't have a good RCT.

Economists are always on the lookout for variables that are correlated with treatments but not with the outcomes they study. These are called "instrumental variables." An example is the Asian economic crisis in Dean Yang's study (sidebar 2.5). Many of the most important development economics questions cannot be studied with the aid of well-designed RCTs. Econometric methods are then used, along with carefully chosen instruments, in an effort to isolate cause and effect. In the rest of this book we will learn about a number of different studies in which economists came up with novel ways to identify impacts without the benefit of an RCT.

James Bond found a more straightforward solution to his identification problem. He quickly shot out all the mirrors until the only thing left was the bad guy, Francisco Scaramanga!

## THE ETHICS OF EXPERIMENTS

Experimenting on people raises ethical considerations. History gives us extreme and frightening examples of incidents in which people have been harmed by research, particularly in the medical and psychological areas. They include deliberate infection with serious diseases, exposure to biological or chemical weapons, human radiation, and many other atrocities. Some are less obviously harmful. A Stanford University study funded by the US Office of Naval Research in 1971 used students as guinea pigs to investigate the causes of conflict between military guards and prisoners. Students participated voluntarily for $15 per day. They were randomly assigned to play the roles of prisoners and guards in a mock prison in the basement of the psychology building, but they internalized their roles too well. By the time the experiment was terminated, the guards were subjecting their prisoners to physical and psychological abuse. The Stanford Prison Experiment often is held up as an example of unethical scientific research.

Today, any time human subjects are part of research, careful measures are required. Institutional review boards (IRBs) have to approve, monitor, and review biomedical as well as behavioral research involving humans. IRB approval is even required in order to carry out most kinds of economic surveys, because when you ask people questions in a survey, the respondents are your research subjects. It is important to remember this anytime you engage in social science research involving people. Guidance on complying with human subjects requirements is available at most universities and from the US Department of Health and Human Services (HHS; www.hhs.gov/ohrp/archive/irb/irb_guidebook .htm).

Despite IRB reviews, as RCTs have become a dominant methodology in development economics, they have raised considerable controversy, including with regard to ethics. Economists Chris Barrett and Michael Carter point out four classes of ethical considerations that arise in experiments by development economists.[20] These are discussed in the following four subsections.

*Adverse Consequences of Experiments*

The first rule in studies involving humans is the "do no harm" principle. Experiments manipulate people's environment in an effort to learn about their behavior. If in doing so they harm people, they are unethical and should not be implemented. This is the primary focus of IRBs.

Often, adverse effects of experiments are predictable and clear-cut. For example, if an RCT would encourage people to do something illegal or would put them in harm's way, it is definitely not ethical. An RCT in India created incentives for people to get driver's licenses without necessarily successfully completing the required training and testing. This potentially put innocent people at risk on the roads.

Other experiments are less blatant but still raise concerns. For example, researchers in China studied the impact of treating kids for iron deficiency (anemia) on school performance. Some children known to have anemia were given iron pills, and others were not. This study would not be approved in the United States because withholding treatment for something like anemia would not be considered ethical.

Barrett and Carter listed a number of cases in which experiments are likely to produce adverse consequences. One experiment tested whether large grants of money to women's organizations change them in ways that lead to the exclusion of poor women, potentially harming poor women. The study's finding that it did lead to exclusion seems to confirm that poor women may have been harmed by the experiment.

Think about the credit experiment we looked at previously, in which some people with low credit scores were given loans. Does it comply with the "do no harm" rule? Fannie Mae (the Federal National Mortgage Association), a US government–sponsored enterprise, made many home loans to people who should not have gotten them. This was a major cause of the "Great Recession" beginning in 2008. Needless to say, it was not a good thing for the people who shouldn't have gotten loans and ended up going into default. Giving loans to people who do not qualify for them can put their property and reputation at risk.

It is hard to imagine doing any harm by giving people good stuff like goats, chickens, or cash. Yet as we have seen, cash transfer programs can potentially harm some nonparticipants, for example, by pushing up local prices for food and other items they buy. This is not to say that these programs should not be implemented—they almost certainly do considerably more good than harm. Nevertheless, when we implement experiments or other programs, we have a responsibility to anticipate possible negative impacts on participants or nonparticipants and do whatever we can to mitigate them. This is part of the "do no harm by doing good" maxim.

### Informed Consent

There is a difference between people being willful participants in experiments and people as subjects manipulated for research ends. The right of informed consent is well accepted; everyone who participates in a drug trial does so voluntarily. In RCTs, people often are unaware that they are (or are not) part of an experiment. IRBs require that participation in research studies, including simply being surveyed as part of an RCT, be strictly voluntary. The question, then, is how much information researchers should give their human subjects before they decide whether or not to be part of an RCT.

### Blindedness

In medical research, people can know they are in an experiment without knowing whether they get treated. The use of a placebo makes this possible: the placebo pill looks the same as the real thing, so no one except the researcher knows who's being treated. Very few RCTs attempt to use a placebo. (For an interesting exception see sidebar 2.6.)

When you give someone an economic treatment, it's hard to keep it a secret. If a person knows she is in an RCT but ends up in the control group, she knows it. Keeping who gets the treatment and who doesn't a secret is a basic tenet of medical research, but it generally is not possible in economic RCTs.

The most important ethical rule, we have seen, is to do no harm. If people know they are in the control group, might they suffer emotional distress because they are not getting the benefits of the treatment? Imagine that you are desperately poor and malnourished. Could there be adverse emotional, psychological, even health consequences of knowing that you have been excluded from a treatment that could significantly improve your situation?

If so, there could be not only ethical but also research concerns. If you know you're in the control group and lose hope as a result, you could end up doing worse than you would have done without the experiment. Thus, the treatment group might look better off compared to you, making it seem like the treatment worked better than it did.

## Sidebar 2.6   What? An Economic Placebo?

Using a placebo is basic in medical research. Treatment and control groups take an identical pill, but no one (except the researcher) knows which pill is the real thing. That's important, because if you know you are (or aren't) getting the treatment, the experiment is likely to get contaminated; for example, your behavior might change (like taking an antihistamine and then riding off into the pollen on your bicycle).

Economic RCTs are different, though. For example, people know whether or not they're getting a cash transfer. It's impossible to give people an "economic placebo."

. . . or is it? Four researchers ran an RCT in which farmers didn't know whether or not they were getting the real treatment. In randomly chosen treatment villages, farmers got a modern high-yielding variety (HYV) of cowpea seed. In control villages, they got the placebo: a traditional variety (TV). None of the farmers knew which seed they were planting. The result? Yields were the same between the treatment and control groups.

In another set of treatment villages, the farmers ran a normal RCT: the farmers knew whether they were getting the HYV or the TV. When farmers knew they were getting the TV, their yields were much lower than when they did not know. Their behavior changed. That is a placebo effect.

High-yielding seeds are designed to produce a bigger harvest when combined with the right combination of inputs: fertilizer, water, and so forth. The experimenters could have given farmers a package of inputs to use along with the seeds. That way, the only difference between treatment and control farmers would have been the seed, itself. Scientists frequently run experiments in which they control all inputs on experiment station plots. They are left with the question: Do experiment station results reflect what really happens out on farmers' fields? If we want to find out how a new seed affects crop yields in the real world, we have to recognize that farmers' input choices will be a key factor shaping the outcome—and those choices will depend on knowing which seed they're planting.

Erwin Bulte, Gonne Beekman, Salvatore Di Falco, Joseph Hella, Pan Lei, "Behavioral Responses and the Impact of New Agricultural Technologies: Evidence from a Double-Blind Field Experiment in Tanzania," *American Journal of Agricultural Economics* 96, no. 3 (2014): 813–30.

Is it ethical to involve people in experiments without their knowledge? If you answer "no" to this question, then you immediately hit another one: Can you reliably measure the impact of a social treatment if people *know* whether or not they are in the experiment? Will people—even people in the control group—change their behavior in ways that tarnish the RCT?

*Targeting*

Development organizations and governments have scarce resources to carry out development projects. It might seem logical (and ethical), then, to efficiently target these resources. Community knowledge can be used to make sure help goes to those most in need. RCTs routinely treat individuals who are not most in need of the treatment, while denying treatment to those who are. Strict randomization thus is viewed by many as being both wasteful and unfair. This can—rightly—be a stumbling block to convincing governments and communities to participate in RCTs.

An additional concern in experiments is the Treat-and-Run Syndrome. PROGRESA left Mexico with one of the world's most comprehensive social welfare programs, one that continues to this day. However, most RCTs are not conducted as part of large-scale government programs; many researchers abandon their research sites once the results of their RCTs are in. What are the long-term impacts of this "treat-and-run" way of doing research? If providing benefits to a treatment group does no harm during an experiment, does ceasing those benefits do no harm in the long run? What are the effects of leaving people behind after an RCT is over?

However you might answer these ethics questions, on one thing we can all agree: anytime we use human beings as research subjects, we have a special responsibility to make sure that we do them no harm, not only during the experiment, but afterward, as well.

### THE INVARIANCE ASSUMPTION

Experiments, in order to be valid, must satisfy the *invariance assumption,* which states that the actual program will act like the experimental version of the program. Often, the purpose of RCTs is to test interventions that, if deemed successful, will be scaled up to a larger—or perhaps the entire—population. Will the large-scale program have the same kinds of impacts as the small-scale RCT? Or is there something about ramping up a project that creates new impacts not captured in experiments?

Actually, there may be. Once the program gets scaled up, the control group disappears. Linkages can transmit impacts of the program through the whole economy. Now everyone is likely to be affected, directly or indirectly, by the treatment. We call the total effect on the economy the "general equilibrium (GE) effect." We look at GE effects of projects at the end of this chapter. GE effects are a major reason why the invariance assumption may be violated. An intervention does not have to be particularly large in order to unleash GE effects; it only has to be important relative to the size of the economy in which it happens. In a poor region, a small project can have a large GE impact.

#### MULTIPLE TREATMENTS AND INTERRELATED OUTCOMES

In the worms experiment there was a clearly defined treatment (for worms) and outcome of interest (children's school attendance). Often, programs have multiple instruments (e.g., a cash transfer plus conditionality and eligibility requirements, or cash transfers and input subsidies or crop-price supports) and interrelated outcomes. In these cases, it quickly becomes difficult to connect specific components of the program with specific outcomes of interest.

Consider the social cash transfer (SCT) program initiated in 2011 in Tigray, Ethiopia. Many of the households eligible to receive the SCT already participated in a different transfer program: the Productive Safety Net Program (PSNP) had been offering them the opportunity to work a limited number of days on public projects in return for food or cash. When a household gets the SCT treatment, it stops getting the PSNP one. The new program crowds out the old, and both coexist within the same (treatment and control) localities. Disentangling the effects of these two programs is essential if we wish to evaluate the SCT's impacts. Some of the best experiments involve multiple treatments, but when there are many different interventions happening simultaneously, RCTs may not be up to the task of sorting out the impacts.

The impacts of most projects and policies are almost certain to be heterogeneous, with both winners and losers. Few experimental studies consider the ways in which some people may gain while others may lose as a result of a policy or program.

## "WHETHER," "WHY," AND "HOW"

Consumer theory gives us a familiar equation relating a household's demand for a good *(D)* with its income *(Y)* and the market prices of this and other goods *(P)*:

$$D = \beta_0 + \beta_1 Y + \beta_2 P$$

This is what we call a structural equation. It is structural because it is derived from a theory of how the household economy works. Thanks to consumer theory, we know why income and prices are in this equation, and we even know what signs to expect on the parameters (for example, $\beta_1 > 0$ if we are dealing with a normal good, and $\beta_2 < 0$ if $P$ is the price of the good in question).

When it comes to estimating this equation, though, we have a problem. Current income is endogenous. It is the result of work and other choices people make, and those choices might be related to consumption decisions in ways other than through income. Thus, when we compare demands among people at different income levels, there is likely to be a selection problem.

In chapter 6 we'll learn about Jacob Mincer, who argued that people's permanent income depends on their schooling *(S)* and work experience *(E)*, which we can treat as given at any point in time:

$$Y = \alpha_0 + \alpha_1 S + \alpha_2 E + \alpha_3 E^2$$

We could substitute this equation into our consumer demand model, eliminating the problem income variable and expressing demand as a function of schooling, experience, and prices:

$$D = \gamma_0 + \gamma_1 S + \gamma_2 E + \gamma_3 E^2 + \gamma_4 P$$

This is what we call a "reduced-form model." In economics, a reduced-form model is what you get once you've solved for the endogenous variables (here, income). In the reduced-form model, the variable of interest (here, $D$) is a function only of exogenous variables. If you do the algebra, you'll find that its parameters are functions of the parameters in the other two equations.

We might use econometrics to estimate this reduced-form model with survey data. We might find, for example, that the demand for smartphones increases with people's schooling. However, we would not be able to interpret the economic meaning of this result without knowing the underlying structural model. There are many reasons why schooling might influence the demand for smartphones. According to the structural model, schooling increases income, which in turn increases cell phone demand. A finding that schooling positively affects cell phone demand would be support for the hypothesis that cell phones are normal goods, based on the structural model.

A common rap against experimental methods is that they are reduced form. In a well-designed experiment, the treatment is exogenous. We estimate its impact on an outcome of interest. Experiments are a good way to test whether a treatment has an effect, but like other reduced-form methods, they do not tell us why. The economist Angus Deaton wrote: "In ideal circumstances, randomized evaluations of projects are useful for obtaining a convincing estimate of the average effect of a program or project. The price for this success is a focus that is too narrow to tell us 'what works' in development, to design policy, or to advance scientific knowledge about development processes."[21]

Designing good policies depends on understanding "why" as well as "whether." It also requires focusing our research on the highest-priority questions.

The best experimental studies not only test program impacts but also try to offer glimpses into the structural reasons why a treatment produces the outcomes it does. For example, in a clever experimental study in Kenya, some farmers were offered free fertilizer delivery early in the season and others not, while still others were offered a fertilizer subsidy. The study found that offering delivery early was more effective at increasing fertilizer use than was a subsidy.[22]

In general, though, it is far more difficult to answer the question of *why* a treatment has the effect it does than *whether or not* there is an effect and *how big* the effect is.

## OPPORTUNITY COSTS

So your RCT finds that a program is effective at achieving its goals. Should the program be scaled up? The answer implicit in most experimental studies seems to be "yes." But is it the best way? Economists often talk about "opportunity costs." The opportunity cost of doing one thing is the value of what you could have done instead. When doing RCTs, it is easy to forget that every project and every way of carrying out a project has an opportunity cost. Finding that a treatment has a significant effect on an outcome of interest does not necessarily mean that the treatment is the best use of scarce public resources. A cash transfer, output price support, technology policy, or fertilizer voucher all might raise incomes in the beneficiary households, but they are unlikely to be equally effective at transforming a dollar of public expenditure into an increase in income in the treatment (or nontreatment) households.

## COST-BENEFIT ANALYSIS

Economics offers a methodology to choose among different actions. It is called cost-benefit analysis (CBA, for short). You probably use CBA all the time without even thinking about it, like when you picked up this development economics book! CBA is the basic tool that development banks use to determine whether a development project is viable before it gets funded, and it can be used to compare the viability of different projects, as well— provided that the costs and benefits of projects can be quantified.

The basic idea behind CBA for development projects is simple: add up all the benefits and costs of the development project and take the difference. If this difference is positive, the project is viable; if not, then there is not an economic basis for undertaking the project. If it is positive for two or more different projects but you can only afford to carry out one of them, pick the project in which the difference between the benefits and costs is greatest.

In practice (like everything in life, it seems), CBA gets complicated. For one thing, most projects involve heavy start-up costs in the short run and benefits that are in the future. A dollar in the future is not worth the same as a dollar today—that's why banks have to pay interest in order to get us to save.

### Discounting and Net Present Value

CBA has a straightforward way to deal with the timing problem: use the interest rate to discount future values and express them in present value (PV). If $i$ is the interest rate, the PV of $100 of income a year from now is $100/(1 + i)$. If the interest rate is 5% (that is, .05), we get $100/1.05 = $95.24. If you had $95.24 today, you could turn it into $100 a year from now by putting it in the bank at 5% interest—and waiting.

What is the PV of $100 two years from now? In other words, how much would you need to put in the bank today to end up with $100 after two years? The answer is $100/(1 + i)^2$. At a 5% interest rate, the PV of $100 two years from now is $100/(1.05)^2 = $90.70. When doing CBA, we convert all future benefits and costs to PV by dividing them by $(1 + i)^t$, where $t$ is the time period: $t = 1$ in year 1, $t = 2$ in year 2, and so on.

Once we have discounted all future benefits and costs of a project, we sum their differences to get the project's net present value (NPV):

$$NPV = \sum_{t=0}^{T} \left( \frac{Benefits^t - Costs^t}{(1 + i)^t} \right)$$

The capital Greek sigma ($\Sigma$) denotes the sum; our formula adds up the discounted difference between benefits and costs from the start of the project ($t = 0$) until the end of the time period over which we wish to perform the cost-benefit analysis ($t = T$).[23]

The NPV formula is the basis for carrying out any CBA. If NPV > 0, the project passes the economic cost-benefit test. If you can only fund one project, on purely economic grounds choose the one with the highest NPV.

### Determining Benefits and Costs

The trick always is in figuring out what the benefits and costs are. Often, a project's costs are immediate and known. For example, it is not hard to determine the cost of running an extension program to train one hundred farmers on how to use a new technology and giving each farmer a technology start-up package (for example, high-yielding seed and fertilizer to plant one acre). Or the cost of building a new school room and staffing it with a teacher. Or of carrying out an immunization program in one hundred villages.

Calculating benefits can be a different matter, though. If you carry out the extension program, how much higher will the farmers' incomes be? If you build the school, will students attend? How many parents will bring their kids to the clinic to get the immunization? If more kids attend school or get immunized, will their future incomes go up because they become more productive?

This is where experiments and the other evaluation methods in this chapter can help. Cleverly designed RCTs can provide estimates of how many farmers will adopt a new technology and how much their yields are likely to increase if they do. The PROGRESA and African cash transfer RCT studies described earlier in this chapter estimate impacts on school attendance. Chapter 6 includes an RCT to evaluate the demand for immunizations.

TABLE 2.1   PRESENT VALUE OF COSTS AND
BENEFITS OF A HYPOTHETICAL PROJECT

| $t$ | Cost(t) | Benefit(t) | Benefit(t)–Cost(t) |
|-----|---------|-----------|--------------------|
| 1 | 100 | | –100 |
| 2 | | 18.18 | 18.18 |
| 3 | | 16.53 | 16.53 |
| 4 | | 15.03 | 15.03 |
| 5 | | 13.66 | 13.66 |
| 6 | | 12.42 | 12.42 |
| 7 | | 11.29 | 11.29 |
| 8 | | 10.26 | 10.26 |
| 9 | | 9.33 | 9.33 |
| 10 | | 8.48 | 8.48 |

NPV: 15.18

Here's a simple illustration of the mechanics of CBA: imagine a project that would cost $100 to carry out, with all of those costs occurring in year 1. Beginning in year 2, based on our experimental or other estimates, we expect the project to produce benefits of $20 per year. Your funding agency requires that the project break even within ten years—that is, the project's NPV, evaluated over a ten-year period, must be positive. Is it?

Using a fairly conservative (10%) discount rate, we can construct a table showing the PV of this project's costs and projected benefits (table 2.1).

The balance of annual benefits and costs starts out negative, because there are only costs in year 1. It turns positive once the project begins to yield the $20 benefit per year. The $20 number doesn't appear in this table, though. Benefits have to be discounted: the PV of $20 after one year is $18.18; after two years it is $16.53, and so on. (If there were costs in years 2–10, they would have to be discounted, too.)

Adding up all of the discounted benefits and costs over the ten-year period, we get an NPV of $15.18. It is greater than zero; thus, the project is economically viable. Whether it is economically optimal will require comparing this to the NPVs of competing projects.

You might want to experiment using the CBA worksheet posted online for this chapter. You would find that this project would not pass the economic cost-benefit test if the benefits were $17 per year, if the interest rate were 14%, or if there were an annual cost of $2 to keep the project going.

In chapter 6 we carry out a simple cost-benefit analysis of going to school for a child in a poor Lesotho village. It is not unlike the CBA you might have carried out while deciding whether or not to study development economics.

### Non-Economic Benefits and Costs

Many benefits and costs cannot be quantified. CBA can be a good tool for evaluating economic costs and benefits and selecting projects on economic grounds. Clearly, there are reasons to carry out projects on other grounds, as well. How can one deny a child education or good health if it is at all possible to provide her with these basic human rights? Non-economic benefits strengthen the argument for carrying out some development projects. Non-economic costs can do the opposite. An example of the latter is an activity that produces negative externalities, for example, a negative environmental impact. Positive externalities, on the other hand, can strengthen the case for a project. For example, "treating" some farmers with information about better cultivation practices could have positive externalities if the "treated" farmers share this information with others. In short, CBA is a useful economic tool, but it may not be the sole criterion for implementing a development project.

### BEYOND EXPERIMENTS: LOCAL ECONOMY-WIDE IMPACTS OF DEVELOPMENT PROGRAMS

Suppose we wish to evaluate the impact of an income transfer program on rural poverty. Poor households receive the transfer, which might entail some sort of conditionality (for example, PROGRESA's requirement that children attend school) or not (the case in almost all of the SCT programs in Africa). Figure 2.1 illustrates the pathways by which this project might impact a local economy. Arrow (a) represents the transfer's direct effect on the income of a recipient (poor) household. This is equal to the amount of the transfer. With higher income, the household's demand for normal goods and services increases. The transfer can affect the household's production activities in a number of different ways. By raising the household's income, it can stimulate consumption demand, including the demand for leisure and goods produced by the household.[24]

For example, an increased demand for food could encourage a subsistence household to grow more food crops, while an increased demand

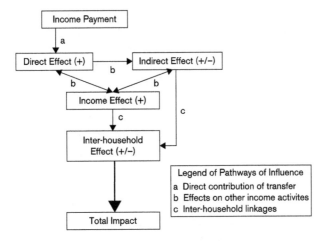

**FIGURE 2.1.** An income transfer project creates both direct and indirect income effects in the treated economy.

for leisure could do the opposite. If leisure demand increases, the household's wage income could fall. The transfer could loosen liquidity constraints on crop production, enabling the household to purchase more fertilizer and other inputs or shift into input-intensive cash crops.[25] Finally, it could reduce income risk, and this might encourage the household to invest more of its scanty resources in risky activities. (We'll learn about agricultural household behavior in chapter 9.) Conditionality could create still other impacts in recipient households. For example, the requirement that children attend school could decrease the family's labor available for crop production.

Arrow (b) depicts these myriad indirect effects of the transfer on the treated household's income from production and labor activities. Experimental methods, when feasible and carefully executed, can provide insights into the net influences represented by arrows (a) and (b).

As the recipient households demand more consumption goods and change their allocation of resources to production and wage activities, others in the local economy invariably are affected. Local markets transmit impacts of the transfer from the recipient to nonrecipient households, as represented by arrow (c) in the figure. Households and businesses supplying goods and services to the recipient households benefit. If the transfer alters the recipient household's wage labor supply, this could drive up wages, or as consumption demand rises, so might local prices. These will affect nonrecipient households in other (possibly negative) ways. As local activities adjust, a new round of changes in input demands, incomes, and household expenditures follows, creating additional rounds of changes in incomes and expenditures. Given income leakages, successive rounds of impacts become smaller and smaller, and the total (direct plus indirect) effect of the program eventually converges to an income multiplier. To the extent the goods demanded by the recipient households are supplied locally, the income transfer could create a multiplier considerably greater than one. On the other hand, if the recipient households purchase goods from outside the local economy, some or perhaps most of the multiplier will go elsewhere. Clearly, the behavior of the households that get the transfer to begin with is critical in shaping the impacts that result from the program, but so is the behavior of the nontreated groups and the structure of the local markets connecting them with each other.

The economic linkages that transmit impacts through economies are called "general-equilibrium feedback effects." In a few cases, RCTs have collected data on ineligible households and found evidence that they are affected by treatments. One such study was done on the effects of Mexico's PROGRESA on the households that did not get PROGRESA transfers. The impact was found to be positive, implying that only focusing on the treated underestimates the program's impact.[26]

To understand the ways in which a treatment affects both treated and nontreated households, we generally have to go beyond RCTs and try to model economic linkages. As the diagram in figure 2.1 illustrates, the direct and indirect impacts of an intervention are shaped by how households change their supply and demand decisions and by the structure of local markets, which in turn reflect various constraints (technology, transaction costs, liquidity, risk). Performing project evaluations in such environments may require integrating models of heterogeneous households into a model of the whole local economy, a local general-equilibrium (GE) model. A model for the economy targeted by the project (village, region, rural sector) can provide a laboratory in which the project is designed and its impacts assessed, using a simulation approach.

There are fundamental differences—some might call these philosophical differences—between RCTs and simulation models. An RCT, we've seen, is like a drug experiment; it can tell us whether something works, but not why. An advantage of experiments is that statistical significance can be attached to RCT findings; for example, "with 95% certainty we can say that the transfer increased food consumption by between $10 and $15 per month." The validity of an RCT depends on getting the experiment right; otherwise, the findings, however significant statistically, may be biased. At conferences where researchers present studies using RCTs, much of the discussion centers around what might have gone wrong in the experiment and how this might have affected the results. This illustrates how much more difficult it can be to run "clean" economic experiments than drug trials. Often, one is left with questions about why a treatment had the effect that it did on those who got the treatment.

Simulation models try to answer the question "why" while capturing complex interactions that shape project outcomes, in ways that often are beyond the reach of experiments. The validity of a simulation model depends on getting the model right. Imagine a flight simulator. Schools do not teach pilots how to fly by hitting them with dangerous real-world situations in mid-air. Pilots can step into a flight simulator. The simulator is programmed with equations representing the physics of flight. It becomes a laboratory in which flight experiments are conducted. If you've ever played a computer game, you know what simulations are all about. If the flight simulator is programmed wrong, well, you won't want to fly with that pilot!

A simulation approach to project impact evaluation highlights the interactions within the local economy that transmit impacts, good or bad, from directly affected actors to others in the economy. We can construct simulation models using data from the same surveys that are used to do RCT research. If our simulation model represents the way in which the local economy works, it can be a valuable tool to understand the full, economy-wide impacts of cash transfers and many other programs and policies.

There are two main knocks against simulation models. One is that they depend on getting the model right, especially how agents behave and how markets transmit impacts from one agent to another (like getting the flight simulator equations right). Another is that it is more difficult (though not impossible) to attach statistical significance to simulation results.

A new method, local economy-wide impact evaluation (LEWIE), uses data from RCT surveys to estimate simulation models and construct confidence bounds around their results. This is a step in the direction of bringing together the best of RCT and simulation methods.

A LEWIE simulation model was used to evaluate the local GE effects of a cash transfer program in the southern African country of Lesotho.

### Sidebar 2.7 Impacts of a Treatment on the Nontreated in Lesotho

When poor people get cash transfers, they spend them. This transmits impacts of cash transfer programs from treated to nontreated households. Lesotho's Child Grants Program (CGP) seeks to improve the living conditions, nutrition, health, and schooling of orphans and vulnerable children. It seeks to accomplish this via an unconditional cash transfer targeted to poor and vulnerable households.

A local economy-wide impact evaluation (LEWIE) found that each $1 transferred to a poor household raises total village income by $2.23, with a 90% confidence interval (CI) of $2.08 to $2.44. Even though all of the cash transfers go to poor eligible households, nearly half of the benefits they create ($1.18) go to ineligible households.

If there are constraints that limit the local supply response, though, higher local demand may push up prices instead of stimulating production. Price inflation reduces the multiplier in real (price-adjusted) terms. (We'll learn how to adjust income for inflation in chapter 3.) It raises consumption costs for everyone in the local economy. If supply constraints are severe, the *real* income multiplier may be as low as $1.36 (CI: $1.25–$1.45). The study found that loosening capital constraints, say, through effective microcredit programs that enable households to buy more crop inputs, can be a key to avoiding inflation and raising the real transfer multiplier.

This study is important because it reveals potential impacts of cash transfer programs that are unlikely to be picked up by RCTs—including impacts on households that do not get the cash. Large local income multipliers suggest that social cash transfer programs promote income growth in poor villages. That's good news for both social welfare ministers and finance ministers in LDCs.

J. Edward Taylor, Mateusz Filipski, Karen Thome, and Benjamin Davis, "Spillover Effects of Social Cash Transfers: Lesotho's Child Grants Program," in *Beyond Experiments in Development Economics: Local Economy-Wide Impact Evaluation*, edited by J. Edward Taylor and Mateusz Filipski (Oxford: Oxford University Press, 2014), 181–202.

It uncovered import spillover effects, including effects on the households that did not get the transfer (see sidebar 2.7).

www.rebeltext.org/development/qr2.html
Learn more about what works and what doesn't by
exploring multimedia resources while you read.

## APPENDIX

### The Math of Selection

The math behind RCTs is not very hard, but it takes most people some time to wrap their minds around it because it involves some "what ifs." Here's how it works:

We want to know whether a treatment (like a development project) affects some outcome of interest (say, income or health). Let's call person $i$'s outcome $Y_i$. If a person gets treated, the outcome is $Y_{1i}$, and if she does not get treated, it is $Y_{0i}$. Each person has both a $Y_{1i}$ and a $Y_{0i}$, but there's a catch: we can only see one of them. If $i$ gets treated, we see $Y_{1i}$ but not $Y_{0i}$. If she doesn't get treated, we see $Y_{0i}$ but not $Y_{1i}$.

Let's make a variable $D_i$ that equals 1 if person $i$ gets treated and 0 otherwise. A concise way to represent the outcomes is:

$$Y_i = \begin{cases} Y_{1i} \ if \ D_i = 1 \\ Y_{0i} \ if \ D_i = 0 \end{cases}$$

The outcome we "see" for person $i$ is whatever it would be without the treatment, $Y_{0i}$, plus whatever effect the treatment has, which is $(Y_{1i} - Y_{0i})D_i$. For short, let's call the actual effect of the treatment $\rho$:

$$Y_i = Y_{0i} + \underbrace{(Y_{1i} - Y_{0i})}_{\rho} D_i$$

The treatment effect, $\rho$, is what we want to find out. It is the change in the outcome that is *caused* by the treatment. (If the person does not get treated, $D_i = 0$, so this second term is zero.)

Now suppose we simply compare expected or average outcomes for people who do and do not get the treatment. In stats talk, the expected or average outcome given that a person gets the treatment is $E[Y_i|D_i = 1]$, and the expected outcome for people who don't get the treatment is $E[Y_i|D_i = 0]$. ("E" means "the expected value of," and the slash marks mean "given that.") The average difference we see between the people who are treated and the people who are not, then, is

$$E[Y_i|D_i = 1] - E[Y_i|D_i = 0]$$

This difference is not the average effect of the treatment on the treated, because it includes selection bias. The average effect of the treatment on the treated is the difference between (1) the expected outcome for people with the treatment, given that they got it ($E[Y_{1i}|D_i = 1]$), and (2) the expected outcome for these same treated people *if they had not been treated* (which we can call $E[Y_{0i}|D_i = 1]$). In other words, the average treatment effect on the treated, which is what we want to know, is

$$E[Y_{1i}|D_i = 1] - E[Y_{0i}|D_i = 1]$$

Imagine the people who get the treatment (that's the first term). If, after they get the treatment, we could put them into an Orwellian time machine, send them back in time, and then not treat them, we'd have the second term. If that person did not change in any other way, the difference would be the true average effect of the treatment on the treated.

Obviously, we cannot both treat and not treat the same people. We have to compare people who get treated to people who don't. This leaves us with selection bias. Selection bias is the difference between (1) the expected outcome for those who got treated, if they hadn't gotten treated (same as the second term in the expression above: $E[Y_{0i}|D_i = 1]$), and (2) the expected outcome without the treatment for the people who didn't get treated ($E[Y_{0i}|D_i = 0]$). In other words:

$$E[Y_{0i}|D_i = 1] - E[Y_{0i}|D_i = 0]$$

In the hospital example, the selection bias is negative, because the people who get the "hospital treatment" (the first term above) are less healthy, on average, than the people who don't get the treatment (the second term). It is reasonable to expect that, on average, the people who went to hospital would have had poorer health without going ($E[Y_{0i}|D_i = 1]$) than the people who didn't go got by not going ($E[Y_{0i}|D_i = 0]$). The people in this last group probably didn't go because they didn't need to.

To sum it all up:

$$\underbrace{E[Y_i|D_i = 1] - E[Y_i|D_i = 0]}_{\textit{Observed difference in average health}}$$

$$= \underbrace{E[Y_{1i}|D_i = 1] - E[Y_{0i}|D_i = 1]}_{\textit{Average treatment effect on treated (positive—we hope!)}}$$

$$+ \underbrace{E[Y_{0i}|D_i = 1] - E[Y_{0i}|D_i = 0]}_{\textit{Selection bias}}$$

What makes this challenging to understand is that the repeated term on the right-hand side of the equation above, $E[Y_{0i}|D_i = 1]$, is hypothetical. We cannot see what did not happen.

Randomization solves the day. If the treatment is truly random, then on average the people who get it are identical to those who do not, so their outcomes without the treatment, on average, are the same: $E[Y_{0i}|D_i = 1] = E[Y_{0i}|D_i = 0]$. The selection bias term disappears, leaving only the average treatment effect on the treated. That's why, in a well-designed RCT, we can estimate the average effect of the treatment on the treated simply by comparing average outcomes for the random treatment and control groups.

# 3

# Income

Economic development entails many different sorts of
outcomes: income growth, poverty, inequality, human
welfare. These outcomes are obviously interrelated. Understanding these interrelationships is a central theme in
development economics. As we shall see, these economic
outcomes can shape one another in complex and important
ways. Before we learn how to study these interactions and
outcomes and before we consider ways to influence them
with policies and projects, we need to know how to measure
them. In this chapter, we focus on measuring income. That
might sound boring and straightforward, but read on—you
may be surprised by how interesting, challenging, and controversial income can be. It is often consequential as well,
because a country's measured income level can determine
whether it gets special privileges or preferential treatment in
international organizations and negotiations.

## ESSENTIALS

- GDP and GNP
- Subsistence goods and shadow values
- Market failures: externalities and public goods
- Development classifications and categories
- Input-output analysis and income multipliers
- Purchasing power parity and price deflators
- Creating and using indexes

## MEASURING INCOME

Income is a basic development indicator. Indeed, it provides the most
obvious distinction between the rich and the poor. It is also an important input in the economic development process, since investments of all
kinds—in people, in society, in innovation, in nature—require resources.

Poor countries have low income and therefore fewer resources available to accomplish their development goals.

Before going any further, we should agree on how to measure income. The most basic measure of a country's income is its gross domestic product (GDP). This concept is based on a fundamental identity (i.e., relationship) in economics: in all economic activities, total income must always equal total expenditures. Every dollar of sales by a shirt factory (income) either goes toward purchasing the inputs used to produce the shirts or gets paid out to the factory's owners as profit (expenditures). Based on this identity, we can calculate a country's GDP in one of two ways.

First, we can add up the value of all *final* goods and services *produced within the country and then sold*. By "final," we mean goods and services that are *not* inputs into the production of some other good. For example, cotton is rarely a final good; it is an input into the production of cloth. Cloth, in turn, is an input into producing clothes. Clothes are almost always a final good—we buy and wear them, rather than using them to produce something else.

You can see the potential for double-counting here. The price of a shirt includes the cost of the cotton fabric to the garment factory as well as the cost of the cotton to the textile mill. If we added the value of the cotton, fabric, and shirt together to calculate GDP, we would significantly overstate the value of what was produced in our economy. We also want to be careful not to count the value of inputs produced in foreign countries. If the buttons on shirts sold in the United States were produced in Mexico, they are part of the GDP of Mexico, not the US. The US-Mexico border really matters in this case, because GDP is meant to capture the geography of economic activity. In short, calculating national income is a lot harder than it sounds.

After we determine which goods to include, we have to add them all together to get a measure of total production. We do this by putting a value on each of the goods. What value do we use for all of these final goods? Economists tend to trust markets to indicate what goods are worth, so, not surprisingly, we use market prices. This gives us the GDP at market prices.

The second way to estimate GDP is to focus on inputs instead of final goods and to add up the cost of all factor inputs (capital, labor, land). Any economic activity takes intermediate inputs (cotton fabric, thread, buttons) and uses factors of production (labor and capital) to turn these inputs into a product (shirts). The income the shirt factory creates is called its "value-added" and consists of the difference between the value of the shirts it sells and the cost of the cotton fabric, thread, buttons, and other intermediate inputs it buys to produce the shirts. This is the value that the shirt factory adds to the cotton fabric and other intermediate inputs once it has turned them into shirts. Value-added is the factory's payments to labor and capital. While adding up all this value-added gives us the GDP at factor cost without running the risk of double-counting, determining value-added, as you might guess, is also not without its complications!

*Input-Output Analysis*

To make the difference between these two approaches crystal clear, let's introduce a new concept: input-output analysis. To be introduced properly to this concept, you should really meet Russian American economist Wassily Leontief, who founded input-output analysis and picked up a Nobel Prize in 1973 for his contribution. Table 3.1 is a Leontief input-output table for a simple economy consisting of only three production sectors: agriculture, industry, and services. In this simple economy, agriculture produces a total output of $920, and industry and services produce $1,425 and $567, respectively. You'll notice that these numbers appear twice, as both the row and column total for each sector.

The columns show the expenditures of each sector, that is, where all the money went. In order to produce its output, agriculture bought $225 in intermediate inputs from itself (e.g., seed), $320 from the industrial sector (e.g., chemical fertilizer), and $75 from services (e.g., contractors and accountants). It spent $100 in wages and purchased $50 in imported inputs. Finally, the agricultural sector generated $150 in profits, for an expenditure total of $920.

The total expenditures must equal the total value of agricultural production. The Agriculture row tells us where this production went, or in other words, who paid money to farms. Reading across the first row you can see that $225 of the value of agricultural output was sold back to agriculture, as intermediate inputs (e.g., seeds), $75 to industry (e.g., as wheat to flour mills), and $2 to services (e.g., food to schools). The difference between the total agricultural production ($920) and these intermediate uses of agricultural goods ($225 + $75 + $2 = $302) is the final demand for agricultural output ($618).

You can interpret the industry and service accounts in exactly the same way.

TABLE 3.1   AN INPUT-OUTPUT TABLE (IN USD)

| Income Account | Agriculture | Industry | Services | Final | TOTAL |
|---|---|---|---|---|---|
| Production Sectors | | | | | |
| Agriculture | 225 | 75 | 2 | 618 | 920 |
| Industry | 320 | 200 | 85 | 820 | 1,425 |
| Services | 75 | 150 | 30 | 312 | 567 |
| Factors | | | | | |
| Labor | 100 | 400 | 275 | n/a | 775 |
| Capital (Profits) | 150 | 300 | 125 | | 575 |
| Imports | 50 | 300 | 50 | | 400 |
| TOTAL | 920 | 1,425 | 567 | 1,750 | |

$775 + 575 = 1,350$ (GDP at factor cost)

$1,750 - (50 + 300 + 50) = 1,350$
(GDP at market prices)

It is easy to calculate GDP from the input-output table, using either of the two methods. GDP at market prices is the sum of the total final demand ($618 + $820 + $312 = $1,750) minus imported inputs ($50 + $300 + $50), or $1,350. GDP at factor cost is just the sum of payments to factors (labor and capital), or value-added: $775 + $575 = $1,350. As you can see, it doesn't matter which way we do it—we end up with the same GDP.

This basic method can be used to calculate the GDP for any economy—a country, state or province, even a village. If the state of California were a country, it would have the eighth largest GDP in the world, just behind Brazil and in a near tie with Italy and the Russian Federation.[1] Some economic surveys of rural households gather all of the data needed to calculate a village's GDP. This can be quite complicated, because many rural households both produce and consume agricultural goods, as we will learn in chapter 9.

*Multiplier Analysis*

In the prior exercise, you not only learned how to calculate GDP, but picked up a little bit about input-output (IO) accounting along the way. As it developed in the twentieth century, IO analysis became the conceptual foundation for socialist planning. From an IO table like this one, it is not hard to derive a Leontief multiplier matrix, which tells us how much each sector in an economy has to produce in order to (1)

TABLE 3.2 LEONTIEF MULTIPLIERS

a. Production

| Production Sectors | Agriculture | Industry | Services |
|---|---|---|---|
| Agriculture | 1.365 | 0.086 | 0.019 |
| Industry | 0.584 | 1.223 | 0.196 |
| Services | 0.182 | 0.143 | 1.079 |

b. Factor Value-Added and GDP

| Factor | Agriculture | Industry | Services |
|---|---|---|---|
| Labor | 0.401 | 0.422 | 0.580 |
| Capital | 0.386 | 0.303 | 0.282 |
| GDP | 0.787 | 0.725 | 0.863 |

satisfy all final demand and (2) supply all the intermediate inputs that are needed by all the production sectors. That's a big part of the central planner's resource allocation problem—and it is no easy task, which is why market economies, which let markets do all this work, have largely outperformed planners.

While masterminding whole economies using IO analysis is no longer in vogue, we've learned that the basic exercise can be very insightful for budding development economists. The appendix to this chapter shows how to derive production, factor value-added (wage and profit), and GDP multipliers from this IO table in three steps, using Excel. The result is shown as table 3.2.

The entries in a Leontief production multiplier matrix are the outputs each row (sector) has to produce in order to satisfy a $1 increase in the column's (sector's) final demand. For example, to meet a $1 increase in final demand for agricultural goods, agriculture must produce an additional $1.36 in output, industry must produce an additional $0.58 in output, and services, $0.18. To produce an additional $1 of industrial output, agriculture must produce $0.09, industry, $1.22, and so on through the table.

From this matrix you can see that in order for production to increase in *any* sector, *all* sectors have to produce more, because each sector demands inputs from other sectors. Only in the extreme case where a sector is an enclave, that is, not connected in any way with other sectors in the economy, would the diagonal element for that sector be 1 and the off-diagonal elements all be 0. Otherwise, economic linkages will transmit impacts from a shock in one sector to all of the other sectors in the economy.

They will also affect wages and profits in the economy. The $1 increase in final demand for agriculture, industry, and services boosts payments to labor by $0.40, $0.42, and $0.58, respectively. Profits increase by $0.39, $0.30, and $0.28, respectively. Adding the wage and profit multipliers together, we get GDP multipliers of $0.79, $0.72, and $0.86, respectively, as a result of the $1 increases in final demands, assuming that all sectors are able to expand their production to meet the new demand.

In addition to providing insights for budding development economists, Leontief IO analysis continues to influence some of the frontiers of development economics. IO analysis inspired Albert Hirschman (chapter 1) to appreciate how economic linkages across sectors can be exploited to help grow whole economies (i.e., by investing in one carefully chosen sector, governments can stimulate growth in other sectors), and these linkages continue to be important to both development economics and development policy. Extensions of IO analysis—for example, the inclusion of households and government, investment, and trade in the form of a social accounting matrix (SAM)—are the starting point for doing almost any kind of economy-wide analysis. Computable general-equilibrium (CGE) models and other types of economy-wide analysis are largely beyond the scope of this book, but we will refer to them from time to time, and when we do, you can remember this simple IO example.

IO tables can be constructed for any economy or activity, from countries or groups of countries (even the entire world!) to villages and agricultural households. With the right data, you could make one for your university, student union, or student farm.

*Other Measures of Income*

You will run across a couple of other names for national income. The gross national product (GNP), also known as gross national income (GNI), is the same as GDP, but it includes the value of goods and services produced by citizens abroad. For example, Mexican migrant workers in the United States send home, or remit, more than $25 billion annually. This is value produced by Mexicans abroad, so it is counted in Mexico's GNP (but not in its GDP). It is removed from the US GDP for calculating the US GNP. For the most part, there is little difference between GNP and GDP, so the two are often used almost interchange-ably. This is not technically correct, though, and in a few cases it mat-ters. For example, in a Mexican village, counting the remittances that flow in makes a big difference in the calculation of village income (the gross village product).

## WHAT'S NOT IN GDP

Now that we know what's in GDP, let's explore what isn't. This might seem technical, but it really matters, especially in poor countries where a lot of what's produced never gets sold and a lot of what people use is never actually purchased in a market.

Look back at our IO table. Everything is in value terms. The GDP at market prices is the value of all *final* goods and services *produced* in a country then *sold*. The GDP at factor cost also was calculated based on goods sold and inputs purchased.

Much of the staple production in poor countries, particularly by the poorest farmers, is for subsistence: it isn't sold. We'll discuss subsistence production and its ramifications in detail in chapter 9. For now, what matters is that, unless a crop is sold, it may not be counted as part of national income. To count subsistence production, we would need not only to expand our definition of national income to include it, but also to find a way to place an economic value on a nonmarketed good. Some countries try to do this more than others.

Since much of the economic interaction and exchange in poor coun-tries is not formalized and documented the way it tends to be in rich countries, several similar complications arise. Many poor households rely heavily on home-produced goods such as agricultural production or small-scale retail shops and roadside stands. Almost none of the fam-ily inputs provided to these operations involve a market transaction. Labor on small farms or in small shops is not hired but supplied by the family members themselves. No wage is paid for this labor, yet clearly it is part of the value-added produced by an economy. What about bar-ter or labor exchanges? Transactions that involve informal trades of one good or service for another are similarly difficult to track and count. Generally, these complications of the informal economy, which account for a bigger share of total economic activity in poorer countries, mean that portions of the value-added that should be part of GDP may simply be missed—and that this missing portion is likely to be bigger the poorer the country.

We can take special steps to count these nonmarket activities in our income calculations, but it won't be easy. For starters, how do we value a subsistence crop? Family labor? Labor exchanged? In a village where most farmers are subsistence producers there might be a few who sell their harvests. Could we use the price they get to value other farmers' subsistence production? This would imply that subsistence farmers value their crops at a market price that they do not—and likely cannot—receive. In chapter 9, we'll see how households are driven into subsistence production when it is too expensive for them to buy and sell on the market. As a result, subsistence producers value their crops at a price that is different—and possibly very different—from the market price. The price of a traditional variety of maize grown by an indigenous farmer in Oaxaca is not the same as the price of corn in a market (it turns out to be higher). To distinguish it from the market price, economists use the term "shadow value" to describe the value of nontraded goods like subsistence crops. Just as you can characterize some features of a tree based only on the shadow it casts in the morning or afternoon sun, so we can sometimes characterize the value a poor farmer places on his maize crop even if he doesn't sell it in the market. His shadow value for the maize he grows cannot be seen directly, but the trade-offs he makes when managing his maize can imply a specific shadow value. With the right data, we can estimate shadow values even though we cannot see them.

What about family labor? Do we look around the village for someone who worked for a wage or hired a wage worker, and use that wage to value family labor? In some cases, households use both family and hired labor to grow crops. Can we assume the two are interchangeable and value both at the same market wage? I might have to monitor my hired workers to make sure they give me the same value product per day as my own (or my family members') labor does (see chapter 11, "Information and Markets"). You can bet that I have know-how about my farming operation that hired workers do not. A day of my labor is likely to be more productive than a day of hired or exchanged labor, and therefore worth more than the market wage. I might be able to squeeze more work out of my family members than I can out of a hired worker.

What if I cannot hire workers, say, because I do not have enough cash to pay them? The labor I have available to work on my farm, then, will be limited by my family's size. Unless I have a big family, I might experience a labor shortage and value family time above the market wage. What if other farmers don't hire? A shortage of work opportunities on other people's farms might trap my family's labor on my farm—

I might have too much labor, and it might be worth less than the market wage. Either way, it is not at all clear that the market wage is the right way to value family labor. In fact, the shadow value of labor is likely to be quite different from the market wage. While we cannot directly observe a farmer's shadow value of family labor, how he manages these labor trade-offs casts a "shadow" that can be used to characterize his underlying shadow value of family labor.

Estimating shadow values for nontraded goods is complicated, so these goods are typically just dropped from national income accounting. Even in rich countries that tend to rely more on market transactions, real goods and services are often missed in income accounting. The same work may or may not contribute to national income, depending on who does it. Last night, Ed and his wife made a nice teriyaki chicken dinner. The value of this home-cooked meal obviously didn't get counted in GDP. However, if we had hired a cook to do the same thing, it would have. Travis can hire a carpenter to fix his house or do it himself (that's what Home Depot is for). In the first case, GDP goes up; in the second, it does not. All the time we spend raising our children doesn't count in the US GDP. If we hired a nanny, the nanny's time would.

You may have noticed a pattern across these examples: often the distinction between what is and what isn't counted in GDP reflects that some things are formalized in market transactions while others involve traditional divisions of labor within the home. In many settings, women are more involved in nonmarket activities than men are, and the many contributions women make are consequently undercounted in GDP. The technical details in national income accounting may seem pretty dry, but some of them strike at the heart of some fundamental development questions, including gender and gender roles.

Then there is the underground economy, which generally does not get counted in the GDP yet in some cases might include a significant part of the economy. In 2012, the US states of Colorado and Washington voted to legalize marijuana. Both states' GDPs increased as a result. Part of this increase may be due to expanded marijuana use, but a sizable portion is due to existing use suddenly being measured as a formal (legal) market transaction.

In 2014, the United Kingdom decided to include the sale of illicit drugs and prostitution in its GDP. This proved to be controversial, but it made the UK's GDP calculations compatible with those of the rest of the European Union, which includes some countries in which narcotics and prostitution are legal (and thus counted in the GDP). Drugs and sex added $16.7 billion to the UK's GDP![2]

You probably never thought measuring national income could be so interesting . . . and controversial!

## PER CAPITA INCOME

Once we know gross national income, we can convert it to per capita income simply by dividing by the country's population. This is very important if we wish to compare standards of living across countries. China's gross GDP was $5.8 trillion in 2010. The US GDP was $14.6 trillion. Yet with a little more than 1.3 billion people (compared to 308 million in the US), China's per capita income was $4,260, while that in the US was $47,140.

Of course, just because we generally use these kinds of comparisons to contrast the standard of living in two different countries does not mean that country-level analysis is always very useful. Both the US and China have rich regions and poor regions. Average differences between two countries can be useful, but they can also be misleading. Thankfully, as we have already mentioned, the same concepts of income accounting apply to other scales of analysis, which enables comparisons of regions or cities within a given country. We explore this kind of inequality in chapter 5.

## EXCHANGE RATES AND PURCHASING POWER PARITY

In the process of making this comparison between China and the US, we confess to using a sleight of hand that we should reveal in the interest of full disclosure. Because all economists use this same trick anytime they make cross-country income comparisons, it is one you should understand. How did we come up with this income figure in dollars for China? After all, they don't use dollars much over there; the currency in China is the renminbi (its basic unit is the yuan). To convert to dollars, we divided the China GDP in renminbi by the nominal exchange rate, which in 2010 was 6.62 renminbi per dollar.

But wait, there's more to the trick. This isn't a fair comparison, you might say, because $4,260 goes a lot further in China than in the US, where the cost of living is higher. You're right—about 78% further, according to the World Bank.[3] If we add this additional "purchasing power" to the per capita income of China, we get 1.78 * $4,260 = $7,570. We call this the purchasing power parity (PPP)—adjusted per capita income. PPP adjustments are essential if we wish to compare incomes and understand differences in standards of living across countries.

How do we make a PPP adjuster? In principle it is not hard: define a basket of goods and services, price it in different countries, and you've got a way to adjust for costs of living. In practice, of course, things are harder. We have to decide what to include in the basket, and in what proportions. Some goods and services are easier to price than others. For example, what is the value of a food crop produced for a family's own subsistence? Prices vary within countries, as well as among them. Do we price our basket in the capital city or in a rural hinterland? The answer to this question will result in vastly differently priced baskets in some cases.

The World Bank does it in three steps. First, it calculates PPP for individual products. For example, a liter of Coca-Cola might cost 2.3 euros in France and $2 in the US, so the PPP for Coke between France and the US is 1.15 (= 2.3/2). Then it averages the PPPs for all goods within a product category. Coca-Cola is in the category of "beverages and concentrates." This gives the PPP for the product category. Finally, it averages the PPPs across product categories to get an overall PPP for each country.

If that sounds hard, you can use a Big Mac to do essentially the same thing (sidebar 3.1).

### PRICE DEFLATING

Besides comparing incomes across countries, we also want to compare incomes in the same countries over time. This is central to studying income growth, the subject of chapter 7. When we do that, we need to adjust for changes in prices over time. Here's an example: between 2009 and 2010, the GDP of the Democratic Republic of the Congo (DRC) rose a hefty 31%, from $12.2 billion to $16.1 billion. But it didn't really grow that much (that is, not in *real* terms). Inflation in 2010 was 22%, which makes the 2010 GDP look higher than it really was. To get the real (inflation-adjusted) GDP growth, we have to take the 2010 GDP and divide it by one plus the rate of inflation: GDP(real) = GDP(nominal)/ (1.22). This gives us a 2010 real GDP of $13.1 billion and a (still respectable) real GDP growth rate of (13.1/12.2) – 1 = 0.07, or 7%. The DRC had an unusually high inflation rate by international standards. In all countries, though, when comparing incomes over time, you have to adjust for inflation.

## Sidebar 3.1    PPP and the Big Mac Index

Ng Yat-chiu, the man who introduced McDonald's hamburgers to Hong Kong, came up with a simple way to compare the cost of living across countries: just look at the price of Big Macs! In 1986 the *Economist* magazine ran an article about the Big Mac Index. It was meant to be a parody of the PPP, but the idea caught on like, well, hamburgers and french fries! The Big Mac Index has been calculated and published every year since then.

For example, in July 2008, the price of a Big Mac was $3.57 in the US and 2.29 pounds, or $4.58 at the current exchange rate, in the UK. That implies a PPP rate of 1.56. By comparison, in Germany a Big Mac traded at 2.99 euros, which at the dollar-euro exchange rate was $3.66; thus, the Big Mac PPP rate between the US and Germany was 1.11.

Is the Big Mac a good basis for constructing a cost-of-living index? In one respect it would seem to be: Big Macs are ubiquitous—what country doesn't have them? How representative Big Macs are of people's expenditures generally is another question, though. The poorer the society, the more Big Macs are a luxury good to which the majority of the population does not have access. Nevertheless, its simplicity and wit have made the Big Mac Index a subject of academic debate as well as a comical analogue to the PPP.

Jiawen Yang, "Nontradables and the Valuation of RMB—An Evaluation of the Big Mac Index," *China Economic Review* 15, no. 3 (2004):353–59.

### GREEN ACCOUNTING AND EXTERNALITIES

Yet another thing missing from national accounts is the environmental cost of producing countries' incomes. Remember that anything not bought and sold in an economy is not counted as part of GDP. This includes the clean air and water that get "used up" when factories belch smoke into the atmosphere and sludge into a river. We call these "environmental externalities." The GDP may miss the depletion of natural resources if the cost of these resources is not properly reflected in market prices. Does the rising world price of oil reflect the fact that we are nearing "peak production?" It can be argued that the cost of natural resource depletion is already factored into rising resource prices. Climate change takes the stakes of not considering environmental costs to a whole new, global, level.

To the extent environmental costs are not reflected in the GDP, the methods described above may overstate income. The economist Robert

TABLE 3.3 AN INPUT-OUTPUT TABLE WITH GREEN ACCOUNTING

| Income Account | Agriculture | Industry | Services | Final | TOTAL |
|---|---|---|---|---|---|
| Production Sector | | | | | |
| Agriculture | 225 | 75 | 2 | 618 | 920 |
| Industry | 320 | 200 | 85 | 820 | 1,425 |
| Services | 75 | 150 | 30 | 312 | 567 |
| Factor | | | | | |
| Labor | 90 | 360 | 247.5 | n/a | 697.5 |
| Capital (Profits) | 135 | 270 | 112.5 | n/a | 517.5 |
| Imports | 50 | 300 | 50 | n/a | 400 |
| Environment | 25 | 70 | 40 | n/a | 135 |
| TOTAL | 920 | 1,425 | 567 | 1,750 | |

Repetto and co-authors wrote that ignoring environmental costs in our GDP calculations "reinforces the false dichotomy between the economy and 'the environment' that leads policy makers to ignore or destroy the latter in the name of economic development."[4] The economist Peter Wood proposed a way to deal with environmental costs in GDP calculations. He called it "green accounting." If we know what the environmental costs of production are, we can include them in our input-output table by adding an "environment account," as in table 3.3.

Notice the new row, labeled "Environment." Think of it as environmental inputs (like clean air) that get used to produce stuff. Now, producing $920 in agricultural output incurs a $25 environmental cost. The environmental costs associated with industrial and service production are $70 and $40, respectively. These environmental costs decrease our GDP from $1,350 to $1,215.

To include this environmental account in our table, we assumed that 10% of value-added in each activity was at the expense of "using up" environmental inputs for which there are no market transactions. This might seem arbitrary, and indeed it is: we do not really know what the true environmental costs of production are (though they're not likely to be zero). This is the greatest challenge to green accounting, though substantial research is going into estimating the environmental costs of various economic activities. If we can figure out a way to create markets for environmental goods, our green accounting problem will be solved (see sidebar 3.2).

Environmental costs are not the only externalities we might want to think about. Obesity, for example, increases the GDP: the more food

## Sidebar 3.2   Green Accounting and the Pollution Drag on GDP

How much does pollution cost an economy? The Environment and Planning Institute of China's Ministry of Environmental Protection decided to use green accounting to find out. It reported that ecological and environmental degradation cost China US$83.5 billion in 2004 and $248 billion in 2010. That's more than 3% of the country's entire GDP up in smoke.

China's efforts have been lauded as one of the most ambitious attempts to do green accounting in any country. However, the approach China uses is not without controversy, which highlights the challenges of doing green accounting. It focuses on three sources of pollution (air, water, and solid waste), calculates the costs of abating them, and adds these up to get an estimate of the total cost of environmental degradation. China did not include tough-to-quantify items like the effect of pollution on public health and workers' productivity, the depletion of aquifers, or the loss of agricultural productivity to soil erosion. If these were counted, the environmental costs of China's rapid economic growth would be even higher.

Vic Li and Graeme Lang, "China's 'Green GDP' Experiment and the Struggle for Ecological Modernisation," *Journal of Contemporary Asia* 40, no. 1 (2010):44–62.

Fergus O'Rorke, "China's Revived Green GDP Program Still Faces Challenges," *CleanBiz.Asia* (March 28, 2013; www.cleanbiz.asia/news/chinas-revived-green-gdp-program-still-faces-challenges#. UvBl5fldWSr).

people consume, the higher GDP becomes. Overconsumption comes at a cost, though: the World Health Organization estimates that 1.5 billion adults twenty and older were overweight in 2008. Sixty-five percent of the world's population lived in countries where being overweight killed more people than being underweight.[5] The health consequences of overconsumption are not reflected in our GDP calculations except, ironically, as a benefit: higher value-added in the health industry! So should we include the negative health consequences of obesity as externalities in our GDP calculations? If so, then where do we stop and call it a day?

#### WHERE DO WE STACK UP? MAKING AN INDEX

Earlier in this chapter we considered how to compare economies in terms of income. In coming chapters we will also compare countries with respect to other outcomes, including poverty, inequality, and human welfare. With 196 countries in the world, that's a lot of outcomes. It gets more complex still when we look at data from surveys of thousands of households within countries. We need efficient, easy-to-understand ways of making sense of all those data. Often, a good way to start is to make an index.

To make an index, we take a variable of interest (say, income, poverty, inequality, or even a composite of different things) and normalize it to have a common starting point or range. You will run across a wide variety of indexes in this book. For most of these indexes, we will take the variable of interest, which typically takes on a wide range of values, and transform it into a measure that ranges from zero to one. This can be an incredibly useful tool to make sense of complex data, as we shall see.

Here's a simple example of how to make an index of country per capita income. It will convey the intuition behind an index, and is the basis for constructing part of the Human Development Index that we will explore in chapter 6. Let $Y_i$ be the PPP-adjusted per capita income of country $i$, $Y_{min}$ be the lowest per capita income of all countries, and $Y_{max}$ be the highest. In 2010, PPP-adjusted per capita incomes in the world ranged from US$409 (Burundi) to $86,899 (Luxembourg).[6] Egypt had a PPP-adjusted per capita income of $6,180. Is this high or low? Clearly, it is a lot lower than Luxembourg's, which other countries could never aspire to. Yet it is considerably higher than Burundi's.

One way of comparing country incomes would be to rank them from poorest to richest. An income ranking would place Egypt sixtieth from the poorest among the 167 countries for which per capita income was available from the World Bank in 2010. We could divide Egypt's rank by the total number of countries, and we would have the share of countries with income at or below Egypt's. This turns out to be 60/167 = 0.359.

Doing this for all countries gives us the cumulative distribution function of per capita incomes. We shall use this to calculate the Gini index of inequality in chapter 5.

A drawback of an index based on rankings instead of actual incomes is that it does not tell us *how much* higher or lower one country's income is than that of other countries. Being the sixtieth from the poorest country doesn't tell us much if we don't know what the distribution of incomes looks like. We can make an index sensitive to income levels for any country $i$ as follows: take the difference between country $i$'s income and that of the poorest country (Burundi), and divide this by the difference between the highest (Luxembourg) and lowest (Burundi) income:

$$I_Y(i) = \frac{Y_i - Y_{min}}{Y_{max} - Y_{min}}$$

This index will range from zero (for the poorest country, the numerator is zero) to one (for the richest country, the numerator is the same as the denominator). It has other nice properties. For example, if country $i$'s income stays the same, while the richest country's income increases, country $i$'s income position as measured by this index will decrease. It turns out that the same thing will happen if country $i$ stays put, but the poorest country's income increases.

For Egypt, the value of our index is

$$I_Y \ (Egypt) = (6,180 - 409)/(86,899 - 409) = 0.067$$

As you can see, Egypt looks much worse off with this index than the one based only on rankings (0.067, compared with 0.359). Many countries are much richer than Egypt. It turns out that Egypt's income makes it more similar to the countries below it than to those above it in terms of income. The last index gives us a better sense of where Egypt finds itself on the global income spectrum.

The average per capita income is one way of measuring welfare. In a microeconomics course we measure consumer welfare using a utility function in which utility depends on consumption. Consumption, in turn, is constrained by income. Thus, rising income translates into higher utility for consumers. Nevertheless, the average per capita income does not tell us anything about how income is distributed: a very equal or unequal income distribution can have the same average per capita income. In chapter 5 we will see how to consider income inequality when we are measuring social welfare.

## DEVELOPMENT TYPOLOGIES AND CLASSIFYING COUNTRIES

Many different terms have been used over the years to classify countries in terms of their income levels. The introduction of the term "development" goes back to the extensive European colonization of Africa that occurred during the nineteenth century. By this time, disparities in living standards between Europe and Africa were becoming obvious (and growing rapidly). Europeans often understood these differences as being different points on a continuum of economic development and indeed invoked this notion as grounds for continued ambitious colonization of Africa, which was fueled by other, less altruistic, motives as well. Europe not only could but *should* help move Africa closer to the European end of the development spectrum—it was commonly argued—and it had a moral duty to colonize Africa as a means to achieve this development, as well as to compensate for four centuries of enslaving Africans: "The merit of a colonizing people is to place the young society it has brought forth in the most suitable conditions for the development of its natural faculties."[7]

For well over a century now, differences in income have generally been framed as differences in "development," even though, as we'll see in subsequent chapters, development involves many things besides income. Within this development framing, though, the specific terms used to classify and contrast countries have changed over the years.

"Third World" has been used to refer to low-income countries, but it is now an unfashionable and rarely used term. It was a product of the Cold War years, in which the world was divvied up into three geo-political-economic groups of countries: the "First World" (high-income western countries: Western Europe, the United States and Canada, and Japan); the "Second World" (a little-used label referring to the USSR, China, and Eastern Europe); and the "Third World" (low- and middle-income countries, which sadly were often the theater in which conflicts between First and Second World countries played out).

"North" and "South" sometimes are used as synonyms for "developed" and "less developed." This simple typology is rather imprecise, though, because there are relatively high-income countries in the South (e.g., Australia and New Zealand) and relatively low-income countries in the North (e.g., Afghanistan and Haiti), depending upon where the line between "North" and "South" is drawn. (Indeed, most of the world's land mass is "North" if one uses the Equator as the geographic delineator.)

"Less developed," "underdeveloped," "developing," and "least-developed countries" (LDCs) are terms often heard at international forums. The first, being comparative, is a broad classification containing any country not included among the "more developed" or "developed" countries. The second has a somewhat pessimistic connotation, implying that the country is less developed than it ought to be, while the third has a more optimistic twist, implying that countries in this group are, indeed, developing. The fourth term, LDCs, is based on an official UN list of countries having the lowest income (GNI per capita [averaged over three years] of less than US$992) and Human Development Index (HDI) ratings in the world. (We will learn about the HDI in chapter 6.) The LDC classification is often used to grant countries preferential status within UN organizations. For example, World Trade Organization (WTO) agreements often grant special exemptions and more flexible terms to WTO members officially recognized by the UN as LDCs.[8]

High-income economies sometimes are called "industrialized"; however, this term is antiquated given that rich countries exist in a postindustrial world in which the biggest share of the economy is services, not industry.

"Transitional economies" are those that once were in the "Second World" but are transitioning toward becoming open-market economies. This term most often is used in reference to Eastern Europe and the former Soviet republics.

The rapidly growing economies of Asia, Latin America, and Eastern Europe are sometimes referred to as "emerging economies." China is a clear example from this group in Asia, Brazil in Latin America. In international policy arenas, five of the most influential emerging economies often coordinate their efforts under an association and refer to themselves as BRICS countries: Brazil, Russia, India, China, and South Africa. With almost 3 billion people and rapidly growing economies, these countries are exerting greater influence in policy circles and negotiations with each passing year.

As you can see, these are broad, imprecise, and somewhat value-laden categories. Moreover, they seem to shift with the shifting sands of political correctness. We need a more objective typology to work with. The World Bank's country classification is based on an objective measure, the income measures we have described in this chapter, and includes four broad categories: low, lower middle, upper middle, and high income. More than simply a descriptive typology, this designation is used in World Bank operations to determine which countries are entitled to receive assistance under different lending terms and which are entitled to different programs. The low- and middle-income economies are also classified by region. The World Bank recognizes that a country's income classification does not necessarily reflect its development status. Nevertheless, its classification is widely used. In 2012, the per capita gross national incomes (defined below) defining each group were as follows:

| | |
|---|---|
| Low income | $1,025 or less |
| Lower middle income | $1,026–$4,035 |
| Upper middle income | $4,036–$12,475 |
| High income | $12,476 or more |

There are clear geographic patterns. African countries dominate the "low-income" category. Haiti is the only country from the Americas in this category. Asian countries in this group include Afghanistan, Bangladesh, Cambodia, Democratic Republic of Korea, Kyrgyzstan, Myanmar, Nepal, and Tajikistan.

As we move up to the "lower-middle-income" group, we see Central American countries and three South American ones: Bolivia, Guyana, and Paraguay. India, Iraq, the Philippines, Pakistan, and Vietnam are in this category, along with a few African countries, including Egypt, Morocco, Sudan, Ghana, and Zambia.

By the time we get to the "upper-middle-income" countries, Africa is barely represented. Here we find Algeria, Angola, Botswana, Libya, Namibia, South Africa, and Tunisia. A number of Eastern European and Middle Eastern countries are found here, along with most of South America, including Brazil, Chile, and Argentina. Mexico straddles the line between "upper-middle income" and "high income." China, Malaysia, and Thailand are the major Asian countries in this category.

At the top tier we find one African country—Equatorial Guinea, an oil producer. There are no Latin American countries. Western Europe dominates this category, along with Canada, the United States, the "Asian Tigers," and a few Middle Eastern oil exporters, including Kuwait, Oman, Qatar, Saudi Arabia, and the United Arab Emirates.[9]

### MEASURING INCOME AT THE HOUSEHOLD LEVEL

From a practical perspective, the World Bank's classification is useful because it gives us precise definitions of which countries belong in which group. These classifications are useful for policy makers and researchers, but they are too coarse for microeconomic analysis in development economics. Many of the questions development economists study require that we track income at the individual level or, more often, the household level.

As we saw in chapter 2, most of the research development economists do to evaluate what works requires data on household-level outcomes. These data are collected in structured and detailed household surveys. The World Bank and other international organizations fund many household data collection efforts throughout the developing world. Very often, researchers collect their own household data to ensure that they get the right information from the right households. With greater detail about household production, assets, expenditure, and livelihoods, development economists can get a much more complete picture of a household's standard of living—one that can include the shadow values of all the nontraded goods and services a household produces or consumes. Getting all these data is not easy. As graduate students quickly learn, research in development economics—especially development *microeconomics*—often requires fieldwork and data collection, which can be extremely demanding but also rewarding.

## POVERTY, INCOME INEQUALITY, AND HUMAN WELFARE

Consider these three statements:

· In 2010, just under 1.3 billion people—22.4% of the world's population—lived on less than $1.25 a day (PPP adjusted).[10]

· In 2010, the low-income countries contained 12.5% of the world's population but controlled less than 1% of its income, while the high-income countries had a little over 16% of its population and 72% of its income.[11]

· In the poorest 10% of countries in 2010, those with GDP per capita less than $1,123, life expectancy averaged 54.4 years (compared to 80 in the richest 10%), and years of schooling averaged 3.2 years (compared to 10.5 years).[12]

These statements present a lot of striking numbers, but they tell us very different things. The first sentence is about poverty, the second is about inequality, and the third is about human welfare. How are they related to one another and to what constitutes economic development? Are they just different sides of the same story? Does inequality imply poverty? Is it sufficient to focus our attention on poverty if our ultimate goal is to improve human welfare? Is income growth sufficient to deal with all these concerns?

In the next three chapters we'll learn how development economists study poverty, inequality, and human welfare and their relationship to income.

www.rebeltext.org/development/qr3.html
Enrich your appreciation of income by exploring
multimedia resources while you read.

## APPENDIX

*Deriving a Leontief Multiplier Matrix in Excel in Three Easy Steps*

Here's how we derived the Leontief multiplier matrix (table 3.2) using Excel:

1. Convert the Leontief input-output matrix into a matrix of coefficients for the three production activities by dividing each element in the original (3 × 3) production matrix by its corresponding column total. For example, the first element in the new matrix is 225/920 = .245. Let's call this new matrix "A" (table 3.A1).

2. Now subtract the A matrix from the identity matrix, which has all zeroes except for ones along its diagonal (table 3.A2). The result is shown in table 3.A3.

TABLE 3.A1   THE LEONTIEF COEFFICIENT (A) MATRIX

| Production Sector | Agriculture | Industry | Services |
|---|---|---|---|
| Agriculture | 0.245 | 0.053 | 0.004 |
| Industry | 0.348 | 0.140 | 0.150 |
| Services | 0.082 | 0.105 | 0.053 |

TABLE 3.A2   THE IDENTITY (I) MATRIX

| Production Sector | Agriculture | Industry | Services |
|---|---|---|---|
| Agriculture | 1 | 0 | 0 |
| Industry | 0 | 1 | 0 |
| Services | 0 | 0 | 1 |

TABLE 3.A3   THE $I - A$ MATRIX

| A | B | C | D |
|---|---|---|---|
| 1 Production Sector | Agriculture | Industry | Services |
| 2 Agriculture | 0.755 | −0.053 | −0.004 |
| 3 Industry | −0.348 | 0.860 | −0.150 |
| 4 Services | −0.082 | −0.105 | 0.947 |

TABLE 3.A4   THE LEONTIEF MULTIPLIER MATRIX
$M = (I - A)^{-1}$

| Production Sector | Agriculture | Industry | Services |
|---|---|---|---|
| Agriculture | 1.365 | 0.086 | 0.019 |
| Industry | 0.584 | 1.223 | 0.196 |
| Services | 0.182 | 0.143 | 1.079 |

The Leontief multiplier matrix, $M$, is the inverse of this $I - A$ matrix. In Excel, we calculate the inverse of a matrix by making a new matrix and in the top left cell with a number in it, enter " = MINVERSE(B2:D5)." Then drag your cursor to select this and the other eight cells, push the F2 key, and hold down "CTRL+SHIFT+ENTER." This completes our construction of the Leontief multiplier matrix. The result is shown in table 3.A4.

*Where It Comes From*

Now that we've got a recipe to make a Leontief multiplier matrix, you might be wondering where it came from. It isn't hard to see if you can imagine the simplest economy in the world, with only one sector, say, corn. Suppose that by planting 5 kilograms of seed you could expect to harvest 100 kilograms of corn. There is only one input-output coefficient in this tiny economy, which we can call $a_c$, and it equals .05. Farmers have to grow a quantity of corn, $y_c$, to meet the final (e.g., households') demand, which we can call $f_c$, plus the seed they'll need to plant in the next period, which is $a_c y_c$:

$$y_c = a_c y_c + f_c$$

Solving this for $y_c$, we can immediately see the multiplier for this economy:

$$(1 - a_c)\, y_c = f_c$$

$$y_c = \frac{1}{1 - a_c} f_c = (1 - a_c)^{-1} f_c$$

This equation tells us that to meet a one-unit increase in final demand, $f_c$, farmers will have to produce an additional amount of corn equal to $(1 - a_c)^{-1}$. As

TABLE 3.A5    FACTOR INPUT-OUTPUT VECTOR $A_F$

| Factor | Agriculture | Industry | Services |
|--------|-------------|----------|----------|
| Labor | 0.109 | 0.281 | 0.485 |
| Capital | 0.163 | 0.211 | 0.220 |

TABLE 3.A6    FACTOR VALUE-ADDED MULTIPLIER MATRIX
$M_F = A_F M = A_F(I - A)^{-1}$

| Factor | Agriculture | Industry | Services |
|--------|-------------|----------|----------|
| Labor | 0.401 | 0.422 | 0.580 |
| Capital | 0.386 | 0.303 | 0.282 |
| GDP | 0.787 | 0.725 | 0.862 |

long as $a_c$ is positive and less than one, as an input-output coefficient should be, this multiplier will be greater than one.

Compare this to the formula for our Leontief multiplier matrix, $(I - A)^{-1}$. The only difference between the two is that the second is for an economy with more than one production sector, so we have to use matrices. Instead of $y_c$, we need a vector with the three sectors' output in it:

$$Y = \begin{vmatrix} y_1 \\ y_2 \\ y_3 \end{vmatrix}$$

We need a vector with three final demands, too:

$$F = \begin{vmatrix} f_1 \\ f_2 \\ f_3 \end{vmatrix}$$

. . . and a matrix of input-output coefficients, which is matrix A, above:

$$A = \begin{vmatrix} a_{11} & a_{12} & a_{13} \\ a_{21} & a_{22} & a_{23} \\ a_{31} & a_{32} & a_{33} \end{vmatrix}$$

Completely analogous to our corn model, the vector of total outputs required to meet the final demand is

$$Y = AY + F$$
$$(I - A)^{-1}Y = F$$
$$Y = (I - A)^{-1}F = MF$$

That's why $M = (I - A)^{-1}$ is the Leontief multiplier matrix. The method is the same no matter how many production sectors there are in the economy—the $I$ and $A$ matrices simply get bigger the more sectors you have.

Once we know the Leontief output multipliers, we can easily calculate a matrix of labor and capital value-added multipliers $(M_F)$ by pre-multiplying the multiplier matrix by the input-output coefficients for labor and capital, which we can arrange in a $(2 \times 3)$ matrix called $A_F$:

$$M_F = A_F M = A_F (I - A)^{-1}$$

To get the input-output coefficients for the two factors, we divide payments to factors by their respective column totals in the original input-output matrix (table 3.A5).

The matrix of factor value-added multipliers is shown in table 3.A6. The last row in this table gives the sums of the factor value-added multipliers, which are the GDP multipliers of changes in each sector's final demand.

4

# Poverty

If you really want to understand something, you must begin by
measuring it. For poverty, this is true not only because we must
have reliable measures of it before we can compare poverty in
different places or track changes in it from one year to the next,
but also because deciding how to measure poverty challenges us
to understand its key dimensions and complexities. In this
chapter, we describe how development economists measure
poverty and some prickly dilemmas we encounter along the
way. We explore how poverty changes over time and why this
dynamic perspective on poverty matters to poor households
and therefore to anyone hoping to alleviate poverty.

**ESSENTIALS**

- Poverty lines
- Headcount poverty index
- Poverty gap
- Foster-Greer-Thorbecke poverty index
- Risk and uncertainty
- Vulnerability
- Wealth dynamics
- Poverty traps
- "Big push" interventions

Alleviating poverty is the single biggest concern confronting development economics. Before we can tackle the challenges of addressing poverty, we have to agree on how to measure it.

On the surface, measuring the poverty rate in a population may seem
straightforward. Count how many people are below the poverty line,
divide this number by the total population, and you've got the share of
people in poverty. If there are $q$ people with income below the per capita poverty level and $N$ people in the total population, this share of
people in poverty is

$$P_H = \frac{q}{N}$$

We call this the "poverty headcount index." In chapter 3, we learned how to make an index for a variable (there it was income) by dividing by the largest value the variable can take on. $N$ is the largest number of poor people there can be—that is, if everyone in the population were poor. Because $N$ is always greater than $q$, the headcount measure will always be less than one, and it will be zero only if nobody is below the poverty line. In other words, it is simply the percentage of the population in poverty. This makes it a good index because it is independent of the size of the population, which gives us a common metric for comparing poverty in big and small countries.

The poverty headcount index is also convenient because it is easy to construct: counting heads is all you need to do to make the headcount index . . . or is it? Suppose you had to construct a poverty index for a remote region of Thailand starting from scratch. This kind of problem comes up a lot in development economics. To make your job easier, suppose that Thailand recently conducted a population census in this region, so you have a good estimate of the region's population. What next? As you might have already realized, before you can go any further you have to answer this question: "Where's the poverty line?"

### FINDING THE POVERTY LINE

Every country has its own poverty line—typically, a level of income that separates the poor from the non-poor. Often there are different poverty lines for urban and rural populations, because it often costs more to survive in a big city than in a rural village. Where exactly do these lines come from? Politics invariably play some role in deciding where the poverty line *is* drawn, but where the poverty line *should be* drawn is fundamentally an economics problem.

Establishing a poverty line requires some careful thinking about the nature of poverty. For starters, let's think about food poverty. How much does it cost to meet a person's minimum food requirements? A nutritionist's answer would be "It depends." There are online calorie calculators by gender, weight, height, and activity level. The World Health Organization (WHO) establishes nutritional guidelines for different countries. As this passage from the WHO website suggests, it is not an easy task: "The [WHO] Department of Nutrition for Health and

Development . . . continually reviews new research and information from around the world on human nutrient requirements and recommended nutrient intakes. This is a vast and never-ending task, given the large number of essential human nutrients. These nutrients include protein, energy, carbohydrates, fats and lipids, a range of vitamins, and a host of minerals and trace elements."[1]

Suppose we agree on the minimum nutrient intake for an average individual in our study area. We could then find all the baskets of foods available that can give us this nutrient level, price each one, choose the cheapest basket, and call this the food poverty line. This food poverty line would be the minimum amount of money needed for a person to meet his or her nutrient requirements.[2]

The trouble is that people do not live on food alone. We have other essential needs: clothing, shelter, cooking fuel and other energy, health care, and, if we want our children to escape from poverty someday, education, too. Where we draw the poverty line will depend on the costs of these things as well as food. Now our job is getting more complicated. But fortunately people are constantly making these kinds of consumption choices—choices that implicitly take these trade-offs into account and that might help us determine where to draw the poverty line so it reflects this more complete consumption context.

Suppose we survey a large sample of people in the population, asking them what foods they consume (a one- or two-week recall is commonly used for this), how much they consume, the prices they pay for each food item, and what their income is. Surveys like this have been done for nearly every country, thanks largely to the Living Standards Measurement Survey (LSMS) initiative by the World Bank.[3] We could take all the food combinations from the survey and convert them into the amounts of nutrients consumed, using conversion coefficients available from the WHO. Then we could graph nutrient demand ($C(Y)$, on the vertical axis) against income ($Y$, on the horizontal axis), as in figure 4.1.

Once we have this graph, we can find $c^*$, the minimum nutrient requirement, and bounce a line off our nutrient demand curve to get the minimum level of income needed to meet the food requirement. This minimum income ($z$ in our figure) would take into account the fact that people spend income on things other than food, so it can be our poverty line.[4] Taking into account how households actually choose to spend their money, both on food and things other than food, leverages a fundamental concept in economics called "revealed preference": observed

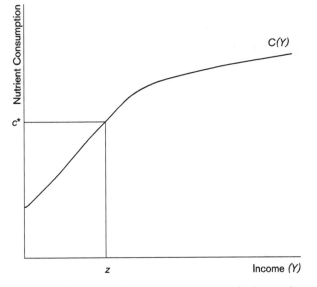

**FIGURE 4.1.** The poverty line, $z$, is the income required to reach the minimum level of nutrient consumption, given households' spending patterns.

patterns of behavior reveal something about an individual's underlying preferences, which are difficult to observe directly.

You might argue that $z$ is too high, because some people spend too much of their income on non-nutritious stuff. For example, if people spend money on alcohol, cigarettes, or fancy clothes instead of food, their income will have to be higher in order to reach a nutrient intake of $c^*$. On the other hand, one also can argue that at very low incomes people do not spend *enough* income on essentials like health, shelter, or education. In that case $z$ will be too low; people really need more money to satisfy their nonfood basic needs. On balance, our figure probably gives a reasonable approximation to the poverty line. In practice, economists construct poverty lines in different ways, but the basic theory that guides the process is essentially captured in this figure. Development economists are constantly building on this logic in an attempt to improve or otherwise enhance our ability to measure poverty. A recent approach proposed by Robert Jensen and Nolan Miller, for example, pushes the "revealed preference" logic even further in order to create poverty measures that are better able to reflect individual or household-level differences in nutritional needs (see sidebar 4.1).

## Sidebar 4.1 The "Hunger Hurts—Need Cheap Calories" Approach to Poverty Measurement

A few limitations of a caloric threshold-based poverty line (i.e., $c^*$ in figure 4.1) stand out as especially problematic. First, there is no clear consensus about what the threshold, if it exists at all, ought to be. Second, the caloric intake threshold for a strapping young man who works ten hours a day on the farm is vastly different than the intake threshold for his grandmother. Third, the background health status of an individual or her household can dramatically shape her ability to absorb and benefit from nutrients. This implies that achieving a minimal caloric *intake* may not be sufficient to make some people healthy. Finally, poor people—just like all of us—are constantly making choices about what foods to consume, and often they will change the composition of their diets drastically if their income changes. These changes typically involve substituting cheap calories with tastier and pricier ones (e.g., fruits, vegetables and animal products) as incomes rise.

Robert Jensen and Nolan Miller use these limitations to motivate an approach to measuring hunger and malnutrition (i.e., food poverty) that is based squarely on peoples' food consumption choices and therefore on "revealed preferences." Their basic idea can be summed up as follows:

When people are below their minimal nutrition threshold, the body protests, which doesn't feel good. Maximizing utility means consuming calories; the marginal utility of calories is extremely high. The cheapest source of calories typically is a staple like cassava, rice, or wheat. Beyond subsistence, though, the marginal utility of calories falls. People start substituting foods that are more expensive calorie sources but provide non-nutritional benefits, like taste.

We cannot "see" people's actual subsistence threshold, but by looking at the choices people make we can figure it out (analogous to inferring a farmer's shadow value of family labor, as described in chapter 3). When people are switching away from staples, they are telling us that their calorie threshold has been met. Thus, "the percent of calories consumed from the staple food source, or the staple calorie share (SCS), can be used as an indicator for nutritional sufficiency."

Jensen and Miller apply their approach to detailed household data from China and find that there is a well-defined SCS threshold at just over 75%. Staples constitute about three-quarters of total calories for very poor people, and this doesn't change much as income rises until a critical income level is reached, at which point SCS falls rapidly because people replace cheap calories with tasty calories.

Robert Jensen and Nolan Miller, "A Revealed Preference Approach to Measuring Hunger and Undernutrition" (working paper no. 16555, National Bureau of Economic Research, Cambridge, MA, November 2010).

At some point in the past decade, you have probably come across headlines that use a $1-a-day poverty line to characterize global poverty. This simple metric emerged from essentially the process described above, along with a bit of "public relations" spin. In the late 1980s, a group of World Bank economists noticed that several developing countries drew their poverty lines at about $370 a year, PPP adjusted. Martin Ravallion, a member of this group and leading expert on poverty measurement, realized that this worked out to roughly $1 a day and that this simple poverty line might be catchy enough to get some real traction in the media and with potential donors. Martin was certainly right about it being catchy: for more than two decades now, this kind of poverty line has shaped the international poverty discourse—including the MDGs described in chapter 1. Of course, these lines have been updated as economic conditions and prices have changed over the years. The average poverty line in developing countries, PPP adjusted, was $2 a day in 2010.[5] Since 2008, the World Bank has set the extreme poverty line at $1.25 in PPP-adjusted 2005 dollars. The official poverty line is much higher in rich than poor countries. For example, the US poverty income for a family of four in 2012 was $23,050 per year, or $15.79 per person per day.[6]

On the other hand, not everyone is enamored by such $1-a-day poverty measures. They are "average averages" (averages over a year averaged across several developing countries). They gloss over individual and regional variation in nutritional needs and the critical fluctuations in income and well-being within the year that make poor households particularly vulnerable.

Lant Pritchett, a development economist at Harvard University, worries that these simple measures have put too much focus on philanthropy and not enough on long-run development: "Instead of promoting prosperous economies, it's about 'how do we identify and target and get transfers to the few people under this penurious line?' which just isn't the way, historically, anybody has ever eliminated poverty."[7] Development economists must often try to strike a balance between the rigor and richness of their methods and the ability to communicate their results in ways that resonate with a broad policy and donor community.

## MORE THAN COUNTING HEADS

Most people think of the incidence of poverty, or headcount index, when they think about quantifying "poverty." The headcount measure is useful, but it doesn't tell us all we need to know in order to analyze poverty and design policies to alleviate it. In practice, we need to know *how poor* people are, not just *whether* they are poor. That is, we need to know the depth of poverty. We could easily imagine two countries with the same poverty headcount but with the poor clustered just below the poverty line in one country and far below the poverty line in the other. A cash transfer to eliminate poverty would have to be larger in the second country, where poor people tend to be very poor instead of a little poor.

The difference between a person's income and the per capita poverty line is called the "poverty gap." If we know poor person $i$'s income $(Y_i)$ and the poverty line $(z)$, we can easily calculate the person's poverty gap; it is

$$z - Y_i$$

The total cost of eliminating poverty is the sum of all poor people's poverty gaps. Summing the gap across all $q$ poor people in our population, we get the total poverty gap:

$$\sum_{i=1}^{q} (z - Y_i)$$

The total poverty gap is critical to know for poverty alleviation programs because it is the cost of bringing everyone up to the poverty line at a given point in time.

The poverty gap gives us more information than the headcount, allowing us to measure the impacts of programs on poverty more accurately. For example, a program might raise a poor person's income but not by enough to get her above the poverty line. A reasonable person would say the program reduced poverty. The poverty gap would decrease as a result of the program, even though the headcount measure would not change.

### The Severity of Poverty

Does the poverty gap give us all the information we need? Consider this scenario: program A reduces the total poverty gap by providing a cash transfer to people just below the poverty line. Program B reduces the poverty gap by the same amount, but it does this by targeting the transfer to the very poorest people in society, that is, people in extreme poverty. The poverty gap does not let us distinguish between the effects of these two programs because it changes by the same amount no matter which poor person gets the cash.

How can we make our poverty measure sensitive to who gets the cash, that is, the severity of poverty?

The easiest way is to square the poverty gap. If we measure poverty using

$$(z - Y_i)^2$$

our index will increase disproportionately as the poverty gap increases. For example, if the gap is $2, the gap squared is $4, but if the gap is $4, the gap squared is $16. Based on this index, a program is more effective at reducing poverty if it raises the income of extremely poor households.

The economists Erik Thorbecke and his students Joel Greer and James Foster proposed a single index that embodies all three of these measures as special cases.[8] The Foster-Greer-Thorbecke (FGT) measure is the most widely used poverty index in economics. Its formula is

$$FGT_\alpha = \frac{1}{Nz^\alpha} \sum_{i=1}^{q} (z - Y_i)^\alpha$$

Where we set $\alpha$ depends on the kind of index we want. You can see the poverty gap, $z - y_i$, to the right of the summation. You can think of $\alpha$ as the weight we attach to this poverty gap while calculating our poverty index. When $\alpha = 0$, the term in the summation equals one for every poor person, since anything raised to the zeroth power is one. We sum up the ones over the $q$ poor people and divide by $N$ (since $z^\alpha$ also equals 1 when $\alpha = 0$). This yields the headcount measure. That is,

$$FGT_{\alpha=0} = \frac{q}{N}$$

It is a useful index because

$$0 \leq FGT_{\alpha=0} \leq 1$$

When $\alpha = 1$, the index equals

$$FGT_{\alpha=1} = \frac{1}{Nz} \sum_{i=1}^{q} (z - Y_i)$$

The right-most term,

$$\sum_{i=1}^{q} (z - Y_i)$$

is the total poverty gap, or the cost of bringing all poor people just up to the poverty line. To make an index, we have to divide this by the largest value the total poverty gap could have. $Nz$, the total population times the poverty line, is what the total poverty gap would be if everyone in the population had zero income. The total poverty gap divided by $Nz$, like the headcount index, lies between zero (nobody is in poverty) and one (everyone is in poverty and no one has any income at all).

To analyze the severity of poverty, we set $\alpha = 2$. In this case, the index becomes

$$FGT_{\alpha=2} = \frac{1}{Nz^2} \sum_{i=1}^{q} (z - Y_i)^2$$

In this version of the FGT index, we weight people in extreme poverty more than people who are just below the poverty line. You can see that this, too, is bounded by zero (nobody is in poverty) and one (everybody is in poverty and no one has any income at all). In the latter case, the term in parentheses is just $z$. It is summed $q = N$ times, and the numerator is $Nz^2$, so the quotient becomes one.

Often, when we perform poverty analyses we report all three versions of the FGT index. The second ($\alpha = 1$) and third ($\alpha = 2$) versions decrease whenever the income of a poor person increases. The third version decreases more if the poor person whose income goes up is extremely poor. The first ($\alpha = 0$) version decreases only if the income gain pops the poor person above the poverty line. Together, the three versions of the FGT provide a comprehensive picture of changes in poverty due to a policy or some other exogenous shock.

*Calculating an FGT Index: A Simple Example*

Suppose we survey a small village consisting of only ten people, with a poverty line of $z = 28$. We find their incomes to be as shown in table 4.1.

TABLE 4.1  INCOMES AND POVERTY MEASURES FOR A HYPOTHETICAL VILLAGE

| Person | Income | 1 if in Poverty, 0 Otherwise | Poverty Gap | Poverty Gap-Squared |
|---|---|---|---|---|
| 1 | 5 | 1 | 23 | 529 |
| 2 | 12 | 1 | 16 | 256 |
| 3 | 22 | 1 | 6 | 36 |
| 4 | 24 | 1 | 4 | 16 |
| 5 | 30 | 0 | 0 | 0 |
| 6 | 40 | 0 | 0 | 0 |
| 7 | 50 | 0 | 0 | 0 |
| 8 | 70 | 0 | 0 | 0 |
| 9 | 80 | 0 | 0 | 0 |
| 10 | 100 | 0 | 0 | 0 |
| SUM | | 4 | 49 | 837 |
| $z$ | 28 | | | |

Using the data in the table, we can calculate the three versions of the FGT index:

$$FGT_{\alpha=0} = 4/10 = 0.40$$

$$FGT_{\alpha=1} = \frac{49}{10(28)} = 0.18$$

$$FGT_{\alpha=2} = \frac{837}{10(28^2)} = 0.11$$

Now let's check the sensitivity of our measures to different cash transfers. Suppose we transfer $5 to person 3, bringing her income up to $27. This is still (just) below the poverty line, so the headcount doesn't change. The poverty gap measure falls by 2 points, from .18 to .16. The gap-squared falls less, from 0.11 to 0.10.

Now what if we gave the $5 to the poorest household instead? The change in the poverty gap is the same as before, because it is insensitive to which poor person gets the cash. However, the gap-squared measure falls all the way to 0.08—a 24% decrease in the severity of poverty!

Because of its sensitivity to changes in extreme poverty, the third measure is the one Mexico uses to measure poverty impacts. In fact, $\alpha = 2$ is in the Mexican constitution, which explains why PROGRESA (chapter 2) targeted the poorest of the poor.

## VULNERABILITY AND POVERTY DYNAMICS

Suppose you're a poor family farmer in the Sahel, with kids to feed. In a normal year, you can get enough out of your grain crop to cover your family's needs, provided you sell an animal or two to supplement your farm income. With a herd of six, including some decent breeding stock, you can do this every year (see sidebar 4.2).

But one year the rains don't come. Your crop fails. You've got six months until you can try your luck planting again and a few months after that until you can even hope to harvest something. How do you keep food on your family's table during this "hungry season?"

You decide to sell one of your animals. Then another, and another. As you plant your next crop, you're down to three animals. The seeds begin to germinate, the rain comes, but your money runs out. You sell another animal, and now you're down to two. With two months to go before harvest, your money runs out again.

What do you do? If you sell your last two animals, your breeding stock, how will you ever rebuild your herd?

Recent research by Travis and colleagues Michael Carter at UC Davis and Chris Barrett at Cornell suggests that, in all likelihood, you won't sell those last few animals. If you do, you know you might never get out of poverty—you'll be caught in a "poverty trap" without a herd and without respect or status among your peers.

But not selling your last two animals brings its own cost: you and your family will have no choice but to skip meals and go hungry. You might survive alright, and so might your spouse and oldest kids. But what about your two-year-old girl? Your newborn baby boy, still unweaned? By preserving your herd in the short run, are you stunting your children's growth and jeopardizing their potential to lead a productive life in the future?[9]

Poor people around the world face these sorts of cruel choices daily. This highlights a very important point about poverty: it is not just that some people are poor and others are not. In our discussion of poverty lines and poverty measurement above, we glossed over a crucial dimension of poverty, namely, that poverty is dynamic, meaning that it changes over time. Some people are never poor. Others always seem to be poor, caught in a "poverty trap." Still others find themselves on the very cusp of poverty, and all it takes is a single shock event to tip them into a poverty from which there may be no coming back.

For decades, development economists have appreciated how important it is to take into account not just static measures of poverty (like the

## Sidebar 4.2    Drought, Poverty, and Inequality: The Sahel

The Sahel is a ribbon of land running east-west across Africa and separating the Sahara desert to the north from the savannas in the south. The contrast between it and the sands of the Sahara are what give this zone its name, which means "coast" in Arabic.

As a transition zone, the Sahel is also a high-risk zone from an agro-ecological point of view. In 1984 a severe drought struck the Sahelian zone of Burkina Faso in West Africa. It was a human tragedy, but its timing was a researcher's dream, because it hit during a multi-year household survey being carried out by the International Food Policy Research Institute (IFPRI). IFPRI had just finished surveying households in a normal year, 1983–84. They surveyed the same households again the next year, after the drought struck. Households in this region practice rain-fed agro pastoralism. The Sahel has extremely variable rainfall, a fragile environment, and poor agro climate. The people living there have learned how to adapt to their environment, doing their best to diversify their incomes beyond crop production. Nothing prepared them for this drought, though.

The IFPRI data give us a unique insight into the impacts of agro-climatic shocks on poor households. Crop income was by far the largest source of income for households in the normal year, constituting 53% of the total. It fell 64% when the drought hit. All of the other income sources increased during the drought, though, as households scrambled to make up for their lost crop income. They sold off livestock: livestock accounted for just 14% of the normal year's income, but animal sales increased 154% during the drought. Local non-farm income, mostly from wages, rose 26%; remittances from migrant work increased 54%; and transfers among households, while very small (1% in the base year), increased 58%.

It comes as no surprise that poverty rose sharply in the drought year. The headcount index shows that the poverty rate more than doubled, from .20 to .51. The severity of poverty increased by a factor of more than 8, from 0.02 to 0.19. The FGT index paints a stark picture of the human toll of drought in the Sahel.

Thomas Reardon and J. Edward Taylor, "Agroclimatic Shock, Income Inequality, and Poverty: Evidence from Burkina Faso," *World Development* 24, no. 5 (1996):901–14.

### Sidebar 4.3   Poverty and Witch Killing in Rural Tanzania

Witch killings are frequent in western Tanzania. Most of the victims are poor, elderly women, and most of the perpetrators are relatives of the victims.

Ted Miguel tested two theories of why these killings occur. The *income shock theory* posits that big negative income shocks associated with extreme weather are the culprit. Most witch killings happen in the pre-harvest period, when households' food stores from the previous harvest are depleted, the next harvest is known, and people realize they'll need food and energy to bring in the next harvest. The *scapegoat theory* predicts that *any* adverse shock witches are believed to control, including disease, should lead to more witch murders, as households eliminate the "cause" of their suffering.

Miguel found that extreme local rainfall shocks (but not disease) negatively impact income. If the income shock theory is correct, then, rainfall shocks—but not disease—should explain witch killings. That is just what Miguel found: "Only the shock that leads to lower income (extreme rainfall) results in more witch murders, while disease epidemics lead neither to lower income nor to witch murders."

This study is important because of the novel identification strategy employed to solve the reflection problem, using random weather shocks to uncover a link between poverty and crime. It has potential policy implications as well. To reduce crime induced by weather shocks, governments might do well to provide poor households with crop insurance, so that when harvests fail they will not have to make the cruel choice of which mouths to feed. Cash transfers, ideally targeted at elderly women (to empower them), also might be effective at reducing witch killings.

Edward Miguel, "Poverty and Witch Killing," *Review of Economic Studies* 72 (2005):1153–72.

headcount measure) but also dynamic poverty measures—measures that capture household vulnerability. There is a large body of work developing concepts and measures of vulnerability. While this research is important and typically covered in advanced development economics courses, our focus here is more conceptual: a household with income just above the poverty line may not be counted as poor, but may be threatened constantly by poverty and destitution. This threat of poverty, this risk of destitution, can be a major source of anxiety and stress and can change the choices people make. Vulnerability and the sense of desperation that can come from seeing future prospects shriveling up before your very eyes can led to desperate—even unthinkable—measures (see sidebar 4.3).

*Out of Poverty—Then Back in Again*

The 2003 Mexico National Rural Household Survey (Spanish acronym ENHRUM) found that 47% of the rural population had income below the poverty line. In 2008, the same households were surveyed again. This made it possible to look at the dynamics of poverty by tracking the same households' poverty status over time. In the five years between these two surveys, poverty in rural Mexico fell. The Mexican government has three different poverty lines, one for food (the food poverty line), another that adds in the cost of health and basic education (the capacities poverty line), and a third that adds in clothing, housing, and energy costs (the asset poverty line). By all three measures, the headcount rate fell by between 3.6% and 4.0%. The other two components of the FGT measure, the poverty gap and severity (gap-squared), also fell, as shown in table 4.2.

This seems like good news—and it is. But it masks the fact that many rural Mexicans were worse off in 2008 than in 2003. Table 4.3 takes all the rural Mexicans who were in poverty in 2003 and shows what percentage were still in poverty in 2008. It does the same for those who were *not* in poverty in 2003. The table reveals some interesting—and troubling—poverty dynamics.

TABLE 4.2 POVERTY DYNAMICS IN RURAL MEXICO

| FGT Index | Food Poverty Line | | | Capacities Poverty Line (Adds Health, Basic Education) | | | Asset Poverty Line (Adds Clothes, Housing, Energy) | | |
|---|---|---|---|---|---|---|---|---|---|
| | *2002* | *2007* | *Change* | *2002* | *2007* | *Change* | *2002* | *2007* | *Change* |
| Headcount[a] ($\alpha = 0$) | 0.47 | 0.44 | –3.6% | 0.54 | 0.50 | –3.9% | 0.70 | 0.66 | –4.0% |
| Depth[b] ($\alpha = 1$) | 0.24 | 0.21 | –2.2% | 0.27 | 0.25 | –2.5% | 0.39 | 0.35 | –3.4% |
| Severity[c] ($\alpha = 2$) | 0.16 | 0.15 | –1.3% | 0.19 | 0.17 | –1.6% | 0.27 | 0.25 | –2.4% |

[a] Share of population in households with income below the poverty line
[b] Also reflects how far below the poverty line poor individuals find themselves
[c] Places greater weight on the poorest of the poor when calculating the poverty index
SOURCE: Analysis of Mexico National Rural Household Survey data, 2003–2008.

TABLE 4.3 A TRANSITION MATRIX OF POVERTY DYNAMICS IN
RURAL MEXICO

|  | Poor in 2008 | Not Poor in 2008 |
| --- | --- | --- |
| Poor in 2003 (47%) | 51% | 49% |
| Not Poor in 2003 (53%) | 30% | 70% |

SOURCE: Analysis of Mexico National Rural Household Survey Data, 2003–
2008.

Of the people who were in poverty in 2003, 51% were still in poverty in 2008. Let's call this "group A." These people—around 24%
(47% * 51%) of the rural Mexican population—seem to be in a state of
persistent poverty (though we would need to track them longer to be
sure). At the other extreme, 70% of those who were *not* in poverty in
2003 were still not in poverty in 2008. This group, which we can call
"group B," seems to be persistently *out* of poverty.

The good news is that 49% of the people who were *in* poverty in
2003 were *above* the poverty line in 2008. These people transitioned
out of poverty during the five-year period, which is the reason why poverty in rural Mexico fell.

The bad news is that 30% of those who were *not* poor in 2003 *were*
poor in 2008. These people transitioned *into* poverty.

Let's call these two transitional poverty groups "group C." They
might not be so different from one another.

Why are poverty dynamics important? First, just because people
transition out of poverty doesn't mean their poverty problem is solved.
Our challenge is not simply to get people out of poverty; it is also to
keep them there, as well as to keep others from slipping into poverty.

Second, it is almost certain that different anti-poverty policies are
needed for each one of these groups. For group A, we need to have
policies to enable people to extricate themselves from what might be
poverty traps. For group B, we need policies that will create opportunities to stay out of poverty.

For group C, those at the margins of poverty, for whom things can
go either way, we need policies that can prevent adverse shocks from
pushing them into potential poverty traps, and keep them out. The
Sahelian farmer-pastoralist in our previous example is a good illustration of the kinds of people likely found in this group. If we somehow
could devise an insurance scheme that could enable people at the fringes
of poverty to feed their children *and* preserve their productive assets at

times of adversity, we might have a big impact on poverty and on preventing people from falling into poverty traps over time.

As economists, we can do better than just characterize and measure vulnerability. We can study the underlying processes that determine where a household can reasonably expect to end up in the future. That is, we can try to understand how a household's context, productive activities, and assets interact to shape its wealth dynamics.

To illustrate this idea, consider the total poverty gap defined above. As we mentioned there, for a given country this gap is literally the total cost of lifting every poor person in the country out of poverty. But if we could implement such an income transfer, what effect would it actually have on poverty? In the short run, a transfer that perfectly targets each poor household with just enough income to lift it above the poverty line would indeed eliminate poverty. In the longer run, however, all bets are off. Why? Because unless the transfer actually changes the wealth dynamics of these households and allows them to create enough wealth to stay out of poverty, they may well slip back into the same poverty they experienced before the transfer.

Rigorous research into poverty dynamics can be tricky, but understanding the underlying concepts is an essential of development economics. Economists typically use recursion function graphs like that shown at the top of figure 4.2 to depict these dynamic forces (we borrow the idea of recursion functions from mathematics and the natural sciences). Be patient as we describe how to understand this figure; we are confident it is worth the effort.

In this recursion function graph, the assets a household owns this year (horizontal axis) determine its assets next year (vertical axis) because assets produce income, which can be invested in more assets. To be more concrete, let's pick up our livestock example again. If the asset in question is livestock, the relationship between your herd size this year and next year is quite clear: the larger your herd, the more income you can make from it by selling animals and milk. It's also true for human capital: the healthier you are and the more education and skills you have, the more productive you can be and thus the higher your earnings. As we saw in the example above, families can "consume" their assets, selling them off to get through a hard time, but that leaves them with less in the next period. They can also lose human capital if, for example, kids go hungry or don't go to school. Human capital can go down if malnutrition impairs children's development and learning. This, too, leaves households with less income in the future.

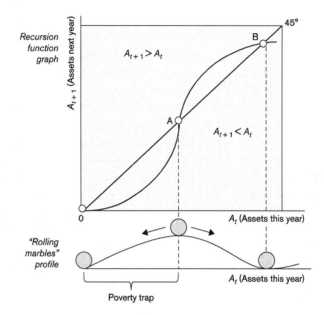

**FIGURE 4.2.** An asset recursion function with a poverty trap. To the right of point A assets grow larger in the next period, driving the household to a favorable steady state at point B. To the left of point A assets decrease, driving the household into a poverty trap.

The 45° diagonal line in this graph plays an important role: it indicates points at which assets next year are expected to be the same as assets this year. In other words, these points represent points of "equilibrium" where we expect assets (e.g., herd size) to remain constant. The S-shaped curve in this figure is the function that maps current assets into expected future assets, which is the recursion function. At each point where the function crosses the 45° line, this relationship is in equilibrium. The recursion function graph in this figure has three equilibria, each denoted by a small white dot (0, A, and B). Whenever there is a gap between the 45° line and the recursion function, we expect assets to be changing over time. Whether assets are increasing or decreasing depends on the direction of the gap. Whenever the function is *above* the diagonal, assets are increasing (i.e., next-period assets are expected to be greater than this period's assets), but when the function is *below* the diagonal, assets are decreasing.

To help you visualize the dynamics that are captured in the recursion function, we have added a "rolling marbles" profile at the bottom of figure 4.2. The three marbles in this profile are each at a different equilibrium asset level. As long as no one bumps the profile, this is where the three marbles will stay (i.e., assets do not change over time). What happens if someone bumps the profile? Can you see that any small bump will cause the marble at A to roll downhill to the right or left? This means that the equilibrium at asset level A is "unstable" because it is not self-reinforcing. In contrast, equilibrium asset levels 0 and B are stable: bumping the profile may cause these marbles to roll around but they will eventually return to their original position.

Now that you understand how this figure is constructed, let's walk through the story it tells. The S-shaped curve roughly captures the herd dynamics for the Borana pastoralists of southern Ethiopia,[10] so we'll tell the story in that context. Suppose a pastoralist has a herd of size A this year. Because this is an equilibrium point, he expects that his herd will have A animals next year as well. Now suppose that a bandit sneaks into the camp one night and steals two animals, which is actually not uncommon. This is like bumping the marble a bit to the left. How does this affect the dynamics of his herd? Next year, he will expect his herd to shrink; same for the year after that. If figure 4.2 is an accurate depiction of herd dynamics in this context, losing two animals puts the herder on a downhill path to the left that ends with him losing his entire herd (i.e., marble ends up at 0).

How does this collapse happen? The dynamics depicted in the figure reflect key features of the underlying production context. In the case of the pastoralist, the collapse is driven by the fact that the only profitable way to manage a herd of livestock on arid rangeland is to migrate with the herd, because this is the only way to take advantage of the best pastures and watering holes. If you can't move your livestock around, you can't survive in this setting as a pastoralist—at which point you must either choose to migrate to the slums of a big city or settle down in a small town with a few chickens. Pastoralists always prefer to stay on the range with their livestock, but their ability to migrate with their animals is a function of their herd size, because you must have enough animals in the herd to sustain a herder (usually a young son) with milk and blood[11] during the migration. This is the key twist in the production context that drives the collapse: with a herd of size A or larger, the herd can sustain a young herder and therefore migrate around to take advantage of greener pastures; but below A the herd is too small to sustain a herder. Thus, it misses out on greener pastures and slowly dwindles.

Our figure thus has two *steady states,* which should be obvious in the "rolling marbles" profile. One of them is at point B. If a pastoralist gets knocked off point B, the asset dynamics will take him right back to it. The other steady state point is zero, the poverty trap. Adverse shocks like theft or a drought can take a household that is near point A and knock it into a poverty trap, possibly driving its assets all the way to zero, from which it cannot easily recover. Adverse shocks can also knock households off point B, but if we've got the dynamics right, they will on average recover and return to the favorable steady state.

## BIG POVERTY TRAPS AND THE "BIG PUSH"

The poverty traps we have described thus far have been microtraps that affect single households. In the pastoralist communities in southern Ethiopia we discussed, different households with different herd sizes are subject to different herd dynamics. The notion of poverty traps is often writ much larger than this. In theory, entire regions or countries could get trapped in poverty.

Some economists argue, for example, that unfavorable geography (e.g., being land-locked) can constrain a country's productive capacity and effectively trap an entire country in poverty. Others argue that cycles of violence, corruption, and weak governance can create big poverty traps that ensnare entire regions or nations. While evidence of micro poverty traps in some contexts seems quite compelling, whether big traps like this exist in practice remains a hot and often contested area of research in development economics. If entire countries were actually trapped in poverty, the policy implications might seem straightforward: the country clearly needs a push from the outside to break free. At this scale, however, things are rarely this simple.

Jeffrey Sachs, a high-profile development economist we will encounter repeatedly in this book, is convinced that big poverty traps exist and should be taken seriously by the development community. Indeed, Sachs sees these big traps as the primary argument in favor of international aid and has succeeded in shaping aid flows in impressive ways in recent decades. This is precisely the motivation behind the United Nations Millennium Villages Project, which Sachs directs and which we will learn more about in chapter 7.

The logic here is simple (much simpler than the research required to test it). If poor countries are effectively trapped in poverty, what they need is a big push from rich countries. This big push—in the form of target investments in infrastructure and education, for example—can catalyze a virtuous cycle of increasing productivity that puts poor countries on a path of economic growth and development. Notice that this is conceptually identical to giving our pastoralist in figure 4.2 enough additional livestock to make his herd larger than $A$, then letting him keep growing his herd to the high equilibrium. The need for this big push should be easy to visualize in the "rolling marbles" profile in this figure.

While the essence of this kind of big push model was developed in the 1940s,[12] Sachs is its contemporary champion. As we encounter him again in later chapters, we'll also learn about some of his detractors, who claim that ambitious external plans are at best ineffective, because they ignore much of the richness and nuance of local context, and at worst destructive, because they can put the rights of autocratic states ahead of the rights of the poor.

www.rebeltext.org/development/qr4.html
Learn more about poverty by exploring multimedia resources while you read.

# 5

# Inequality

As humans, we often feel an irresistible impulse to compare
ourselves to others. Sometimes these comparisons are vain
and superficial, but they can often be much more consequential. Disparities in income can have real economic consequences by shaping the opportunities and well-being of
individuals and affecting more broadly the way markets and
governments function. As we have already seen, efficiency
and equity objectives are often difficult to achieve separately
because they are interrelated in important ways in developing
countries. In this chapter, we focus on how economists
measure inequality and how different forms of inequality
matter in development economics, including gender inequality within households.

### ESSENTIALS

- Distinction between poverty and inequality
- Inseparability of efficiency and equity
- Gini coefficient
- Social welfare analysis
- Definition of a household
- Gender inequality

Inequality matters to people everywhere. It was inequality that fueled
the passion of the Occupy Movement, which struck cities around the
world in the fall of 2011 with the rallying call "We are the 99 percent!"
There are several reasons why inequality is important from an economic
(or political-economic) point of view:

- *Social justice.* Many people believe it is unfair for the benefits of
  economic growth to be concentrated among a select few.
- *Relative deprivation.* Economists usually assume people optimize:
  firms maximize profits, households maximize utility from con-

suming more goods. But sociologists have long recognized that being deprived of goods that others have can make people unhappy. Suppose you live in a poor village and your income does not change while your neighbor's does. You see him remodel his house, his kids start dressing well, and a parabolic TV dish sprouts from his rooftop. Do you feel as well off as before?

- *The structure of economies.* Different income groups have different spending patterns, and how income gets spent can help shape the structure of economies. (This is less the case in countries that open up to trade, as we shall see in chapter 13.) Research from India, Mexico, and other countries reveals that poor and middle-income households are more likely to spend their income on goods and services that were produced within their country and that stimulate local employment. Rich households are more likely to use their income to buy imports, to buy goods produced in more capital-intensive industries, or to save abroad. Changes in the distribution of income can thus have important effects on production and employment in poor—as well as rich—countries.

- *Economic efficiency.* Economic efficiency is likely to depend on how income is distributed—particularly in poor countries where assumptions about perfectly functioning markets break down. If there is no bank willing to loan money to the poor, then their ability to buy fertilizer probably depends on whether or not they have the liquidity (cash) to "self-finance" their production. If you have the cash, you use the optimal amount of fertilizer. If you don't, you don't and your productivity (efficiency) will suffer. The inseparability of efficiency from equity is an ongoing theme in this book.

- *Growth and poverty alleviation.* Inequality can directly shape how overall economic growth of an economy translates into poverty alleviation. Because it can affect both the efficiency and the structure of any economy in ways that disadvantage the poor, inequality can channel the benefits of growth away from the lower socioeconomic classes. Ensuring that growth reduces poverty in practice requires policies that explicitly take inequality into account—either by countering the effects of inequality on economic structure and inefficiency or through targeted transfers and other redistribution programs. Improving human development outcomes without growth in poor countries requires redistribution.

## INEQUALITY IS NOT POVERTY

You might think inequality matters in development economics because the more unequally income is distributed the more poor people there are. But that's not true: inequality is different from poverty. A society could have an unequal distribution of income with no one living below the poverty line, or a very equal distribution with everyone living in poverty. Poverty, as we explored in chapter 4, is about individuals' well-being relative to a set standard of living. Inequality is about individuals' well-being relative to each other.

To reinforce this idea, consider a situation in which changes in inequality and poverty are related. Imagine an egalitarian society (i.e., there is no inequality) with enough income to maintain everyone in the population *just above* the poverty line. In this fictitious society, everybody gets the per capita income, which in turn is just above the poverty line. In this case, the introduction of *any* inequality would also bring poverty to the society. This implies that, in general, the richer a country is, the more inequality can increase without increasing poverty.

Most countries in the world have per capita incomes well above the poverty line, which makes this *theoretical* and mechanical connection from increasing inequality to increasing poverty irrelevant in practice. This does not imply that there is no relationship between inequality and poverty. Indeed, characterizing and understanding this relationship is an important area of research in development economics. What it does imply, instead, is that the relationship is *empirical* and context dependent: it is positive in some cases, negative in others, and apparently nonexistent in still others.

To illustrate how this important relationship between the distinct concepts of inequality and poverty depends on context, we'll return to the drought in Burkina Faso described in chapter 4 later in this chapter and see that it simultaneously increased poverty and decreased inequality. But first we need to establish ways to measure inequality empirically. Exploring these measures requires us to carefully define inequality and—just like the poverty measures we discussed in the last chapter—this provides a natural opportunity to learn more about this essential concept of development economics.

## MEASURING INEQUALITY

When we compared the index of per capita income with income rankings in chapter 3, we saw that the distribution of global income is very unequal. Can we use what we learned there to construct a useful index of income inequality? Inequality can be measured in different ways. Some of these measures make eye-catching headlines. The Occupy Movement slogan "We are the 99%" is a good example of such a measure: the richest 1% of Americans owned about a third of the country's wealth. Measures that make headlines, however, do not always prove useful for comparing inequality across countries or in the same country over time. The workhorse measures of inequality in the development economists' tool kit are based on frequency distributions of income.

### Frequency Distributions

Often, just eyeballing the distribution of income in a country is illuminating. This is precisely what frequency distributions allow us to do (in addition to serving as the basis of the most common inequality index). To construct such a graphical depiction, you simply rank everyone in the country from poorest to richest, group them into income groups, and make a bar chart showing the percentage of the population in each income group. You just created a frequency distribution for income.

Figure 5.1 shows frequency distributions for Albania, Nicaragua, Tanzania, and Vietnam. Looking at frequency distributions of different countries like the ones shown in the graph can give you a sense of differences in income inequality, but we typically want a more precise way to compare income inequality across countries. We want an index measure of inequality.

A first step toward creating such an index and comparing income distributions is to group the population into equal parts along the horizontal axis. This allows us to turn income frequency distributions measured in dollars (figure 5.1) to income frequency distributions measured in *percentiles*. These percentile frequency distributions allow for more direct comparisons of inequality within countries with different income levels. Figure 5.2 compares frequency distributions of income for Mexico (left) and Sweden (right), in which the population has been divided into ten equal parts, or deciles.[1]

You can see in the picture that the poorest decile of Mexico's population received a small fraction of the income: the height of the smallest

Frequency Distributions of Income

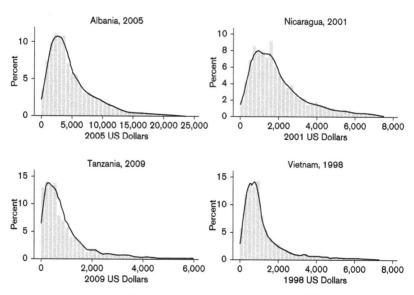

FIGURE 5.1. Comparison of frequency distributions of income for Albania, Nicaragua, Tanzania, and Vietnam.

bar is 1.2, telling us that the poorest 10% of the population gets 1.2% of the income. None of the bottom seven deciles gets anywhere near its proportional share (10%) of income. At the other extreme, the richest 10% get 42.2% of the income.

When we know what to look for in frequency distributions, they give us a convenient snapshot of inequality. In a perfectly equal income distribution, all the bars would be the same height. This clearly is not anywhere near the case in Mexico. It is not even the case in Sweden, which has the world's most equal income distribution.

Sweden's distribution seems more equal than Mexico's, but how much more equal is it? Is Mexico's more or less equal than, say, Tanzania's? How can we track changes in income inequality in the same countries over time? This is why we need an index of inequality.

If you've taken statistics you might already know some measures of dispersion that could be applied to income: the variance, standard deviation, or coefficient of variation. It turns out that these are not very good indexes. The variance has no bounds and is sensitive to the units we use to measure income. For example, suppose we calculated the

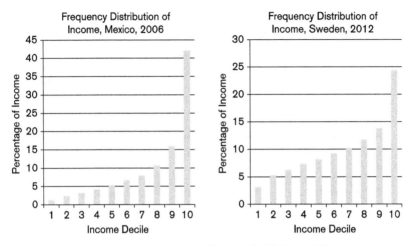

FIGURE 5.2. Decile frequency distributions of income for Mexico and Sweden.

variance of China's income. We could do this either in yuan or, using the 2013 exchange rate of a little more than 6 yuan per US dollar, in dollars. Either way, it would be a huge number. If we calculated the variance of China's income in yuan instead of dollars, it would come out $6^2$ (or 36 times) larger!

The standard deviation (SD) is the square root of the variance. It has the same problems as the variance for comparing dispersion or inequality across countries. Sometimes we try to normalize the SD of a variable like income by dividing by the variable's mean. This gives us the coefficient of variation (CV). It doesn't solve the problem, either: the CV of income for a country can take on any positive value.

In short, these conventional statistical measures of variance don't help us compare inequality across countries (or in the same country over time).

### Gini in a Nutshell

The most commonly used measure of inequality is the Gini coefficient. Not only is it a neat index, with values between zero and one, but it satisfies all five properties that an inequality index should have. These properties, incidentally, were established by economists to provide guidelines for how a measure of inequality should and should not behave in order for it to be useful. As you'll see, these properties—often called axioms or "self-evident truths"—are intended to be so uncontroversial that they are essentially impossible to reject as guidelines.

1. Pigou-Dalton transfer principle: Inequality, as measured by the index, should increase when income is transferred from a low-income household to a high-income household.

2. Symmetry: The measured level of inequality does not change when individuals trade places in the income distribution.

3. Independence of income scale: A proportional change in all incomes (like measuring income in dollars instead of yuan) does not alter inequality.

4. Homogeneity: A change in the size of the population will not affect measured inequality.

5. Decomposability: We would like to be able to use our index to understand how income from different sources (wages, profits) affects inequality. This means we should be able to decompose it with respect to income sources.

Several measures of inequality satisfy these given assumptions. The Gini coefficient is the most intuitive among them, as we shall see. It is also a measure of dispersion, like the variance. In fact, it has been argued that we should use it instead of the variance for portfolio analysis and other types of research.[2] That doesn't mean that the Gini coefficient is perfect; it is an aggregate measure, and there are some important dimensions of income inequality that it does not pick up, as we shall see below.

### RECIPE FOR MAKING A GINI COEFFICIENT

Here's how to make a Gini coefficient: First, remember in chapter 3 when we lined everyone in the country up from poorest to richest? Let's do that again and make everyone stand on top of a horizontal axis (specially designed to support their weight!), as in figure 5.3.

Pick a person—say, person $i$. Starting at the far left, add up how many people are to the left of person $i$. That's how many people are poorer than person $i$. Add one and divide by the country's total population and you get the share of people with income at or below that of person $i$. Do this for every person and you have the cumulative popula-

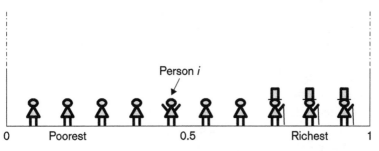

Person *i*

0   Poorest   0.5   Richest   1

**FIGURE 5.3.** Ranking of population from poorest to richest.

tion share from poorest to richest. For person *i* in our figure you can see that the share is 0.5, and for the far-right (richest) person it is 1.0.

Now figure out what share of the country's income each of these people has. To get the cumulative income shares, add up the income shares, starting at the far left, for each person in the population. Plot the cumulative income shares above each person, as in figure 5.4.

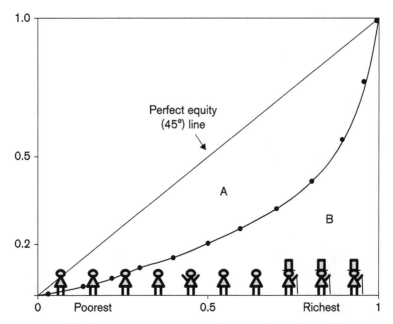

**FIGURE 5.4.** The Lorenz curve relates population shares (horizontal axis) to cumulative income shares (vertical axis). The Gini coefficient of income inequality is the area between the perfect equity (45°) line and the Lorenz curve (area A) divided by the area of the triangle below the perfect equity line (area A + B).

For person $i$, the cumulative income share is 0.2. In other words, one-half of the population has income at or below person $i$'s, but those people control only 20% of the country's total income. By the time we get to the very richest person, we have 100% of the country's population and income.

Connecting the dots, we get what is called the Lorenz curve (LC). It shows what share of income each cumulative population share controls, from poorest to richest. The more unequal the country's income distribution, the more bowed the LC will be toward the southeast corner of the unit box. The possibilities are bracketed by two extremes:

*Perfect Equity.* No society has it, but perfect equity means that each population share would have an equal share of total income: the poorest 20% would have 20% of the income, the poorest 50% would have 50%, and so on. (Really, they wouldn't be the poorest 50%, because everyone would have the same income.) The "perfect equity line" is just the diagonal running from the origin to the top right corner of the box.

*Perfect Inequality.* No society has this, either, because all but one person would starve to death. In a world of perfect inequality, no one has anything except for the richest person, who has it all. The "line of perfect inequality" is just the outside border running across the horizontal axis and up the right-hand side of our box.

Now look at the area in between the LC and the perfect equity line (area A) and the area between the LC and the perfect inequality line (area B). Add them together and you get a triangle forming the southeast half of the box. The ratio

$$\frac{A}{A + B}$$

is the Gini index (or coefficient) of inequality. As a good index, the Gini index always lies between zero and one. It equals zero only if there is perfect equity, so that the LC is the perfect-equity line (area A is nil). It equals 1.0 only if there is perfect inequality, so the LC is the outside border of the box (area B is zero).

Because $0 \leq G \leq 1$, the Gini coefficient is a useful way of measuring inequality, not only of income but of other things, as well, including wealth and assets. For example, a high Gini coefficient of land tells us

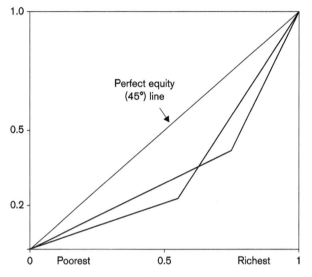

**FIGURE 5.5.** With intersecting Lorenz curves, different income distributions can give the same Gini coefficient.

that land is unequally distributed, and a low Gini for land indicates the opposite.

Still, it is important to keep in mind that, like per capita income, the Gini coefficient is an aggregate measure, a summary statistic. It does not tell us everything we might want to know about the distribution of whatever it measures. Many different distributions can give the same Gini coefficient. In fact, the same Gini can come from an infinite number of different Lorenz curves! To illustrate this, look at figure 5.5. Low-income households have a smaller share of total income in the economy depicted by the Lorenz curve that starts out lower. Yet the two Lorenz curves in this figure give the same Gini coefficient: the ratio $A/(A + B)$ is the same for both. The Gini coefficient could go down because income rises in a very poor or middle-income household, or because the income of a rich household drops. Looking only at the Gini coefficient, we do not know which. We also do not know how *polarized* a society is; income inequality and income polarization are two different concepts (sidebar 5.1).

Nevertheless, with Gini coefficients we can get a pretty good sense of how different countries stack up in terms of inequality. It might seem hard to calculate the area between the Lorenz curve and perfect equity line, but

### Sidebar 5.1    Income Polarization Is Not Income Inequality— and Why It Matters

To be precise, the Occupy Movement we describe was motivated at least as much by income polarization as it was by income inequality. You might think these two concepts are one and the same, but they are not. And since we are focusing on how economists measure income inequality, it is worth taking a minute to understand why the Gini coefficient picks up income inequality but not income polarization.

Much of Marx's thinking about society and economics hinged on the idea of polarization—a process by which society breaks up into hostile, antagonistic classes: the bourgeoisie and the proletariat. These classes become progressively more internally homogeneous while also becoming more distinct as separate camps. This is income polarization.

Economists Joan-María Esteban and Debraj Ray have studied the measurement of income polarization. To understand why polarization is not income inequality, let's return to figure 5.3. Suppose we numbered each of the 10 individuals depicted in this figure 1, 2, 3, . . . , 10 from poorest (left) to richest (right) and assigned each individual an income that was proportional to his number—for simplicity, $1, $2, $3, . . . , $10. This society obviously is not polarized into income groups. Now suppose that we wanted to polarize the income in this society by redistributing income. Specifically, we create a proletariat class from individuals 1–5 by taking from the rich (4 and 5) and giving to the poor (1 and 2) so that everyone in this class has $3, and we create a bourgeoisie class by doing the same with individuals 6–10 so each of their incomes is $7.

Esteban and Ray point out that while the polarized society we have created certainly "feels" quite different from the one we started with— it may even appear to have higher income inequality—in the process of polarizing this society we actually made the Gini coefficient go down! To see why, notice that our redistribution satisfies the Pigou-Dalton transfer principle, because every transfer involved the richer giving to the poorer. Have they convinced you that income inequality is different from income *polarization?*

Lest this sound like a very technical distinction, it is worth pointing out that highly polarized societies with clear concentrations of money and power function very differently than less polarized societies, even if their Gini coefficients are identical! In addition to the (Marxian) risks of social and political conflict, Tewodaj Mogues and Michael Carter, for example, show how polarization in social norms and networks can create feedback loops that in turn dial up income inequality.

J.-M. Esteban and D. Ray, "On the Measurement of Polarization," *Econometrica* 62, no. 4 (1994):819–51.

T. Mogues and M. R. Carter, "Social Capital and the Reproduction of Economic Inequality in Polarized Societies," *Journal of Economic Inequality* 3, no. 3 (2005):193–219.

TABLE 5.1  A HYPOTHETICAL
INCOME DISTRIBUTION

| Person | Income $(Y_i)$ | $F(Y_i)$ |
|---|---|---|
| 1 | 79.6 | 0.1 |
| 2 | 128.7 | 0.2 |
| 3 | 153.1 | 0.3 |
| 4 | 177.8 | 0.4 |
| 5 | 200.3 | 0.5 |
| 6 | 223.6 | 0.6 |
| 7 | 249.4 | 0.7 |
| 8 | 284.2 | 0.8 |
| 9 | 332.8 | 0.9 |
| 10 | 587.9 | 1 |

| | |
|---|---|
| Cov$(Y,F(Y))$ | 34.48 |
| Mean Income | 241.74 |
| Gini Coefficient | 0.28 |

there's an easy way: after ranking everyone in the economy, just take the covariance between their income $(Y_i)$ and the cumulative distribution of income $(F(Y_i))$, double it, and divide by mean income $(\mu)$. That is,

$$G = \frac{2\,Cov(Y_i, F(Y_i))}{\mu}$$

For example, take a little economy with ten people and incomes, as in table 5.1. The first column ranks people from poorest (1) to richest (10). The second column gives each person $i$'s income, $Y_i$. The third gives the cumulative distribution of income, or share of people with income at or below $Y_i$, which we denote $F(Y_i)$. If we take the covariance between the last two columns (34.48), double it, then divide by mean income (241.74), we get the Gini coefficient.[3]

### WHAT'S UNEQUAL? INTERNATIONAL COMPARISON OF INEQUALITY

In our little example, the Gini coefficient is very low: 0.28. That's around where the Gini for Sweden is, which is not surprising, because for our example we took the income deciles for Sweden and pretended they were people. This actually gives us a rough approximation of the Swedish income Gini. It isn't a very efficient use of our formula, though, because we lose a lot of information by lumping everybody into deciles.

TABLE 5.2 GINI COEFFICIENTS FOR SELECTED COUNTRIES

| Country | Source | Year | Gini Index | Country | Source | Year | Gini Index |
|---|---|---|---|---|---|---|---|
| Very Low Inequality | | | | Medium Inequality | | | |
| Serbia | WB | 2008 | 0.28 | Thailand | WB | 2009 | 0.40 |
| Kazakhstan | WB | 2009 | 0.29 | Russian Federation | WB | 2009 | 0.40 |
| Pakistan | WB | 2008 | 0.30 | Philippines | WB | 2009 | 0.43 |
| Egypt, Arab Rep. | WB | 2008 | 0.31 | Argentina | WB | 2010 | 0.44 |
| Bangladesh | WB | 2010 | 0.32 | United States | CIA | 2007 | 0.45 |
| Low Inequality | | | | High Inequality | | | |
| Poland | WB | 2009 | 0.34 | Mexico | WB | 2008 | 0.48 |
| Niger | WB | 2008 | 0.35 | Costa Rica | WB | 2009 | 0.51 |
| Sudan | WB | 2009 | 0.35 | Chile | WB | 2009 | 0.52 |
| Vietnam | WB | 2008 | 0.36 | Brazil | WB | 2009 | 0.55 |
| Japan | CIA | 2008 | 0.38 | Very High Inequality | | | |
| Turkey | WB | 2008 | 0.39 | South Africa | WB | 2009 | 0.63 |
| Burkina Faso | WB | 2009 | 0.40 | Namibia | CIA | 2003 | 0.71 |

SOURCE: World Bank (http://data.worldbank.org/indicator/SI.POV.GINI); Central Intelligence Agency (www.cia.gov/library/publications/the-world-factbook/fields/2172.html).

We'd be better off having a row in our data table for every single Swede. (A random sample of Swedes would do.)

Sweden is pretty much the lower bound on the world's Gini coefficients, because it has about the most equal income distribution on the planet. The US Gini is a lot higher—around 0.45. If we grew the Swedish economy by one-third and gave *all* the new income to the richest decile, we'd get a Gini coefficient like that of the United States. (To do this in our example, just increase the top decile's income by 798.) Or we could grow the economy by 50% and split it between the top two deciles. Or we could just take away 70% of the poorest three deciles' income and give it *all* to the richest decile. There are many ways to transform Sweden's income distribution and end up with the same Gini as the United States has, but any one of them would be a huge redistribution in favor of the rich.

Table 5.2 lists some Gini coefficients from other countries. It shows a wide range of Gini coefficients around the world, from below 0.30 for the most equitable countries to as high as 0.71 for the countries with the most unequal income distributions.

You might wonder what the Gini coefficient for *the whole world* is. Would it be higher or lower than most country Ginis? Think about it:

world income inequality includes both inequality within countries (which is what we have in our table) and inequality among countries, which is big: just look at the range of average per capita incomes we saw in chapter 3. A recent study put the global income Gini coefficient at around 0.62, which would put the world in our "very high inequality" category.[4] The good news, however, is that this global Gini has been falling in recent decades. In what might seem like a contradiction, global inequality has fallen even as income gaps between countries have widened.[5]

## INEQUALITY AND POVERTY

In the last chapter we saw how a severe drought in the Sahel affected poverty. The poverty rate increased significantly, regardless of whether we measure it using the headcount or the severity measure. What happened to inequality? Was rising poverty in the Sahel accompanied by rising inequality?

Table 5.3 compares the impacts of the drought on poverty, as measured by two variants of the FGT measure, and on income inequality, using the Gini index. It might come as a surprise that the drought had an equalizing impact on household incomes. The Gini coefficient for this region fell slightly, from 0.34 to 0.31. Virtually all households were hard hit by the drought. As the headcount shows, many households fell into poverty, while the severity index reveals that many poor people became much poorer. In relative terms, though, high-income households took a bigger hit. This explains why the Gini coefficient fell.

These findings illustrate the lack of a mechanical relationship between poverty and inequality. When poverty increases, inequality may either

TABLE 5.3 IMPACTS OF DROUGHT ON HOUSEHOLD
INCOME INEQUALITY AND POVERTY IN BURKINA FASO

| Year | Poverty | | Gini |
|---|---|---|---|
| | *Headcount* | *Severity* | |
| Normal Year | 0.20 | 0.02 | 0.34 |
| Drought Year | 0.51 | 0.19 | 0.31 |

SOURCE: Thomas Reardon and J. Edward Taylor, "Agroclimatic Shock, Income Inequality, and Poverty: Evidence from Burkina Faso," *World Development* 24, no. 5 (1996):901–14.

increase or decrease depending on the context. As we mentioned earlier, however, one thing about the context that conceptually matters in this relationship is the rate and severity of poverty before a shock like a drought hits. In the Sahel, desperately poor households may have simply had little income to lose—even if the little they lost really hurt. Less poor households, by contrast, had more to lose and still lacked any real protection from the drought. By contrast, imagine the same drought hitting a richer country with fewer people at subsistence levels and drought insurance for richer households. Can you see how the same drought could both increase poverty *and* increase inequality in such a context?

### INEQUALITY AND SOCIAL WELFARE

At the end of chapter 3 we noted that the average per capita income often is used as an indicator of social welfare. This is true, but it is only a rough indicator because it does not take into account how income is distributed. Now that we have a convenient measure of inequality, we can do better. One way to bring income inequality into a social welfare function is to use the Gini coefficient of income inequality *(G)*:

$$W = y(1 - G)$$

. . . where $W$ represents social welfare and $y$ is the average per capita income in the economy (country, region, village, or whatever level we want to carry out the welfare analysis on).[6] This social welfare function has the properties that either an increase in income of any member of society or a transfer of income from a rich to a less-rich person will increase social welfare, no matter what the original income distribution looks like.[7] Of course, there are lots of other ways to combine income and inequality in a social welfare function. One of the critical features of any of these functions is how much "weight" we put on income relative to inequality. Differences in political opinion and philosophy can translate into very different weights, but for our purposes let's run with this simple welfare function.

Using this welfare function instead of per capita income makes a big difference in measuring the impacts of income changes on welfare. For example, let's take the economy in table 5.1 and give thirty units of income (an amount equal to 5% of the richest decile's income) first to the poorest and then to the richest decile (leaving all other deciles

TABLE 5.4 IMPACTS OF AN INCOME INCREASE ON PER CAPITA INCOME,
INEQUALITY, AND WELFARE IN A HYPOTHETICAL ECONOMY

| Impact on Per Capita Income, Inequality, and Welfare | Transfer of $30 (5% of Richest Decile's Income) to | |
| --- | --- | --- |
| | *the Poorest Decile* | *the Richest Decile* |
| Change in Average Per Capita Income | 1.2% | 1.2% |
| Change in Gini | –5.0% | 2.6% |
| Change in Welfare ($W = y(1 - G)$) | 3.2% | 0.2% |

unchanged). The results are shown in table 5.4. In both cases, adding an amount equal to 5% of the richest decile's income raises average household income by 1.2%. However, the Gini coefficient falls when this income goes to the poorest decile, and it increases if the cash goes to the richest decile. Welfare increases 3.2%—more than the percentage increase in average income—if the cash goes to the poorest decile. It goes up by only 0.2% if the same income goes to the richest decile. With this welfare measure, adding new income to an economy will not make welfare decrease, even if there is a negative effect on inequality; however, a negative effect on inequality drags down the measured welfare impact.

## WHAT IS A HOUSEHOLD?

Because households are the basic unit of society, they also tend to be a useful unit of analysis for understanding income and income inequality. Even though we often use per capita income—the average income per *person*—to compare the income levels of different countries, the income level of the average or median *household* can be easier to interpret. In the case of income inequality, the household is almost always the unit of analysis, which consequently requires that we clearly define what constitutes a household.

Development economists typically define a household as a group of people who share a common pot of food or who otherwise share or pool productive resources. In many developing countries, particularly in rural areas, households by this definition can be quite large and include several nuclear families residing in the same compound. As you can imagine, this can really complicate the process of filling out detailed household survey questionnaires!

To illustrate how important the definition of a household can be for measuring inequality, consider a place like Niger (Gini coefficient of 0.35; table 5.2), which typically has large households that include several family units (usually, brothers and their families). What would happen if richer households suddenly got smaller (i.e., had fewer kids)? If we computed the Gini coefficient based on the average income per household member, would this change raise or lower the Gini? The answer is that it would raise measured inequality. In contrast, average per capita income for Niger (shockingly low at $246 in 2012) is impervious to how individuals group into households.

In the past forty years, the composition of households has changed dramatically in the US and other developed countries. You won't be surprised to learn that this can have big effects on measured inequality. Since 1970, the Gini coefficient in the US has increased from 0.39 to 0.48, but part of this increase reflects a steady evolution in the composition of US households. We have many more single-mother households and many more dual-income households today than we did in 1970. Since these two types of households are overwhelmingly low and high income, respectively, the change in household composition pushes up the US Gini coefficient.

In developing countries, household structure has changed less in recent years, but there are changes brewing that could have important implications for how we measure inequality. In many cities, the structure of households is beginning to change. In rural areas, out-migration has reshaped many households. In the next decade or two, it will become increasingly important for development economists to take these demographic changes into account when computing inequality measures and comparing them over time.

## THE SOURCES OF INCOME INEQUALITY

Earlier in this chapter we said that one of the properties we would like our inequality index to have is decomposability. If we want to know what explains income inequality, we had better be able to represent inequality as a function of income from different sources, like profits, wages, cash transfers, or a new development project. It turns out that this is easy to do in the case of the Gini coefficient. The appendix to this chapter shows how to decompose the Gini coefficient by income sources. Here's what we end up with:

$$G = \sum_{k=1}^{K} S_k G_k R_k$$

The interpretation of this formula gives us insight into what determines income inequality.

- $S_k$ is the share of income from source $k$ in total income in the economy. The larger the income source is relative to total income, the bigger the impact it can potentially have on inequality.
- $G_k$ is the Gini coefficient of inequality for income source $k$. It tells how unequally income from a source is distributed. In order for an income source to have a big effect on income inequality, it has to be unequally distributed. If income from a particular source is perfectly equally distributed, its Gini coefficient is zero and it cannot affect income inequality.

  You might think that an income source that is large and unequally distributed would increase inequality. But what about welfare payments? Consider social cash transfers, like Mexico's PROGRESA (chapter 2). They are large relative to total income in many poor villages. They are unequally distributed, because only the poorest of the poor get the transfers; thus, the Gini coefficient for social cash transfers is high. Yet we would expect welfare programs to decrease income inequality because of who gets the payments. Social cash transfers target the poorest.
- $R_k$ tells us who gets income from source $k$. It is the Gini correlation between income from source $k$ and total income. It ranges from −1 (income from source $k$ has a perfect negative correlation with households' total-income rankings) to 1 (a perfect positive correlation). For $k$ = profits, we'd expect $R_k$ to be positive, because profits tend to flow disproportionately to richer households. For $k$ = welfare income, $R_k$ should be negative—provided the right households get the cash.

When does a development project reduce income inequality in an economy—say, in a village? When it has a large positive effect on village income, when this effect is unequally distributed across village households, and when it favors those at the bottom and middle of the village income distribution. The same is true for migration (see sidebar 5.2).

### Sidebar 5.2   Remittances and Inequality

The migration of labor off the farm is a universal feature of economic growth, as we'll see in chapter 10. Each day thousands of people throughout the developing world migrate out of their villages seeking work in other parts of the country (internal migration) or abroad (international migration). If they are successful at finding a job, they are likely to send home part of their earnings as migrant remittances.

How do migrant remittances affect rural income inequality? If remittances increase across the board, does the rural income Gini coefficient increase or decrease? There is a long-standing debate on this question. Ed teamed up with two other economists, Oded Stark and Shlomo Yitzhaki, to provide an answer using a Gini decomposition of village incomes. They hypothesized that remittances affect inequality differently at different stages of a village's migration history. Migration—especially international migration—entails high costs and risks. The first migrants are likely to come from relatively well off village households; when they send back remittances, inequality in the village is likely to increase. Over time, though, the pioneer migrants can help others migrate by providing information and assistance. If access to migrant labor markets eventually spreads to other households in the village, remittances could become less unequalizing—or even equalizing—over time.

To test this migration diffusion hypothesis, household survey data were used to perform a Gini decomposition of income in two Mexican villages, one with a long history of sending migrants to the United States, and the other a relative newcomer to international migration. The study found that remittances increased income inequality in the village that was just beginning to send migrants abroad, but they reduced inequality in the village that had a long history of US migration. In the first village, remittances from migrants in the US constituted 16% of village income ($S = 0.16$). They were unequally distributed, with a Gini coefficient of 0.90, and they were highly correlated with total income ($R = 0.86$). In the village with a long US migration history, remittances represented a larger share of village income ($S = 0.21$), but the Gini coefficient was lower ($G = 0.68$), and the correlation with total income was much lower ($R = 0.33$). The authors showed that a percentage increase in remittances from the US, due for example to a peso devaluation or an improvement in US labor markets, would increase the Gini coefficient of income inequality in the first village while decreasing it in the second.

O. Stark, J. E. Taylor, and S. Yitzhaki, "Remittances and Inequality," *Economic Journal* 96 (1986):722–40.

## INTRA-HOUSEHOLD INEQUALITY AND GENDER

Income inequality at different scales matters for different reasons. By far, countries are the most common unit of analysis for inequality measurement, but inequality analyses at subnational levels can also be instructive. Do you think the Gini coefficient for your hometown is higher or lower than for New York City? If you guessed lower, you are almost certainly right: New York City has the highest income inequality of any major city in the US, with a Gini of 0.504. Which city has the lowest inequality? Salt Lake City, with a Gini of 0.417.

But why stop at cities? There is a yet deeper level that is a common unit of analysis for inequality research in development economics: the household. One of the greatest sources of inequality in poor countries is not between households but within them: gender inequality between men and women living in the same household.

Women are less likely to go to school, less likely to work, less likely to earn the same wage for comparable work, more likely to be in poverty, and less likely to hold political positions. In many countries, they lack basic legal rights, like the right to own property or even travel without their husband's permission.

And then there are the millions of women who are missing. What do we mean by "missing"? The female share of the world's population is lower than it would be if women had access to the same resources as men and if parents did not practice selective abortion. Amartya Sen coined the term "missing women," and Esther Duflo called it "the starkest manifestation of the lack of gender equality . . . Most of these missing women are not actively killed," she writes. "They die from cumulative neglect."[8]

Understanding and addressing the inequality between men and women is a major concern in development economics. Gender inequality both is affected by economic development and can directly hinder development. For example, if poor couples are less likely to value girls, rising incomes should favor more gender equality. But discrimination against women can hinder development in the first place. When women lack the same legal protections and access to resources as men, they are not as productive as they otherwise could be. But the missed opportunity is deeper than just underutilized resources. Women tend to have greater influence over future generations than men, through their effect on families and, by extension, societies.

A key theme of this book is that it generally is not possible to separate issues of equity and efficiency in poor countries. This inseparability of efficiency and equity is perhaps easiest to see within the household, where continued suppression of women makes households less productive and less efficient. Gender inequality thus hinders economic development, as well as being exacerbated by underdevelopment.

www.rebeltext.org/development/qr5.html
Learn more about inequality by exploring
multimedia resources while you read.

**APPENDIX**

*Deriving the Gini Decomposition*

Here's how we derived the Gini decomposition by income sources. First, take our formula for calculating the Gini coefficient:

$$G = \frac{2Cov(Y_i, F(Y_i))}{\mu}$$

Second, represent household income, $Y_i$, as the sum of income from $K$ different income sources:

$$Y_i = \sum_{k=1}^{K} y_{ki}$$

For example, $k = 1$ could be wages; 2 could be profits; 3, welfare income; and so forth. We add these up over all $K$ sources to get a household's total income. Now substitute this for $Y_i$ in the formula for the Gini coefficient:

$$G = \frac{2Cov(\sum_{k=1}^{K} y_{ki}, F(Y_i))}{\mu}$$

Now we're taking the covariance between a sum of things (the $y_{ki}$) and something else ($F(Y_i)$). This equals the sum of covariances between each income source and the cumulative income distribution:[9]

$$G = \frac{2\sum_{k=1}^{K} Cov(y_{ki}, F(Y_i))}{\mu}$$

In a mathematical sleight-of-hand, we multiply this by a couple of rather interesting names for one, namely:

$$\frac{\mu_k}{\mu_k}$$

and

$$\frac{Cov(y_{ki},F(y_{ki}))}{Cov(y_{ki},F(y_{ki}))}$$

where $\mu_k$ is the mean income from source $k$, and $F(y_{ki})$ is the share of households with source-$k$ income at or below $y_{ki}$. If we do this we get a crazy plateful:

$$G = \frac{2\sum_{k=1}^{K} Cov(y_{ki},F(Y_i))}{\mu} \cdot \frac{\mu_k}{\mu_k} \cdot \frac{Cov(y_{ki},F(y_{ki}))}{Cov(y_{ki},F(y_{ki}))}$$

But after regrouping terms we get a new formula, which decomposes the Gini coefficient into each of its $K$ income sources:

$$G = \sum_{k=1}^{K} S_k G_k R_k$$

where

$$S_k = \frac{\mu_k}{\mu}, 0 \le S_k \le 1$$

$$G_k = \frac{2Cov(y_{ik},F(y_{ik}))}{\mu_k}, 0 \le G_k \le 1$$

$$R_k = \frac{Cov(y_{ki},F(y_i))}{Cov(y_{ki},F(y_{ki}))}, -1 \le R_k \le 1$$

**6**

# Human Development

If this book had ended with the previous chapter, we might
be accused of seeing income as an end, instead of a means to
an end. This would be misleading. There is a rich, decades-
long record of work in development economics that distin-
guishes between income and the deeper dimensions of human
development that ultimately matter most. Nobel laureate
Amartya Sen has led this charge to consider "development as
freedom." As he has forcefully argued, income may be a
potent predictor of individuals' quality of life, but we
misunderstand key aspects of economic development if we
focus exclusively on income. Sen inspired the creation of a
measure of human development—the Human Development
Index—which has been a centerpiece of international
development since its launch in 1990. We describe the
construction of the Human Development Index in this
chapter as a way to explore how development economists
think about development as deeper than just income.

### ESSENTIALS

- Human Development Index (HDI)
- Human capital
- Market failures: Externalities and public goods
- Opportunity cost
- Conditional cash transfers
- Cost-benefit analysis
- "Development as freedom"

Poverty is about income. Economic development ultimately is about
people. In 1990, the Pakistani economist Mahbub ul Haq began urging
the United Nations Development Program (UNDP) to create a broader
measure of development that focused on human outcomes. He felt this
was necessary in order "to shift the focus of development economics
from national income accounting to people-centered policies" (p. 9).[1]

The measure Haq proposed had to be simple to understand, and it had to encompass both economics and human well-being. Above all, it had to be an *index* which would make it possible to compare improvements in well-being across countries. The Nobel laureate Amartya Sen provided the conceptual framework for this project. Actually, Sen initially opposed the idea, worrying that it would be too difficult to capture the full complexity of human development in a single index. In the end, Haq swayed Sen by persuading him that only a holistic development index could shift policy makers' and researchers' attention from economics to human well-being. Only a concept that confronts GDP head-to-head, as a single number, could get real traction in the policy process. That is how the Human Development Index (HDI) was born.

After considerable discussion and debate, the UNDP decided on an index that included the following economic and human outcomes:

*Life expectancy at birth* (years; LE). Because it is measured at birth, this index is affected by high infant mortality rates in some countries.

*Education,* composed of two separate measures: expected years of schooling for children (EYSC), and mean years of schooling for adults (MYSA). By having a separate measure for expected education of children, this index can reflect improvements in low-education countries that invest in expanding educational opportunities for kids. Mean years of schooling for adults would reflect such improvements only after many years have elapsed.

*Income* (GNI), measured as the gross national income per capita, PPP adjusted to take into account cost-of-living differences among countries.

Table 6.1 shows the highest and lowest outcomes for each of these variables across the globe in 2010. It reveals massive disparities in human development indicators. People in the highest-ranked countries live more than 75% longer, have more than ten times more schooling, and make more than 350 times more income, on average, than people in the lowest-ranked countries.

We can argue about whether these variables are sufficient to capture the most critical differences across countries in terms of their human development. Surely, you can think of other variables that might be included in an HDI. A good index does not have to include every human outcome we can think of, though. A few well-chosen ones should do, as long as they are correlated with the other important outcomes that get

TABLE 6.1  THE TWO ENDS OF THE HUMAN DEVELOPMENT SPECTRUM

| Min/Max and Country | Life Expectancy at Birth (LE, Years) | Expected Years of Schooling (of Children) (EYSC, Years) | Mean Years of Schooling (of Adults) (MYSA, Years) | GNI Per Capita in PPP Terms (Constant 2005 International $) |
|---|---|---|---|---|
| Minimum | 47.4 | 2.4 | 1.2 | 260 |
| Country | Sierra Leone | Somalia | Mozambique | Liberia |
| Maximum | 83.2 | 18 | 12.6 | 93,383 |
| Country | Japan | Australia | Norway | Qatar |

SOURCE: Data from United Nations Development Program (http://hdr.undp.org/en/statistics/data/).

left out. For example, access to health care is an essential part of development. But because life expectancy is closely related to health care, we do not necessarily have to include both life expectancy and health care in our index.

There is a difference between having a long life and a healthy life, though. Other measures have been proposed to capture both the length and quality of life. One is the disability-adjusted life year (DALY). People with disabilities lose time to premature death and spend time disabled by disease. One DALY is equal to one year of healthy life lost, due either to death or disability. Health research based on DALY highlights the importance of psychiatric and neurological conditions as well as physical disabilities that take away healthy life years. In some cases, the health of countries with a long life expectancy does not look as impressive when researchers adjust for DALY. DALYs have not been included in the HDI.

One variable that has been added to the HDI is inequality. The Inequality Adjusted Human Development Index (IHDI) discounts each dimension of the HDI (income, health, and education) by the degree of inequality in that dimension. When there is no inequality in any dimension, the IHDI is equal to the HDI; otherwise, it is lower. Wide variability in per capita incomes, life expectancy, and education across a population can substantially reduce the population's HDI.[2] Countries with low human development tend to have high levels of inequality in more dimensions.

CONSTRUCTING THE HDI

Creating the HDI raised a challenging technical question: How do you construct an index from such qualitatively different outcomes as income, education, and life expectancy? The HDI is an index of indexes, one for each outcome. The outcomes in it are diverse, are measured in different units, and take on a very wide range of values.

Actually, we've already learned pretty much everything we need to make the HDI. At the end of chapter 2 we constructed an income index. We calculate our gross national income index to include in the HDI for each country $i$, which we can call $I(GNI_i)$, as follows:

$$I(GNI_i) = \frac{Ln(GNI_i) - Ln(GNI_{min})}{Ln(GNI_{max}) - Ln(GNI_{min})}$$

This is just like the income index in chapter 2 except that it takes the natural log of each GNI. There is a good reason to do this. We just saw that the country per capita incomes for the 2010 HDI ranged from $260 (Liberia) to $93,383 (Qatar). That's a big range. We would expect that an increase in income in rich countries won't affect human development as much as the same increase in poor countries. Taking the natural log of each country's income accomplishes this. It compresses the income range, since $Ln(260) = 5.56$ and $Ln(93,383) = 11.44$.

Notice how we've used the highest and lowest GNIs to construct this index. The UN uses the highest and lowest incomes any country had between 1980 and 2010 ($163 and $108,211, respectively). We can use the same method to construct indexes for life expectancy at birth and the two education variables. For life expectancy, the UN uses a minimum value of 20, which from a practical point of view is about the lowest a society could have and still reproduce itself. The maximum LE is 83.2 (Japan in 2010). For the mean years of schooling for adults, it uses a maximum of 13.2 (the United States in 2002), and a minimum of zero (since, in theory, a society could survive with zero schooling). For expected years of schooling for children, the maximum is 20.6 (Australia in 2002), and the minimum, as for the other education variable, is zero.

In all these indexes, a country with an outcome equal to the minimum gets a value of zero, while a country with an outcome equal to the maximum gets a value of one. All other countries have values between zero and one.

The last step is to combine these four indexes to make the HDI. We could just take the average of the four. The problem with that approach is that a country could do well on one component but miserably fail on another and still come out looking alright. If a country really fails on one human development dimension, we want our index to reflect this.

TABLE 6.2  COUNTRY HDIS BY
PER CAPITA INCOME QUINTILE

| Quintile | HDI Range | |
|----------|-----|------|
|          | Low | High |
| 1 | 0.22 | 0.44 |
| 2 | 0.45 | 0.61 |
| 3 | 0.61 | 0.69 |
| 4 | 0.70 | 0.78 |
| 5 | 0.78 | 0.91 |

(Richer ↓, rows 1–5)

The UN opted for using geometric means. The geometric mean of $N$ variables is the $N$th root of the product of the $N$ variables. This sounds pretty mathematical, but the math we choose depends on what we want our index to say about society.[3]

Here's how to make the HDI: first, the two educational indexes are combined, using a geometric mean, to make a single educational index, which we can call $I(E_i)$. It is computed as

$$I(E_i) = \sqrt{I(EYSC_i) * I(MYSA_i)}$$

The HDI is calculated by taking the geometric mean of the three indexes, $I(GNI_i)$, $I(LE_i)$, and $I(E_i)$:

$$HDI_i = \sqrt[3]{I(GNI_i) * I(LE_i) * I(E_i)}$$

(Notice that this is the cubed root, since we are dealing with three indexes.) The HDI, like each of its components, ranges from zero to one. It is zero if a country has a zero for any of the three component indexes. It can only equal one if a country maxes out on all three indexes. We can take all 187 countries for which we have data, sort them from lowest to highest HDI, and divide them into quintiles (fifths). Table 6.2 shows the HDI ranges for each quintile; the HDI and its components for selected countries appear in table 6.3. Among all countries (click on the QR code at the end of this chapter), the lowest quintile is dominated by African countries; in fact, with only a handful of exceptions (Afghanistan, Haiti, Nepal), all of the countries in the lowest quintile are African. With the exception of a couple of oil-producing and Asian countries, all in the top quintile are European or North American. In between is a diverse group of countries, including some that do well on one or two HDI components but not on the other one or two.

TABLE 6.3 OVER- AND UNDERPERFORMERS IN HUMAN DEVELOPMENT

| Country | LE[a] Level | Index | EYSC[b] Level | Index | MYSA[c] Level | Index | GNI[d] Level | Index | HDI | GNI Rank (Lowest to Highest) | HDI Rank (Lowest to Highest) | GNI Rank −HDI Rank |
|---|---|---|---|---|---|---|---|---|---|---|---|---|
| **Worst Performers** | | | | | | | | | | | | |
| Equatorial Guinea | 50.8 | 0.49 | 7.7 | 0.37 | 5.4 | 0.41 | 16,908 | 0.71 | 0.51 | 143 | 54 | 89 |
| Kuwait | 74.5 | 0.86 | 12.3 | 0.60 | 6.1 | 0.46 | 46,428 | 0.87 | 0.73 | 181 | 129 | 52 |
| Botswana | 53.3 | 0.53 | 12.2 | 0.59 | 8.9 | 0.67 | 12,479 | 0.67 | 0.61 | 124 | 74 | 50 |
| Oman | 72.8 | 0.84 | 11.8 | 0.57 | 5.5 | 0.42 | 22,633 | 0.76 | 0.68 | 150 | 100 | 50 |
| South Africa | 52.2 | 0.51 | 13.1 | 0.64 | 8.5 | 0.64 | 9,257 | 0.62 | 0.59 | 109 | 66 | 43 |
| Angola | 50.7 | 0.49 | 9.1 | 0.44 | 4.4 | 0.33 | 4,659 | 0.52 | 0.46 | 79 | 40 | 39 |
| Gabon | 62.3 | 0.67 | 13.1 | 0.64 | 7.5 | 0.57 | 11,771 | 0.66 | 0.64 | 121 | 83 | 38 |
| Qatar | 78.2 | 0.92 | 12 | 0.58 | 7.3 | 0.55 | 93,383 | 0.98 | 0.80 | 187 | 153 | 34 |
| Bhutan | 66.8 | 0.74 | 11 | 0.53 | 2.3 | 0.17 | 5,060 | 0.53 | 0.49 | 82 | 49 | 33 |
| United Arab Emirates | 76.4 | 0.89 | 13.3 | 0.65 | 9.3 | 0.70 | 59,819 | 0.91 | 0.82 | 185 | 158 | 27 |
| Trinidad and Tobago | 69.9 | 0.79 | 12.3 | 0.60 | 9.2 | 0.70 | 22,979 | 0.76 | 0.73 | 151 | 125 | 26 |
| Average | 64.35 | 0.70 | 11.63 | 0.56 | 6.76 | 0.51 | 27,761 | 0.73 | 0.64 | 137 | 94 | 44 |
| **Best Performers** | | | | | | | | | | | | |
| Cuba | 79 | 0.93 | 17.5 | 0.85 | 9.9 | 0.75 | 5,253 | 0.53 | 0.74 | 84 | 131 | −47 |
| Georgia | 73.5 | 0.85 | 13.1 | 0.64 | 12.1 | 0.92 | 4,535 | 0.51 | 0.69 | 76 | 111 | −35 |
| Grenada | 75.8 | 0.88 | 16 | 0.78 | 8.6 | 0.65 | 6,914 | 0.58 | 0.71 | 93 | 121 | −28 |
| Palau | 71.5 | 0.81 | 14.7 | 0.71 | 12.1 | 0.92 | 9,617 | 0.63 | 0.75 | 110 | 138 | −28 |
| New Zealand | 80.5 | 0.96 | 18 | 0.87 | 12.5 | 0.95 | 23,776 | 0.77 | 0.87 | 153 | 180 | −27 |
| Madagascar | 66.5 | 0.74 | 10.7 | 0.52 | 5.2 | 0.39 | 840 | 0.25 | 0.44 | 11 | 37 | −26 |
| Average | 74.47 | 0.86 | 15.00 | 0.73 | 10.07 | 0.76 | 8,489 | 0.54 | 0.70 | 88 | 120 | −32 |

[a] Life expectancy at birth (years).
[b] Expected years of schooling (of children; years).
[c] Mean years of schooling (of adults; years).
[d] Per capita GNI in PPP terms (constant 2005 international $).
SOURCE: Analysis of data from the UNDP Human Development Report (http://hdr.undp.org/en/statistics/data/).

INCOME AND HUMAN DEVELOPMENT

As we emphasized at the outset of this chapter, income is important because it is a means to an end—to meaningful, healthy, and empowered existence. But just *how* potent a means to human development is income? With only income, can we predict human development, or do countries at similar income levels often have different human development outcomes? There is clearly a built-in relationship between income and the HDI because one of the HDI's components is income. There is also almost certainly a relationship between income and both life expectancy and educational attainment. We can see evidence for this in figure 6.1, which graphs different countries' HDIs (vertical axis) against their per capita gross national incomes (horizontal axis).

It is clear that the HDI rises sharply with per capita income, but it tapers off sharply at higher income levels, which is precisely the motivation for using log transformations of income. Nevertheless, there are some wide variations in human development outcomes among countries even at the same income levels.

Let's dig more deeply into the UNDP data and look for countries in which the connection between income and human development is not so clear. This might offer us some insights into why some countries have managed to do a better job of meeting their human development challenges than others. One way to do this is to rank countries first in terms of per capita GNI, then in terms of HDI, and then take the difference between the two rankings. A positive difference means that a country was ranked relatively high in terms of income but low in terms of the HDI. You can think of these as the underperformers: they seem to have gotten disproportionately little human development out of their incomes. If the rank difference is negative, a country overperformed: it was ranked higher in HDI than income.

Table 6.3 shows the countries with the biggest rank differences, positive or negative. You could draw the line on what "biggest" means wherever you wish; we chose countries that have a rank difference of more than 25 (positive in the top panel, negative in the bottom).

Look at Equatorial Guinea. Its income rank is very high: it had the forty-fourth highest income among the 187 countries in our data. It is the richest country in Africa in terms of per capita income, with a PPP-adjusted per capita income of $16,908. You'd think it would score high on life expectancy and education, the other two components of the HDI, but it doesn't. Its average life expectancy is a dismal 50.8 years, and the average adult has only 5.4 years of schooling.

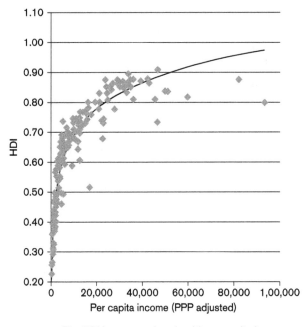

**FIGURE 6.1.** The HDI increases sharply with per capita income and then tapers off.

What's the story in Equatorial Guinea? It is one of the largest oil producers in Africa, but its considerable oil wealth is in the hands of relatively few people. Most of the population lives in rural areas, where subsistence production predominates. (We will look at subsistence production in chapter 9.) Getting quality data on Equatorial Guinea is problematic. A Gini coefficient for income is not available from the World Bank or the CIA. However, the Vision of Humanity's Global Peace Index estimates a Gini coefficient of 0.65, making Equatorial Guinea one of the most unequal countries in the world.[4]

It might seem surprising that a country with so much oil wealth would have a relatively poor record in terms of the HDI, but Equatorial Guinea is not the only one. The United Arab Emirates, Kuwait, Angola, and Qatar are among the top twenty oil exporters in the world, and all of them are on our "underperformers" list. So are Gabon and Trinidad and Tobago, two other oil exporters. Oil riches do not seem to buy human development—or, perhaps more accurately, having easy oil money can shape the structure of an economy and society in ways that slow human development gains.

Another standout on the worst performers' list is South Africa. It has the largest economy in Africa, and the World Bank ranks it as an upper-middle-income country. But it also has one of the world's most unequal income distributions (a Gini coefficient of 0.63, according to the World Bank), and an alarmingly high HIV infection rate (on the order of 20%). You can see in the table that South Africa does relatively well in terms of education, but its life expectancy at birth is only 52.2 years.

It is harder to find countries that significantly overperform in terms of human development. The world's greatest overperformer is Cuba, ranking forty-seven places higher in terms of human development than income. This is a country where the PPP-adjusted per capita income is $5,253, about half of South Africa's and less than a third of Equatorial Guinea's. Yet Cuba has one of the highest life expectancies in the world (79 years). The average Cuban child can expect to end up with 17.5 years of schooling, more than the average US child (16 years). Overall, there are only six countries whose HDI ranking beats their GNI ranking by more than twenty-five places, but there are eleven in which the HDI ranking is twenty-five places lower than the GNI ranking.

In short, there are large variations in human development outcomes among countries. There are also large discrepancies within countries. In particular, human development outcomes tend to be most dismal in rural areas of poor countries, where most of the world's poverty is found. Still, there's no denying that income appears to be a key correlate of human development. Income growth is a key for improving human well-being in the world's poorest countries.

Income growth is the topic of our next chapter. The rest of this chapter will focus on the two other components of the HDI: education and health. We will learn why each is important, not only in and of itself but also in *determining* other development outcomes. We'll also learn how development economists think about the role of government in providing people with education and health, and how economists study the determinants of education and health as well as the impacts of each on economic development.

## EDUCATING A COUNTRY

Why are you here? We don't mean the big cosmological question—we mean here, as in this school, taking this class, reading this book. You would probably answer something like: "to learn development economics," or "to get a good job someday," by which you might mean a high-paying job or perhaps a fulfilling one, or both. No one to whom we've asked this question ever answered "to make other people more productive." Yet from a societal point of view, that's one of the important things education does. By becoming more educated, we become more productive, which is why we can hope to get paid more. But people become more productive when they have other educated people to work with, too.

This is what we call a positive externality, a social benefit that your private decision creates. When people decide how much schooling to get, they do a sort of cost-benefit analysis, as we shall see later on in this chapter. But we only consider the private costs and benefits in our calculation—how much it costs us to have another year of school, and what we can expect to get out of it. We do not normally consider the social benefit that our schooling investment creates by making other people more productive. Because people do not take the social benefits into account, left to their own devices they will tend to underinvest in education.

In the presence of externalities, there is a compelling case for governments to get involved in the market with policies designed to make people take social benefits and costs into account, or at least nudge them closer to the social optimum. If we were rewarded for the social good our schooling creates, we might be willing to invest more in schooling. Economists call this *internalizing the externality*. That essentially is what public education does by making the cost of getting schooled lower than it would be in a private school system. Public investment in education is the principal way in which countries try to solve the education externality. But there are other ways, as we shall see. Simply building new classrooms and putting teachers in them might not be sufficient to make the students come, especially if their families are poor.

When deciding whether or not to send their kids to school, parents weigh the costs and benefits. To achieve the millennium development goal of universal primary education and beyond, policy makers need to understand what kinds of interventions will get kids into the classroom and make them learn. That means getting the costs and benefits right.

### The True Cost of Going to School

How much does it cost to send a kid to school? You might be imagining the costs of books, supplies, uniforms, transportation to and from school, meals, and tuition. These costs can easily be prohibitive for poor people, but they are only part of the cost of sending kids to school. They are what we would call the *direct costs* of education. There's also an *opportunity cost* of spending time in the classroom and studying. In economics, the opportunity cost of going to school is the benefit foregone by not doing the next best thing. If you weren't studying economics, you might be playing a sport or engaging in a hobby that you enjoy, in which case your opportunity cost would include the utility loss from having less leisure. Maybe you would have a job, in which case the opportunity cost of going to school would include your lost wages.

For a poor family in an African village, the opportunity cost of sending kids to school almost certainly includes the value of the labor that kids would provide at home—helping in the fields, watching animals, taking care of siblings, and so forth—if they were not studying. Even attending a school that is free has its costs. For a very poor household, the opportunity cost of sending kids to school might be insurmountable.

*The Benefits of Going to School*

At any moment in your education, you could stop going to school and get a job. You continue studying because, as you perceive it, the benefits outweigh the opportunity cost of not working plus the "hard costs" of going to school. What are the benefits of going to school?

Human capital theory provides a useful framework for understanding the benefits of going to school. Human capital is the set of knowledge and skills that make workers productive. To these we can also add health, without which it is hard for even highly skilled people to be productive, and less tangible things like the values we hold that make us work hard, take risks, and embrace new ideas (or not).

If schools impart useful knowledge, skills, and values, then we accumulate human capital by going to school. By making people more productive, schooling raises their wages. This basic tenet of human capital theory comes straight out of the microeconomics of the firm. A firm will not hire a worker unless the additional value he produces (his marginal value product of labor, or MVPL) is at least as large as what it will have to pay the worker (that is, the wage, $w$). Figure 6.2 illustrates this classic "MVPL = $w$" rule. It shows the MVPL curve, which is downward sloping due to diminishing marginal productivity of labor. The firm hires labor up to the point where the market wage just equals the MVPL. Characteristics that raise workers' productivity, like schooling and work experience, therefore, should bring higher wages.

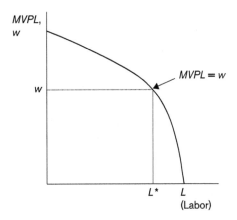

**FIGURE 6.2.** Firms optimize by hiring labor up to the point where, at the margin, the value of the marginal product just equals the market wage.

Jacob Mincer, a labor economist, invented what has become one of the most famous empirical models in all of economics. The Mincer model posits that people's wages are a function of their human capital, in particular their years of schooling and work experience. Econometric studies consistently find that, on average, more highly educated people have significantly higher earnings. Schooling raises earnings proportionately *more* in poor than rich countries, because human capital is scarcer in poor countries.

This gives us a way to understand schooling decisions. Once we know the costs of going to school, including the opportunity costs, we can compare them with the private benefits, which are the future stream of earnings gains that will result, discounted to reflect the fact that income in the future is worth less to people than income earned now. That is, we can perform a cost-benefit analysis, similar to what we did for project evaluation in chapter 2. Knowing how to apply cost-benefit analysis to different situations is an essential of development economics. The basic method of cost-benefit analysis is the same no matter what the analysis is for: a new airport, road, irrigation system, tourism project, or going to school. Applying this method to schooling can give us insights into the challenges to achieving educational goals in poor countries.

*A Cost-Benefit Analysis of Going to School*

The appendix to this chapter takes us through a cost-benefit analysis for the following case: consider a twelve-year-old child in a poor country (we picked Lesotho because we have good data from a recent survey Ed helped carry out there).[5] She has just finished primary school and is deciding whether or not to continue on and do three years of secondary (middle) school.

If children are not in school, often they work, especially if their family is poor. Our data show that the average annual wage for a working child (younger than sixteen years of age) in rural Lesotho in 2012 was 487 maloti (around US$64) per year for boys and 279 maloti (US$52) for girls. We use these as the opportunity costs of going to school.

We estimated a Mincer wage equation for the whole sample of working-age adults. (We control for the fact that many people do not work for a wage.) It found that each additional year of schooling raises the wage by 9.8% for males and by much more—18.6%—for females. Three additional years of schooling thus translate into a 29% increase in the wage for males and a 56% increase for females. That turns out to be an annual wage gain of 142 maloti for males and 218 for females, compared to the adult wage for someone with only primary schooling.

Unfortunately, we do not see these wage gains until after the student finishes secondary school—that is, until the fourth year and after. To perform a cost-benefit analysis, future benefits and costs must be discounted back to the present, using a discount factor that reflects how much weight people place on the future compared to the present. Our survey does not provide information on how heavily people discount the future. In real life, as we shall see in chapter 12, different people have different ways of thinking about the future, and thus different discount rates. Poor people with pressing, life-and-death needs today may put little weight on costs and benefits that are off in the future—that is, they may discount the future using a personal discount rate that is very high.

It is common practice in cost-benefit analysis to use the prevailing interest rate to discount future benefits and costs. That's because the interest rate is the economy's price for waiting. It is what a bank has to pay us to keep our money for a year, and it is what consumers have to pay for their impatience when they take out a loan. To keep things simple in our example, we'll use an interest rate of 4.4%, which was the real (inflation-adjusted) interest rate in Lesotho in 2012 according to the World Bank's Indicators.[6] We can use this rate to discount future costs and earnings.

Under the best of circumstances there is a public secondary school nearby, and the direct costs of going to school might be small. But remember, the individual (and her household) lose the wage earnings during the three years she is in secondary school.

Should she do it?

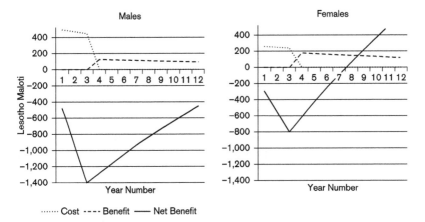

Males                                    Females

Lesotho Maloti

Year Number                              Year Number

······ Cost  ---- Benefit  —— Net Benefit

**FIGURE 6.3.** Students incur opportunity costs during the three years they are in secondary school. Girls recoup these costs by year 8, while boys still have not recouped the costs in year 12.

Our cost-benefit analysis concludes that secondary schooling is worth the opportunity cost for both boys and girls (see appendix). The net present value of investing in secondary schooling, or difference between total discounted future benefits and opportunity costs, is 958 maloti for boys. It is considerably larger (2,816 maloti) for girls, who have a higher estimated wage gain from schooling and a lower opportunity cost of going to school.

Even though secondary school passes our cost-benefit test, it takes a while—quite a while in the case of boys. We can calculate the break-even point, or the year in which the net benefits turn positive. Figure 6.3 shows that for a girl, the break-even point on investing in a three-year secondary education is not until five years after she leaves school. For boys, it is much later. The figure shows that in year 12, boys still do not reach the break-even point. In fact, it takes fifteen years from the time they graduate for males to recoup the opportunity cost of completing secondary school. That's a long time to wait—too long for many poor families. It's no wonder that secondary school enrollment rates are low for children in rural Lesotho (28.0%), especially for boys (21.3%; the rate for girls is 35.5%).[7]

*Some Caveats*

Bear in mind that we assumed a discount rate of 4.4%. If poor people in rural Lesotho discount the future more heavily than that, which is likely, the break-even points will shift farther out. Having to pay for books and supplies, school uniforms, and other school items would also shift the break-even point rightward.

We further assumed that schooling is exogenous when we estimated the Mincer equation. That would be the case if years of completed schooling were somehow randomly sprinkled across the population of young people, as in an RCT (chapter 2), but that obviously is not the case. There is a selection problem: the people who go to school are different from the people who do not in ways that we cannot see in our data. If high-ability people choose to go to school, we cannot say with certainty whether the economic returns we estimated are from schooling or ability. High ability could lead to high earnings with or without schooling. Ideally, we would like to control for ability in the Mincer regression.

Our cost-benefit analysis was for a sample of rural households in Lesotho. Its findings would not necessarily apply to other countries or to urban areas in Lesotho, like the capital of Maseru. There, wages as well as the economic returns to schooling are considerably higher than in the remote rural villages from which most of our sample was drawn. Factory jobs create a demand for educated workers that is apparent to urban children as well as to their parents. Poor rural households have a demand for labor on the farm that does not have an analogue in most urban households, and lower poverty might make parents in urban areas more amenable to investing today in order to reap gains in the future.

On the other hand, it is possible that the true economic returns to rural education are higher than what we could capture in our analysis, because those who are most successful after leaving school might not stick around for us to survey. We shall see in chapter 9 that schooling significantly raises the odds of young people migrating out of rural areas. People (logically) tend to take their human capital to the labor market where it is likely to bring them the greatest economic rewards. This usually is in urban areas rather than on the farm, and for some people it is in foreign lands. The schooling-then-migrate decision might well yield higher economic returns than schooling alone.

*Policy Options: Building Schools and Beyond*

If the opportunity cost of sending kids to school is high and the rewards from doing so are in a future that seems far away from the immediate demands of feeding a family, how can poor countries hope to signifi-

## Sidebar 6.1   Do More Schools Mean More Education?

Indonesia launched a huge school-building campaign between 1973 and 1978, adding more than sixty-one thousand new schools. What effect did this have on educational attainment and earnings? That is a hard question to answer, because the number of schools increased for *everyone* in Indonesia. It's like the reflections in a hall of mirrors; we can't separate cause from effect. To determine the effect of the new schools, we'd need a treatment group of people who got more schools and a control group that didn't. But we don't have that, right?

Actually, we do. It occurred to economist Esther Duflo that new schools wouldn't affect schooling for people who were too old to go to school, but they would have an effect on kids who were just the right age to benefit from them. She looked at children 2 to 6 years old in 1974 and found that they got significantly more schooling than people who were older at the time the new schools were built. It's pretty random how old a person was at the time of the school-building craze. That's what made it possible to isolate cause and effect. Nature provided the randomization. Duflo also found that the new schools had a big effect on wages.

This study not only answered an important development question but also provided an imaginative way to identify impacts of school construction without the benefit of a randomized controlled trial.

Esther Duflo, "Schooling and Labor Market Consequences of School Construction in Indonesia: Evidence from an Unusual Policy Experiment," *American Economic Review* 91, no. 4 (September 2001), 795–813.

cantly raise educational attainment? Our cost-benefit analysis offers some insights.

First, since people do not factor the social benefits of schooling into their cost-benefit analysis, and the hard costs of schooling easily can tip the scales against sending kids to school for poor, cash-constrained households, countries need to provide universal and free education. Building schools and staffing them is a necessary first step. An imaginative study by Esther Duflo found that the expansion of schools in Indonesia significantly increased educational attainment—as well as wages—for the people who were young enough at the time to benefit from it (see sidebar 6.1).

Second, governments need to ensure that there is a high economic return to schooling. That means growing the nonfarm sectors of the economy, where the productivity gains from schooling are highest, as well as creating an infrastructure—transportation, information, communications—that will get people to jobs there.

Third, governments need to ensure that people do not discount their futures so heavily as to diminish the present value of future income gains from going to school. This means following sound macroeconomic policies that reduce economic uncertainties—and build hope—in people's futures. High unemployment and inflation environments tend to do the opposite. So does poverty. Desperately poor people naturally tend to be preoccupied with keeping food on the table now, which leaves little room to think about investing in a better future.

Finally, governments need to consider the opportunity cost of going to school. That is what pushes the break-even point out so far in our cost-benefit analysis. Child labor and school attendance laws, if effectively enforced, can reduce the opportunity cost of sending kids to school by denying parents the option of working their children on the farm. However, such laws do not change the fact that very poor households depend on their children to make ends meet. When parents depend on their children's labor to survive, laws prohibiting child labor and requiring school attendance can be very difficult to enforce.

How can governments reduce or eliminate the opportunity cost of sending children to school? Mexico's PROGRESA, which we learned about in chapter 2, tried to do just that. By giving ultra-poor women cash payments conditional upon their children being enrolled in school, PROGRESA turned what would have been an opportunity cost into an economic gain for poor households. Social cash transfer programs in Lesotho and other African countries hope to accomplish the same end, but without conditions. Lesotho's Child Grants Program gives poor households with children a transfer of 360 maloti (US$48) per quarter. This is three to four times greater than the opportunity costs we calculated from our survey data and used in our cost-benefit calculation. It seems that conditions matter for some things (see sidebar 6.2), but RCTs are already showing significant and positive impacts of unconditional cash transfers on school attendance in poor African countries.

## MAKING A COUNTRY HEALTHY

The architects of the HDI recognized that human development is all about enabling people to lead productive and healthy lives. The "life expectancy at birth" component of the HDI is intended to capture health as broadly

## Sidebar 6.2   Do Conditions Matter?

If a government program gives cash—enough to compensate for the opportunity cost of sending kids to school—will it be enough to get the kids into the classroom? Or does the cash have to come with strings attached, in the form of a requirement that the kids go to school in order for the poor parents to get the cash? That's a big question, because monitoring people's behavior is costly, and there is always a potential for corruption when some local official, like a school administrator, has to sign off before a poor person can get her cash.

Two research teams carried out RCTs to answer this question. In each one, a randomly selected treatment group of poor people were given cash without conditions, while a second treatment group received cash, but receipt was conditional upon kids being in school. Both were later compared to a random control group that did not get any cash.

In Burkina Faso researchers found that conditionality didn't matter when it comes to kids with high ability or whom parents tend to prioritize anyway, including boys and older children. However, attaching conditions did make transfers more effective at improving the enrollment of children who are less likely to go to school, including girls and younger or lower-ability children.

A cash transfer program in Malawi found that when poor people were given cash unconditionally, fewer of their children dropped out of school than in a control group that got no cash. However, this effect was much smaller than for those who got cash conditional upon their children being in school. There was a surprise, though: teenage pregnancy and marriage rates were substantially *lower* in the group that got the cash without any conditions, compared with the control group. There's a logical explanation for this. When girls in the conditional group dropped out of school, the payments stopped. The girls in the unconditional group who dropped out of school continued to benefit from the cash payments. Apparently, continuing to get cash transfers made girls significantly less likely to marry or become pregnant.

These interesting findings suggest that there is no simple answer to the question of whether to attach conditions to cash transfer programs. It depends in part on what the objectives of the programs are.

Sarah Baird, Craig McIntosh, and Berk Ozler, "Cash or Condition? Evidence from a Cash Transfer Experiment," *Quarterly Journal of Economics* 126, no. 4:1709–53.

Richard Akresh, Damien de Walque, and Harounan Kazianga, "Cash Transfers and Child Schooling: Evidence from a Randomized Evaluation of the Role of Conditionality" (policy research working paper no. 6340, World Bank, Washington, DC, 2013).

as possible in a single indicator. The Millennium Development Goals (chapter 1), not surprisingly, place more emphasis on health outcomes than on any other goal, including child health (MDG 4), maternal health (MDG 5), and combating HIV/AIDS and other diseases (MDG 6).

We saw earlier in this chapter that life expectancy at birth ranges from a high of more than eighty-three years in Japan to a low of just over forty-seven years in Sierra Leone. What explains this huge disparity in health outcomes? How directly involved should governments become in managing their people's health? And most importantly, how do you make a poor country healthier?

### The Market for Health

Everybody wants to be healthy. Nevertheless, left to their own devices, people are likely to invest less in health than is optimal from society's point of view, for two reasons. First, there are externalities in health, just as there are in education. If you are healthy, the people you live, work, and study with are more likely to be healthy, too (and vice versa). Health, like schooling, is a key component of human capital. Indeed the two are strong complements: even an educated person will find it hard to be productive if she is in poor health. Thus, when you are healthy, you and the people you work with are more productive. When you are not, you can make others sick by going to work and interacting with them in other ways. When deciding how much to invest in health, will individuals consider the benefits and costs for the rest of society? Not likely—we often take into account how our health affects those closest to us, but rarely does this extend to society at large.

A second reason why people underinvest in health is because making people healthy requires some large-scale investments with big fixed costs followed by low or negligible marginal costs of service use. An example is a potable water system. The big cost is tapping into the water source—a distant river, maybe, or a subterranean aquifer—and delivering clean water to a village. Once this investment is made, people can collect water from the system at little, or virtually no, marginal cost. All they have to do is turn the tap of the public spigot. A public sanitation system is another example: once the treatment plant is constructed and the sewers are laid, the cost of treating an additional family's waste is small. These are examples of increasing returns to scale. The greater the use, the lower the average cost of providing the service, because the large fixed cost gets spread across more and more users.

Potable water and sanitation systems are like bridges. Once a bridge is built, it costs virtually nothing to let another car cross it. This means that the standard rule of profit maximization—equating the market price with the marginal cost—does not work here. Moreover, you might be able to keep a car off the bridge, but once the water system is in place, anyone can turn the spigot, so it may be hard (and unethical) to exclude people from it. This creates a free-rider problem, similar to what happens in firefighting. If you could choose whether or not to pay for fire protection, you might decide not to, knowing that if your house catches fire, the fire will have to be put out to keep it from spreading to other houses. If asked to contribute toward a public works project, you might choose not to on the assumption that others will. If everyone thinks that way, of course, the project doesn't happen.

A similar problem arises with respect to disease. If a communicable disease hits some part of the population and is not contained, it is likely to spread, much like a fire. Will the first people who become ill do what is necessary to keep the disease from spreading? (Probably not.) If a new immunization becomes available to keep people from getting a disease, will people choose to be inoculated? If I know others around me are inoculated, it is highly unlikely that I will contract the disease from them. So will I get inoculated, too? What if it costs me money and time (and maybe a little pain) to get the vaccine?

Free-rider problems crop up when it comes to public licensing and health inspections of food establishments, food processors, and phytosanitary control of food imports. Clearly, when it comes to health, market failures abound. Most of us make our health decisions without considering their ramifications for the rest of society, and it is hard for private investors to make a profit supplying public health services. This is a fundamental reason why countries have health departments, public disease treatment, and immunization programs.

Figuring out how to improve health outcomes in poor countries is one of the highest priorities in development. It is hard to imagine anything as central to people's welfare, or to economic growth. Health is human capital; healthier people have the potential to be more productive and to earn more income, which enhances human development even more.

*The Economic Benefits of Good Health*

Some researchers have tried to estimate the effect of health on earnings and compare this to the effect of schooling on earnings for individuals.

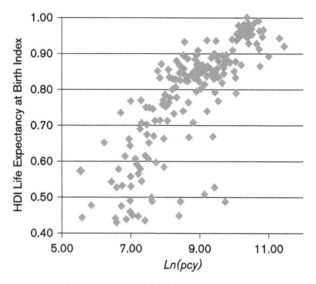

**FIGURE 6.4.** Life expectancy at birth in various countries (vertical axis) rises sharply with per capita income (horizontal axis). Source: Analysis of HDI data.

Others have taken a more aggregate view and tried to test whether country-wide health outcomes (typically, life expectancy at birth) explain income growth.

There is no question that life expectancy and other measures of good health correlate positively with per capita incomes; poor populations are less healthy than rich ones. Figure 6.4 shows that the component of the HDI that measures countries' life expectancy at birth increases sharply with per capita income. Even within rich countries, life expectancy is not the same everywhere. A recent study by the US Centers for Disease Control (CDC) found that people who live in southern US states, where poverty is relatively high, can expect to live fewer years—and more importantly, fewer healthy years—than people who live in other parts of the country.[8] It seems that the best predictor of your life expectancy in the United States is your zip code of residence.

This raises a question that is crucial for development policy: does poor health *cause* low incomes, or do low incomes cause poor health, or is the truth some combination of the two? There is a classic reflection problem (chapter 2): each of these two variables affects the other in ways that are difficult to isolate. Poor countries spend less on public health than rich countries do. Poor households have less access to good nutrition, health services, and information about how to stay healthy. Many lack access to clean water and sanitation and face environmental risks, for example, the use of traditional fuels like firewood that can have negative health consequences. Places with high poverty rates tend to be the kinds of places where life expectancy is shorter, populations are less healthy, and health services are less available. We can imagine many variables that influence both health and income, as well. How can we identify the health-income relationship?

There is no RCT here: we cannot do an experiment in which one group of people is randomly treated with good health while another is not. We can, however, randomly increase some people's income and not the income of others, as in the social cash transfer projects described in chapter 2. Moreover, health experiments offer some insights into how policies can be effective at improving health and nutritional outcomes. RCTs are commonly used by health scientists to test the effectiveness of specific health treatments, including spillover effects on people who do not get the treatment (see sidebar 6.3).

It's hard to design an experiment to test whether measures to improve people's health lead to higher incomes, but Edward Miguel and Michael Kremer's worms study (chapter 2) found a health intervention that increased school attendance, which we have seen is a key to increasing people's productivity and incomes down the road.

If people underinvest in health, then economic incentives may be required to nudge them toward making a more socially optimal level of health investment. "Investment" here means not only investing money (which poor people lack) in health (e.g., medical services), but also making the effort to get family members to public health services (e.g., free immunizations) if they are available, using bednets provided by an aid program, feeding children and pregnant and lactating mothers the most nutritious diet possible subject to a family's budget, and practicing good sanitation at home. Malaria once covered the world. In rich countries, development got rid of it.

Researchers have carried out a variety of experiments to test how various kinds of economic incentive structures can encourage people to invest in health. Two examples of health-related RCTs follow.

*Immunizations*

Immunizations are one of the most effective ways to save lives, yet the World Health Organization reports that 27 million children don't get

### Sidebar 6.3  Bednet Spillovers

Malaria is a fact of life—and a taker of lives—in tropical Africa. Bednets treated with insecticide can provide protection to the people who use them as well as to people around them (by killing off malaria-carrying mosquitoes and depriving them of access to people's blood). But if a development program gives people bednets for free, will they use them? If people have to share in the cost—paying a subsidized price for getting a bednet—will the program be less wasteful, because only those who really need and will use a bednet will buy one? These are big questions, given the scarce resources development programs have to work with.

Two economists decided to find out, by running a randomized controlled trial in Kenya. Prenatal clinics sold bednets treated with antimalarial insecticide to pregnant women at randomized prices. The study found no evidence that getting a bednet for free made women less likely to use it. There was no evidence that women who needed a bednet more were more likely to purchase one. However, cost-sharing significantly reduced the demand for bednets. The researchers found that free distribution could save many more lives. Not only that, more widespread use of treated bednets would create a positive externality by reducing the likelihood that others contract malaria. Once this externality is taken into account, it appears that free distribution would actually be a *more* economical way to save lives; it would result in a lower cost of bednets per life saved.

Jessica Cohen and Pascaline Dupas, "Free Distribution or Cost-Sharing? Evidence from a Malaria Prevention Experiment," *Quarterly Journal of Economics* 125, no. 1 (2010):1–45.

essential immunizations each year. Immunizations are a centerpiece of work by the wealthiest foundation in the world (the Bill and Melinda Gates Foundation), and governments as well as donors invest considerable resources in them. So why do so many poor children not get immunized? Is it that parents do not believe in immunizations, or is it something else?

It could be what Esther Duflo calls "the last mile." Parents procrastinate, health centers usually are a good walk away, and once people get there, lines are long and the health center is certain to be understaffed and may not even be open when it is supposed to be. The cost (including time) of getting to immunization centers and unreliable service there create disincentives for parents to get their children immunized. Researchers at J-PAL designed an RCT to test this (see sidebar 6.4).

## Sidebar 6.4   The Last Mile?

Researchers Abhijit Banerjee and Esther Duflo hypothesized that eliminating disincentives would make the difference between children getting or not getting immunized. In Udaipur, Rajasthan, India, a new project set up monthly "vaccination camps" in randomly selected treatment villages. These camps were well publicized and sure to be open rain or shine. The idea was to replicate an ideal health-delivery system. It also gave some randomly chosen people an extra incentive: a kilo of lentils. Then researchers compared immunization rates between the treated villages and a randomly selected group of control villages where there were no vaccination camps.

The percentage of vaccinated kids tripled, from 6% to 18%, in the villages with camps. When lentils were thrown in, the percentage rose by a factor of more than six, to 39%. An unexpected benefit of the program was that the cost of immunizations fell by half, as the same number of nurses was able to immunize many children. That is, the researchers found increasing returns to scale in this health-care intervention.

This project's research contribution was not so much to show that economic incentives work; we already knew that from PROGRESA and other CCT programs. It was to demonstrate that a small incentive, like a few lentils, can have a big effect on people's demand for crucial health services like immunization.

Abhijit Banerjee and Esther Duflo, "A New Look at an Old Problem: Why Do So Many Poor Children Miss out on Essential Immunizations?" UNICEF, *Child Poverty Insights* (June 2011; www.povertyactionlab.org/sites/default/files/ChildPovertyInsights_June2011_EN%281%29.pdf).

## HIV/AIDS

In 2010 an estimated 22.9 million people in sub-Saharan Africa were living with HIV and 1.2 million died of AIDS, leaving 16.6 million children orphaned. Rates of HIV infection among adults 15–49 years old were 17.8% in South Africa, where 5.6 million adults were infected, and reached as high as 23.6% in Lesotho, 24.8% in Botswana, and 25.9% in Swaziland.[9] Besides being a human tragedy of epic proportions, AIDS can have a major impact on countries' economic prospects because it strikes at the heart of the working-age population and thus takes a particularly heavy toll on human capital. A study in Mozambique concluded that the disease reduced total economic growth by as much as 1% per year. Estimates for other sub-Saharan African countries range from 0.56% to 1.47% lost income growth per year, and these estimates may be low.[10]

RCTs are giving us important insights into how to fight HIV/AIDS in poor countries. Lack of education and economic dependence on men ("transactional sex") are believed to be important causes of HIV infection among young women. An RCT tested whether cash transfers to young women reduced infections among school-age girls in Malawi, where 11% of the adult population has HIV/AIDS. It found strong evidence that they did, if they target young unmarried women still in school (see sidebar 6.5).

## PUBLIC WORKS PROJECTS TO IMPROVE HEALTH

The impacts of large-scale health projects with big fixed costs can be challenging to evaluate. It is rare to find such projects rolled out in a random fashion, like social cash transfers often are, so that their impacts can be evaluated without running into the selection problem. Take water, for instance. Intestinal diseases traceable to unsafe drinking water supplies and a lack of sanitation systems are a major cause of death in poor countries, especially among children. There is little doubt that governments and international aid agencies should invest in tube wells, hand pumps, and village taps to provide people with access to groundwater protected from the contaminants found in surface water, including lakes and streams. The problems of increasing returns to scale and public goods make these kinds of investments unlikely unless governments or aid agencies step up and do them. But will a public works project solve the problem?

Surprisingly, evaluations find mixed impacts of water projects on illnesses linked to waterborne pathogens. Some find large impacts on morbidity, while others find little impact at all. Katrina Jessoe wanted to find out why. The answer, she hypothesized, lies in what people do to the water once it is inside their homes (see sidebar 6.6). Simply providing people with clean groundwater, it seems, may not be enough to keep them safe.

## NUTRITION AND HEALTH

It is difficult to imagine anything as fundamental to health and economic development as people's nutrition. The American economic historian and Nobel laureate Robert Fogel showed that over time, people's

### Sidebar 6.5 A Cash Transfer Program for AIDS

It is widely believed that poverty and a lack of education increase the risk of HIV infection among school-age women by making them economically dependent on older sex partners. This is often referred to as the "sugar daddy" phenomenon. If it is true, then giving cash to young women who are enrolled in school should reduce their incidence of HIV and other sexually transmitted diseases (STDs).

A team of researchers from US universities and the World Bank set out to test this hypothesis in Malawi. They took a sample of 1,289 females aged 13–22 years who were enrolled in school and never married, randomly assigning some to get cash payments (the treatment group) and the others (the control group) to get nothing. Women in the treatment group, in turn, were randomly divided into two subgroups, one getting the cash unconditionally and the other conditional upon staying in school. The payments ranged from US$1 to $5 monthly, and the women's parents were also given $4 to $10 per month.

After eighteen months, 1.2% of the treatment group and 3.0% of the control group tested positive for HIV or herpes simplex virus 2 (HSV-2). The difference between the two groups was statistically significant. Among the women who got cash, the study found no significant difference in HIV infection between those required to continue in school to get the cash and those who got the cash regardless of school attendance.

You might conclude from these findings that only the cash matters—not school attendance. To test whether that is true, the study also followed 417 women in the same age group who already had dropped out of school before the experiment. Among those women, the cash transfer had no significant effect at all, revealing that school enrollment does, indeed, matter.

These findings show that cash transfer programs, which do not directly target sexual behavior, can reduce HIV and HSV-2 infections among adolescent schoolgirls in a poor country. To be effective, however, the cash transfer program must target adolescent women while they are still in school. Once they have dropped out, it is too late.

Are cash transfers and education enough? Almost certainly not. For one thing, the "sugar daddies" are still out there. If cash transfers and school attendance take some poor young women out of the transactional sex market, what will happen to the rest?

This study is important in showing that a cash transfer program, not targeted at sexual behavior, can be an important complement to other interventions to reduce the spread of STDs.

Do findings from a small research experiment like this one hold up in a large-scale government cash transfer program? In chapter 2

*(continued)*

(sidebar 2.2) we learned about the Kenyan government's large scale Cash Transfers for Orphans and Vulnerable Children (CT-OVC) program, which gives cash to ultra-poor households. Four researchers at the University of North Carolina found that the CT-OVC transfers lowered the odds of sexual debut among men and women 15–25 years old by a significant 31%. Thus, large-scale cash transfer programs with poverty alleviation objectives may reduce HIV risk among young people.

Sarah J. Baird, Richard S. Garfein, Craig T. McIntosh, and Berk Özler, "Impact of a Cash Transfer Program for Schooling on Prevalence of HIV and HSV-2 in Malawi: A Cluster Randomized Trial," *Lancet* 379, no. 9823 (April 2012):1320–29 (www.thelancet.com/journals/lancet/article/PIIS0140-6736%2811%2961709-1/abstract).

Sudhanshu Handa, Carolyn Tucker Halpern, Audrey Pettifor, and Harsha Thirumurthy, "The Government of Kenya's Cash Transfer Program Reduces the Risk of Sexual Debut among Young People Age 15–25," *PloS one* 9, no. 1 (2014): e85473.

average height is linked to changes in standards of living, mortality, and perhaps even morbidity. As nations' incomes grow, people get taller! The average height of mature people in the United States, Côte d'Ivoire, Brazil, and Vietnam rose by between .75 and 1.5 centimeters per decade during the twentieth century.[11] Fogel argued that height is a useful index of a population's well-being, both between and within countries. When there are large variations in adult height within countries, he claimed, we learn something about how the benefits of economic growth have been distributed across the country's population. In the poorest regions, people tend to be less healthy—and shorter.

Not only that, history shows that taller people earn more. In Brazil, for example, a 1% increase in height is associated with an 8% increase in people's wages, according to two development and health economists, John Strauss and Duncan Thomas. Taller people also are better educated, and we have already seen that education increases earnings. In Brazil, for example, these economists found that a ten-centimeter difference in height corresponds to a 25% increase in completed schooling.[12]

If these findings are correct, then improving people's—especially children's—nutrition could have multiple benefits. By improving health, better diets make people happier and more productive. Higher productivity, in turn, can provide people with the income they need to eat healthy diets. On

## Sidebar 6.6  Keeping the Water Safe

Jessoe hypothesized that when people get access to cleaner water, they feel less of a need to treat their water at home, and this reduces health benefits from water projects. She compared in-home treatment of water, including boiling (the most effective way to kill pathogens), between households with and without access to improved water sources in rural India.

Ideally, this study would have used an RCT. You can imagine an experiment in which projects to deliver clean groundwater are carried out in a random group of treatment villages. Changes in at-home treatment and health outcomes before and after the projects could be compared to changes in a random sample of control villages that did not get water projects. Unfortunately, no such experiments are available in rural India. To complicate matters, water projects in rural India tend to target disadvantaged places with few health services. These are likely to be the kinds of places with poor health outcomes with or without new water projects. Because of this selection problem, it might not be surprising to find poor health outcomes in places that get water projects!

Without an RCT, the trick is to find an instrumental variable that is highly correlated with households' drinking water source but not with health outcomes or water treatment behavior except through the source. Jessoe found an unusual instrument: the type of rock underneath the communities she studied. Substratum rock types determine what type of water source a community has. However, there is little reason to think that it affects people's water-treatment behavior or health outcomes except through the drinking water source effect.

Using this instrument to predict water source, this study found that households are 25%–27% less likely to treat their water at home when they get the water from an improved source. Apparently, they feel that they don't have to. The practice of boiling water falls by 18%. These changes in treatment at home offset a large part of the gains from public investment in water projects; the improvement in water quality at home is smaller than would be the case if people did not change their water-treatment behavior.

This study is important because it teaches us that public investments in water projects may not be enough to combat waterborne disease. Information campaigns and other economic inducements to get people to practice safe water treatment at home also may be required.

Katrina Jessoe, "Improved Source, Improved Quality? Demand for Drinking Water Quality in Rural India," *Journal of Environmental Economics and Management* 66, no. 3 (2013):460–75.

the other hand, low incomes lead to poor nutrition, health, productivity—and thus low incomes in the future. That sounds suspiciously like a health poverty trap, akin to the poverty trap we learned about in chapter 4.

Econometric studies have estimated the impact of people's income on their nutrient intake (which economists call "nutrient demand"). In China, Ed and World Bank economist Xiao Ye found that as income rises, people's calorie intake also rises—although more slowly. A 1% rise in income increased total calorie demand by 0.45% in the poorest household group. (By contrast, it had almost no effect on calorie intake in the highest-income rural households.)[13]

The big impact was on *where* people get their calories. Calories from meat jumped 1.43%, while calories from grain rose only 0.28%. As people shift from grain to animal products, the average cost of the calories they consume goes up. The United Nations considers the share of people's energy provided by animal products as a key indicator of diet quality, because calories from animal products come with an almost complete package of vitamins and minerals essential to a good diet.

Some RCTs are beginning to confirm these findings in other contexts. For example, the Malawi study cited in sidebar 6.2 found that dietary diversity increased in the households that got cash transfers.

## THE BIG PICTURE: HEALTH AND INCOME GROWTH

Whether better health causes higher incomes, or whether it is the reverse that explains most of the positive association we see between health and income, is very hard to determine. Nevertheless, we saw in chapter 2 that programs that randomly give cash to poor households improve children's nutrition (as well as their schooling). We can see the impacts on people's diets fairly quickly—within the one or two years of the start of a cash transfer program. Impacts on morbidity and mortality are likely to take more time to materialize, and impacts on child growth stunting and adult height take considerably more time than evaluations usually cover. Nevertheless, there is some early evidence that cash transfers to poor households reduce children's illness in some countries.

When it comes to the big question of how health affects economic development and vice versa, researchers have tried to find econometric strategies to try to identify causal impacts. One way is to see whether periods of rapid income growth are followed by improvements in health outcomes in countries. For example, we can calculate changes in income (that is, income growth) over a given period and changes in mortality rates over a following period for a sample of countries, then test whether one explains the other. This is called a "difference in difference" approach. We can also find instruments that explain income growth but arguably do not directly affect health except through income.

Two World Bank economists, Lant Pritchett and Lawrence Summers, used both these strategies to get an estimate of how much income affects child mortality.[14] One of the instruments they employ is the ratio of countries' investment to GDP. They find that this variable significantly explains income growth. And when they use it as an instrument for income growth, they find that income growth significantly decreases child mortality. In chapter 8 we'll see how two other economists, Daron Acemoglu and James Robinson, considered the opposite direction of causation, arguing that mortality resulting from malaria in colonial settlements affected countries' economic performance in the very long term.

In chapter 2 we learned that natural experiments can offer a way to identify impacts. If a health shock strikes some people but not others— or some people more than others—we might be able to compare people's economic outcomes later in time and gain insights into how health affects incomes. That's what two teams of development and health economists did, using China's great famine to evaluate the long-term impacts of malnourishment in utero on people's economic outcomes (see sidebar 6.7). Their findings underline the importance of nutrition in shaping economic outcomes in the long run.

#### SEN'S "CAPABILITIES APPROACH" AND "DEVELOPMENT AS FREEDOM"

We started this chapter with a hat tip to Amartya Sen, whose work inspired the creation of the HDI and now three generations of development economists. Sen worried about development economists' "overarching preoccupation with the growth of real income per capita."[15] In the 1980s, he and several collaborators proposed an alternative framework for understanding development in distinctly human terms—a framework that has come to be known as the "capabilities approach." We alluded to this framework at the beginning of this chapter. To conclude the chapter, we describe the capabilities approach in greater detail and evaluate how well the HDI captures its essence.

Sen's framework has three key elements. *Functionings* are the *actual* "beings and doings" of life, what a particular individual chooses to do with her life. *Capabilities* are the *possible* "beings and doings" of life,

## Sidebar 6.7  The Long-Term Effects of Famine

Documenting the long-term effects of famine is challenging because it requires tracking individuals over long periods of time. This has not deterred development and health economists from teaming up to test how much of an impact childhood malnutrition has on adult outcomes in poor countries, though.

China's Great Leap Forward policies (1958–1961), including the abolition of land ownership and diversion of peasant labor to industry, created the worst famine in history: between 16.5 and 30 million people perished. What human capital legacy did the famine—and the ill-designed policies that caused it—leave behind?

One study tested the effect of being exposed to the famine in utero on people's economic and health outcomes. The famine was widespread, and it was not random. However, whether or not an individual happened to be in her mother's womb at the time of the famine, one could argue, was random. The researchers followed cohorts of children born during the famine (1956–1964) into their adulthood, using data from the 2000 Chinese population census.

The results show that there are long-term economic and health consequences when mothers are exposed to famine. Males exposed to famine in utero were significantly more likely to be illiterate, less likely to work, and less likely to be married four decades later. Females were also more likely to be illiterate and less likely to work, and they tended to marry men with less education. Fetal exposure to famine also substantially reduced the sex ratio; males are more vulnerable to maternal malnutrition, so fewer males survived.

The adverse impacts of famine did not end with the generation exposed in utero. The authors uncovered what they call an "echo effect" of the famine on the *next* generation. Women who had been exposed to famine in utero, once they became mothers, were more likely to give birth to daughters.

In Zimbabwe, three development economists used a more direct approach. They followed siblings who faced different civil war and drought shocks that led to different nutritional outcomes during their preschool years. Children who, because of these shocks, had lower height-for-age as preschoolers also had lower height as young adults, and they completed fewer years of school. If preschool Zimbabwe children in this study had had the same stature as an average developed-country child, they would have been 3.4 centimeters taller as adolescents, completed an additional 0.85 grades of school, and started school six months earlier.

Maternal malnutrition is a major problem throughout the developing world. These studies provide insights into some of the long-term consequences not only of famine, but of maternal malnutrition in general.

Yuyu Chen and Li-An Zhou, "The Long-Term Health and Economic Consequences of the 1959–1961 Famine in China," *Journal of Health Economics* 26, no. 4 (2007):659–81.

Harold Alderman, John Hoddinott, and Bill Kinsey, "Long Term Consequences of Early Childhood Malnutrition," *Oxford Economic Papers* 58, no. 3 (2006):450–47.

everything an individual realistically could choose to do with her life. *Agency* is an individual's *freedom to choose* what to be or to do according to what she considers to be meaningful or valuable in life. True development enriches lives by building agency and expanding capabilities so that individuals can be and do what they want to be and do. Clearly, income can only be a means to an end in this approach.

The difference between voluntary and involuntary fasting illustrates this approach. A person who fasts (skips meals) because he has no food is obviously in very different circumstances from those of a person who fasts because of a deeply held personal conviction. Many religions encourage adherents to fast periodically for spiritual or religious purposes. Protesters often use hunger strikes to achieve social or political objectives. When fasting is a choice—an expression of a person's agency—we see it as empowering and enriching. But when fasting is imposed by one's circumstances, we rightly see it as degrading, deplorable, and disturbing.

Sen's framework sees freedom as being both instrumentally and inherently valuable. If you only cared about having greater freedom because it allowed you to be or do more (because it expanded your functionings), there would be little need for capabilities and agency in the framework. But freedom is valuable in and of itself, too. A bit of introspection will surely confirm to you that having greater freedom just plain feels good. Having options and being empowered to choose among those options based on what you think makes life meaningful feels good, because freedom is inherently valuable.

In 1996 and 1997, Amartya Sen gave a series of lectures at the World Bank on "development as freedom" and described this perspective on development:

> Viewing development in terms of expanding substantive freedoms directs attention to the ends that make development important, rather than merely to some of the means that, inter alia, play a prominent part in the process . . . Development requires the removal of major sources of unfreedom: poverty as well as tyranny, poor economic opportunities as well as systematic social deprivation, neglect of public facilities as well as intolerance or overactivity of repressive states. . . . Freedom is central to the process of development for two distinct reasons. (1) The evaluative reason: assessment of progress has to be done primarily in terms of whether the freedoms that people have are enhanced. (2) The effectiveness reason: achievement of development is thoroughly dependent on the free agency of people.[16]

Now let's return to the HDI. With Sen's broader thinking about development as freedom in mind, can you see why he initially resisted the idea of a crude index composed of only income, life expectancy, and educational outcomes? Although the HDI certainly sacrifices some important dimensions of human development, it has the virtue of being easy to communicate, which in large part explains how it has successfully shaped the international development dialogue since 1990. And because so many other dimensions of human empowerment and freedom are correlated with the HDI, the index seems to strike about the right balance between simplicity and usefulness.

As we'll see in the next chapter, a good model—like a good index— must strike a balance between simplicity and usefulness. An index like the HDI necessarily glosses over some of the richness of reality, but it does so to achieve a clear purpose. The same holds for model building.

www.rebeltext.org/development/qr6.html
Learn more about human development by
exploring multimedia resources while you read.

**APPENDIX**

*A Cost-Benefit Analysis of Getting a Secondary Education*

These are the critical numbers we need in order to perform our cost-benefit analysis of getting a secondary education in rural Lesotho:

*Opportunity costs:* According to our data, average wages for kids fifteen and under are 487 maloti for boys and 279 for girls.

*Direct schooling costs:* To keep things simple, we assume these are zero. In real life, parents may have to pay costs of school supplies, books, and uniforms to attend public schools, so our assumption here may give an overly optimistic cost-benefit result.

*Returns to schooling:* The Mincer model we estimated showed expected returns to an additional year of schooling equal to 9.8% for boys and 18.6% for girls.

*Wages without secondary schooling:* Average wages for adults (eighteen and older) with primary schooling (5–6 years) are 549 for males and 307 for females. These, along with the percentage returns to schooling, permit us to estimate the gains from an additional year of schooling as 9.8% * 549 for boys and 18.6% * 307 for girls.

*The discount rate:* We use the real interest rate for Lesotho, which according to the World Bank was 4.4% in 2012. If poor people discount the future more heavily than this, our analysis will be overly optimistic about the benefits of going to secondary school.

Now we are ready to do our cost-benefit analysis of completing secondary school. We will do this separately for boys and girls, since they have different opportunity costs as well as different expected returns from going to school. In the abbreviated table 6.A1, the analysis for boys is in columns B–E, and for girls, columns B′–E′. (This table is also available as an Excel file in an online appendix for this chapter. You can use it to explore how sensitive the results of this cost-benefit analysis are to the interest rate, secondary schooling costs, and the economic returns to schooling.)

During the first three years, parents incur the opportunity cost of sending their kids to school in the form of lost children's wages. We calculate the present value (PV) of these lost wages by dividing them by $(1 + i)^{t-1}$, where $i$ is the discount rate and $t$ is the year number. So the PV of the year 1 opportunity cost of sending a boy to secondary school is $487/(1+.044)^{1-1} = 487$, whereas in year 2 it is $487/(1+.044)^{2-1} = 467$, and in year 3 it is 447. For girls, the discounted opportunity costs are 279, 267, and 256, respectively, over the first three years. The discounted opportunity costs appear in columns B and B′.

The discounted wage gains from the three years of secondary schooling appear in columns C and C′ of the table. For a male the gain is $142/(1+.044)^{4-1} = 125$ in year 4, the first year out of secondary school. It is $142/(1+.044)^{5-1} = 120$ in year 5, and so on. The discounted future wage gains for girls are 191, 183, 176, and so on.

Columns D and D′ report the net benefit of going to secondary school each year, or the difference between that year's benefit and cost. You can see that these are all negative (equal to the discounted opportunity cost) for the years the child is enrolled in secondary school and assumed not to work. They turn positive, equal to the PV of the wage gain from secondary schooling, after that.

To create figure 6.3, we need to keep a running account of the discounted costs and benefits year by year. Columns E and E′ report this. For boys, the cumulative gain from three years of secondary school is negative until year 18, fifteen years after secondary school graduation. For girls it turns positive by year 8.

TABLE 6A.1 RESULTS OF A COST-BENEFIT ANALYSIS OF SECONDARY SCHOOLING IN LESOTHO

| | Males | | | | Females | | | |
|---|---|---|---|---|---|---|---|---|
| Year (A) | Opportu-nity Cost (B) | Benefit (C) | Benefit Minus Cost (D) | Cumula-tive Net Benefit (E) | Opportu-nity Cost (B') | Benefit (C') | Benefit Minus Cost (D') | Cumulative Net Benefit (E') |
| 1 | 487 | 0 | −487 | −487 | 279 | 0 | −279 | −279 |
| 2 | 467 | 0 | −467 | −954 | 267 | 0 | −267 | −546 |
| 3 | 447 | 0 | −447 | −1,401 | 256 | 0 | −256 | −802 |
| 4 | 0 | 125 | 125 | −1,276 | 0 | 191 | 191 | −611 |
| 5 | 0 | 120 | 120 | −1,157 | 0 | 183 | 183 | −428 |
| 6 | 0 | 114 | 114 | −1,042 | 0 | 176 | 176 | −252 |
| 7 | 0 | 110 | 110 | −932 | 0 | 168 | 168 | −84 |
| 8 | 0 | 105 | 105 | −827 | 0 | 161 | 161 | 77 |
| 9 | 0 | 101 | 101 | −727 | 0 | 154 | 154 | 232 |
| 10 | 0 | 96 | 96 | −630 | 0 | 148 | 148 | 379 |
| 11 | 0 | 92 | 92 | −538 | 0 | 142 | 142 | 521 |
| 12 | 0 | 88 | 88 | −450 | 0 | 136 | 136 | 657 |
| 13 | 0 | 85 | 85 | −365 | 0 | 130 | 130 | 787 |
| 14 | 0 | 81 | 81 | −284 | 0 | 124 | 124 | 911 |
| 15 | 0 | 78 | 78 | −206 | 0 | 119 | 119 | 1,030 |
| 16 | 0 | 74 | 74 | −132 | 0 | 114 | 114 | 1,144 |
| 17 | 0 | 71 | 71 | −61 | 0 | 109 | 109 | 1,254 |
| 18 | 0 | 68 | 68 | 8 | 0 | 105 | 105 | 1,359 |
| . . . . . . . . . . . . . . . . . . . . . . . . . . . . . . . . . . . . . . . . . . . . . . . . . . . . . . . . . . . . . . . . . . . . . . . . . | | | | | | | | |
| 40 | 0 | 26 | 26 | 958 | 0 | 41 | 41 | 2,816 |

We can sum up the net benefits over a child's working life to see whether secondary schooling is worthwhile. The sum of columns D and D' is the Net Present Value (NPV) of completing the three years of secondary school. (It is also the bottom number in the running total in columns E and E'.) If it is positive, secondary schooling passes the cost-benefit test, and if it is negative, it does not. The cost-benefit analysis comes out favorable for both boys and girls. The NPV for boys is 958 maloti. For girls, it is 2,816.

# 7

# Growth

If we could trace the history of modern economic thought to a single question, it would almost certainly be the one implied by Adam Smith in the title of his magnum opus, *An Inquiry into the Nature and Causes of the Wealth of Nations*. The Industrial Revolution brought profound changes to production systems and lifestyles that have created ever-growing disparities between rich and poor countries. Obviously, since these countries were essentially the same not so many centuries ago, this gap is explained by rich countries growing faster than poor countries over many, many years. But how did they do it? In the words of Nobel laureate economist Robert Lucas (p. 5), "The consequences for human welfare involved in questions like these are simply staggering: once one starts to think about them, it is hard to think about anything else."[1] This chapter explores the models economists use to identify and understand the determinants of economic growth. Since the drive to find these determinants is commonly motivated by the desire to improve human welfare, growth models are often used as the basis for policy action—and debates about policy action can get contentious and controversial!

## ESSENTIALS

- Value and use of models
- Production functions
- Neoclassical (Solow) growth model
- Regression
- Innovation and technology adoption
- Spillovers and agglomeration effects
- "Big push" interventions
- "Planners vs. searchers"
- Endogenous growth theory
- Incentives

The average per capita GDP in 2000 was $35,082 in the United States, $450 in India, and $256 in Uganda. Where do such vast differences in economic performance come from? For one thing, workers were a lot more productive in the United States than in India, and they were more productive in India than in Uganda. The average worker in the United States produced $70,102 of income (GDP) in 2000. By contrast, the average worker in India produced $1,211, and in Uganda, $611.

But why was worker productivity so different? For one thing, US workers had a lot more capital to work with (i.e., equipment, machinery, tools, etc.) than Indian workers, and Indian workers had a lot more than Ugandan workers. The average US worker had about $146,640 worth of capital to work with. The average worker in India had $6,848, and in Uganda, $536.[2] There is no question that capital makes workers more productive. Does this mean that capital is the key to development?

As we saw in chapter 1, many early development economists thought so. They saw investment in capital as the key to growth. We have seen that income is an important ingredient in what we think of as economic development (though not the only one). Without economic growth, making real development progress and improving household outcomes becomes very difficult. If countries could accumulate capital through investments in equipment and machinery that enhance productivity—investments that are perhaps partly provided by big infusions of international aid—would their economies grow faster?

In this chapter, we'll learn what the best-known growth economist, Nobel laureate Robert Solow, thinks. ("No.") We'll explore the basics of neoclassical growth theory, which Solow pioneered in the 1950s; the relatively recent field of endogenous growth; and theoretical versus empirical growth models. The big questions we want to answer here are these: "What makes economic growth happen?" and "Why do some countries grow so much faster than others?"

Lurking behind these questions is another, perhaps bigger one. If the economic returns to capital are as high as they seem based on comparisons of places like the US, India, and Uganda, why don't poor countries with so much opportunity to grow attract investors in droves? Why do some economies invest so much in capital, while others invest so little?

### WHAT A DIFFERENCE A CENTURY MAKES

Imagine a country where the life expectancy at birth is 47.8 years. Out of every 1,000 babies born, 150 die within their first year of life. Ten percent of the population is completely illiterate, and only 7% ever graduate from high school. One-third of homes have running water, 15% have flush toilets, and only 3% are lit by electricity. Women comprise only 18% of the paid workforce. Flu and pneumonia are common causes of death. The average per capita income is around $18.15 per day.

Is this country real? It might strike you as bizarre. For one thing, a per capita income of $18.15 per day (about like Egypt's) is high for a country with such poor human development outcomes.

It is real, though—or more accurately, was. The country described above is the United States in the year 1900.[3]

What happened during the twenty-first century that catapulted the US economy into a completely different realm? As Robert Lucas pointed out, the vast consequences of questions like this can make them irresistible. Providing answers to them is the great challenge of modern growth theory.

## THE NEOCLASSICAL GROWTH MODEL

You may have noticed that economists often rely on models to help them make sense of how markets work, how individuals make decisions, and how markets and people interact to create outcomes that shape society. Of course, models are fundamental to just about any human endeavor. Trying to recognize and interpret patterns in order to make sense of the world is a fundamental human impulse. Most of the time, the resulting models remain loose mental constructs. When they are formalized, however, models can provide a very useful platform for exploring and understanding the complexity of our world.

Many economic models look and feel like models from the hard sciences, especially physics. Yet, because economics is a social science, things are inherently less precise than in physics. Thus, economic models cannot predict the future the way a model of gravity can predict an object's terminal velocity. They can, however, help us understand which factors shape future outcomes and why.

As we explore growth models in this chapter, beginning with the neoclassical growth model, keep in mind that, as development economists (like economists generally), we use models like these to generate insights about complex patterns in the world. Like the famous statistician George Box, we acknowledge that "essentially, all models are wrong, but some are useful."[4] The usefulness of models of economic growth ultimately hinges on whether they point us to effective policy tools to stimulate growth.

## The Production Function

To analyze why incomes grow over time, we need a model of how income gets "produced." In other words, we need an *income production function*. Income production functions take many forms and are estimated on different levels, from countries to households. Here we'll learn about the aggregate growth model, which is what most people think about when they hear the word "growth." First, though, let's go out to the farm and learn what a production function is.

A *production function* in economics summarizes the technological relationship between inputs and outputs. You can think of it as taking different combinations of inputs and determining the maximum level of output attainable with those inputs. Alternatively, you can think of it as telling us the minimum combinations of inputs required to produce a given level of output.

Figure 7.1 shows a simple production function for a firm (e.g., a farm) that produces an output, $Q$ (say, kilograms of corn), using only two inputs: days of labor *(L)* and hectares of land *(K)*. That is, the production function illustrated in the figure looks like this: $Q = F(L,K)$. The function itself *(F(·))* represents the technology that turns inputs into output. To make things even simpler, let's assume land is fixed; the farmer cannot change how much land she plants in corn, at least not in the short run. The assumption of fixed land (or other capital) is often reasonable; for example, most crops have to be planted at a certain time of year, and once you plant the crop, you're stuck with it until after the harvest. We can show land is fixed by putting a bar over the $K$.

This figure illustrates two important things about production functions. First, the production function slopes upward, indicating that it is increasing in the inputs. Land is fixed, but you can see that as labor increases, so does output. The slope at any point (say, at $L'$ days of labor) gives the change in output from a small change in the input, or the marginal product of the input (here, the marginal product of labor, or $MP_L$). If you're math-minded, you'll recognize this as the derivative of output with respect to the input, and it's positive.

The other important thing to notice is that the marginal product of labor is not the same for all input levels; it decreases as the amount of

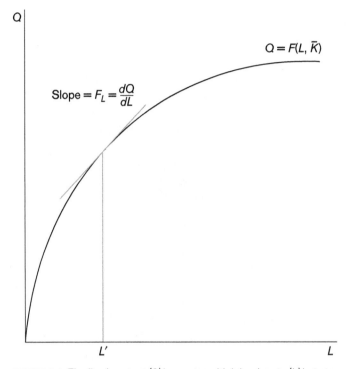

**FIGURE 7.1.** The firm's output (Q) increases with labor inputs (L) but at a decreasing rate.

labor increases. In math speak, this is a *concave* function: join any two points along the curve with a line segment, and all the combinations of labor and income on the segment will be feasible—they will lie below the curve. Think of a fixed plot of land, say, one hectare large. Without any labor, you cannot produce anything on it. Add a little labor, and you start getting output; you can till the land, plant seeds, add fertilizer, weed, and harvest. After a point, though, each hour of labor you add to this single hectare of land will get you less of an increase in output than the previous hour of labor you added. Geometrically, the slope gets flatter as we move out to the right in our diagram. We call this *decreasing marginal returns* to inputs. (Mathematically speaking, the second derivative is negative.) Off to the right of our picture the curve flattens out completely. At that point, the $MP_L$ is zero. Beyond it, the $MP_L$ could even become negative: more labor, less output (as when too many workers get into each other's way or trample the crops).

*An Aggregate Production Function*

Imagine adding up the value of everything produced in the whole econ-omy (that is, the GDP), as well as all the labor and capital used to pro-duce it. This gives you an *aggregate production function*. Just as farms, industries, and service firms take labor, capital, and other inputs to pro-duce a quantity of output (tons of corn, millions of motherboards, or billions of Facebook messages), so entire economies combine their labor and capital to produce a GDP. Aggregate production functions are used to describe the relationship between inputs and income in national economies. Neoclassical growth theory is all about how aggre-gate production grows over time, and where it will end up if a policy or other event (say, war or earthquake) shocks it in one direction or another.

We will use the simplest aggregate production function, which is the staple of the neoclassical growth model. It relates aggregate income ($Y$) to labor ($L$) and capital ($K$): $Y = F(L,K)$. Under certain conditions, you could increase all inputs by the same factor and output will increase by that factor. Double all inputs, and output will double. This is called "constant returns to scale" (CRS). (There are also *decreasing returns to scale* [DRS] and *increasing returns to scale* [IRS], but as in neoclassical growth theory, we'll assume CRS here.)

If there are CRS, we could multiply all the inputs by any number, for example $1/L$. Output would increase by a factor of $1/L$, so our aggre-gate production function would become $Y/L = F(L/L, K/L)$, or just $y = f(k)$, where $y$ is the output-to-labor ratio ($Y/L$) and $k$ is the capital-to-labor ratio ($K/L$). In an economy with constant returns to scale, output per worker depends on capital per worker. We could do the same thing to the production function of our individual farm, above, as long as it also exhibits CRS. (We'll revisit farm production functions in chapter 9, "Agriculture.")

It's important to keep the distinction between returns to scale and returns to one of the factors of production clear. When we talk about returns to scale, we're talking about increasing *all* of the inputs by the same multiple, for example, doubling both labor and capital in our simple two-input case. Even if we have constant (or increasing) returns to scale, we typically have decreasing returns to any single input. Suppose doubling your labor and your capital allows you to double your output. Then imag-ine doubling only your labor: without also increasing your capital, you won't be able to double your output. It's like increasing the number of

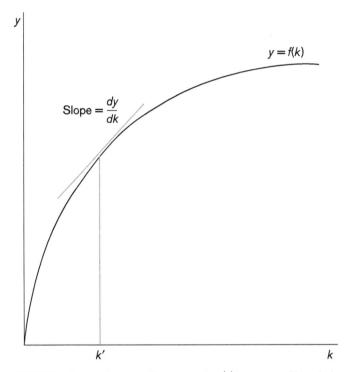

**FIGURE 7.2.** Aggregate production per worker *(y)* increases with capital per worker *(k)* but at a decreasing rate.

cooks in a crowded kitchen; eventually they won't have enough pots and pans to go around and they'll start getting in each other's way.

We can draw a picture of an aggregate production function (figure 7.2). Given the two properties of production functions we discussed earlier (output is increasing in inputs, but at a decreasing rate), this aggregate production function will look a lot like the individual firm's production function shown in figure 7.1.

Figure 7.2 shows output per worker increasing with capital per worker. At any point along the curve, the slope is the change in output per worker that results from a small increase in the amount of capital available per worker in the economy. More capital/worker means more output/worker. But as was the case for an individual farm, for the whole economy, there are diminishing marginal returns to *k*, that is, to capital/worker.

You can see how important capital is in this model. With no capital per worker, there's no GDP! Since neoclassical growth models share the basic structure we've laid out thus far, the factors that explain the amount of capital per worker in an economy become the main focus of these models. These factors include the following:

- the amount of investment per worker, which is what creates capital
- the population growth rate, which adds workers and dilutes the amount of capital per worker
- the capital depreciation rate (how quickly capital wears out during the production process), which steadily erodes the capital stock and implies that economies have to keep investing in new capital just to stay in the same place—as if they were on a treadmill of sorts

We need a way to represent these factors in our model. Investment comes from savings. In national accounting, total investment always equals total savings (which could include some foreign savings or investment, but let's set that aside for now). Let's use $s$ to represent the savings rate in the economy. Thus, for every dollar/worker that gets created in the economy, $s$ gets saved and turns into investment, or capital. Savings per worker, then, is just $s * y$. We can show savings per worker on our graph, as in figure 7.3.

Next we have to add the population growth rate and the rate of depreciation. Let's call the population growth rate $n$, and the rate of depreciation $d$. Suppose we start the year with 2,000 units of capital and 20 workers, so $k = 2000/20 = 100$ units of capital per worker. By the end of the year, 200 units wear out ($d = .10$). That leaves a total of 1,800 units of capital, or 90 per worker. Meanwhile, the labor force grows by one worker ($n = .05$), so now there are 21 workers sharing 90 units of capital. Depreciation of capital and growth of the workforce thus results in the capital/worker ratio falling to 85.7 (1800/21).

The economy will need a minimum of $(n + d)k$ in savings per worker just to stay in the same place. We can put this in our graph, too. It's a straight line with a slope equal to $(n + d)$, as shown in figure 7.4.

Nothing catches an economist's eye like two lines crossing in a graph. You can see a crossover at point A, where the savings per worker *(sy)* just equals what's needed to keep the capital/worker ratio stable $((n + d)k)$. This point, at the capital/labor ratio of $k^*$, is the economy's steady state. When the economy is at this point, output per worker is constant over time.

To the left of the steady state point, savings *exceeds* what is needed to keep up with depreciation and labor force growth (the savings line *sy*

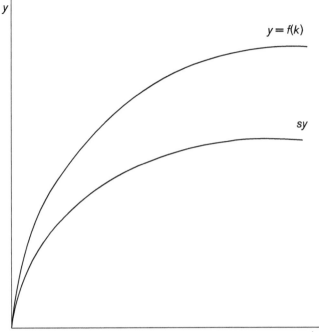

**FIGURE 7.3.** Savings per worker is output per worker times the savings rate, *s*. Since the savings rate is less than 1, the *sy* curve lies below the *y* curve.

is above $(n + d)k$, so the capital per worker will increase until we get to $k^*$. To the right of the steady state, there is not enough savings to keep up with depreciation and labor-force growth, so the capital per worker will fall back to $k^*$.

In short, once the economy is at $k^*$, there is no reason for it to go anywhere else in this simple model, and if something throws the economy off of $k^*$, the economic forces at work in our diagram will always bring it back to the steady state. This is the famous Solow growth model, named after its cofounder, the Nobel laureate Robert Solow. (It is also called the Solow-Swan model after T. W. Swan, who independently came up with a similar model at the same time.)

The big question we want to take on now—indeed the question that became an obsession to Robert Lucas—is how to make growth happen. What does the Solow model have to say about this?

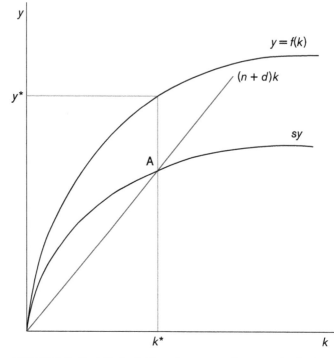

**FIGURE 7.4.** To the left of point A, savings per worker exceeds what is needed to keep up with labor force growth ($n$) and depreciation ($d$), so capital per worker increases. The opposite is true to the right of A. Thus, A is the steady-state income and capital per worker in the economy.

At the steady state in our picture the economy is growing just enough to keep up with depreciation and labor force growth. Income per worker is $y^*$. How can we make it increase?

One thing we can try is raising the savings rate, say, from $s$ to $s'$. This pivots the savings-per-worker curve upward, from $sy$ to $s'y$, as in figure 7.5.

At the existing capital-worker ratio $k^*$, the amount of savings in the economy jumps from point A to point B. Point B is not a steady state, though, because savings is higher than what is needed to keep up with depreciation and labor force growth. Capital per worker thus goes up, and with it, so does income per worker. The economy moves up the $s'y$ curve to point C. The new capital-labor ratio is $k'^*$, and output per worker is now $y'^*$.

Notice that increases in the labor force growth rate or depreciation rate have the opposite effect. If $n$ or $d$ goes up, say, to $n''$ or $d''$ (see figure 7.6),

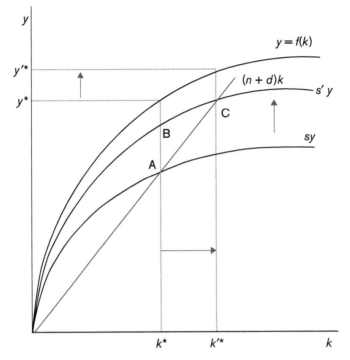

**FIGURE 7.5.** An increase in the savings rate leads the economy to a higher steady-state capital-labor ratio and income per worker.

the $(n + d)k$ line gets steeper. This shifts the steady state from point A to D, driving down both output and capital per worker. This does not mean that labor doesn't make the economy grow—it does. The aggregate production function is increasing in labor. But if the workforce is growing faster than total income, income *per worker* will decrease. It should come as no surprise that income per worker is lower in countries where the workforce is growing rapidly.

*Technological Change in the Solow Model*

We opened the chapter with a snapshot of the US in 1900 to contrast how much life has changed in just over a century. What one word best explains these dramatic changes? Our pick: technology. Since technology clearly matters in practice, it must show up somewhere in growth models. What does technology change do to our Solow diagram?

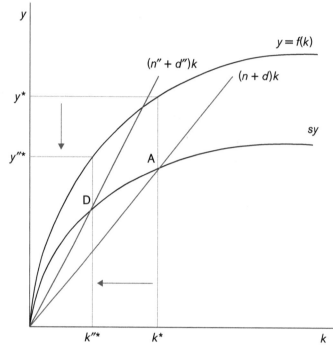

**FIGURE 7.6.** An increase in the labor-force growth or depreciation rate takes the economy to a lower steady-state income and capital per worker.

Assume as before that, at any point in time, there are diminishing marginal returns to capital per worker, so the basic shape of the $y$ and $sy$ curves does not change. However, technological change and the accumulation of human capital increase productivity, shifting the income per worker $(y)$ curve upward over time. Assuming a constant savings rate, the $sy$ curve follows the $y$ curve upward, as illustrated in figure 7.7. The figure shows how the economy's steady state shifts up toward the northeast, raising both $k$ and $y$ as the productivity of labor and capital in the economy increases.

## TESTING THE NEOCLASSICAL GROWTH MODEL: FROM THEORY TO EMPIRICS

As we warned earlier, this model—like all models—is essentially wrong because it abstracts from the richness of the real world. The right question

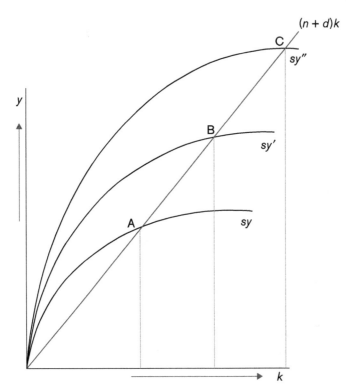

**FIGURE 7.7.** As productivity in the economy increases, the steady-state capital and output per worker rise from point A to B to C.

to ask is whether it is useful. A useful growth model should provide insights that are tough to see without the model, and it should hold up well enough to real-world tests that these insights might inspire sensible action.

The Solow model does offer some important insights. In order to grow, countries need both capital and labor. A poor, labor-abundant country is unlikely to increase its income per capita without increasing its capital per worker. "Capital" includes physical capital (e.g., machines) as well as human capital (education and skills). And don't forget public capital like roads, irrigation, and the Internet. These are known as *public goods* because they typically benefit everyone. Governments usually have to make investments in public goods, because private firms cannot capture and profit from many of their benefits; thus, left to the private sector, there will not be enough investment in them.

If you look around the world, you'll find that the major success stories, like the Asian Tigers and now China, involved substantial investments

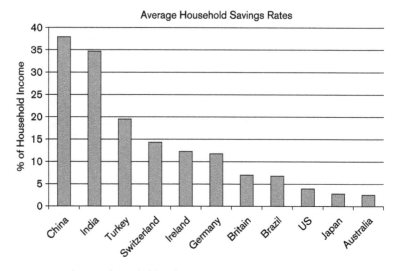

Average Household Savings Rates

**FIGURE 7.8.** Average household savings rates vary widely across countries. Source: "Savers and Spenders: How Household Savings Stack Up in Asia, the West, and Latin America," *BloombergBusinessweek* (June 10, 2010; www .businessweek.com/magazine/content/10_25/b4183010451928.htm; compiled from data provided by OECD, World Bank, Standard Chartered, Turkish State Planning Office, and British Office for National Statistics).

providing workers with capital that they did not have before. These investments were financed, at least in part, by domestic savings. Savings rates vary widely across countries, as shown in figure 7.8. China, one of the fastest-growing economies in the world, also has a very high savings rate: in 2010, households in China saved an average of 38 cents out of every dollar of income they received!

Increases in capital per worker lead to higher wages, because with more capital, workers produce more value, and employers will not pay a worker a wage that exceeds the value she produces. It's telling that real wages are rising so fast in China (about 10% a year) that they are nearly as high as Mexico's now, as you can see in figure 7.9.

Where population is growing rapidly, more investment is needed just to keep pace; otherwise, income per worker may stagnate or even decline. You can't deny that labor is a key input into the production of GDP, but without capital, there are diminishing returns to labor in the production process. It's no surprise that high-population-growth countries tend to have low per capita incomes.

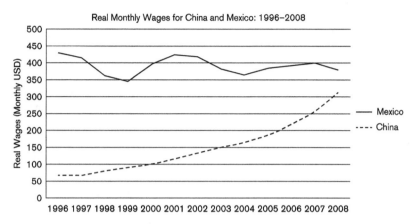

FIGURE 7.9. Real monthly wages in China and Mexico converged between 1996 and 2008. Source: Compiled from the International Labor Office (ILO), *International Labor Statistics* (http://laborsta.ilo.org/).

Now what about real-world tests of the neoclassical growth model? We test models by taking their predictions and seeing whether they hold up in the real world. A number of key predictions come out of the Solow model.

One prediction is that when major shocks like war or natural disasters strike, economies will return to their steady state. Rich country economies tend to bounce back quickly from natural disasters. Post–World War II Europe is a good example (with a little help from the Marshall Plan). There is some evidence that this is true even in poor developing countries (see sidebar 7.1). However, the long-term impact of disaster is challenging to identify, the data to do this are hard to come by, and largely because of this it is a little-researched area in development economics. Recovering from disaster in other ways (e.g., psychologically) is an entirely different matter.

Other predictions of the Solow growth model do not hold up so well. For example, look at the aggregate production function again. It implies that growth in aggregate income can be explained by growth in labor and growth in capital. In the real world, do changes in labor and capital explain all or most of the differences in economic growth we see among countries and in the same countries over time?

The empirical growth economist Xavier Sala-i-Martin says no. By running nearly 2 million econometric regressions, he found twenty-two different variables that appear to be significant in explaining differences in income growth among countries! These variables include capital

**Sidebar 7.1  The Growth Legacy of the Vietnam War**

The Vietnam War involved the heaviest aerial bombardment of any war in human history. War destroys capital. Neoclassical growth theory predicts that when exogenous events destroy physical and human capital, countries will recover, with no long-term impact on their steady-state equilibrium. Of course, the horrors of war include more than the destruction of capital. War impacts psychology, technology, social institutions, and other outcomes in complex and possibly long-term ways.

A unique study by Edward Miguel and Gérard Roland tested the long-term impact of US bombing in Vietnam. The authors used actual US military data on bombing intensities in different districts in Vietnam. (The data were provided by the Vietnam Veterans of America Foundation and the Vietnam Ministry of Defense Technology Center for Bomb and Mine Disposal.) The study tested whether districts that were more heavily bombed during the war had higher poverty rates, lower consumption, poorer infrastructure, more illiteracy, or lower population densities three decades later.

The econometric results showed no significant difference in growth outcomes between heavily bombed districts and the country's other districts. The legacy of war did not prevent Vietnam from recovering and experiencing rapid economic growth. Such findings are consistent with a return to the steady state following a major economic shock, as predicted by the neoclassical growth model. The authors warn, however, that Vietnam may have unique features that help explain its postwar economic success, and they advise caution in generalizing their results to other countries.

Edward Miguel and Gérard Roland, "The Long-Run Impact of Bombing Vietnam," *Journal of Development Economics* 96, no. 1 (September 2011):1–15.

investment, but they also include a diverse list of other things, from openness to trade to political rights, black markets, colonial legacy, war, and religion (see sidebar 7.2).

Another key prediction of neoclassical growth models is that the income levels of poor countries will tend to catch up, or *converge,* with the income levels of rich countries over time. For this to happen, poor countries would have to be growing faster than rich ones. Are they?

In figure 7.11, we plot countries' annual change in per capita GNI between 1990 and 2010 (vertical axis) against their initial (1990) per

## Sidebar 7.2  The Man Who Ran 2 Million Regressions

Econometricians use real-world data to model relationships among variables and test key hypotheses that come out of their theories. For example, if some variable such as capital investment *(X)* increases income growth *(Y)*, we should be able to take data on these two variables, make a scatter plot, and fit a line (or curve) to the data, as in figure 7.10.

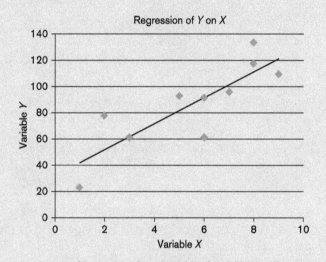

**FIGURE 7.10.** Illustration of a regression of variable *Y* on *X*; we can use the values of *X* to predict values of *Y*. *X* might be capital investment, and *Y* income growth.

Econometrics is about finding the best way to model relationships, which usually involve not just two but many variables. (You can learn about econometrics in *RebelText: Essentials of Econometrics* or any number of expensive econometrics textbooks.)

Empirical growth economists have found many variables that seem to correlate with countries' economic growth, but often correlations lose their statistical significance when new variables are included in the growth model.

Xavier Sala-i-Martin's big contribution was to come up with a way to estimate many different models, with every conceivable combination of variables, and find the variables that come out significant most often in explaining economic growth. Here's the list he came up with and the sign of the correlation between each variable and economic

*(continued)*

growth (you can learn more about these variables and how he measured them by reading his article, cited below):

| | |
|---|---|
| Equipment investment (+) | Black-market premium (−) |
| Number of years open economy (+) | Primary exports in 1970 (−) |
| Fraction Confucian (+) | Degree of capitalism (+) |
| Rule of law (+) | War (−) |
| Fraction Muslim (+) | Non-equipment investment (+) |
| Political rights (−) | Absolute latitude (+) |
| Latin America (−) | Exchange-rate distortions (−) |
| Sub-Saharan Africa (−) | Fraction Protestant (−) |
| Civil liberties (−) | Fraction Buddhist (+) |
| Revolutions and coups (−) | Fraction Catholic (−) |
| Fraction of GDP in mining (+) | Spanish colony (−) |

Xavier Sala-i-Martin, "I Just Ran Two Million Regressions," *American Economic Review* 87, no. 2 (May 1997):178–83.

capita income (horizontal axis). If the convergence hypothesis is correct, the points in this graph should form a clear downward-sloping line.

But that is not what the figure shows. Growth rates are all over the place, especially for poor countries. An econometric regression of 1990–2010 growth against 1990 income shows no significant relationship between the two. There is, however, one important caveat to this interpretation of the data. The graph in figure 7.11 uses countries as the unit of analysis and therefore implicitly weights China and Chad equally, even though China is more than one hundred times bigger in population. If we resized the dots in this figure so they reflected the population of the country they represent, your eye would likely pick up a downward sloping tendency because the two biggest countries in the world—China and India—were poor in 1990 and grew faster than the average in the subsequent two decades.[5]

Although empirical growth studies focus on differences in economic performance across countries, there are tremendous disparities in income growth within countries, too. Almost every country in the world has its "left-behind" regions, from western China to southern Mexico

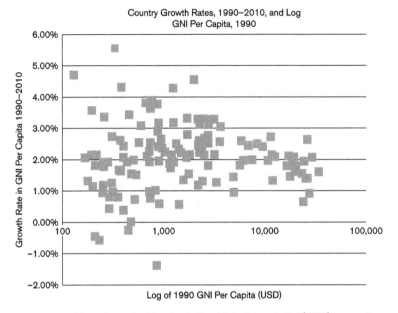

Country Growth Rates, 1990–2010, and Log
GNI Per Capita, 1990

**FIGURE 7.11.** There is no significant relationship between initial (1900) per capita income and country growth rates between 1990 and 2010. Source: Constructed from World Bank data (http://data.worldbank.org/indicator/NY.GNP.PCAP.CD).

to, as remarkable as it sounds, California's Central Valley, the richest agricultural land in the world, where many towns have per capita incomes lower than Mexico's! Economists have not done much work on why we do not see economic convergence within countries. As in the case of intercountry comparisons, it seems that the facts are inconsistent with the predictions of neoclassical growth models.

### REVISITING THE ASSUMPTIONS

Why doesn't the neoclassical growth model describe what actually happened in terms of economic growth? The model is internally consistent: the math behind it all works. If its predictions do not hold up, we have to look at the model's assumptions. Incidentally, this is another benefit of using models: they force us to make our assumptions transparent. Perhaps our model left out something that stimulates income growth in relatively high-income countries and/or impedes it in poor countries, thereby preventing convergence from happening.

To check on the model's assumptions, let's go back to where we started. We had an aggregate production function describing a CRS technology in which output depends on labor and capital (the $F(L,K)$ function). One assumption behind the convergence theory is that countries share the same or similar technologies. Another is that the production function does not change. If rich and poor countries have different production functions, or if technologies are changing in ways that favor rich countries, convergence may not occur. Still another assumption is CRS. What if the returns to scale are increasing instead of constant? Could it be that the more an economy grows, the faster it is able to grow in the future? Economies of scale describe a situation in which the larger the economy becomes, the more efficiently it is able to turn inputs into outputs.

Rich countries give us plenty of examples where "game-changing" technologies transformed the relationship between inputs and outputs and created enormous production and income gains. Between 1908 and 1915, the Ford Motor Company introduced the assembly line, which transformed the production function for making cars. Suddenly, the same labor and capital investment could turn out vastly greater numbers of cars, and mass production made automobiles available to middle-class consumers. In the 1980s and 1990s the Internet transformed all facets of production and consumption, laying the foundation for new production activities never even imagined before. New startups sprouted up where information and technology production already was concentrated, as in California's Silicon Valley.

Today, social networking is transforming the production landscape of the city of San Francisco. Where else in the world could a company like Facebook become a hundred-billion-dollar-plus company within eight years? Facebook produces social networking. Down the road sits Google, which produces searches. How much labor and capital are required to create an additional hundred messages or searches? An additional million? With a gross income of $38 billion in 2011, Google would rank eighty-third among countries, above Ghana and about the same as Costa Rica. (Apple would rank fifty-fifth, just ahead of Vietnam.) What country in the world has an income production function that looks anything at all like Google's?

It is indeed hard to argue that the technologies that combine inputs to create outputs are similar in rich and poor countries, or that they stay the same over time. Even though we can represent technological change as improvements in labor productivity in a Solow growth model, as we did above, this is clearly too constraining a depiction of technology and its impact. Thus, the far-reaching technological advances in high-income countries that have transformed lives and lifestyles do not really seem to have a place in the neoclassical growth model. This shortcoming was not lost on economists, who appreciate the depth of these technological transformations as much as anyone.

### ENDOGENOUS GROWTH THEORY

A new generation of growth theory, endogenous growth theory, emphasizes technological change and "knowledge spillovers" while explaining differences in income growth over time and among different countries. The economist Paul Romer, who along with Robert Lucas helped found the new growth theory, describes what he did this way: "Robert Lucas . . . and I . . . cited the failure of cross-country convergence to motivate models of growth that drop the two central assumptions of the neoclassical model: that technological change is exogenous and that the same technological opportunities are available in all countries of the world." He goes on to argue: "Each unit of capital investment not only increases the stock of physical capital but also increases the level of the technology for all firms in the economy through knowledge spillovers" (p. 4).[6]

This is a good example of how new theories build upon old ones that do not stand up to tests against real-world data and events. In the Solow model, investment raises the stock of capital. In endogenous growth theory, it also raises the level of technology for all firms by creating knowledge spillovers, new ideas that make people more productive. Just think of the knowledge spillovers the Internet created! When there are significant knowledge spillovers, the whole production function changes when capital investment goes up. There are incentives for new activities to set up around existing ones, as in California's Silicon Valley, where Internet start-ups are drawn together like iron to magnets. The benefits of setting up where other successful firms already operate are called "economies of agglomeration."

Neoclassical and endogenous growth theory stress different determinants of economic development. In neoclassical theory, as Romer (p. 543) writes, "nations are poor because they lack valuable objects like factories, roads, and raw materials." In endogenous growth theory, "nations are poor because their citizens do not have access to the ideas that are used in industrial nations to generate economic value." Romer calls the first explanation an "object gap" and the second an "idea gap."[7] Closing the object gap requires savings and investment, as emphasized by the Solow model. Closing the idea gap requires focusing attention on "the patterns of interaction and communication between a developing country and the rest of the world." Some measures, including good macroeconomic policies, educational investments, and the development of well-functioning legal institutions, can help close both gaps. In Romer's view, closing both the idea and object gaps is the key to achieving the upward shifts in productivity illustrated in figure 7.7.

Endogenous growth theory builds upon neoclassical growth theory by incorporating new elements of economies of scale, technology change, and agglomeration. In the neoclassical growth model, an increase in capital per worker raises output per worker, which in turn generates savings that are used to invest in new capital. Endogenous growth theory adds a new "technology loop." New investments in capital, including human capital, lead to technological change and create spillover and agglomeration effects, which in turn stimulate new increases in incomes. This is the way most economists think about economic growth today. We've noted that countries with rapid population growth have lower growth in per capita incomes. Endogenous growth theory explains why this is true. Rapid labor force growth retards income growth because it creates *negative* spillover effects. When there is plenty of labor, producers don't have an incentive to invest in labor-saving innovations that can generate positive spillover effects in the economy. Without a good reason to invest in labor-saving capital and technologies, productivity per worker stagnates.

In practice, endogenous growth models have directly shaped development policy. Because these models hinge on spillovers and agglomeration effects, they suggest that location can really matter. Based on evidence of these location effects during the 1980s and 1990s—particularly in sectors that depend heavily on knowledge and technology—economist Michael Porter formalized the study of clusters and cluster development. This work has strongly influenced the way countries around the world and across the income spectrum approach economic development.

Silicon Valley, the standard example for illustrating how these locational effects play out, has come to epitomize cluster development. Pick just about any industry (e.g., food processing, biotechnology, call centers, etc.) and you can probably find a country with an explicit strategy to create the next "Silicon Valley" of it by providing infrastructure, other public goods, and industry-specific incentives to attract a critical mass of firms in the industry to a specific cluster. Once this critical mass is achieved, it is hoped that spillovers and agglomeration effects will kick in and catalyze sustained regional growth.

Some places in some countries have seen spectacular success using this strategy, including regions of Japan, South Korea, Singapore, China, and India. What about the rest? When we think "endogenous growth," will Zimbabwe ever come to mind? Is there any hope for countries that are not likely to become tech leaders anytime in the foreseeable future? Can they still manage to raise their living standards and be a productive part of the global economy?

### GROWTH MODELS AND THE PRACTICE OF DEVELOPMENT

The growth models we have encountered throughout this chapter and the economists behind them hope ultimately to improve policy and development outcomes. How much of an influence have they actually had on development policy and on the practice of development? Has this influence led to improved outcomes? The first question is easier to address than the second for the reasons we described in chapter 2, but both are worth some attention as we conclude this chapter.

Many of the growth models we have described have had important effects on development policy and practice. In the decades after World War II, the neoclassical growth model directly shaped the emergence of international aid. In more recent decades, endogenous growth models and their basic insights have had enormous impact on national and regional development strategies. But the process of influencing policy and practice and evaluating this impact can be both controversial and contentious. To make this point, let's revisit economist Jeffrey Sachs, whom we met in chapter 4, now that we've had the benefit of studying growth models.

Go back and look at figure 4.2 in chapter 4, which describes Sachs's poverty trap model. It looks different from the curve in the Solow model. It is an S instead of a nice convex growth curve. To the left of point A in that figure, the curve is not convex. Join any two points along it with a line segment and you get outcomes that are not feasible (assets next year that are not possible given assets this year). Assets—and thus, income—don't grow to a favorable steady state unless we somehow get the country past point A in the poverty trap diagram. Big push growth models—which, in contrast to the models we covered in this chapter, are characterized by poverty traps—influenced development policy and practice before the 1980s, but they then fell out of favor because big push recommendations didn't seem to work. But Sachs is convinced that entire countries in sub-Saharan Africa are trapped, and he is the current champion of big push development approaches to help villages, regions, and entire countries escape these traps.

Specifically, with the right policies and carefully targeted aid interventions—including the diffusion of technologies from rich to poor countries—Sachs believes it is possible to eliminate extreme poverty within a couple of decades. He points to China, where the number of people living on less than $1.25 per day plummeted from 85% of the population in 1981 to 16% in 2005. To Sachs, a key to eradicating extreme poverty is to dramatically increase foreign aid, with a focus on providing subsistence farmers with improved seeds, irrigation, and fertilizer, as well as supporting microcredit and health programs.

To make the point, Sachs founded the United Nations Millennium Villages Project (MVP). The project started by setting up twelve "research villages" in ten African countries. Each village gets a flood of assistance equivalent to US$250 per villager per year based on the MVP motto: "No single intervention is enough . . . we must improve them all." Here's how the MVP website describes the project's goals:[8] "The Millennium Villages are based on a single powerful idea: impoverished villages can transform themselves and meet the Millennium Development Goals if they are empowered with proven, powerful, practical technologies. By investing in health, food production, education, access to clean water, and essential infrastructure, these community-led interventions will enable impoverished villages to escape extreme poverty, something that currently confines over one billion people worldwide."

William Easterly, an economics professor at New York University, disagrees vehemently with this orchestrated approach to development. Instead, he favors focusing on incentives and taking into account who has power and how they wield it. In his book *The Elusive Quest for Growth* he writes:[9]

> Many times over the past fifty years, we economists thought we had found the right answer to economic growth. It started with foreign aid to fill the gap between "necessary" investment and saving . . . [we] thought investment

in machines was the key to growth . . . education was a form of "human machinery" that would bring growth . . . population control . . . loans to induce countries to do policy reforms. Finally . . . debt forgiveness.

None of these elixirs has worked as promised, because not all the participants in the creation of economic growth had the right incentives. (p. 23)

Easterly argues that without the right incentives for people to work hard, be creative, and invent and adopt new technologies, development won't happen. He is a harsh critic of foreign aid, arguing that the billions of dollars spent on it have little to show for themselves and certainly have failed to foster sustainable growth. Aid, he argues, often operates from a "do-good" mentality instead of trying to create an environment in which markets provide people with the incentives needed to make growth happen.

Who's right, Sachs or Easterly? This question is much deeper than two bickering, high-profile economists. The question is deeply rooted in development economics and, indeed, in economics, political science and philosophy more broadly.

Let's first consider this question as it applies to the MVP. Has the project been successful? For a variety of reasons, it is remarkably hard to tell. The project was intentionally not designed as an RCT (see chapter 2) because, according to Sachs, the idea "that one can randomize villages like one randomizes individuals [is] extraordinarily misguided."[10] This makes it difficult for any analysis to provide conclusive evidence of success. We are instead left with a growing collection of mixed reports of limited success at best, the possibility of negative effects, and the standard implementation challenges that beset many big push attempts. Not surprisingly, Sachs is confident that his project is succeeding and that there will be enough empirical evidence in the coming years to convincingly document this success. For now, however, the jury is still out when it comes to the MVP.

More broadly, the debate about the MVP underscores two very different philosophical approaches, which Easterly characterizes as "planners vs. searchers." According to Easterly, big plans like the MVP are destined to fail—they always have been and they always will be. Among other reasons, planners fail because they lack sufficient knowledge about complex local processes and don't have enough skin in the game (i.e., they lack the right incentives). Searchers, on Easterly's other hand, are locals who have a potent combination of local knowledge and incentives. We will take up the "knowledge problem" that lurks behind the failure of many big plans in a future chapter. But let's take up his concern about incentives here.

Is getting the incentives right the key to making development happen, as Easterly argues? China's remarkable progress in combating poverty would be unimaginable without the far-reaching economic reforms that unleashed markets throughout the country and gave people powerful economic incentives that they did not have before. Yet, China also made major top-down investments in its rural areas, with new roads, communications, schools, marketing infrastructure, and productivity-increasing agricultural research—and hundreds of billions of dollars of foreign investment didn't hurt. It even had its own "model villages" along the way. Even with that, massive disparities persist. Shanghai is a developed global city, with per capita income similar to Italy's, while some rural areas in China still have per capita incomes on par with Ghana's, as illustrated brilliantly by Hans Rosling (to see the Rosling clip, use the QR code or URL at the end of this chapter).

In reality, most economies today rely on some degree of planning and government intervention, because markets that function well often require a supporting infrastructure (more on this in the next chapter). Where countries have successfully developed clusters of innovative firms, planning, public investment, and government action commonly have played a role in this success. But Easterly's concerns about big plans are certainly important to keep in mind: the history of international development is riddled with plans and projects that failed spectacularly owing precisely to the concerns he raises.

In a more recent book,[11] Easterly argues that the problem with big plans is not only that they rarely work but also that they tend to ignore or even trammel fundamental rights of the poor to govern their own lives. That is, they put states' rights ahead of individual freedom. The classic state-versus-market dichotomy cannot easily accommodate this critique, he claims, because many autocratic rulers embrace market reforms in order to stimulate growth, while simultaneously disregarding the political and economic freedom of individuals, especially the poor, who have little or no connection to the ruling elite. Instead of state-versus-market, Easterly proposes a continuum of total state power at one extreme and full individual freedom at the other. Framed in this way, it is easy to see just how deeply the roots of the planners-versus-searchers debate run—and how they ultimately tap into political and even philosophical positions.

With some introspection, you may be able to see the fingerprints of your own political views and your own philosophical leanings on the lens through which you perceive this debate in development practice.

www.rebeltext.org/development/qr7.html
Learn more about growth by exploring multimedia resources while you read.

**8**

# Institutions

Our lives are largely governed and heavily influenced by
things we don't often see or appreciate. As you learned in
elementary school, the persistent contractions of the involuntary muscles of your vital organs keep you alive. All of your
favorite electronic devices require mountains of complex code
to function. As you live your life—working, playing, studying, engaging in markets, and interacting with others—there
is a largely hidden set of norms and rules of engagement that
help you function. In this chapter, we explore the influence of
these "institutions" on economic development. Their
influence on developing countries and your own little world
is likely to be far greater than you have previously appreciated. And woe is the development economist who underestimates how fundamentally they shape the process of economic
development!

**ESSENTIALS**

- Corruption
- Institutions and transaction costs
- Incentives
- Dynamics
- Instrumental variables
- Entrepreneurship
- Innovation and technology adoption

If you have ever had to park your car on the streets of New York City,
you know how bewildering it can be. Driving in Manhattan is hard, but
parking in Manhattan can be almost impossible. In addition to being
exorbitantly expensive, it is complicated: there are layers of parking
laws that govern where you can park, when, and for how long.

Now, imagine that you were living and working in Manhattan and
were granted blanket immunity from parking citations. You could park

anywhere you wanted on any public street at any time for as long as you'd like. If you parked illegally, you could still get a parking ticket— but you could safely ignore any tickets you got because of your "immunity status." How many parking tickets do you think you'd rack up in your first month of immunity?

This kind of parking citation immunity may seem far-fetched (a bit like the remote control Travis always wanted that would turn any traffic light green), but until 2002 UN diplomats enjoyed precisely these parking privileges as part of their diplomatic immunity. Raymond Fisman and Edward Miguel spotted a cool research opportunity. Even though the NYC police issued parking citations to these diplomats, they didn't have to pay them, so cultural norms were the only thing keeping the diplomats in line. Because the NYC police kept a record of these violations, it was possible to know how many citations each diplomat received.

Which diplomats abused this privilege? Fisman and Miguel wanted to know whether the parking behavior of a country's diplomats reflected its "corruption culture" as measured by Transparency International's Corruption Perceptions Index, which ranks countries from least to most corrupt. In the 2013 rankings, for example, Denmark and New Zealand came in first place as least corrupt, the United States tied with Uruguay in 19th place, Mexico was 106th, Egypt 114th, and Somalia, North Korea, and Afghanistan were in a dead heat for most corrupt among the 175 countries evaluated.

Using this index, Fisman and Miguel discovered that diplomats from highly corrupt countries were much more likely to rack up parking citations than those from less corrupt countries.[1] In London, where diplomats also have immunity, one Egyptian diplomat, who drove a Mercedes C Class, racked up £10,000 in fines.[2] In contrast, if Swedish diplomats get tickets (they don't, according to Fisman and Miguel's data), their government requires them to pay the fine.[3]

Corruption is an example of what economists call "institutions." When you hear the word "institution" it might conjure up something more concrete than corruption. We call universities "institutions of higher learning." There are research institutions, banking institutions, philanthropic institutions. When we hear someone got institutionalized we often think of a mental health facility, or maybe a prison.

If you have taken a political science course, you know all about political institutions. Democracy is one: popular voting, parliamentary procedures, government checks and balances—these are institutions. You may even have bumped into institutions in a zoology course; animal behaviorists sometimes speak of animal institutions in the wild.

Anthropologists study many kinds of informal institutions. Here's an example: "Human social life is . . . guided by less formally codified institutions in the forms of symbolically mediated practices. These include, for instance, codes of dress, modes of greeting people, and symbolic communication systems such as spoken language. Central to both legally codified and uncodified modes of coordination are their normative quality . . . Social conventions and institutions do not specify what 'is done,' but rather what 'ought to be done.'"[4]

Institutions act like operating systems for societies and economies: they provide a platform of rules, conventions, norms, and processes that enable people to know what they can reasonably expect as outcomes from their decisions and interactions with others. They can have a profound effect on how individuals and groups make decisions, how their decisions affect others, and how all these decisions and interactions work together to create markets and the broader society. They often function in the background of our lives and go underappreciated—that is, until they get buggy and crash.

Now, let's return to corruption, which can be a pervasive institution because it creates norms and expectations about what are acceptable courses of action for oneself and for others. In this sense, the Egyptian diplomat was simply reflecting norms of conduct that he had internalized from "cutting his teeth" in a context where corruption was prevalent.

The institution of corruption bends the rules of the game in favor of some people and to the detriment of others—and ultimately to the disadvantage of society as a whole. It can create serious obstacles to economic development by diverting the energy of clever people into corrupt instead of productive pursuits, and by turning laws and law enforcement into opportunities for personal gain instead of broader social benefit. In their book *Economic Gangsters*, Fisman and Miguel write: "The concurrence of violence, corruption, and persistent poverty is so pervasive that it is almost impossible to separate the study of poverty from these other social ills" (p. 15).[5]

You might think that once people realize an institution is bad, they'll change it. After all, it's people who create institutions in the first place, right? In reality, though, it can be tough to change a norm that has become "institutionalized," even if it is not the best way to do things (see sidebar 8.1). In the case of corruption, for example, those who

## Sidebar 8.1   Typing, Eating, and "Path Dependency"

One example of an institution is literally shaping what I am doing right now: typing this sentence. The layout of the keys on this keyboard conforms to the dominant QWERTY convention, which emerged in a curious manner. (If you haven't noticed, the first six letter keys on your keyboard are Q-W-E-R-T-Y.)

As the US Civil War was ending, a tinkerer in Milwaukee named Christopher Latham Sholes was inventing the first typewriter. An early prototype had a mechanical problem that Sholes solved by arranging the keys in a specific way. The problem was that the typebars (metal rods with letters mounted on them, which hit the paper when the corresponding key was pressed) would clash if two neighboring keys were pressed in rapid succession. Sholes realized he could remedy this problem by configuring the keyboard in a way that put a safe distance between letters that commonly appear in pairs (like *T* and *H*). With some help from a local educator, QWERTY was born. QWERTY keyboards were popular on early mechanical typewriters because they reduced clashing and thereby made for faster typing.

The original motivation for QWERTY keyboards has long since faded, but we stick to this convention. Overlapping generations (i.e., our kids) learn to type on such keyboards. Several "better" alternative configurations have been developed in the past decades, but none have dethroned QWERTY.

Here's a second, equally tangible example: how we eat. You may have noticed that Europeans and Americans follow different conventions. Most Europeans hold the fork in their left hand and knife in their right. Many Americans start this way, holding the knife in their right hand to cut, then switch the fork from left to right hand before eating a bite. When Ed was a kid growing up in California, he thought that was inefficient, so without even knowing how Europeans ate he taught himself to eat like one. Ed's American friends have made fun of him ever since!

Travis came across an explanation for this American "zig-zag." Archeologist James Deetz claimed that it stemmed from the belated arrival of the table fork in American colonies. Americans had to use a spoon instead of a fork to pin down food while cutting with a knife. Once a piece was cut, eating it required more dexterity with a spoon than a fork, so Americans took to switching the spoon from the left to the right hand between cutting and eating. What explains forks arriving late in the colonies? It seems that British mercantilist policies are to blame for table forks being a luxury in the colonies, long after they were ordinary utensils in Europe. Curiously, even though forks are

*(continued)*

now as common and cheap in America as in Europe, table manner differences persist.

There are conventions that govern both how we type and how we eat. They are a type of "institution" in the way economists use this term. They help us formulate expectations and make decisions—albeit not consequential decisions that can shape the growth of an economy. They are also prone to "path dependency." A particular set of conditions that prevail at a given moment in history may explain the emergence of an institution, but it can persist long after these conditions fade because conformity pays dividends in social and economic interaction. As Karl Marx observed, "Men make their own history, but not of their own free will . . . The tradition of the dead generations weighs like a nightmare on the minds of the living."

Paul A. David, "Clio and the Economics of QWERTY," *American Economic Review* 75, no. 2 (1985):332–37.

Travis J. Lybbert, "The Economic Roots of the American 'Zigzag': Knives, Forks, and British Mercantilism," *Economic Inquiry* 48, no. 3 (2010):810–15.

Karl Marx, "The Eighteenth Brumaire of Louis Bonaparte," in *Karl Marx: Surveys from Exile*, edited by David Fernbach (New York: Vintage Books), 146.

benefit most are typically powerful, and they resist changes that would erode their control and ability to profit from continued corruption.

In this chapter, we explore development economics as seen from the profound perspective of institutions. As we shall see, institutions matter enormously to development. Perhaps the most concise explanation about why institutions matter to the development process comes from a famous bank robber named Willie Sutton, who had a reputation of being a real gentleman during his robberies.[6] When a reporter asked him why he robbed banks, Sutton said, "Because that's where the money is." Institutions determine "where the money is" in a given society—they shape the incentives individuals and organizations face and can have profound effects on development outcomes.

## HOW MUCH DO INSTITUTIONS MATTER TO DEVELOPMENT?

For centuries, many economists—beginning with Adam Smith—have appreciated how fundamentally institutions affect the way individuals and organizations interact in markets and how these interactions translate into economic performance. More recent insights from several economists, including four Nobel laureates (Ronald Coase, Douglass North, Elinor Ostrom, and Oliver Williamson), led to the emergence in the 1970s of "New Institutional Economics" as an influential field of study. The New Institutional Economics encompasses a broad range of topics. Several directly relate to contemporary development issues, including property rights, social norms, governance and transparency, corruption and rent seeking, enforcement of contracts, and transaction costs.

Institutions seem to be so fundamental to development that the success of just about any development policy, project, or intervention is shaped by them. Development economists broadly agree that institutions matter. But just how much they matter, compared with other potential factors, is a point of contention. It is difficult to settle by relying on empirical evidence because of the challenges described in chapter 2. Confounding factors and selection bias can undermine even careful attempts to estimate how much institutions *cause* economic growth—and therefore how much they explain about differences in development outcomes across different countries or time periods. Institutions shape economic development, but economic development can enable countries to invest in stronger institutions (like better law enforcement). It's a chicken-and-egg problem.

Take crime and corruption. They can undermine economic development; how can a country hope to eliminate poverty if government officials skim development assistance to Swiss bank accounts, or if the threat of theft—or worse, death—plagues the countryside? It's easy to imagine why crime keeps poor countries from developing. But poor countries also tend to have more crime. Poverty and weak legal institutions tend to go hand in hand. The nonprofit Transparency International found that in Liberia, with a per capita income of $1.16 per day, more than 95% of the people say their police are corrupt. In eight of the nine most corrupt nations, more than four out of five people say the police are corrupt.[7]

So do corruption and crime cause underdevelopment, or does underdevelopment cause corruption and crime? We dare you to design an RCT to answer this question! What about randomly sprinkling different districts or villages in a country with criminals or corrupt police officers and then measuring what happens to poverty?

Is isolating the impact of poverty on crime or corruption a Sisyphean task, then?[8] This empirical challenge has sparked vigorous debate among some of today's best economists and other social scientists.

*Institutions Matter Big Time*

Over the course of fifteen years of research, Daron Acemoglu (MIT) and James Robinson (Harvard) have wrestled with historical data on economic growth from around the world to try to understand what explains the patterns of economic development we see today (sidebar 8.2). They recently assembled much of this evidence into a book entitled *Why Nations Fail.*[9] As the title suggests, the authors do not shy away from claiming to know why some countries are rich and others are poor. They argue that differences in economic and political institutions are *the* dominant explanation for these patterns. There are several strands in this argument that are worth appreciating—strands that in our judgment qualify as essentials of development economics.

First, much of Acemoglu and Robinson's argument hangs on the distinction between "inclusive" and "extractive" institutions. Inclusive institutions begin with political systems that are pluralistic, protect individual rights, and create the conditions that reward innovation and entrepreneurship, including secure private property and competitive markets. In contrast, extractive institutions (as you might guess) are characterized by concentrated political power and economic institutions that reinforce and often enrich the powerful few. Such institutions are extractive, like mining: gold mining extracts but does not create gold. In a similar manner, the governing elite of extractive institutions opportunistically extract value from the resources they control (land, minerals, monopoly rights, public coffers, people, foreign aid, etc.), with little regard for making investments that create value and improve welfare for the broader society. To be sure, societies with inclusive institutions also have governing elites who try to cash in on their power and influence for personal profit. However, this impulse is constrained by the checks and balances of an "operating system" that limits such opportunities and provides incentives for productive and creative investments.

A second strand of Acemoglu and Robinson's argument is that institutions can be a potent economic force because of the positive or negative dynamics they trigger. For example, inclusive institutions are much better at fostering and encouraging innovation than are extractive institutions. In Acemoglu and Robinson's argument, this innovation dynamic is precisely what makes institutions the dominant development factor. As with any dynamic process, small differences today often become big differences tomorrow. If a ship sailing out of the San Fran-

## Sidebar 8.2   How Malaria Became Central to the Institutions Debate

When trying to use data to make sense of the world, economists some-times rely on seemingly strange connections between events. A connec-tion between malaria (and other tropical diseases) and colonization plays a pivotal role in the debate over how important institutions are to economic growth and development.

It is relatively easy to show that institutions *correlate* with eco-nomic growth. It is much harder to show that they *cause* it. Acemoglu and Robinson teamed up with colleague Simon Johnson to figure out how institutions *cause* economic growth. They used an instrumental variables identification approach (see chapter 2). Their challenge was to find a variable, or instrument, that affects growth *only through its effect on institutions.*

The crux of their approach is the observation that as European powers were colonizing much of the world in the seventeenth, eight-eenth, and nineteenth centuries, the kinds of institutions they imported to a given place depended on how pleasant they found the place to be. If Europeans could live in a place without a constant threat of tropical diseases or other hazards, they tended to import more inclusive insti-tutions (after all, Europeans would expect nothing less). If, instead, mortality risks kept Europeans from settling en masse in a location, they opted for more extractive institutions, putting a few colonial masters in place to maintain (heavy-handed) order.

Could "settler mortality risk" be a good instrument for extractive institutions? Acemoglu, Robinson, and Johnson argued that it could be. They found that higher settler mortality caused Europeans to put extractive colonial institutions in place. Places that had extractive colonial institutions, in turn, had lower income per capita in 1995. This is the central tenet of their strong claim about institutions *causing* economic growth.

Recall from chapter 2 that in order for settler mortality risk to be a valid instrument, it must be correlated with extractive institutions (which it is) *and* not have a direct effect on 1995 income. In the case of malaria, a major determinant of mortality risk, this means that malaria-prone places were more likely to have extractive institutions, but malaria cannot directly affect present-day income.

Since this paper was published in 2001, several critics have claimed that mortality risk is not a valid instrument because it can directly affect current income levels. Many places that had high malaria risks two hundred years ago continue to have malaria risks today, and cur-rent disease pressure in a society can directly affect current income through lost productivity. Thus, it is not clear whether extractive insti-tutions or malaria caused the lower incomes.

*(continued)*

So what does this all mean? The analysis shows conclusively that nineteenth-century mortality is correlated with income levels in 1995, but it is less clear whether this effect comes from the institutions European powers left behind or the current disease ecology.

Daron Acemoglu, Simon Johnson, and James A. Robinson, "The Colonial Origins of Comparative Development: An Empirical Investigation," *American Economic Review* 91, no. 5 (2001):1369–1401.

cisco Bay changes its course by only a few degrees, it might well end up in Sydney instead of Shanghai!

Third, some policies are widely recognized to be "bad" in the sense that they hamper the economy and keep people poor. Often there are known remedies to these bad policies. "If only" policy makers and leaders knew how to fix bad policies, the power of the market would be unleashed and economic development would take off. While some elites may simply not know how to improve things, Acemoglu and Robinson point to a more basic problem: elites may not *want* things to improve, since genuine improvements may deteriorate their power. Almost by definition, the status quo "rules of the game" benefit the elites (that is how they became elite!). Recognize, however, that the "elite" in this sense includes everyone with enough power or influence in society to potentially undermine the control of the ruling party or family, who often have to shower rival elites with financial and other goodies in order to retain their grip on power. For much of the past fifty years, the risk of being overthrown in a coup has been high enough that the top priority of the ruling elite in many developing countries was to keep their rivals either fat and happy or silent (dead or in jail). Either approach reinforces harmful institutions and hampers economic growth.[10] The fact that changes to these existing institutions may threaten their status and influence does not, however, mean that the ruling elite can get away with doing nothing. They often have to *pretend* to want to change and even *publicly advocate* it—while privately ensuring that little actually gets done.

### The Dissenting View: Institutions Aren't Everything

The strong position staked out by Acemoglu and Robinson is not without its critics. You'll remember Jeffrey Sachs from the last chapter. He argued that massive aid is needed to promote development in poor countries. Aid is not likely to be the answer if institutions are the cause of underdevelopment. In a lively debate that started as a formal review of *Why Nations Fail* and then morphed into something like an academic street brawl in the blogosphere, Sachs offered a counterargument to Acemoglu and Robinson.

First, he argued that they "incorrectly assume that authoritarian elites are necessarily hostile to economic progress" (p. 142).[11] He cites several examples of dictators who launched economic and political reforms that made institutions more inclusive—albeit typically as a response to threats to their power. These threats come from inside a country (e.g., instability), as well as pressures from other countries.

Second, while inclusive institutions do encourage innovation much more effectively than extractive ones, Sachs argues that the diffusion of technology from other countries sometimes matters more than innovation, particularly at early stages of development. In fact, most recent episodes of dramatic economic development, like South Korea, began with the adoption and reverse-engineering of existing technologies rather than new inventions. And dictators sometimes speed rather than impede the diffusion of new technologies.

Finally, Sachs agrees that corrupt politicians might not want things to change, but he sees other big constraints on development and economic growth. Even if we could magically turn institutions from extractive to inclusive, unfavorable geography and other factors may continue to constrain growth and development. His Millennium Village Project, as we saw, aims to relax the constraints that Sachs believes are the root causes of poverty traps: lack of access to practical technologies, health, food production, education, clean water, and other essential infrastructure. Sachs accuses Acemoglu and Robinson of acting "like doctors trying to confront many different illnesses with only one diagnosis" and argues that "the key to troubleshooting complex systems is to perform what physicians call a 'differential diagnosis': a determination of what has led to the system failure in a particular place and time" (p. 145).

## WHERE DO INSTITUTIONS COME FROM?

Even Sachs agrees that, at a fundamental level, institutions matter to economic development. So why is there continued debate over whether they are *the* driver or only *one* of the drivers of development? And, if there is general agreement, can't we use our basic appreciation for the importance of institutions in development to help the poor in some way? The answer to both of these questions hinges on deeply rooted political and even philosophical differences—differences that can entrench positions, fuel passionate disagreement, and lead to marked differences in policy recommendations to help the poor. This rift largely traces its origins to the question: "Where do institutions come from?"

In the last chapter we met William Easterly, who left the World Bank because he was critical of what he thought were its misguided efforts to aid poor countries. Where institutions come from is at the foundation of his critique and frustration with international aid.

Easterly provides a caricature of two opposing views on the origins of institutions, but acknowledges that most thoughtful viewpoints lie somewhere in between these extremes. (After we describe the views, decide where your views lie on this spectrum!) He calls these opposing views "top down" and "bottom up."

The top-down view maintains that institutions are created by leaders and legislators who govern and establish laws. The bottom-up view, in contrast, sees institutions as emerging and constantly evolving, based on the social norms, traditions, values, and beliefs of individuals as they interact and exchange with each other in a society. In this view, laws are codified and accepted as laws after (and because) they seem reasonable and useful to people. The political and philosophical differences between these viewpoints were prominently on display during the eighteenth century Enlightenment, when French philosophers Jean-Jacques Rousseau and Nicolas de Condorcet advocated the top-down view and Irish philosopher Edmund Burke espoused the bottom-up view.

These two views on the origins of institutions lead to dramatically different positions on how to solve problems and improve society—differences that continue to generate an endless stream of political commentary in the media. According to the top-down view, leaders and legislators can directly and decisively determine a society's institutional path. In extreme cases, they even get "do-overs," in which they scrap the existing laws and start afresh with new and improved ones. We call such episodes revolutions.

According to the bottom-up view, institutions only change gradually, as individuals change their values or beliefs. Astute leaders and legislators formalize these institutions into laws and regulations, perhaps attempting to nudge them in one direction or another. In Easterly's words, bottom-up institutions are "evolutionary rather than revolutionary." Adam Smith emphasized a similar process of institutional evolution that is directly shaped by the size of the market. As the volume of goods and services traded in a market expands, specialization and division of labor emerge and raise productivity. This more sophisticated economy both enables and is enabled by the emergence of institutions that help to govern market transactions.

### INSTITUTIONS AND THE PRACTICE OF DEVELOPMENT

These opposing views have direct implications for what we do professionally as development economists. The top-down view implies that experts are needed to help craft and refine institutions. The bottom-up view suggests that there is little that experts can do to create institutions. Much like Acemoglu and Robinson's argument that dictators know what changes would help their country as a whole but resist them because these changes would also undermine their own power, the bottom-up view sees little room for experts to engineer institutions to solve social or economic problems.

As Easterly points out, the extreme version of either view may not provide a useful description of reality. In practice, effective policy making often borrows insights from both positions. Nevertheless, the distinction between these opposing viewpoints raises a couple of important implications for development economists.

First, imposing institutions from the top down in the form of laws and regulations may be effective in some circumstances, but only with an appreciation for the richness and complexity of preexisting bottom-up norms, values, and beliefs. They may not be formally codified and may be difficult to see, but bottom-up institutions govern individual behavior and social interaction in profound ways—and they exist for specific reasons. Woe unto the policy maker who thinks the legislative pen is mightier than these foundational institutions! The emergent bottom-up norms that exist in a society often determine what kinds of top-down institutions can realistically be imposed by leaders and legislators. If a law strays too far from preexisting norms, it is likely to be either unenforced and ignored or disruptive and ultimately ineffective. As Easterly says, "Even if the bottom up economists can think of NO reason why a particular institution exists, they are still cautious about changing existing institutions abruptly . . . with the knowledge that there is SOME reason, not yet understood and perhaps never to be understood, for their existence. As Richard Dawkins said about the analogous exercise in evolutionary biology of trying to understand the rationale for the anatomy of each species, 'evolution is smarter than you are'"[12] (p. 96).

Second, the distinction between bottom-up and top-down origins of institutions—combined with an appreciation for how importantly institutions shape economic outcomes—can inform how we use and what we mean by the term "development." President Harry Truman first introduced the metaphor of a development continuum in his post–World War II "Four Point Plan." This continuum ranged from undeveloped countries on one side to developed countries on the other and implied a linear development process from one side to the other, similar to Rostow's stages of economic growth, which we learned about in chapter 1. This is consistent with a top-down view of institutions, in which developed countries look alike and the development process consists of adopting developed-world institutions. By contrast, "The bottom up view of institutions is more open to the possibility that societies evolve different institutions even in the long run" (p. 96). Diverse informal institutions arise when formal institutions are missing (sidebar 8.3). The rapid rise of China since 1990, with its unique mix of political and economic institutions, seems to fit better into this latter view. The combination of China's ever-expanding influence and its unique institutional makeup ensures that there will continue to be lively debates on these issues.

### LAND OWNERSHIP INSTITUTIONS AND ECONOMIC DEVELOPMENT

Thus far, we've mainly discussed institutions in the abstract. Let's get more concrete. Since many of the world's poor live in rural settings and rely on agricultural production, economists have thought long and hard about land and land ownership. In many places, complex institutions govern who has access to land, when, and what bundle of rights comes with the land, for example, to buy and sell, rent in or out, use as collateral for a loan, keep or share the harvest, or simply decide what gets cultivated, and how. Many economists see reforming land institutions as a prerequisite to spur productivity growth in agriculture and encourage soil conservation, because security of land ownership has such an important effect on people's incentives to invest in the land—or not. Figuring out how land rights affect investments is not easy, though (see sidebar 8.4).

Even as poor countries become more urbanized, these land issues remain crucial, not least because a family's home and the land it occupies

**Sidebar 8.3  How Market Institutions Make It
Tough to Do Business in Sub-Saharan Africa**

Imagine for a moment how it might be to run a T-shirt factory in
Ghana. You might first think about where to locate your factory, how
to hire workers, and how to manufacture your T-shirts. While these
and a thousand other decisions would be part of running a successful
factory, there are some critical, deeper dilemmas that are easy to overlook if you have not spent time in places like Ghana—dilemmas that
arise because of the institutions that govern markets and market transactions. Marcel Fafchamps, a leading development economist, has
shed more light on this topic in countries throughout sub-Saharan
Africa than anyone else.

Which supplier will you turn to for cotton fabric? How will you pay
for your supplies? What will you do if a supplier cheats you by mixing
inferior cloth in with your more expensive roll of cloth? How many
workers will you hire? These questions raise serious dilemmas in Ghana.

Legal contracts are rarely used and difficult to enforce, which
means that firms often look only for suppliers from their own "social
networks"—from people they trust because of a shared ethnicity or
tribe. This introduces frictions and inefficiencies. When your first priority is finding a supplier who is unlikely to cheat you because you
have no legal recourse, it is tough to select suppliers based on standard
features such as price, quality, and service. Without the competitive
forces of the market, deliveries are often late, quality is often bad, and
customer service is often lacking. So-called crony capitalism can
emerge naturally in such a setting. Connections can matter more than
competition.

Missing or purely informal market institutions make it difficult to
find access to loans to cover inventory, which leads to a host of inefficiencies. They also make it difficult to decide who and how many
workers to hire. For example, Fafchamps finds that many manufacturing firms hire fewer workers than would be optimal because that's
how they reduce the risk of theft. Fewer workers are easier to monitor.

Fafchamps's work has challenged development economists to look
more carefully at the diverse informal institutions that emerge to regulate market transactions when the formal institutions of well-developed markets are missing. These market institutions profoundly shape
how businesses are run and whether and how they respond to opportunities. Fortunately, some of these insights are starting to filter into
intervention and policy design.

Marcel Fafchamps, *Market Institutions in Sub-Saharan Africa: Theory and
Evidence* (Cambridge, MA: MIT Press, 2004).

## Sidebar 8.4 Do Land Rights Make People More Productive?

Where people have secure rights to their land, are they more productive? That turns out to be a hard question to answer because of the *selection problem* (chapter 2). We could compare how productive farmers are in places where land rights are secure and in places where land rights are insecure. The trouble is, if land institutions are different between two places, chances are that a lot of other things are different, too—things that might affect productivity. We might look for a place where institutions changed. After the Mexican Revolution (1910–1920), Mexico created a communal land-holding system called the *ejido*. People could not own *ejido* lands. This changed in the 1990s—but so did a lot of other things in Mexico. If we see a change in productivity, how can we know it's because of the *ejido* reform and not some other change in agricultural policy that happened at the same time?

Three researchers spotted an opportunity to learn about land tenure insecurity and productivity in rural China. At the time of their study, local leaders periodically redistributed lands from some farmers to others in the same villages. Decisions to expropriate (take away) some farmers' lands varied across villages and, the authors argued, they were largely exogenous from the farmers' point of view. A farmer doesn't know if or when his land will be taken away.

Farmers can invest in making their land more productive by applying organic fertilizer—some combination of manure, dredged soil, decayed vegetable matter, and other wastes from the farm yard. The benefits of doing this (unlike chemical fertilizer application) can last several years. Are farmers who live in places with a low threat of expropriation more likely to make this investment?

The answer, it seems, is yes. The authors used an econometric model to estimate the risk of expropriation in a sample of villages in China. They found that farmers invest more intensively in organic fertilizer where their threat of expropriation is low. This confirms that land tenure security affects productive investments. However, the authors also found that eliminating the risk of exploitation is not enough to raise productive efficiency in a big way. Public investments, like irrigation, drainage, and terracing, are critical, and these do not depend on individuals' plot rights in rural China.

Hanan G. Jacoby, Guo Li, and Scott Rozelle, "Hazards of Expropriation: Tenure Insecurity and Investment in Rural China," *American Economic Review* 92, no. 5 (2002):1420–47.

constitute one of its most valuable assets and can provide a potent source of financial leverage. Without a formal title of ownership, the family is unlikely to be able to use property as collateral to get a loan, which can make it hard to start or expand a small business, for example.

For much of the past century, increasing land tenure security through land titling has been a policy priority. The logic is simple: better security provides an incentive for people to make productive investments in their land. Yet, despite decades of devoted effort to impose land titles from above, only a tiny fraction of land in Africa is registered under a formal system. Moreover, even where titling has happened, the anticipated boost in investment has largely been absent. Does this mean the simple logic is flawed? Not likely. Instead, it probably says something about the complexity of land ownership institutions.

In Europe and North America, we have a relatively simple concept of land ownership: a plot of land either belongs to an individual or organization or it belongs to the state. In much of the developing world, land ownership concepts are much more complex. In the argan forests of southwestern Morocco, for example, the land is formally "owned" by the government, but locals have usufruct (use) rights to collect fruit and dead wood from the forest and to graze their livestock in the forest. These usufruct rights change from one season to the next, however, so determining who has the right to do what on a given plot of land depends not only on the location of the plot but also the month of the year. These usufruct rights can be bought or sold, but they are also passed down through inheritance.

Generations of inheritance transfers add further complexity to land rights. In the argan forests, use rights to a given tract of forest land can be shared between several different families, and the sharing arrangement can change from one season to the next. Nearly all of the informal ownership institutions that govern locals' use of the argan forest have emerged from the bottom up, based on local norms and religious (Islamic) notions of ownership and inheritance.

In contexts with rich bottom-up institutions governing land rights, what happens when top-down land titles are imposed by the state? One common outcome is local resistance and even conflict. Many a landtitling program has failed to formalize land ownership or has fallen far short of its intended coverage because of frictions with preexisting informal ownership institutions. Even when a program succeeds in titling land, these land titles—which to the outsider seem to offer much greater tenure security—do not seem to induce much additional investment. In practice, these titles can introduce confusion and uncertainty into land ownership because it is often unclear how they will change local informal norms in practice.

## ENTREPRENEURSHIP, INSTITUTIONS, AND INSTITUTIONAL INNOVATION

For several years, Travis has asked the students in his Introduction to International Economic Development class the question, "How entrepreneurial are Americans?" After collecting their responses on a scale of 1 to 10, he asks them the same question for Europeans and then for Africans. The answers for a recent class are shown in figure 8.1.

Are Americans really more entrepreneurial than Europeans? Are both really that much more entrepreneurial than Africans? While this is clearly not a rigorous survey, the pattern of perceptions is consistent across classes and offers an interesting perspective on how institutions shape economic development.

The word "entrepreneur" traces its origins to seventeenth-century France, where the term described a government subcontractor who supplied specified goods or services (from "entre," between, and "preneur," taker). The payment to the subcontractor was fixed and determined by the contract, so he had to find creative ways to keep his own costs low in order to make a profit. The risk of making or losing money on the proposition was borne by the entrepreneur, which provided strong incentives for him to lower costs as much as possible. Those who study entrepreneurship often point out that this ability to solve problems by exerting ingenuity and making connections in order to earn a profit is an ever-present aspect of human activity, an innate impulse.[13] Some people are simply better entrepreneurs than others, but just as with innate math or music skills, the concentration of this trait is no greater on one continent than another. But if this is true, what explains the patterns in figure 8.1? Perhaps they are simply misperceptions of reality, but let's dig deeper than that.

To address this question, recognize that while human nature changes very little from one continent to another, institutions can change dramatically—and institutions direct human ingenuity and impulses in specific directions. In Willie Sutton's language, institutions determine "where the money is" in a society and thereby channel the entrepreneurial capacity of a people. Local norms and values can also powerfully shape whether people recognize entrepreneurial opportunities, as well as whether and how they respond.

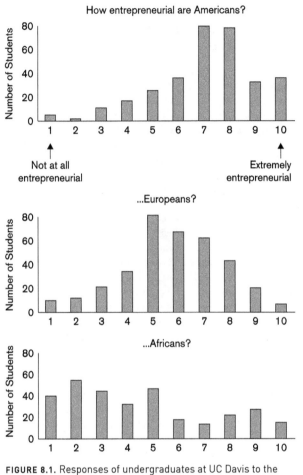

**FIGURE 8.1.** Responses of undergraduates at UC Davis to the question, "How entrepreneurial are _____?"

In part, the patterns in figure 8.1 reflect the way we sometimes romanticize entrepreneurship. Entrepreneurs innovate and create new products and jobs. They connect people to goods, services, and other people in new and cheaper ways. They may get rich, but they improve or contribute to society in the process. While capitalism reveres entrepreneurs as a result, their incentives are not always aligned with those of the broader society. Indeed, some institutional configurations encourage entrepreneurs to focus all their energies on creating new rent-seeking procedures. In this sense, bad institutions like cronyism and corruption can spawn impressive and genuinely innovative entrepreneurship.

## Sidebar 8.5 Entrepreneurial Monks and the "Innovation Machine"

Thinking about differences in entrepreneurship in America, Europe, and Africa generates some useful insights into what entrepreneurship entails and what influences it. In a similar way, looking over time at different forms of entrepreneurship can be very enlightening. One of the most influential modern economists, William Baumol of New York University, did precisely that in an entertaining article and insightful book.

Baumol compares different historical episodes of entrepreneurship—including Ancient Rome, Medieval China, and Middle Age Europe—and tells some intriguing stories. For example, monks may not strike you as entrepreneurs, but the Cistercian monks of the Late Middle Ages in Europe were as entrepreneurial as any of their contemporaries and were "the spearhead of technological advance."

How did this happen? Baumol explains that the rules of the game offered large economic rewards to the exercise of Cistercian entrepreneurship. Specifically, instead of getting direct support from royal coffers, these monks received exemptions from the ruling elite from all river and road tolls and from payment of tithes. This raised marginal returns to investment and led the order of monks to operate and develop new water mills, among other productive pursuits.

In related work, Baumol characterizes capitalism as an "innovation machine" that, while imperfect, is better at encouraging innovation and productive entrepreneurship than any other economic system. In order to function, capitalism requires institutions such as rule of law, property rights, and market exchange. Economists have long recognized the efficiency of markets to allocate goods and services. Baumol argues convincingly that these institutions have an even more potent dynamic virtue: they channel entrepreneurial effort into, and reward, innovation, which is the basis of long-run economic growth.

W. J. Baumol, "Entrepreneurship: Productive, Unproductive, and Destructive," *Journal of Political Economy* 98, no. 5, part 1 (October 1990):893–921.

W. J. Baumol, *The Free-Market Innovation Machine: Analyzing the Growth Miracle of Capitalism* (Princeton: Princeton University Press, 2002).

The problem, of course, is that creative rent seeking is not only unproductive; it can undermine legitimate productive economic activity.

If we perceive Americans to be more entrepreneurial than Africans, perhaps it is because we restrict our definition of entrepreneurship to productive pursuits—and one can make a compelling case that there is more productive entrepreneurship in the US than in most African countries. (Wall Street's creative concealment of subprime mortgages in innovative securities, which triggered the 2008 financial crisis, weakens this case!) Our mistake, then, is to exclude innovative rent seeking from our definition of "entrepreneurship" and thereby overlook the substantial share of African entrepreneurial effort that is unproductive for society as a whole but lucrative for the entrepreneur. History also teaches us about how the "rules of the game" help define entrepreneurship (sidebar 8.5).

Innovation and entrepreneurship are in many ways the lifeblood of the global economy. Sustained economic growth and genuine economic development require healthy institutions, because innovation and entrepreneurship are shaped so fundamentally by these rules of the game. Whether one agrees with Acemoglu and Robinson that institutions are *the* dominant determinant of economic growth or not, inclusive institutions are clearly better than extractive ones at encouraging productive, dynamic entrepreneurship and innovation. The best inclusive institutions not only resist capture by special interests and the elite, they also have built-in mechanisms to adapt to new economic forces and technological opportunities in resiliently inclusive ways.

www.rebeltext.org/development/qr8.html
Learn more about institutions by exploring
multimedia resources while you read.

**9**

# Agriculture

In 1979, development economist Theodore W. Schultz won
the Nobel Prize. The opening lines of his Nobel Prize lecture
provide the perfect springboard for this chapter: "Most of the
people in the world are poor, so if we knew the economics of
being poor, we would know much of the economics that
really matters. Most of the world's poor people earn their
living from agriculture, so if we knew the economics of
agriculture, we would know much of the economics of being
poor."[1] The 1960s and 1970s brought unprecedented
agricultural productivity gains thanks largely to investments
in international aid. In the 1980s and 1990s, the role
agriculture plays in economic development was frequently
ignored—but it was remembered anew in the 2000s.
Throughout these cycles, poor farmers kept farming. These
agricultural households have some important economic
features that are worth understanding. They face distinct constraints that shape the way they farm and how they are
affected by markets and government programs.

**ESSENTIALS**

- Structural transformation
- Production functions
- Risk and uncertainty
- Green Revolution
- Innovation and technology adoption
- Food security versus self-sufficiency
- Agricultural household model
- Subsistence goods and shadow values
- Gender inequality
- Inseparability of efficiency and equity
- Market interlinkages

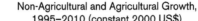

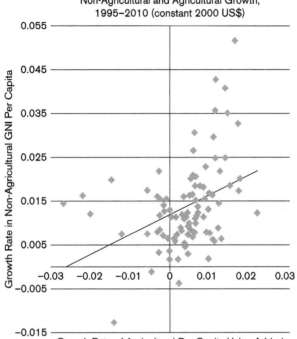

FIGURE 9.1. There is a positive association between countries' agricultural and non-agricultural economic growth. Source: Analysis of World Bank data (data.worldbank.org).

Seventy percent of the world's poor live in rural areas, and in the poorest countries most rural households are involved in agriculture. Agriculture is a fascinating and crucial sector of the economy. Virtually all countries start out with economies based primarily on agriculture, but agriculture's shares of GNI and national employment fall as economies grow. It would seem, then, that agriculture starts out being important, but becomes less so over time.

There is, however, an important connection between agriculture and economic growth. You can see it in figure 9.1, which relates countries' growth in agricultural GDP with growth in non-agricultural GNI over time. There is wide variation in both agricultural and non-agricultural growth rates across countries, but the figure shows a significant positive relationship between the two. Agricultural and non-agricultural growth seem to go hand in hand; the countries that had the highest agricultural GDP growth also tended to have the highest non-agricultural GNI growth. If we do an econometric regression using the data in this picture, we find that a 1% increase in agricultural growth is associated with nearly a half (0.45) percentage point increase in non-agricultural growth.[2]

This does not necessarily mean that agricultural growth *causes* total income growth. In fact, it could be the reverse: countries that do well overall might be better at growing their agricultural sector. More likely, it is some combination of the two. Increases in agricultural production facilitate growth in other sectors of the economy, and this, in turn, has a positive feedback effect on agricultural growth. In addition, there may be other factors, like technological change or—as we learned in the last chapter—healthy institutions such as clear and stable rule of law, that make both sectors grow.

Decades of experience have shown that most countries need to grow their agriculture if they want to grow their economy as a whole. Agriculture continues to be the main source of income and employment for many people in the world today, making agricultural households an important market for manufactured goods. Agriculture is the principal source of food and labor to fuel expanding urban economies. It provides essential intermediate inputs such as fruits, vegetables, and grain to food processors. When a large part of the economy is agricultural, where else are the savings to invest in industry going to come from? As evidence of the crucial cash that can be generated by the agricultural sector, countries around the globe have devised a variety of means to "tax" agricultural income as a way to support industrial sectors. Japan, in the Meiji period (1868–1912), taxed its farmers directly. The former USSR taxed farmers indirectly by paying them prices below the world price for their crops. This model of state enterprises ("parastatals") paying farmers low prices (and selling at high prices) in order to fund other activities has since been followed by many developing countries.

This chapter is an introduction to how economists study agriculture as it relates to economic development. The first thing we'll learn is that agriculture is different from other parts of the economy, and agricultural producers in poor countries are also households. They are neither pure firms nor pure consumers, but rather a combination of the two. The microeconomic theory of the firm does not describe their behavior, but neither does the theory of the consumer. We will learn how to model the dual nature of agricultural households as producers and consumers, and what this means for designing policies to address rural poverty and food security.

Next, we'll look inside the household. Building on our discussion in chapter 4 on intra-household inequality, we'll see how unequal access to resources can affect not only how the household's economic pie gets divvied up among household members (equity), but also how big the pie is (efficiency). We'll see that gender divisions within households can result in significant losses in agricultural productivity. Similar losses of economic efficiency and income can occur in other domains as well, which can create unintended consequences for development projects in both agricultural and non-agricultural settings.

Finally, we'll look beyond the household and see how diverse households interact within rural economies. We'll see how economic linkages transmit impacts of policy and market shocks among households, often with surprising outcomes.

## HOW AGRICULTURE IS DIFFERENT

Agriculture is different from other sectors of the economy in ways that have far-reaching ramifications for both development policy and economic analysis.

To start with, let's think about the production function. In most sectors of the economy, the production function represents a knowable engineering relationship between inputs and outputs, like how many copies of RebelText can be produced from a given amount of paper, ink, capital (printing machines), labor, and so on. The agricultural production process is biological and filled with uncertainty. Farmers rely heavily on inputs from nature, including weather. The good news is that nature provides inputs like sunshine and rainfall for free. The bad news is that you never know when the rains won't come, the sun won't shine, or a swarm of locusts will devastate your crop. Adverse shocks break the engineering relationship between inputs and outputs. Agricultural economists pay a great deal of attention to incorporating risk into the production function. In agriculture, the production function is random, or stochastic (from the Greek word "στόχος" [stóchos], meaning "guess" or "target"). Stochastic production analysis is beyond the scope of this book, but as you read on it is important to bear in mind this critical difference between agriculture and other sectors. We will introduce some dimensions of risk in this chapter and save the details of the topic for chapter 12.

Agricultural production involves long time lags—often many months— between purchasing and applying inputs and harvesting outputs. Neither the size of the harvest nor (usually) the output price is known at planting time. Farming requires land, so agriculture is spread out over wide geographic areas. Because agricultural production is spread out, seasonal, risky, and involves long time lags, reliable and timely access to markets is critical. These include markets for inputs such as seeds and fertilizer, crop outputs produced by farmers, and financial markets for savings and credit to finance input purchases, as well as insurance to protect against crop failures. Imagine, then, the challenges farmers face in poor countries, where markets don't work well (coming in chapter 11), banks won't lend money to small farmers, and formal insurance is nonexistent (coming in chapter 12).

Some sectors, like energy, steel, or automobiles, are dominated by a few large producers. The minister of industry might be able to get key industry players to sit down around a table and discuss industrial development policies. Agricultural production is carried out by large numbers of farmers with unequal access to resources, from large agribusinesses (sometimes referred to as "factories in the fields") to smallholder farmers with tiny plots. To get agricultural policies right, we have to understand the behavior of thousands, millions, or (in China and India) hundreds of millions of heterogeneous actors whom the minister of agriculture couldn't possibly get around a table! Influencing agricultural outcomes thus requires having good economic models of diverse agricultural producers and knowing how they are likely to respond to different kinds of policies. To complicate matters, as we shall see, what's good for big farmers can be bad for small ones.

Perhaps the biggest difference between agriculture and other sectors in poor countries is that agricultural production decisions are almost always made within economic units that also function as households. That is, unlike firms that are focused exclusively on production decisions, agricultural households jointly and simultaneously make both production and consumption decisions. This may seem like a technical distinction, but as we'll see it is actually a real "game changer" when it comes to economic analysis.

## THE AGRICULTURAL HOUSEHOLD MODEL

In rich countries, most agricultural producers are firms that produce for the market. Agricultural households in poor countries are different from rich-country farmers as well as from their non-agricultural counterparts, because they consume part or all of what they produce. They also supply many of their own inputs, particularly land and labor. You can think of them as a hybrid of firm and household. Our models therefore have to reflect agricultural households' dual nature as both producer and consumer to provide a reliable basis for understanding the agricultural economy and offer guidance for designing policies.

The analysis of agriculture and development in this way leads to surprises, because what is good for agricultural households as producers often is not good for them as consumers. When the price of food goes up, most crop producers in poor countries are *not* better off, because they also face higher prices as food consumers. Failure to understand the workings of agricultural households has been a source of many ill-fated development policies.

*The Household as Consumer*

The agricultural household model is the staple for any kind of microeconomic analysis of agriculture in poor countries. Let's start with consumer theory. Figure 9.2 shows the famous indifference curve and budget constraint in the consumer model, which you'll remember from your microeconomics classes. The axes measure the quantities of food (horizontal axis) and other stuff (vertical axis) the household demands. We could have more categories of goods, but each new good adds a dimension to our figure, which makes it hard—or impossible—to draw, so let's keep it at two. Our findings will generalize to more than two goods.

The straight line represents the household's budget constraint. In a standard consumer model, we almost always assume the household's income is fixed. In an agricultural household model, though, it includes profits from producing food. Remember this—it's an essential part of the household-farm model.

The point where the budget constraint hits an axis (the intercept) is the maximum amount of the good on the axis that the household could consume if it spent all its available income, $Y^*$, on that good. To see where the budget constraint hits the two axes, just divide income by the price per unit of each good. The maximum amount of food this household could consume, which we'll call $X_a^{max}$, is the household's income divided by the price of food. For example, if your income is $100 and food costs $2 per kilo, the most food you can consume if you don't buy anything else is 50 kilos. The line between those two points shows all the combinations of food and other stuff the household can afford if it spends all of its money.

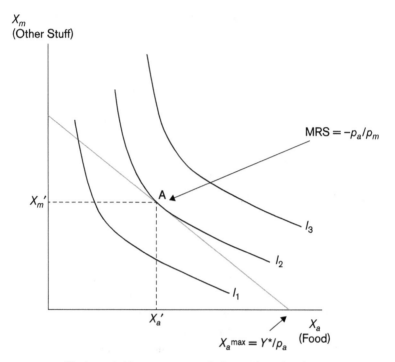

**FIGURE 9.2.** The household as consumer optimizes at the point of tangency between the indifference curve and budget constraint. At point A, its marginal rate of substitution between goods equals the (negative) ratio of market prices.

The budget constraint has a slope equal to the (negative of the) price of food (or whatever's on the horizontal axis) divided by the price of other stuff (or whatever's on the vertical axis). You can see that this line tells us the rate at which the market trades off food for other stuff. Its slope tells us how much other stuff we could buy if we gave up one unit of food (and vice versa).

The basic precept of consumer economics is that at the optimum, every household consumes at the point where its own personal (subjective) trade-off between food and other stuff equals the rate at which the *market* trades off the two goods. The market's rate of trading off food for other stuff is just the slope of the budget line, or the (negative of the) ratio of market prices.

How should we depict the household's preferences, or rate of trade-off in terms of satisfaction (what economists call "utility")? Should it be a line, like the budget constraint? Probably not. Your trade-off in preferences will almost surely not be constant because of the law of dimin-ishing marginal utility. The more you have of something, the less utility you get from having one more unit; thus, the more you'd be willing to trade to get an additional unit of something else. That's why you'll almost never end up consuming at either end of your budget constraint. You won't spend your whole budget on food (unless you face a very severe nutritional constraint that forces you to do so in order to sur-vive). And you'll never end up at the other end of the budget line, either, because you obviously need to spend some of your budget on food.

Given diminishing marginal utility, we need a curve, not a line, to depict consumer preferences. An indifference curve ($I_1$, $I_2$, or $I_3$ in the figure) depicts all the combinations of food and other stuff that leave the house-hold equally well off; that is, along each indifference curve, the house-hold's utility is constant. There are many (really, an infinite number of) indifference curves. As we move from the origin up to the northeast in the diagram, we hop onto indifference curves providing higher levels of utility. Most, like curve $I_3$, describe bundles of food and other stuff that the household cannot afford given its budget constraint. Others, like $I_1$, describe bundles of goods the household can afford, with money left over.

Point A in the figure is the bundle that gives the highest utility the household can attain given its budget constraint. That's the point where the household's marginal rate of substitution (MRS) between food and other stuff just equals the (negative of the) price ratio. It is where the household's trade-off in preferences equals the market trade-off. Every household will set its trade-off in preferences equal to the ratio of prices. In an economy where every household faces the same market prices, everyone will consume at the same MRS between food and other stuff. When that happens, consumption is said to be Pareto efficient: no house-hold can be made better off without making another one worse off.

What happens if the price of food increases? Modeling how an out-come changes when some exogenous variable (here, the price of food) changes is called "comparative statics." If the household allocated its whole budget to food, it would be able to buy less than before. How-ever, if it spent all its income on other stuff, it could still buy the same amount as before, so the vertical intercept does not change. As a result, the budget line pivots inward, as in figure 9.3.

You may remember that the comparative statics of a price change from microeconomics. Faced with a higher food price, the household substitutes other stuff for food. If it could stay on the same indifference curve as before, the new ratio of prices would drive it from A to B in the

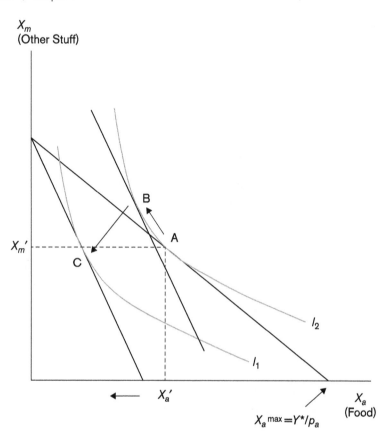

**FIGURE 9.3.** In the consumer model, a rise in the price of food triggers substitution (A → B) and real income (B → C) effects that reinforce one another; the quantity of food demanded decreases.

diagram. This is called the "substitution effect," because consumers substitute away from the good that has gotten more expensive in favor of other goods, which have become less expensive relative to food. In our figure, the substitution effect decreases food demand.

The household cannot afford to consume at point B, though. With the higher food price, its real income falls, forcing it down to a lower indifference curve (point C). A negative real-income effect reinforces the negative substitution effect. That's why demand curves slope downward: as the price of food (or pretty much any good) increases, consumers demand less of it.

That's the end of the comparative statics of an own-price change in the consumer model—but not in the household-farm model. Remember,

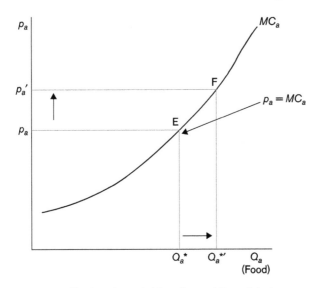

**FIGURE 9.4.** The farm household produces at the point where the food price equals the marginal cost of producing food. When the food price rises, so does food production.

agricultural households also produce food. How does this change things? An increase in the price of food hurts consumers, but it makes producers better off, because farm profit goes up.

*The Household as Producer*

To show the production-side effect of the price change, we need to borrow a curve from producer theory. You'll recognize the one in figure 9.4. The marginal cost (MC) gives the cost of producing an additional unit of food. A profit-maximizing firm produces where the MC equals the market price. At different prices (vertical axis) we can determine the supply response (horizontal axis) from the MC curve. Thus, the MC curve is also the firm's supply curve.

The $p$ = MC rule makes good sense. The price is the reward the firm gets for producing one more unit. If the price is higher than the MC, the firm will want to produce more. If the MC is higher than the price, it will cut back on production until it brings MC down to the market price. As a producer, our agricultural household will have the same incentive to do this as a firm would.

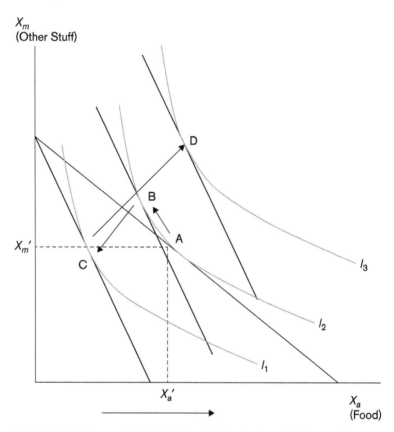

**FIGURE 9.5.** The farm profit effect shifts out the budget constraint, possibly resulting in a positive effect of food prices on the household's food demand.

At the food price $p_a$, our household farm maximizes its profit from food production at point E, producing a level of output equal to $Q^*_a$. Its profit, $\Pi = p_a Q^*_a - MC_a$, is the more-or-less triangular area above the marginal cost curve but below the price in our figure.

What happens when the price of food goes up? At the higher price, $p_a'$, price equals MC at point F. Output jumps to $Q^*_a{}'$ and profit increases (you can see that the triangle below the new price line is bigger).

This is not the end of the story either, because remember: profit is part of the household's income. When the price of food goes up, the household's income goes up because of the profit effect. To see what that does to our comparative statics, we have to go back to our indifference curves.

Before we considered the profit effect, the household was at point C in figure 9.5. We show an increase in income as a parallel outward shift in the budget constraint (an increase in income changes the point where the budget constraint intersects the axes because the household can afford more of either good). This increases the demand for both food and other stuff, as long as both are normal goods.

To determine the overall effect of a price change on demand we need to know how much the budget constraint shifts due to the profit effect. If the increase in profits only shifted the budget constraint a little, food demand would remain lower than before the price increase. But it could shift the budget constraint out farther, maybe all the way to where it's tangent to indifference curve $I_3$. At point D, the household consumes a bundle that is actually to the right of where it started, at point A. That means its food demand increased when the price of food went up. An agricultural household's food demand curve can slope upward if the profit effect is big enough! In fact, often when economists estimate household-farm models with real-world data, they find that it does slope upward (see sidebar 9.1).

### THE AGRICULTURAL HOUSEHOLD MODEL AND DEVELOPMENT POLICY

The agricultural household model changes the way we think about most of the agricultural producers in the world. It also has some important lessons for agricultural development policy.

First, if a government wants to increase the supply of food for its urban consumers, raising the price of food will not necessarily help. The amount of food available from domestic producers to the market, or marketed surplus $(MS_a)$, is the difference between what the farm household produces and what it consumes; that is, $MS_a = Q_a - X_a$. Assuming the household does not face serious production constraints, production increases when the price goes up. This would increase the marketed surplus if the farm household's demand stayed the same—but it doesn't. The more the household farm's consumption increases because of the profit effect, the smaller the marketed surplus effect. Governments often are disappointed when they offer farmers expensive price supports but the market supply doesn't change much.

Second, most people—including economists—assume that if the price of food goes up, that's bad news for urban consumers but good for farmers. The agricultural household model shows that this might not be the case. If a household is to benefit from higher food prices, the positive profit effect has to outweigh the negative consumption effect. In order for that to happen, the household has to be a net seller of food—that is, its marketed surplus must be positive.

## Sidebar 9.1   Upward-Sloping Demand Curves?

A generation or two of graduate students in development economics learned how to understand and use the agricultural household model from economists Inderjit Singh, Lyn Squire, and John Strauss. In their classic book on the topic, they demonstrated the importance of taking into account the relationship between production and consumption decisions with a comparison of findings from agricultural household models for Taiwan, Malaysia, Korea, Japan, Thailand, Sierra Leone, and Northern Nigeria. Four of the seven studies found a positive own-price elasticity of demand for agricultural goods. In those cases, the positive profit effect was stronger than the negative real income and substitution effects. In all seven cases, the profit effect substantially lowered the effect of a food-price increase on the marketed surplus of food.

This may not be the first time you've heard of upward-sloping demand curves. Most introductory microeconomics textbooks mention the possibility of "Giffin" goods that also have upward-sloping demand curves—although for a distinctly different reason. Understanding the distinction may help reinforce the logic behind the agricultural household model.

Until recently, such Giffin goods were treated a bit like the Loch Ness monster because no one had ever actually *seen* them in the real world. In 2008, economists Robert Jensen and Nolan Miller, who devised the revealed preference measure of poverty (Staple Calorie Share) we encountered in chapter 4, provided convincing evidence of Giffin behavior using data from 1,300 poor households in China. They found that as the price of rice increased, extremely poor households actually consumed *more* rice.

What's the explanation? The agricultural household model cannot explain this result for one simple reason: these were *urban* poor who did not reap a profit benefit from higher rice prices. Instead, this appears to be driven by subsistence concerns: as the price of rice—their main source of calories—increases, the food budgets of these poor households tighten, and they start cutting back on other food purchases. But to survive, they must make up the calories somehow and choose the cheapest calories available: rice!

Inderjit Singh, Lyn Squire, and John Strauss, eds., *Agricultural Household Models, Extensions, Applications and Policy* (Baltimore: Johns Hopkins University Press, 1986).

Robert T. Jensen and Nolan H. Miller, "Giffen Behavior and Subsistence Consumption," *American Economic Review* 98, no. 4 (2008):1553–77.

TABLE 9.1 NET BENEFIT RATIOS BY RURAL HOUSEHOLD GROUP IN FOUR
CENTRAL AMERICAN COUNTRIES

| | Country | | | |
|---|---|---|---|---|
| Household Group | *El Salvador* | *Guatemala* | *Honduras* | *Nicaragua* |
| Landless | –0.16 | –0.36 | –0.63 | –0.49 |
| Subsistence | –0.01 | –0.32 | –0.78 | 0 |
| Small Commercial | 0.31 | –0.12 | –0.13 | 0.39 |
| Medium Commercial | 1.2 | 0.07 | 1.01 | 0.62 |
| Large Commercial | 3.88 | 0.64 | 1.71 | 1.79 |

SOURCE: J. Edward Taylor, Antonio Yúnez-Naude, and Nancy Jesurun-Clements, "Does Agricultural Trade Liberalization Reduce Rural Welfare in Developing Countries? The Case of CAFTA," *Applied Economic Perspectives and Policy* 32, no. 1 (2010):95–116.

It might surprise you to learn that most of the world's farmers produce less food than they consume. The development economist Chris Barrett compared findings from twenty-three agricultural household surveys in eastern and southern Africa. He found no case in which most farmers were net sellers. The percentage of agricultural households that sold their crops ranged from a high of 45% (maize in Zimbabwe) to lows of 10%–12% (barley, sorghum, and wheat in Ethiopia). This means that most farmers—those who produce less than they consume— lose if the price of the crops they grow goes up.[3]

Another development economist, Angus Deaton, came up with a handy way to determine how much welfare increases if the price of food crops goes up: the ratio of net agricultural sales, or marketed surplus (MS), to the household's total expenditures on all goods (E). He called this the net benefit ratio (NBR):

$$NBR = \frac{MS}{E}$$

The NBR can be interpreted as the percentage change in welfare resulting from a 1% change in the crop's price. Table 9.1 gives the NBR for different rural household groups in El Salvador, Guatemala, Honduras, and Nicaragua.

The NBR is almost always negative for small-farm households. For subsistence producers in Honduras, a 1% increase in food prices *reduces* welfare by 0.78%. An important implication of these findings is that trade agreements that lower import tariffs on food actually benefit most food producers in these Central American countries.

A third lesson from agricultural household models is the importance of the production response. When we talk about agricultural households we mean small farmers. Big corn farms in the United States are family operated, but for all practical purposes they are pure firms because they consume a negligible part of their harvest. Farm households, in order to survive and help feed the burgeoning urban population in their countries, have to be able to increase their production in response to price changes.

*Feeding the World: The Elasticity of Agricultural Supply*

The MC curve is the household's supply curve. The flatter (more *elastic*) it is, the more it will respond to an increase in price by producing more. In the extreme case where the supply curve is vertical (perfectly *inelastic*), no change in price will lead to an increase in output.

Why would an agricultural household ever have a vertical, or nearly vertical, supply curve? In the real world, small farmers face many different kinds of production constraints that large farmers in rich countries typically do not face. A few of the most common ones are as follows:

- limited access to land, and especially irrigated land
- poor land quality
- technological limitations, including lack of access to high-productivity seeds
- limited access to modern inputs like fertilizer
- a lack of cash to purchase inputs, and limited or no access to credit
- limited or no access to insurance to protect against crop failure
- labor constraints

Typically, a constellation of constraints restrict small farmers' capacity and willingness to increase production and shift into higher value crop activities. Small landholdings mean high administrative costs for banks and limited collateral to offer them as security against loans to pay for inputs, as we'll see in chapter 12. High production risks and a lack of crop insurance make banks even more unwilling to lend to small farmers. All of these constraints can also make small farmers unwilling to "risk the farm" and take out loans, even if banks are willing. Households that lack the cash to hire workers from their village, or who face a limited supply of potential workers, have to farm their land themselves; families with few, old, or unhealthy members often then have little choice but to leave land fallow. The result can be a vicious cycle between poverty and production, leading to a poverty trap.

Our agricultural household models need to include these constraints if we want them to reflect the way agricultural economies work. This is necessary for our models to be a useful basis for designing policies to increase food production and combat poverty in agricultural areas. In fact, there have been many extensions of the agricultural household model to incorporate these constraints.

*Agricultural Technology: Improving Production Potential of Crops*

Let's begin with the most fundamental constraint on agricultural production: technology. Technology is reflected in the production function, which specifies the maximum output obtainable from a given set of inputs. Graphically, it is reflected in the shape and position of the supply curve. When new technologies come along enabling farmers to get more output from the same set of inputs (or use fewer inputs to get the same output), an inelastic supply curve can shift outward, as illustrated in figure 9.6.

Agricultural production technologies took a great leap forward with the advent of the Green Revolution. The Green Revolution began as a series of agricultural research initiatives started in 1943 by Norman Borlaug, an agronomist and eventual winner of the Nobel Peace Prize who has been credited with saving more than a billion lives.[4] Borlaug set out to breed new varieties of plants—especially rice and wheat—that could produce more food. Most plant breeders aspire to doing something like this, but Borlaug succeeded like no one before him ever had. His work began in Mexico, but his ideas were put to the test in India, which in 1961 was on the brink of mass famine. Its rice yields at the time were only around two tons per hectare. By the mid-1990s, Indian rice yields had tripled, rice prices had fallen (despite continuing population growth), and India had become a rice exporter.

How did this huge technological change happen? New rice varieties developed at IRRI (the International Rice Research Institute in Los Baños, Philippines) were bred to more efficiently exploit soil nutrients. This, together with an expanded use of fertilizer and irrigation, vastly increased the world's ability to feed itself—and then some. Rice isn't the only crop that experienced a Green Revolution. Between 1950 and

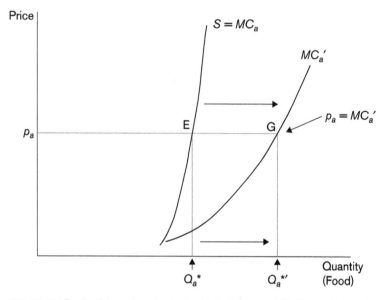

**FIGURE 9.6.** Productivity-enhancing technological change shifts the agricultural supply (marginal cost) curve outward to the right, increasing the quantity supplied at a given price.

2005, wheat yields in the world rose from around 750 kilograms per hectare to more than 2,500.[5] Today, a network of international crop research institutes, called the CGIAR (www.cgiar.org), continues to seek new solutions to feeding the world's still growing population. The CGIAR's main job is to continue shifting out the agricultural supply curve. Today, in an era of climate change, this means taking on environmental as well as biological challenges.

### AGRICULTURAL TECHNOLOGY ADOPTION

Once crop scientists have succeeded in breeding high-yielding varieties that are well suited for a given location, it might seem like farmers would be drawn quickly to these new technologies. Such a "build it and they will come" approach to agricultural technology may work with rich farmers, but things aren't so simple with poor farmers. Even after high-yielding varieties are available, there are several constraints that can prevent small-holder farmers from adopting them. One of the most active research areas in development economics—agricultural technology adoption—seeks to understand these other constraints.

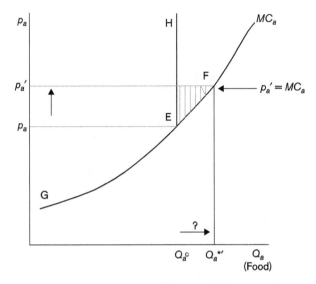

**FIGURE 9.7.** A liquidity constraint (segment EH) can result in suboptimal production and a welfare loss.

### Financial Adoption Constraints

Let's consider a liquidity (cash) constraint in our comparative statics example above. Suppose that at the initial food price, the household is spending all the cash it has to buy inputs. It faces a liquidity constraint. A basic problem in agricultural production is that inputs have to be purchased many months before the harvest comes in. Unless the household can borrow against the harvest, which poor small households cannot, its input demand is constrained by its available cash. In figure 9.7, the food price goes up, but the liquidity constraint prevents the household from increasing production. The liquidity constraint is represented by the vertical line in the diagram. The MC curve is the same as before, but because the household cannot expand production beyond the constrained level, its supply curve effectively is "kinked," so it is given by GEH. The shaded triangle is the welfare loss to the household from not being able to adjust its production to the higher level. The only way to increase production and raise the household's welfare in this case is to loosen the liquidity constraint.

A lack of access to credit, insurance, or hired labor may reflect market failures due to information and other problems, which we will look at in chapters 11 and 12. The household also may face high transaction costs in selling its output or purchasing inputs, for example, if transportation to markets is very expensive. If transaction costs are high enough, the household's best bet may be to withdraw from the market completely and become a subsistence producer.

### Information Adoption Constraints

In addition to these financial and economic constraints, there are several potential information and even cognitive constraints to technology adoption. Obviously, a farmer must learn about new technologies or new production practices before she can adopt them. How do poor farmers learn about new seeds? In some places, they may first hear about a new technology from an official agricultural "extension agent," but they typically are only willing to adopt it after seeing someone else's experience or testing it out on a small piece of their own land. Social learning and learning by doing are therefore important topics in this area of development economics and often shape the design of farmer training and extension programs (see sidebar 9.2).

We opened the chapter with a quote from Theodore Schultz's 1979 Nobel Prize lecture. In that lecture and indeed throughout his career, he emphasized how critical it was that farmers be able to learn and adapt to changing circumstances. As he saw it, "While land *per se* is not a critical factor in being poor, the human agent is," because smarter farmers who have learned how to learn, and who look for new ways to enhance their productivity, can take advantage of new opportunities.[6]

What makes the economics of technology adoption complicated and challenging is how the various constraints on technology development and adoption interact. Here, we have presented these constraints in an order that seems logical: first, new and improved technologies must be developed. Then, the constraints keeping small farmers from adopting these new technologies need to be addressed. But in practice, things are more complex: the presence of farm-level constraints discourages investments in the development of new technologies. Why would any profit-minded company invest in creating new seed varieties and other technologies, knowing that small farmers are too constrained to adopt them? This is why investments in international agricultural research are unpopular as private-sector investments. They are more likely to be provided as a form of development assistance. Indeed, agricultural research and development are among the most cost-effective ways of reducing rural poverty.

## Sidebar 9.2    Learning from Others

The Green Revolution brought new high-yielding seeds to India's farmers, whose production technology had changed little for decades. Many did not adopt the new seeds, even though agronomic field tests had shown them to be significantly more productive than traditional seed varieties. Andrew Foster and Mark Rosenzweig, using data that tracked farmers over time, found that a lack of knowledge about how to manage new seeds was a significant deterrent to adoption. The profitability of the new seeds for farmers increased as their neighbors gained experience growing them. Because of this, farmers whose neighbors had experience growing the new seeds planted more of their own land in high-yielding varieties. Thus, the authors concluded, farmers who adopted the new technology created benefits not only for themselves but also for others, by providing important "knowledge spillovers."

In a more recent study, Timothy Conley and Chris Udry investigate the role of social learning among pineapple farmers in Ghana. Many of these farmers began growing pineapple in the 1990s, learning through trial and error how much fertilizer to use to maximize their profit. By analyzing data on social networks and this trial-and-error process, they found that farmers do indeed learn from their "information neighbors," but only when their neighbors get a surprisingly good or bad result from trying a particular fertilizer dosage rate.

These studies have documented how the spread of information about new technologies can be critical in making farmers in poor countries more productive. They have influenced the design of agricultural extension programs—and sparked several follow-up studies by development economists seeking a yet deeper understanding of the information and cognitive constraints that impede technology adoption.

Andrew D. Foster and Mark R. Rosenzweig, "Learning by Doing and Learning from Others: Human Capital and Technical Change in Agriculture." *Journal of Political Economy* 103, no. 6 (1995):1176–1209.
Timothy G. Conley and Christopher R. Udry, "Learning about a New Technology: Pineapple in Ghana," *American Economic Review* 100, no. 1 (2010):35–69.

## FOOD SECURITY AND SELF-SUFFICIENCY

Food security is the most fundamental of all human rights and the most basic objective of economic development. Food self-sufficiency is not. The two have nothing to do with each other—as long as markets exist, that is. Ed has a measly garden that yields a few organic greens and herbs, along with an orange or lemon from time to time. Ed is certainly not self-sufficient in food, but he is not food insecure. If something happens that keeps markets from working, however, food security and food self-sufficiency have everything to do with each other.

The point that food security and self-sufficiency are different concepts might seem obvious, but over the years many countries have confused one with the other and launched expensive programs in an effort to achieve self-sufficiency in food production. Japan has strived to achieve self-sufficiency in rice by offering farmers up to ten times the price farmers in other countries get. In 1980, Mexico launched an expensive program called SAM (Sistema Alimentario Mexicano) to reduce its dependence on corn imports. It became so expensive that it was aborted in 2002.

We can use our agricultural household model to learn why self-sufficiency is normally a bad idea. The *Oxford Dictionary* defines self-sufficiency as "needing no outside help in satisfying one's basic needs, especially with regard to the production of food." What happens when our agricultural household has to be self-sufficient?

To explore this question, suppose the household can allocate its fixed resources (for example, land) between two production activities. When Ed conducted surveys in China's Jiangsu Province, he saw many family farms converting some of their rice fields into fish ponds, so let's consider rice cultivation and fish ponds as an example. Land is not perfectly transformable between these two activities; there are likely to be decreasing returns to scale in each one. (If you're smart, you'll dig out your least productive rice land for fish ponds.) The various combinations of rice and fish production the households in a region can produce are given not by a straight line, but instead by a concave production possibilities frontier (PPF), as in figure 9.8. Where the PPF touches the axes, it tells us how much of each good the region could produce if it produced only that good. If we start where it crosses the $x$-axis (the economy is producing only rice) and move along the PPF, we see how much fish could be produced as less rice is produced. The PPF is curved due to diminishing marginal returns: each subsequent unit of fish requires the economy to give up more rice as land more suited to rice cultivation is converted to fish ponds.

Where along the PPF will our households produce? If they are self-sufficient, they will produce exactly as much as they consume. We'll need to bring in an indifference curve to figure out where the optimal production (which equals consumption) choice will be.

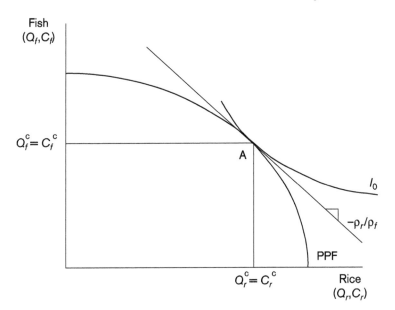

**FIGURE 9.8.** A self-sufficient household will produce at point A, where the marginal rate of transformation in production equals the marginal rate of substitution in consumption. Notice that the production possibility frontier (PPF) takes the place of a household budget constraint.

The slope of the indifference curve $I_0$ in this figure describes the households' trade-off in preferences between rice and fish: how much of one it would *be willing to give up* to get one more unit of the other. The slope of the PPF is its technological trade-off: how much of one good it would *have to give up* in order to *produce* an additional unit of the other. The point of tangency between the two is the optimal solution to the households' problem given self-sufficiency. It is where the slope of the PPF, the marginal rate of transformation (MRT) of rice into fish, equals the MRS of rice for fish. There are no market prices; however, the slope at this optimum equals the (negative of the) ratio of household shadow values, or subjective valuations of rice $(\rho_r)$ and fish $(\rho_f)$.

Suppose now that the households can trade rice and fish at the going market prices of $p_r$ and $p_f$, respectively. The market trade-off between rice and fish is the ratio of these two prices, represented by the price line in figure 9.9.

With a market to trade in, the households no longer have to be self-sufficient in rice or fish. They can sell one and buy the other. The market makes it possible to decouple production from demand, just like you do

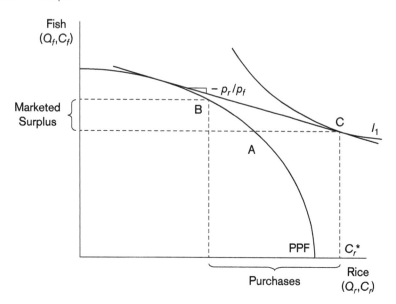

**FIGURE 9.9.** Markets enable the household to increase its welfare by separating its production and consumption decisions.

and just like we do (we being professors who pay other people to grow our food).

On the production side, the households will now equate their MRT with the ratio of market prices. They'll produce at point $B$. Notice that at point $B$ they produce more fish and less rice than when they have to be self-sufficient. Then they can trade along the price line and climb onto the highest indifference curve they can reach. On the consumption side, they'll end up at point $C$. They've produced more fish than they demand and traded fish for rice. As a result, they consume more rice than they could possibly produce: $C_r^*$ is to the right of where the PPF hits the rice axis.

The moral of this story is clear: markets let our household farms trade up to a higher indifference curve ($I_1$) than they could reach if they were constrained to be self-sufficient. In other words, markets improve welfare. This, in a nutshell, is the argument for free trade. We'll come back to this argument (as well as its limitations) in chapter 11. For now, think about how important food markets are to you in your everyday life.

Protective trade policies, like import tariffs and quotas, prevent countries from trading. For agricultural households, prohibitive costs of buying and selling prevent trade. In Tigray in the 1980s, the cost of trading was that you'd likely be shot on sight if you walked the highway. For most agricultural households, it's far less dramatic than that. Poor roads, communications, and information make it too expensive to get produce to or from the market, which might be tens of kilometers away over roads that are impassible part of the year. As Adam Smith wrote, "The division of labor is limited by the extent of the market."[7] The gains to specialization and trade are significant, but they must be preceded by infrastructure and institutions that expand the "extent of the market."

When it comes to food, it turns out that very few households are truly self-sufficient; everyone seems to buy and sell little bits here and there in their village, in weekly markets or through "door-step trade." However, many villages and regions are largely cut off from outside markets. When droughts strike, instead of markets drawing in food from other places, local prices skyrocket, food stocks dwindle, and families' nutrient intake falls. The consequences can be dire and long term, especially for children, as we saw in chapter 6.

Food aid may rush in to try to fill the vacuum. As we'll explore in greater detail in chapter 13, emergency food relief, while of course necessary to keep famines in check, can set back local farming by driving prices to zero. Development practitioners can labor for years helping to develop more vibrant local farm production systems, only to see their efforts set back when drought hits and food aid rushes in.

Imagine an alternative world in which farmers have access to crop insurance and agricultural households are integrated with outside markets. A drought hits, insurance pays off, and the payoff is used to buy food that the market brings in the minute prices begin to rise. At most, the local price of, say, rice, would rise to whatever the world price is at the nearest port, plus the cost of getting the rice out to the village.

In short, food insecurity and its extreme form, famine, are not just a production problem. They are a problem with markets, and ultimately, governments. Amartya Sen, whom we encountered in chapters 1 and 6, focused much of his research on this topic—and earned a Nobel Prize for his work. Oxfam, one of the world's major aid and development organizations, explains it this way:[8] "Famine is the 'triple failure' of (1) food production, (2) people's ability to access food and, finally and most crucially (3) in the political response by governments and international donors. Crop failure and poverty leave people vulnerable to starvation—but famine only occurs with political failure. In Somalia years of internal violence and conflict have been highly significant in creating the conditions for famine."

## INSIDE THE HOUSEHOLD

So far we've been considering households as if they were single, homogeneous units. But in real life, they are a composite of individuals, each with different access to resources and with their own preferences and needs. Human development depends on the distribution of food and other resources within as well as among households. Households bring together groups of individuals, usually family members, who can share in production and consumption. But power asymmetries within households can profoundly influence how resources get allocated. They not only determine who gets to consume what; they also can determine whether households act in ways that can make the pie as big as it can be. In other words, household dynamics can affect efficiency as well as equity.

Nutritionists focus on individuals, not households. A new generation of agricultural household models has emerged that takes into account conflict within households and its ramifications for efficiency as well as equity.

### Nash-Bargained Household Models

In the agricultural household model we just learned about, income was pooled, and consumption decisions were made as though the household acted as a single unit. That model works if the household members share the same preferences. Alternatively, in the "dictator model," one person has all the power, and his or her preferences determine expenditures. We call these "unitary households."

In the Nash-bargained household model, in contrast, different members have different preferences and access to income. (This model is named after Nobel laureate mathematician John Nash, subject of the Hollywood film *A Beautiful Mind*, who invented the game-theoretic model on which it is based.) Household members naturally influence expenditures in ways that reflect their preferences.

How do we model such a household? Two people, person $m$ and person $f$, decide whether to stay single or form a household. Let $v_m$ be person $m$'s utility or welfare if they do not form a household, and let $v_f$ be person $f$'s. If they form a household, they'll combine their income and spend it on things either or both care about. Person $m$'s welfare will be $U_m$ and $f$'s will be $U_f$. Neither one will want to form a household unless there's a positive welfare gain in it, so both $U_m - v_m$ and $U_f - v_f$ must be positive (that is, unless it's a forced marriage).

Once the household is formed, $v_m$ and $v_f$ are "threat points," the utilities that each person would have if they were single. The higher a person's threat point, the more bargaining power he or she has in the Nash-bargained household. Thus, anything that affects a person's threat point can help explain what the household spends its income on. If my threat point is high, I should be able to influence my household's spending in a big way.

What's in a threat point? Lots of things, potentially, but one of them certainly is unearned income. Earned income, like wages, might be affected by what one's spouse earns, but unearned income (from assets, for example) is the same regardless of whether or not a person is part of the household. If I'm independently wealthy, my threat point will be high. If I'm penniless, it will be low.

In a unitary household model it wouldn't matter who had the unearned income because all the income would get pooled. In a Nash-bargained household, it would matter. Who controls the unearned income determines who has the most bargaining power within the household, and therefore how much money gets spent on what. Tests for whether we've got a unitary or Nash-bargained household boil down to this question: Does who controls the non-earned income explain household expenditures? Or is total household income the only thing that matters—that is, a rupee is a rupee, no matter who controls it?

A number of studies find that it does matter who controls the income (see sidebar 9.3). Their findings demonstrate that power asymmetries within households can profoundly affect spending and equity.

### Are Households Efficient?

Does who has control within the household also affect efficiency? When economic power within households is unequal, does this affect the size of the economic pie as well as its distribution?

The Nash-bargained model described above assumes there is no reason why households would not maximize their incomes, even if power relations within households affect expenditures. If I exert a large influence on how my household's income gets spent, shouldn't I try to make that income as large as possible? And if I do not, wouldn't I still want my household's income to be large? Having a little influence over a larger pie is better than having a little influence over a little pie.

**Sidebar 9.3  Who Controls the Cash?**

A number of studies find that it matters who in the household controls income. Using data from a household survey in Brazil, Duncan Thomas tested whether unearned income controlled by fathers and mothers had the same effect on how households spent their money. He found significant differences between the two. Income controlled by mothers had a much bigger positive effect on children's health than income controlled by fathers. The effect of mother's income on child survival probabilities was almost twenty times larger. This is one reason why cash transfer programs in developing countries often give the money to poor women instead of men. (We learned about cash transfer programs in chapter 2). The study also found that mothers are more likely to spend their income on daughters and fathers on sons.

A study from Thailand found that the more property income males had, the more likely they were to marry. But for women, unearned income had the opposite effect. It seems marriage is an "inferior good" for Thai women!

Both of these studies were influential in showing that, at least for some types of research, the assumption of unitary households may not be appropriate.

Duncan Thomas, "Intra-Household Resource Allocation: An Inferential Approach," *Journal of Human Resources* 25, no. 4 (1990):635–64.

T. Paul Schultz, "Testing the Neoclassical Model of Family Labor Supply and Fertility," *Journal of Human Resources* 25, no. 4 (1990):599–634.

This is an important question. If someone in the household could be made better off without making others worse off, the household economy is said to be not Pareto efficient.

Testing whether who controls income and wealth within households affects expenditures is easier than testing whether it affects efficiency. A pioneering study in the African country of Burkina Faso found a way, though. It concluded that power asymmetries within households reduce efficiency. The economic pie in such a context would be larger if women controlled more of the assets (see sidebar 9.4).

### BEYOND HOUSEHOLDS

Households do not exist in isolation from one another. Diverse, heterogeneous households interact within rural economies, like individual

**Sidebar 9.4    Bad to Be a Female Plot**

In many African countries, crops are produced on plots controlled by different members of the household. Pareto efficiency implies that these plots are managed so as to maximize income—that is, make the pie as big as it can be, however it might end up being divvied up. Are household economies Pareto efficient? Chris Udry explored this question using data on male and female plots in Burkina Faso households. If the household is efficient, it will allocate its fertilizer such that the benefit of the last bit of fertilizer (the marginal product) is the same on all plots. Udry's econometric analysis refuted this. It found that plots controlled by women were farmed much less intensively than the male-controlled plots; yields were 30% lower on female plots within the same household. This study was influential because it demonstrated that heterogeneous preferences and access to resources within households affect not only equity, but also efficiency.

Christopher Udry, "Gender, Agricultural Production, and the Theory of the Household," *Journal of Political Economy* 104, no. 5 (October 1996):1010–46.

cells that together make up a complex organism. When a policy, market, environmental, or some other shock strikes one household, its effects reverberate through the economy, like ripples in a pond. The models we have looked at so far in this chapter focus on individual households; they ignore linkages among households.

To illustrate the importance of these linkages, suppose a poor household receives a 100-peso transfer from a government welfare program like the ones we looked at in chapter 2. The immediate effect of the transfer is to raise the poor household's income by the amount of the transfer. But that is not the end of the story, because the poor household spends the money. Suppose it spends 50 pesos to buy meat from a herder in the same village. The herder's income goes up by 50 pesos. So far, the 100-peso transfer has increased village income by 150 pesos. Now suppose that the herder spends half of her new income in the village, hiring a mason to fix her house. The mason now has 25 pesos. As the money circulates through the village, it creates more income. Some of the money leaves the village along the way, contributing to income somewhere else in the country (or world). But the money that stays in the village has a multiplier effect on income in the village. Most people spend most of their income closer to home. If people spend half of their income in the

**Sidebar 9.5    The Mystery of Maize in Mexico**

In 1995, Mexico did away with policies that guaranteed farmers high prices for their maize and other basic crops. The producer price of maize in Mexico immediately fell by around 40%, but this was followed by a record-high maize harvest that couldn't be explained by the weather. Why would maize production increase after the price fell?

A study by three UC Davis economists offered an answer. Most maize producers do not sell their crop; they are subsistence farmers. When the price of maize fell, farmers who were not in the market were not directly affected.

Typically, villages have many subsistence farmers and a few commercial ones. They interact with each other in local labor markets, as subsistence households hire out labor to commercial farms.

When the price shock hit, commercial maize farmers cut back their production and hired less labor. This transmitted a negative impact to the subsistence households, even though they did not sell maize. Unable to find employment, subsistence farmers had to find another use for their labor. Their solution? Grow more maize for home consumption!

The result seemed paradoxical: the price of maize fell, but maize production on subsistence farms increased. The authors refer to this as a "retreat into subsistence." Across Mexico, maize production went up on rain-fed lands, where subsistence farmers are concentrated. Despite higher maize production, though, Mexico's maize farmers were worse off after the price plunge.

George A. Dyer, Steve Boucher, and J. Edward Taylor, "Subsistence Response to Market Shocks," *American Journal of Agricultural Economics* 88, no. 2 (2006):279–91.

village, it can be shown that every peso of income transferred to a poor household ends up creating two pesos of income in the village.

If you have taken a macroeconomics class, you might recognize this story. It is just like the Keynesian income multiplier, which became an important part of economic policies in rich countries following the Great Depression and, most recently, in the United States, "Obamanomics."

A relatively new area of research in development economics takes models of individual households and "nests" them within models of the larger economies of which these households are part: villages, regions, or nations. Economy-wide impacts created by interactions among economic agents, like income multipliers, are called "general equilibrium effects." General equilibrium effects can take many forms, and they can dramatically alter the ways development policies affect incomes, employment, and welfare in poor economies (see sidebar 9.5). We'll look at general equilibrium effects again in chapter 10.

www.rebeltext.org/development/qr9.html
Learn more about agriculture by exploring
multimedia resources while you read.

# Structural Transformation

Poverty and wealth dynamics are fundamental to development economics. In prior chapters, we described how a
household's wealth today can shape its wealth trajectory into
the future. The same can be true for villages or even countries. The dominant driver of these large-scale dynamics is the
transformation of an economy from agriculture to manufacturing and services. Today's developed countries underwent
this transformation in the past century or so. Developing
countries are undergoing this transformation before our
eyes—some at an incredible pace. As a result, for the first
time in human history more people now live in cities than on
farms. This raises new challenges in the form of strain on
already weak infrastructure, environmental pressures and
congestion of different forms, but also opens new opportunities for leveraging economies of scale, spillovers, and
agglomeration effects. In this chapter, we explore the insights
development economists have gained on this fundamental
economic transformation process.

### ESSENTIALS

- Elements of structural transformation
- Dual-economy (Lewis) model
- Migration
- Human capital
- Specialization and diversification
- "Supermarket revolution"
- Market interlinkages

In January 2006 the United Nations Food and Agricultural Organization (FAO) held a workshop called "Beyond Agriculture." To appreciate
how striking this is as a title of an FAO conference, consider the FAO's
mandate: "to raise levels of nutrition, improve agricultural productivity,

better the lives of rural populations and contribute to the growth of the world economy."[1]

For years, with most of the developing world's population living on farms, one could assume these were compatible objectives. For example, high-yielding seeds could raise agricultural productivity, reduce poverty, and provide people with more secure access to food.

The FAO was telling us that wasn't the case anymore.

On May 23, 2007, the world became more urban than rural.[2] That's the day that, according to the United Nations, more than half of the globe's population was living in towns and cities—for the first time ever.[3]

Not only is the world becoming less rural; rural populations are becoming less agricultural. Rural households in Malawi and Ghana still get 55%–56% of their income from crop production, but the crop share is 41% in Vietnam, 21% in Nicaragua, and only 15% in Bangladesh.[4] In Mexico, the share of agriculture in rural household income was 14% in 2002 and 11% in 2007; only around 2% came from corn.[5] In these settings, substantial gains in agricultural productivity may benefit poor households that rely more heavily on agricultural production, but these gains are unlikely to raise the average income for rural households very much when most income is non-agricultural.

The FAO found itself grappling with the question of how to achieve multiple objectives that, in the modern world, are less and less related to one another.

How did we get here?

The growth models in chapter 7 give an aggregate, bird's-eye view of income growth and why some countries grow faster than others. The empirical growth model of Sala-i-Martin suggests that growth involves a complex array of variables, and there may be more than one way to make growth happen. As endogenous growth theorists point out, there are important feedbacks that shape growth in different countries. Economic incentives are important in shaping these feedbacks. Poverty trap models suggest that exogenous "big push" interventions like Jeffrey Sachs's Millennium Village Project are required to kick-start asset accumulation and income growth.

Unfortunately, aggregate models mask far-reaching transformations that have to occur within economies in order to make growth possible and that are themselves a product of growth. Countries start out being mostly agricultural in terms of where people derive their income and where they are employed, with most people living in rural villages. As economies grow, they morph into manufacturing-and-service economies. That is, the structure of the economy changes.

The structural transformation from largely agricultural to non-agricultural societies is one of the most fundamental features of economic development. The Nobel laureate W. Arthur Lewis (whom we will learn about below) called it the heart of the development process. Whatever nostalgia you might have for picturesque farming villages and the rural way of life, you'd better get over it, because economic development leads inescapably to people leaving the farm. (Of course, a society can invest in trying to keep picturesque villages alive, as France has, but it will not be cheap, and not very many people will live in them.)

Figure 10.1 drives home the point. It shows a scatterplot of countries at different levels of per capita income (PPP adjusted, measured on the horizontal axis) and shares of the workforce employed in agriculture (vertical axis). Each country is represented by a ray whose starting point tells us where the country was in 1990 and whose tip shows where it was in 2005. The very top arrow belongs to Burundi, with a per capita income of $620 per year and 94% of the workforce in agriculture. The right-most rays correspond to countries with very high per capita incomes and almost none of their workforces in agriculture. There you would find the United States and even France and Japan, which have expensive government programs to support farmers and rural villages.

As country per capita incomes rise, the share of the workforce in agriculture doesn't just decrease—it drops off a cliff. First, look at how the arrows line up. With no exceptions, the countries with low per capita GDPs have high shares of their workforces employed in agriculture. As per capita incomes rise, the arrows fall sharply, forming a hyperbolic curve. Not only that—almost all the arrows slope toward the southeast. (If you see an exception, there is a unique story behind it, like a resource-extracting country without agriculture, or a former Soviet republic struggling to adjust to a postsocialist existence.)

The sloping arrows tell us that between 1990 and 2005, per capita incomes increased while farm labor shares fell. At high per capita incomes, the arrows converge toward the horizontal axis, where agriculture's share of the workforce is zero. No country ever reaches zero— you can't grow crops without *any* workers. However, some rich countries have agricultural labor shares of 2% or less. Some of the smallest farm workforce shares in the world are in countries with expensive gov-

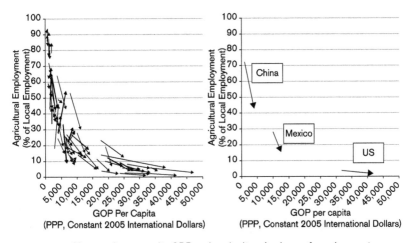

**FIGURE 10.1.** Changes in per capita GDP and agriculture's share of employment, 1990–2005. As countries' per capita incomes increase, the share of the labor force doing farm work decreases. Source: World Development Indicators (WDI), World Bank (http://data.worldbank.org/data-catalog/world-development-indicators).

ernment programs to support agriculture, like the US, the EU countries, or Japan, whose domestic price of rice is as high as seven times the world price.

The right-hand diagram removes all but three of the countries on the graph: China, Mexico, and the United States. China is the economic miracle, with income growth exceeding 10% in some years. You can see that it starts out in 1990 with over 75% of its workforce in agriculture. In 2010, 49% of Chinese workers had farm jobs—and the farm share was falling fast. Mexico began the period with a higher income and a much smaller workforce share in agriculture than China. Its income continued to grow and its farm employment share fell, though at a slower rate than China's. The United States began the period with one of the world's highest per capita incomes and around 2% of its workforce in agriculture. Most hired farmworkers in the United States are from Mexico.[6]

## MODELING THE TRANSFORMATION

In order to understand what drives this economic transformation, we need to dig underneath the aggregate growth numbers we looked at in chapter 7. Multisector models allow us to study the interactions between agriculture and the non-agricultural sectors in an economy, including the movement of people between them. They offer insights into what has to happen to get growth going and how economic growth transforms poor economies. We'll see what development economists have to say about how the transformation from agricultural to industry-and-service economies unfolds and the ramifications for economic development research and policy.

The simplest multisector models involve only agriculture (often called the "traditional sector") and the non-agricultural sectors (the "modern sector"). Because they have only two sectors, these are called dual-economy models. They are a good starting point for learning about interactions between sectors. Today, though, almost all multisector models used in development economics have many different sectors as well as many different actors: households, governments, and others. After learning about two-sector models we'll take a look at multisector models and how they are being used for development policy and research.

*Leaving the Farm*

Francisco is a farmer in a village in southern Mexico.[7] He and his wife Alde have a three-hectare (about 7.5 acre) plot of good land, three sons, and two daughters. A horse, a team of oxen, and some goats and chickens fill out the family.

A construction job opens up in the city of Oaxaca fifty miles away, and a contractor comes to the village to recruit able-bodied villagers willing to work. Francisco and Alde's seventeen-year-old son, Alejandro, asks if he can go. His best friend migrated to Oaxaca a few months earlier. Alejandro reminds his parents that his friend sends home $50 a month to help his family. "I could do the same thing," he assures them.

Should they let him go? Alejandro's fifteen-year-old brother, Ramiro, says he can fill in for Alejandro on the farm. "There isn't enough work for all of us here, anyway," he says.

The next morning Alejandro hops on the bus for Oaxaca.

A month later, Francisco and Alde's daughter Alicia's friend heads off to work in an electronics plant in Tijuana. Alicia says she's already sending back $25 a month to her parents. "I could do that, too," she tells them.

"But if you go, who will watch the animals and help me around the house?" her mom asks.

"I will," her little sister, Silvia, assures her.

The next week, Alicia is gone. Within a month, Francisco and Alde get $75 a month in migrant remittances, the income sent home by their two kids. Not only that, they now have fewer mouths to feed. Ramiro and his dad have no trouble bringing in the harvest, with a little help from the younger daughter, Norma, and her little brother Tomás. The extra income from Alejandro and Alicia helps pay for Norma and Tomás to go to school.

A year later, Alejandro comes back to visit for the fiesta of the Virgen de Guadalupe. "The work's good," he tells Ramiro. "Ever think of going to the city?"

"Don't think of it!" Alde tells them. "Who will help your father in the field?"

"I will!" little Tomás and Norma exclaim in unison. "I'm *never* leaving home!" Norma insists.

Their father shakes his head, knowing all too well that kids with schooling don't stick around the village. "I'm not getting any younger, Ramiro. If you go, I fear there will be no harvest," Francisco sighs.

Ramiro stays, gets married, and his new wife moves into Francisco and Alde's house. Little by little Ramiro takes over the farm, with some financial help from his migrant siblings when there's an investment to be made or when the harvest isn't good. Tomás and Norma both migrate to the city the summer after their high school graduation.

This story is a composite of families all over rural Mexico, and indeed, the world. It's so universal that there's a well-known economic model that describes precisely this story.

### The Lewis Model

The economist W. Arthur Lewis, a Nobel laureate, wrote a famous paper called "Economic Development with Unlimited Supplies of Labor."[8] Lewis looked at the surplus labor in rural areas and recognized its tremendous potential for economic development. He argued that the marginal product of labor in the subsistence sector (agriculture) is virtually zero—or at least very low compared to the "subsistence wage," or what it takes to keep a person alive in the rural economy. This means that, at the margin, agricultural workers produce next to nothing, yet naturally everyone has to consume enough food to survive (a "subsistence bundle"). Think of the subsistence wage, $w_s$, as the cost of this subsistence bundle.

An employer in the city, in theory, only has to offer a wage equal to the cost of subsistence—plus maybe a little extra for the bus fare and the higher urban cost of living—in order to induce a worker to move off the farm and migrate to a modern-sector job.

The power of Lewis's argument is this: workers can move out of the subsistence sector without the economy suffering any loss in agricultural output. In effect, the movement of labor off the farm could provide a seemingly endless supply of labor to the expanding modern (industrial and service) sectors, and farms would still be able to produce the food to feed them (as long as there are good markets to get the food to the city; see chapter 11). As the urban economy expands, urban employers do not have to offer higher wages to get more workers to come, as long as there is a surplus of labor ready to move off the farm. The supply of labor to urban jobs, therefore, is perfectly elastic: the urban labor supply curve is horizontal. If urban capitalists create jobs, the workers will come—from the farm to the city. And if urban wages stay low, this is precisely what capitalists will do. Low wages mean high profits, which in turn can be reinvested to make the urban economy grow even more.

Figure 10.2 illustrates the Lewis model. The horizontal axis in each graph represents labor. The economy starts out with an amount of labor equal to $\bar{L}$, all of it in the traditional (or agricultural) sector. Since the economy starts out with virtually all its labor in the traditional sector, any gain in labor to the modern sector implies a loss of labor from the traditional sector.

The top figure represents agriculture. You should start out at its southeast corner and read from right to left. The curve depicts the marginal value product of labor (MVPL) in agriculture, given the other inputs (land, capital) available to farms. This curve is drawn steeply to reflect sharply decreasing marginal returns to labor under traditional technologies. For the first few workers, the MVPL in agriculture is high. These workers would include Francisco and Ramiro. As more and more people work the land, the contribution of the last worker becomes smaller. Eventually, Lewis argues, it bottoms out at zero; there is surplus labor, and the agricultural MVPL curve flattens out along the horizontal axis. Over the flat range of the MVPL curve, workers can leave the farm without having any adverse effect on agricultural output.

The bottom graph is about the modern (industrial and service) sector. We have to read it from left to right because any gain to the modern-sector workforce implies a loss for the traditional-sector workforce. This figure shows three MVPL curves in the modern sector, each cor-

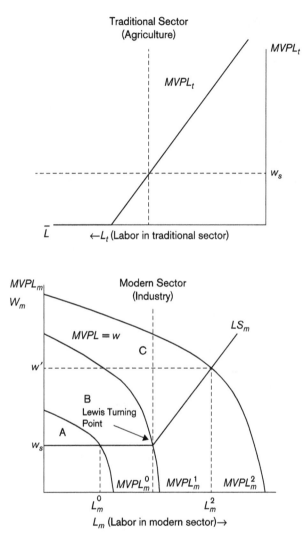

**FIGURE 10.2.** In the Lewis model, as the demand for labor in the modern sector increases (bottom), surplus labor is drawn from the traditional sector (top) without putting upward pressure on wages until the Lewis turning point is reached.

responding to a different level of capital investment. As more capital is invested in new plants and equipment, the MVPL shifts out to the right. Like the MVPL curve in agriculture, each modern-sector MVPL curve is decreasing with labor: an additional worker adds less and less to output at a given level of capital. New investments increase this MVPL, though.

In addition, the bottom graph shows the labor supply (LS) curve for the modern sector. You can also think of it as the wage curve: for each wage (vertical axis), we can read off this curve the amount of labor the traditional sector is willing to supply to the modern sector. It will not supply any labor if the wage is less than subsistence.

Lining the bottom graph up with the top graph, you can see that the modern-sector LS curve is horizontal until the traditional-sector MVPL exceeds the subsistence wage. Over this range, the traditional sector will supply all the labor the modern sector demands—that is, until the labor surplus dries up and the agricultural MVPL rises above the subsistence wage. This is called the "Lewis turning point."

Beyond the Lewis turning point, if more workers leave the farm, the value of agricultural production goes down by more than the subsistence wage. Modern-sector employers will have to pay higher wages to induce more workers to move off the farm. They'll have to convince people like Ramiro. That's why the LS curve turns upward beyond the Lewis turning point.

How much labor will the modern sector hire? The MVPL for the modern sector tells us how much revenue will increase if another worker is hired. The wage line tells us how much industries will have to pay for that additional worker. Modern-sector firms will hire additional workers up to the point where their MVPL just equals the wage they have to pay. The modern sector starts out with a low level of capital, at $MVPL_m^0$, paying a wage equal to $w_s$; thus, it demands $L_m^0$ workers.

The difference between the MVPL and the wage at each level of labor use is the marginal worker's contribution to profit. Cheap labor creates high profits.

For any MVPL curve, profits are the area underneath the curve but above the wage (or labor supply) curve, and wages are the area underneath the wage line. At $MVPL_m^0$, the modern sector's profit is given by area A, and wages are the area of the box defined by $w_s * L_m^0$. Part of this profit is invested in new plant and equipment, which shifts the MVPL curve out to $MVPL_m^1$. You can see that the new profit, depicted by areas A + B, is much larger than the original profit (A). Modern-sector growth, then, is self-perpetuating, as long as a large part of the profit is reinvested.

Eventually, the surplus labor in the traditional sector becomes exhausted. Once the MVPL in agriculture exceeds the subsistence wage, the modern sector has to offer higher wages to attract new workers. At that point, the income distribution begins to shift in favor of labor. At

$MVPL_m^2$, total modern-sector wages are the box given by $w'* L_m^2$, and profits are given by the area above the $w'$ line (C).

With this brief description of the Lewis model under your belt, let's take some time to digest the model, which has been very influential in development economics, policy, and practice. Why exactly was this model important? The Lewis model gets us inside the "black box" of the aggregate growth models we presented in chapter 7. It illustrates what has to happen in order for incomes to grow: the economy has to transition from a traditional, agricultural one to a modern, industrial-and-service one. Growth in the modern sector cannot be understood in isolation from the traditional sector. Lewis pioneered what is known as "dual-economy" or "two-sector" economic models. As income grows, the workforce shifts out of the traditional sector.

The Lewis model is not without its critics or limitations. Theodore Schultz, an economist we met in chapter 9 who shared the Nobel Prize with Lewis, questioned the assumption of a zero marginal value product of labor in agriculture. More generally, Lewis largely ignored the importance of agriculture in his model. An influential study by Gustav Ranis and John C.H. Fei pointed out that agricultural production has to be sufficient to support the whole economy with food and raw materials—otherwise, rising food and raw-materials prices will choke off the expansion of the modern sector.[9] Their work shows the importance of investing in *agriculture* if a country wants its *modern* sector to grow. Agricultural investments can make it possible to produce more with fewer workers, thereby freeing up labor for the growing modern sector.

Although dual-economy models offer new insights into the economic and social transformations accompanying growth in poor economies, they are still aggregate models (though less so than the models in chapter 7). They do not tell us much about what has to happen on a micro level to enable people to move up economically by moving off the farm, or how to feed them once they are in the city. For food to be available to urban workers, markets have to work. Market failures are a quintessential feature of poor countries, especially in rural areas (chapters 11 and 12).

Can countries continue feeding themselves as people leave the farm? The answer to this question depends on farmers' ability to produce more food more efficiently—to raise productivity. Limited access to credit, insurance, and markets for inputs and output severely constrains small farmers' capacity to invest in new technologies and production

**Sidebar 10.1   Can China Feed Itself as People Leave the Farm?**

If agriculture is past the Lewis turning point, farm households cannot sacrifice labor to the nonfarm sector without losing production. A study of agricultural households in the northeast of China found that crop yields fell sharply when family members migrated from farm to nonfarm jobs. However, the study also found that those who left the farm sent home remittances, and remittances, in turn, raised crop yields. This finding suggests that the income family members send home loosens financial constraints on investing in fertilizer and other inputs that raise crop production. This study concluded that, on balance, the migration of labor off the farm has only a small effect on the aggregate supply of food in China.

Scott Rozelle, J. Edward Taylor, and Alan deBrauw, "Migration, Remittances, and Agricultural Productivity in China," *American Economic Review* 89, no. 2 (May 1999):287–91.

activities. Via remittances, family members who migrate can provide farmers with capital they need to raise productivity. There's no place for this kind of feedback of migration on agricultural investment in Lewis's or Fei and Ranis's models.

How does the Lewis model hold up when tested against hard data? Finding data to test how off-farm labor affects crop production is not easy, because few household surveys provide good information on both migration and crop production. The studies that do, though, almost unanimously reject the Lewis hypothesis of zero marginal value product of labor in agriculture. However, they also find that off-farm work may help farmers overcome the lost-labor effect and raise productivity (see sidebar 10.1).

#### FROM FARMER TO FACTORY WORKER

The skill demands of modern-sector jobs are different from those of subsistence production. The Lewis model leaves us with big questions in this regard. There's no human capital in the Lewis model—only hands. (This stands in stark contrast to Schultz, who believed human capital was as important for farmers as it was for anyone else.) Lewis does not offer insights into who leaves the farm and who does not. Do countries have to invest in preparing people to enter nonfarm jobs? Without investments in education, people will not be prepared to work in the modern sector. China had an unusual situation when its market reforms happened: a massive workforce with secondary education, ideal to fill factories with skilled workers and make China the world's workshop. Ireland had a similar situation but at a higher skill level. Its policy of free university education created a very highly trained workforce, and it became the headquarters for many corporations positioning themselves to supply the European Union's markets.

Research shows that the people who migrate off the farm look different from those who stay behind. These differences teach us about the things people—and countries—need in order to make the transition from an agricultural to a manufacturing-and-service economy.

### Who Leaves, Who Stays, and Who Succeeds?

In a happy world, there would be jobs for people wherever they wanted to work, and people would have whatever skills they needed to fill those jobs. Reality is not much like that, even in the best of worlds. A student may love Davis, but the chances of finding a job in a small college town after graduation are low. In poor countries, millions of people leave their villages to work in the city and end up unemployed because they do not have the right skills, the jobs aren't there, or they just aren't in the right place at the right time. The transition from agricultural to industrial-and-service economies involves huge dislocations and wrenching adjustments. Hundreds of millions of people move off the farm and have to compete and live in a very different, urban, world. As populations shift from rural- to urban-based activities, pressures on food production and public services in urban areas increase. Many people—though a tiny minority of the world's population—migrate to other countries.

Industry and service jobs may not materialize because investors do not believe that workers with the right skills will be available. In the 1989 Hollywood movie *Field of Dreams,* an Iowa corn farmer (Kevin Costner), hearing voices, interprets them as a command to build a baseball diamond in his fields; he does, and the players come. Good players. If you build a factory, will the right workers come?

In the story of Francisco and Alde, Alejandro and Alicia both migrate to nonfarm jobs, one in construction, the other in an electronics factory. In real life, can *any* kid raised for farm work simply shift over to a nonfarm job? How did Francisco know that his two youngest kids would migrate away as soon as they finished school?

The Lewis model doesn't answer the questions of who migrates and who does not, or whether factories in the city can get the quantity as well as the quality of labor they need. Instead, it treats workers as homogeneous and ignores human capital.

Human capital theory (see chapter 6) can help us answer these questions. Econometric evidence confirms that there are significant and high economic returns to education in the modern sector—higher than in farmwork. At the very least, basic literacy, and possibly schooling beyond the primary level, may be required for a person to become a productive factory worker.

If this is true, then a human capital migration model would predict that people with more schooling are more likely to migrate from the traditional to the modern sector. Empirical studies consistently find this to be the case (for example, see sidebar 10.2).

## THE "DE-AGRICULTURALIZATION" OF RURAL ECONOMIES

As people move off the farm, rural households diversify their income sources. A poor rural household in Burundi is likely to get most or all of its income from farming. But in Latin America, Asia, and increasingly even sub-Saharan Africa, it is hard to find households that specialize in farming. Most are income diversifiers. Table 10.1 illustrates this for several countries in Africa, Asia, and Latin America.

It is clear from these data that when we think "rural" we should not automatically think "agricultural." To end up with average shares as high as these, many households must have nonfarm income shares that are very high indeed.

High shares of non-agricultural income in rural households have important implications for development policies as well as for research. The following sections discuss two of the most important ones.

### Productivity and Poverty

If poor rural households get a large share of their income from agricultural production, raising agricultural productivity could have a big effect on poverty. In general, poor rural households get a larger share of their income from agriculture the poorer a country is. However, in a transforming rural economy, raising agricultural productivity and raising rural incomes become different policy goals—even when it comes to poor households. For example, take a poor household that gets

### Sidebar 10.2   Who Migrates and Who Doesn't?

A study using survey data from rural Mexico found that migration is highly selective: the characteristics of those who migrate off the farm are different from those who stay, in ways consistent with human capital theory. As in the story of Francisco and Alde, migration seems to be a household strategy. Household heads are significantly less likely to migrate to the city than their children. Each year of additional schooling raises the likelihood that a child migrates by 0.6%. This is not a small effect considering that 7% of all rural Mexicans were found to be internal migrants. (Another 6.7% were international migrants, working in the United States.) An additional year of work experience also increases the likelihood of migration. Thus, a child with ten years of schooling and work experience is more than 11% more likely to migrate to the city than a person without any schooling or experience. The probability of migrating is lower for women than men, and it is lower the more land the family has (why?). If one family member migrates, the likelihood of another family member migrating rises. Each family migrant raises the odds that another family member will migrate by 3.5%. Thus, migration is a network-driven process.

Human capital theory would predict that schooling would have the largest effect on migration to jobs where it raises workers' productivity the most. The study found that higher schooling *decreased* the likelihood of migrating to farm jobs. Schooling was found to have *no significant effect* on the likelihood of migrating to the United States. Most people who migrate from rural Mexico to the United States do so illegally, and education does not help much if you're working abroad as an undocumented immigrant. Schooling significantly *increased* the likelihood of migrating to urban areas within Mexico, however.

Jorge Mora and J. Edward Taylor, "Determinants of Migration, Destination, and Sector Choice: Disentangling Individual, Household, and Community Effects," in *International Migration, Remittances, and the Brain Drain,* edited by Çağlar Özden and Maurice Schiff (New York: Palgrave Macmillan, 2005), 21–52.

20% of its income from growing and selling staples. Suppose a new technology (say, a Green Revolution seed variety) raises staple productivity by 10% for this poor household. How much will its income go up? The immediate effect of the new technology will be to raise this household's income by 10% * 20% = 2%. In other words, the income

TABLE 10.1 NONFARM INCOME SHARES OF SELECTED LDCS

| Country | Year of Survey | Nonfarm Income Share |
|---|---|---|
| Mozambique | 1991 | 15 |
| Gambia | 1985–86 | 23 |
| Malawi | 2004 | 23 |
| Tanzania | 1980 | 25 |
| Nigeria | 1974/75 | 30 |
| Rwanda | 1990 | 30 |
| Vietnam | 2002 | 37.7 |
| Sudan | 1988 | 38 |
| Ghana | 1998 | 39.1 |
| Nicaragua | 2005 | 43.1 |
| Guatemala | 2000 | 50 |
| Mozambique' | 1988-89 | 59 |
| Bangladesh | 2000 | 63.1 |
| South Africa (former homelands) | 1982/86 | 75 |
| Botswana | 1985/86 | 77 |
| Lesotho | 1976 | 78 |
| Kenya | 1987/89 | 80 |

SOURCES: Thomas Reardon, "Using Evidence of Household Income Diversification to Inform Study of the Rural Nonfarm Labor Market in Africa," *World Development* 25, no. 5 (1997):735–47; Erik Jonasson, Mateusz Filipski, Jonathan Brooks, and J. Edward Taylor, "Modeling the Welfare Implications of Agricultural Policies in Developing Countries," *Journal of Policy Modeling* 36, no. 1 (2014): 63–82.

effect is much smaller than the production effect. In time, the household might be able to put more effort into staple production and get a higher return from the new seeds. But the point is clear: in a rural economy where a large share of income does not come from growing staples, raising productivity in staples might not be the best way to move households out of poverty.[10]

In a diversified economy, households' income sources can span different activities as well as different locations. The key to moving out of poverty might well be to move out of agriculture and into higher paying non-agricultural jobs. Policies that stimulate non-agricultural activities inside rural areas, or that encourage kids to go to school so they can grow up to have nonfarm jobs, can play an important role in combating rural poverty. So can employment growth in urban areas, which may benefit poor urban households as well as rural households, through migration. Keeping ties with rural households might be an important form of livelihood insurance for migrants in distant labor markets.

### Consumers versus Producers

Some countries try to support their rural households by offering farmers artificially high prices for their crops. In many cases, this means that crop producers get higher prices, but consumers pay more for food. Agricultural households are both producers and consumers of food. We saw in chapter 9 that when the price of food goes up, these households win as producers but lose as consumers. If only a small share of income comes from food production, the consumption effect will outweigh the production effect, and higher food prices will hurt rural (as well as urban) households. Many rural households do not have land and do not grow crops at all. For them, like urban consumers, higher food prices are almost certainly welfare-reducing. Never assume that higher food prices are necessarily good for rural households, particularly the rural poor.

Another implication of diversification away from agriculture concerns the benefits of technological change. Consider a new technology, like a high-yielding seed, that raises crop productivity. If everyone is a farmer, the main benefits of this new technology will be on farms. As more and more people move away from farming, they benefit indirectly, through lower food prices.

### Who Diversifies and Who Doesn't?

Economists often talk about the gains from specializing. The economist David Ricardo advised countries to specialize in producing goods in which they enjoy a "comparative advantage" and trading to get whatever else they wish to buy. As rural economies diversify, it is natural to ask whether the same advice applies to rural households. Mark Twain once said: "Put all your eggs in one basket—and watch the basket." Clearly, most rural households do not follow Twain's advice. Should they?

An economist would look at diversification and conclude that it is welfare-maximizing. Otherwise, why would households diversify? Or maybe households would like to specialize wherever their comparative advantage lies, but for some reason they cannot. Perhaps there is a market failure or some other barrier to maximizing income. (Market failures will be a topic of chapters 11 and 12.)

An action can be welfare (or constrained-welfare) maximizing even if it does not maximize income. For example, a household might be willing to sacrifice income in order to reduce income risk. In that case, its welfare depends not only on expected income but also on income uncertainty, which might be measured by the variance of income or the probability that income will fall below some minimum subsistence threshold. Does aversion to risk prevent poor households from making the investments needed to lift themselves out of poverty? This is an important question in development economics.

What is the relationship between diversification and income? The answer to this question depends on why households diversify. Are they "pushed" into diversifying for some reason other than to increase their income? Or are they "pulled" into diversifying because they can get higher income by investing in non-agricultural activities?

The "diversity push" view mostly emphasizes risk. A poor farmer could put all his effort and cash into crop production, but if the crop fails, he will not be able to put food on the table for his family. Poor farmers around the world lack any access to crop insurance. If the crop fails, that's it. Diversification allows a poor household to fall back on its other income sources should the crop fail.

The "diversity pull" view stresses diminishing marginal returns in crop production or intra-household considerations. Beyond a point, the more you invest in crop production, the smaller the marginal returns to that investment—whether it is cash spent on fertilizer or family labor. If a farmer could earn more by working an additional day for a wage or in some noncrop production activity than in his own fields, it makes sense for her to diversify into wage work, or noncrop production. The same applies to different family members. A strong son with little schooling might be a productive crop producer but have few prospects as a factory worker, whereas his sibling (sister, perhaps) with secondary schooling would be ill-placed in the fields.

These two theories of why households diversify provide different hypotheses, which might be testable using survey data. If the diversity push view is right, we would expect that households most vulnerable to risk (and with the least access to other forms of income security) would

**Sidebar 10.3    Do Nonfarm Activities Increase Inequality?**

A survey of findings from several African countries found that many rural households diversify into nonfarm activities, including nonfarm rural enterprises like food processing that rely on agriculture for inputs. In most areas, nonfarm wage work and nonfarm production generate higher income than agricultural work, and they constitute an important part of rural household incomes. However, poor households face severe barriers to entry into these nonfarm activities. Taking a chance on a nonfarm investment entails risks and requires capital, both financial and human. Getting access to a nonfarm wage job requires schooling and skills. These are all things that the poorest households generally cannot afford. Thus, most of the gains from diversifying into nonfarm activities bypass the poor, and as a result, off-farm income increases inequalities in rural areas.

Thomas Reardon, "Using Evidence of Household Income Diversification to Inform Study of the Rural Nonfarm Labor Market in Africa," *World Development* 25, no. 5 (1997):735–47.

diversify, and this would lead to lower incomes relative to households less vulnerable to risk. If the diversity pull view is correct, we would expect diversification into noncrop activities to be associated with higher incomes. That's what a survey of research findings from African countries found—but not everyone can diversify into nonfarm activities (see sidebar 10.3).

### The Transformation of Agriculture and the National Economy

The economist Peter Timmer identified four stages of the transformation of agriculture and its role in national economies.[11] First, agricultural productivity per agricultural worker begins to rise, creating an economic surplus. Second, this surplus is tapped in ways discussed in chapter 9 (taxes, surplus labor migrating to the city, or government price policies). The second stage is the main focus of the dual-economy models, like the Lewis model. In stage 3, the agricultural sector becomes increasingly integrated with other sectors of the economy. This happens as markets develop, linking agriculture with the urban economy, and also as the rural economy diversifies into non-agricultural activities, as

**Sidebar 10.4  The Supermarket Revolution**

Supermarkets used to be the rich country consumer's place to shop, but not any longer. In Asia, Latin America, and Africa, the spread of supermarkets is transforming food markets within and across countries. And the transformation is happening fast. The supermarket growth that took five decades in the United States happened in a single decade in Latin America; by 2000, supermarkets there accounted for 50%–60% of total retail food sales. In East and Southeast Asia it is happening even faster. It is just beginning to unfold in some African countries.

The supermarket transformation of agricultural markets has big implications for economic development and development policy. Can small farmers compete in a world dominated by Walmart and other big players with centralized procurement, for whom quality and timing are paramount? How can development projects help small producers, processors, and traders succeed in this new world instead of being excluded from new market opportunities? As the leading economist studying supermarkets and development, Thomas Reardon and his colleagues write: "Development models, policies, and programs need to adapt to this radical change. Development agencies must understand that 'product markets' will mean 'supermarkets'" (p. 1140). "Market oriented programs and policies" will in fact be "supermarket-oriented" (p. 1146).

Thomas Reardon, C. Peter Timmer, Christopher B. Barrett, and Julio Berdegué, "The Rise of Supermarkets in Africa, Asia, and Latin America," *American Journal of Agricultural Economics* 85, no. 5 (2003): 1140–46.

discussed earlier in this chapter. Eventually, in stage 4, agriculture is just another sector of the economy. As Timmer writes: "The role of agriculture in industrialized economies is little different from the role of the steel, housing, or insurance sectors" (p. 6).

Even in poor countries, it is important to view agriculture in the context of an increasingly diversified and integrated national economy. Perhaps the most concrete way to appreciate the transformation of agriculture in developing countries is through a place you have likely patronized at least once in the past month: a supermarket (see sidebar 10.4).

As we shall see next, viewing agriculture as one of many interacting sectors in a complex economic system changes the way we think about, and model, developing economies.

## RURAL-URBAN LINKAGES

In chapter 9 we learned about the how important agricultural development is to the urban economy. In this chapter we met W. Arthur Lewis,
who demonstrated agriculture's importance as a source of labor to the
expanding urban industrial sector. Then we met Gustav Ranis and
John Fei, who used a dual-economy model to show how agricultural
production has to keep up with the demand for food and raw materials
in the rest of the economy. In 1976, John Mellor—then an economics
professor at Cornell University—showed that the rural economy was
critical in another respect: poor countries depend on demand in rural
households to provide a market for the goods produced in the urban
sector.[12]

From these and other studies a new picture of developing economies
emerged. Economists began to recognize that the rural and urban economies of developing countries become integrated in complex ways.
Each sector depends upon the other. A shock in one sector gets transmitted to the other. A poor harvest adversely affects urban households
through high food prices. An expansion in urban employment affects
agricultural households by drawing workers off the farm; these workers, in turn, share part of their urban earnings with rural households,
through migrant remittances.

Market linkages between sectors play a useful role in economies by
diffusing the impacts of shocks through the whole economy. To give an
example, in chapter 5 we saw that when a drought hit agricultural
households in Burkina Faso, remittances from migrants increased
sharply to help compensate for the rural income loss. In chapters 11,
12, and 13 we'll learn about the important role markets and international trade can play in helping people adjust to adverse shocks.

Connections between rural and urban households do not always lead
to beneficial outcomes, however. For example, you would think that people would not migrate to cities if work was not available there—but in
practice many choose to migrate despite high urban unemployment. In
the 1950s and 1960s, governments became overwhelmed by rising urban
unemployment and, at the same time, urban population growth fed by
increasing streams of rural-to-urban migrants. Urban slums proliferated.
Government revenues could not keep up with the demand for public services, from sanitation to schools. By the end of the 1990s, one slum in
Mumbai, India, covered 175 acres with a population density of an

astounding 1,200 people per acre![13] By 2003, nearly a third of the world's urban population—almost 1 billion people—lived in slums, according to the United Nations.[14] In many of the world's slums, most people live in makeshift dwellings on land they are not authorized to occupy.[15]

Increasing rural-to-urban migration in the face of rising urban unemployment does not make any sense in the models of Lewis and Ranis and Fei. Why leave the farm and migrate to a city in search of jobs that aren't there?

In 1970, economists John Harris at MIT and Michael Todaro at the University College of Nairobi came up with an explanation for this seemingly irrational behavior.[16] When deciding whether or not to migrate, people compare their expected wage in the city to their marginal value product on the farm. The expected wage is the actual wage times the probability of finding a job. For example, if the going wage for a migrant worker in the city is $6 per day, and a new migrant has a 50-50 chance of getting a job at that wage, her expected wage is 50% × $6 = $3. If the income she could generate on the farm is less than $3, she will migrate; otherwise, she will stay on the farm. (In real life, other considerations factor into the migration decision, including the economic and psychic costs of moving.) That's why migration happens even if the urban unemployment rate is high.

The Harris-Todaro model shows how a rational decision by an individual to migrate to the city can lead to an outcome that is inefficient for society. If a person can produce something on the farm but migrates to a crowded city slum and ends up unemployed, society obviously would be better off if he had not migrated.

It also has big policy implications. What should governments do to reduce urban unemployment? Create new jobs in the city? That will raise the probability of employment and bring more migrants in, driving the unemployment rate back up again. A country would be better off creating jobs for people in rural areas.

Many topics in the development economics literature fall under the "rural-urban linkages" area. They include the functioning of labor markets, the role of the informal economy, entrepreneurship and microenterprises, slums, the creation of infrastructure, migrant remittances and their impacts, and the sustainability of cities. New approaches that make creative use of technology and people will be critical if poor countries hope to accommodate their expanding urban populations (sidebar 10.5).

**Sidebar 10.5 Smart Cities**

Cities in developing countries will have to absorb enormous new populations in the next two decades, including an additional 350 million people in China, 250 million in India, and 380 million in Africa. How they do that will shape how people interact in their urban environments, how livable cities will be (and for whom), the competitiveness of cities and nations, and the environment—80% of global carbon emissions now come from cities. Anyone who has breathed the air in Cairo or Beijing or sat in a São Paulo or Nairobi traffic jam understands how daunting the challenge is.

Making cities "smart" is the key to responding to this challenge. In rich countries the term "smart cities" conjures up images of intelligent buildings, thousands of networked devices gathering real-time information, even sensors in trash cans to tell garbage collectors where to go. In poor countries, smart development means delivering more services to more people in a more efficient and effective way, using whatever technology is available at the moment. Invariably, this means involving citizens in planning, managing, and collaborating with local governments to provide better services. For example, the touch of a smartphone app can take the place of a remote sensor to provide information that is fed into systems to improve the design and delivery of urban services.

World Bank, "Building Smarter Cities" (https://blogs.worldbank.org/ic4d/building-smarter-cities).

World Bank, "Urban Development" (www.worldbank.org/en/topic/urbandevelopment).

## BEYOND THE DUAL ECONOMY: ECONOMY-WIDE MODELS IN DEVELOPMENT

Empirical research using survey data finds that rural households engage in an array of farm and nonfarm activities as well as rural-to-urban migration. Urban economies are more complex, with a large number of interacting production sectors, factors, labor types, and households. An economy is really a complex organism, a vast marketplace in which millions and millions of decisions by a diversity of actors lead to both aggregate (for example, national) and micro (for example, household-level) economic outcomes. The interplay of demand and supply determines both prices and quantities of goods as well as factors of production.

Both aggregate growth models and dual-economy models miss these complex interactions, which are the essence of modern economies. Over the past quarter-century, a new breed of economy-wide models has emerged to enable researchers to simulate the ways in which development policies impact whole economies and the actors within them. These models are called "computable general equilibrium" (CGE) models, and they have become a staple of development policy analysis.

CGE models are complex, and building one is beyond the scope of this text.[17] Like climate models and even computer games, constructing CGE models requires having an understanding of the system being modeled (in this case, the workings of the economy) and the mathematical and programming skills to create the simulation model.

Nevertheless, development economics students, researchers, and practitioners are likely to come across them at some time or another, so having a basic understanding of how they work has become an essential of development economics. Mary Burfischer, in the preface to her "how-to" book on CGE modeling, writes: "A CGE model is a powerful analytical tool that can help you to gain a better understanding of real-world economic issues. . . . Economists today are using these models to systematically analyze some of the most important policy challenges and economic 'shocks' of the twenty-first century, including global climate change, the spread of human diseases, and international labor migration" (p. xiii).

*The Anatomy of a CGE Model*

So what is a CGE model? Actually, we already saw a miniature one in chapter 9. An agricultural household model, estimated with real-world data, is a CGE model for a very small economy: that of a household farm. It includes both supply and demand. If agricultural households are involved in many different kinds of activities, both farm and non-farm, the household-farm model can be expanded to include these activities. Then it is a multisector model. A household-farm model can be used to simulate the impacts of policies and other shocks on the agricultural economy.

Now imagine combining a household-farm model with similar models of *all* producers and consumers in the national economy. There would be models for urban as well as rural households, and urban firms as well as rural household farms. Most CGE models are national. Some even link models of several nations into an international CGE model.

They commonly include several different household groups and scores of different production sectors.

To a non-expert, CGE models are likely to seem like complex black boxes. In this sense, they are like any simulator, from flight simulators to *World of Warcraft* (or whatever your favorite computer game is). All involve a set of equations describing the behavior of the system they are simulating. For example, a flight simulator contains equations describing the physics of flight and aerodynamics. As long as these equations are correct, the simulator can teach pilots how to fly. Similarly, a CGE model with equations describing the behavior of an economy can teach us how economies function, how they evolve over time, and how they adjust when "shocked" by a policy, market, or environmental change. Of course, in many ways an economy with millions of consumers and producers is more complex than flying an airplane, so these simulations—like all models—are not perfect. But even imperfect simulators can be quite useful.

A CGE model is an "economy-wide model" because it is created to represent the economic behavior and interactions among *all* of the actors in an economy, producers as well as consumers.

Let's take a brief tour through a typical CGE model to see how it works, using the tools we already know from microeconomics courses and previous chapters of this book.

### Producers (Firms or Farms)

The behavior of producers in a CGE model is represented by production functions describing the technologies that combine inputs to produce output (for example, Cobb-Douglas production functions), as well as the classic conditions for profit maximization: that firms demand inputs at the point where their marginal value products just equal their prices. Each sector in the economy has its own set of equations in the model.

To produce output, firms purchase inputs. Payments for intermediate inputs become demands for the output of other firms. The income firms generate, above and beyond these intermediate input costs, is the firms' value-added, which we saw in chapter 3 adds up to a country's GDP. Firms also pay taxes, for example, sales taxes, also called "indirect taxes." They also may save (retained earnings). At the end of the day, each firm's total revenue must equal its total expenditures; all of the money has to go somewhere.

## Households

The value-added generated by firms gets channeled into households, in the CGE model as in the real world. It, along with any other income households might receive, determines households' budget constraints. Expenditure functions in a CGE model describe how households spend their income, as a function of their income as well as prices. The equations describing households' expenditures are derived from the maximization of household utility functions, subject to the budget constraint. In addition to demanding goods and services, households save and pay taxes (called "direct taxes"). At the end of the day, households' total expenditures must equal their total income (plus borrowing). Each household group in the economy has its own set of expenditure equations in a CGE model, and sometimes there are many different groups, depending on the model's focus. Households can be grouped using many different criteria, for example, by their main economic activities, demographic makeup, ethnicity, location, or poverty status.

## Governments

The taxes paid by firms and households determine the government's budget constraint. Governments use their income (often supplemented by borrowing) for many purposes, most of which involve demanding goods and services in the economy or transferring income back to households.

## Investors

Savings by households and firms (perhaps supplemented by other sources, including foreigners) turn into investments. Investments, in turn, create a demand for goods and services in the economy. For example, construction investment involves the purchase of materials as well as labor and capital.

For every economic agent, total income must equal total expenditures. This fundamental identity of economics is critical in building CGE models, just like the input-output model in chapter 3.

When incomes increase, so do the demands by households, government, and investors, and this stimulates the production of goods and services in the larger economy, which in turn creates new incomes, and so on. Everyone is part of the circular flow of goods, income, and spending in an economy. As in any ecosystem, an exogenous shock to any

### Sidebar 10.6 Climate Change and Poverty

A team of economists and climatologists at Purdue and Stanford Universities used a CGE model to study the effects of climate change on poor households in fifteen different developing countries. Climate change alters crop yields. This can affect poor households directly, if they grow crops, as well as indirectly, by changing food prices. Even poor urban households, which are not involved in crop production, may suffer if food prices rise.

Understanding the impacts of climate change on poverty requires a systems approach that integrates climate science with CGE modeling. Climate simulation models give us predictions of the effects of climate change on key variables affecting crop yields, particularly temperatures and rainfall. These climate predictions are used as inputs into CGE models, which then simulate the impacts of the resulting crop production changes on the incomes of different household groups as well as the prices they must pay for food and related products.

Under one climate change and food production scenario, prices for major staples rise 10% to 60% by 2030. The effects of these higher food prices on poverty are different in different countries. In some non-agricultural household groups, the poverty rate rises by 20% to 50% in parts of Africa and Asia. Meanwhile, in other parts of Asia and in Latin America, some households specializing in agriculture actually gain as a result of climate change. Climate change, like most everything else in life, creates winners as well as losers.

This study was unique in bringing together experts in CGE modeling and climate science. Its findings have been influential in alerting policy makers to the adverse effects climate change is likely to have on poverty. The CGE findings also offer insights into where government policies might focus their efforts to protect the most vulnerable households from the negative effects of climate change.

Thomas W. Hertel, Marshall B. Burke, and David B. Lobell, "The Poverty Implications of Climate-Induced Crop Yield Changes by 2030," *Global Environmental Change* 20, no. 4 (2010):577–85.

part of the economy reverberates through the economic system, carrying impacts from one actor to another.

A CGE model "solves" to find the set of prices and quantities at which the economy is in equilibrium. This is the point at which the quantity supplied equals the quantity demanded for all goods and factors, like at an enormous auction.

Once we have a CGE "base model," we can use it to run experiments. For example, we can ask what is likely to happen if the government implements a particular policy, if there is a change in world food prices, or if climate change reduces crop production. Each of these policies "shocks" the CGE model and throws it out of equilibrium, but the model adjusts, through a series of iterations, to find a new equilibrium set of prices, quantities, and incomes. If the model is detailed enough, it can show us how different shocks are likely to affect different production sectors and household groups, as well as the overall economy (see sidebar 10.6).

www.rebeltext.org/development/qr10.html
Learn more about transformation by exploring
multimedia resources while you read.

11

# Information and Markets

International development debates, just like domestic policy debates in most countries, often reveal how much we trust markets, on the one hand, and governments, on the other, to improve society. Framing these debates as either–or may be good political strategy, but it is often a false dichotomy that is ultimately not very helpful. To function efficiently, markets rely on a host of institutions, many of which require some form of government intervention to offset basic market failures. Conditions in developing countries frequently magnify these market failures. Development economists must appreciate how markets function in practice in poor countries and where they fail to function well, because these market failures can prevent the poor from reaping the big benefits markets can bring—benefits that planning without markets could never match.

### ESSENTIALS

- Specialization and diversification
- Market integration and efficiency
- Institutions and transaction costs
- Market failures: asymmetric information
- Subsistence goods and shadow values
- Market failures: externalities and public goods
- The "knowledge problem"

Imagine you wake up one day and there are no markets. Not for food or other stuff. No credit, either—not that it would matter, without access to goods to spend money on. You'd eat whatever your plot of land gave you—no more, no less. You would be *your own* market; your internal balance of supply and demand would determine how much you consume and produce.

It also would determine how much you value things. If you're running low on food, you'd value it highly. In economics jargon, your

**Sidebar 11.1 Famine and Missing Markets in Tigray**

Between 1983 and 1985 a widespread famine took more than four hundred thousand lives in northern Ethiopia. The blame for the famine often is put on drought. However, the drought did not strike until months after the famine was already under way. In fact, as northern Ethiopia suffered famine, record harvests were reported in other parts of the country. Civil conflict against the Derg government and repressive policies shut down rural markets, forcing peasant households into self-sufficiency. When record low rainfall hit, markets could not function to fill the region's food deficit, and the rural population was left without access to food.

In January 2012 Ed visited a village in Tigray, the hardest hit province. The village had only a few hundred inhabitants, but this was market day. Thirty thousand people filed in from smaller villages as far away as twenty miles, all on foot. The line of people coming and going stretched off into the distance as far as he could see. Some hoisted bags of grain over their shoulders, others carried bags of produce or bunches of live chickens bound at their feet, and a few led goats on leashes fashioned from rope.

Ed asked his guide, an official in the state government, what this market looked like during the famine years. He sighed and said, "You do not understand. The soldiers would not let anyone walk the roads then. There was no market."

Alex de Waal, *Evil Days: Thirty Years of War and Famine in Ethiopia* (New York and London: Human Rights Watch, 1991), and personal interviews in Tigray province.

"shadow price" of food would be high. If your plot produces too many tomatoes, your shadow price of tomatoes will be low.

I don't know about you, but I'd be in serious trouble without a food market. When people in Tigray province, Ethiopia, lost their access to food markets in 1983, the result was catastrophic (see sidebar 11.1).

Things would be better if we could get everyone in town together and form a market. You grow food, we do something else (like teach economics!). Someone else could make us candles, and others could bake us bread (assuming there's wax and wheat around), fire bricks, or carve furniture (assuming there's wood to be had). Having a local market, we could all begin to specialize.

With more far-flung markets, we'd get access to stuff we couldn't possibly produce locally and be able to sell stuff we produce best or have too much of. Tomatoes could be rotting on the vine in your yard, but in a mill town in the next valley over there might be a tomato shortage. They'd pay dearly for your tomatoes and you for their wood, if only the two of you could discover one another, get together, and trade.

These insights about how the size of a market shapes incentives to specialize is a fundamental economic truth, but markets demand more than just buyers and sellers. Markets are based on specialization and trade, which require coordination and information. Buyers and sellers need to know about each other. If your "thing" is doing carpentry, you need to know where your buyers are and, in turn, where to get the food you'll need to eat.

One way to coordinate production across space is through centralized planning, as in the former Soviet Union and pre-reform China. Central planners faced an enormous task: coordinating production and demand across millions of producers and consumers and typically very large spaces (those countries were big!). They turned out not to be very good at it, as evidenced by their persistent use of rationing (exemplified by the long bread lines in Moscow in the 1960s), their inefficiency, and ultimately the demise of large centrally planned economies altogether.

Interestingly, large corporations in the world today face serious coordination challenges reminiscent in some ways of the ones faced by centrally planned economies. (Imagine the coordination it takes to make a Boeing 747!) Over the years, corporations have tended to oscillate between having highly centralized and decentralized decision models. They have come up with innovations to deal with their information and coordination demands, including structures that mimic markets and, of course, extensive use of computers and the Internet to track and coordinate activities.

Since ancient times, markets have been the answer to overcoming local resource constraints and gaining access to new goods. Archeologists have uncovered prolific evidence of ancient trade. For example, ceramic pottery and silver coins from fifth-century Athens are still being unearthed all around the Mediterranean Sea, from Egypt to Sicily. In ancient Athens, the Long Walls connected the city to its port, Pireaus, so that citizens would never be cut off from trade by sea, which provided most of the Athenians' food supplies. When Athens did lose control of the sea in the Peloponnesian War (404 BC), it quickly fell to Sparta and its allies—a vivid illustration of how critical access to markets is.

Today, markets are seen as the key to economic efficiency even in the world's former centrally planned economies. Why is this?

The Nobel laureate economist Friedrich August von Hayek had a simple answer to this question. He argued that markets effectively pool information from many different sources—more than any single person could easily understand—into a convenient measure of market conditions: a price (see sidebar 11.2). To most people, a price is nothing more than what you pay to buy something or what you get from selling it. To an economist, prices aggregate and convey information more effectively than any one person (or computer for that matter) could. A high price tells producers there is excess demand for their good, so they should produce more, and it tells consumers to cut back and seek out consumption substitutes. High input prices tell producers to seek out input substitutes while creating incentives for others to develop these substitutes. As we will see, this insight about markets has important implications for development policy and practice.

Markets are critical to economic welfare because they bring together sellers and buyers, integrate vast amounts of information, and distill that information into prices. In rich countries life would be unimaginable without access to a wide array of reasonably well functioning markets, from food to credit and insurance. It is almost never the case that a rich-country household has to produce something in order to consume it, or that its members cannot sell their labor for a salary or wage. Credit markets function for small businesses and farms to finance their investment projects. People pop out credit cards for convenience, to get through a tough time, or to buy things they can't afford at the moment. Insurance markets help protect people from unexpected income and health shocks. Every day more and more people interact in "virtual marketplaces," where buyers and sellers find each other and transact online, like on eBay and Amazon.com.

Missing markets create inefficiency. When markets don't work, prices vary from one place to another. Wages are high in my town but low in yours; food prices are low in my town but outrageously high in yours; I lack a forest but you have cheap wood. Almost nothing catches an economist's eye more quickly than price differences across space, because of the obvious efficiency implications. Widely varying prices for the same goods suggest that there is poor market integration and an opportunity to increase the economic pie for everyone.

Access to markets is just as compelling for a poor rural household in Rwanda, India, or Peru as for someone in a high-income country. With-

## Sidebar 11.2    All in One Price

As a number of countries were experimenting with centrally planned economies, Friedrich von Hayek was looking "inside" prices. What he found there can tell us a lot about why centrally planned economies failed and why, without well-functioning markets, the economic prospects for poor societies are dim.

Think of anything that can shift around a supply or demand curve: changing technology, population, ethnicity of consumers, people's expectations, government policies, the weather, a war, the Internet, whatever. So many things that it's impossible to keep track of them all. Yet in a market, the intersection of supply and demand determines the price. If any of the multitude of things affecting supply or demand changes, we see it in the price. The Beatles said, "All you need is love." Economists say, "All you need is price." That's why market economies are better coordinated than centrally planned economies.

The price system, Hayek argued, is a "communications network" and the most efficient means of making use of economic information. It transmits information from one part of the market to another. For example, a drought might cause a grain-crop failure in one region, pushing up the grain price there. The higher price immediately communicates information to *other* regions where prices are lower. Astute traders see an opportunity to *arbitrage* (buy cheaply in one region and sell dearly in the other). In so doing, they resolve the excess-demand problem in the drought region while driving down prices there. If the market works very efficiently, a local drought will have almost no effect at all on local grain prices—the minute the price goes up, grain will rush in from other regions, driving it back down again. All because of the way prices convey information. The key to making prices play this valuable economic role is the rough-and-tumble process of market agitation that Hayek called "market competition."

Even well-developed market economies sometimes experience system-wide coordination failures leading to artificial booms and busts and even collapse into economic depression. These failures, Hayek argued, stem from coordination problems. Coordinating activities over time is more difficult than coordinating them at a given point in time. For example, producers have to make decisions today anticipating what other producers and consumers will do in the future. It turns out that prices are better at conveying information at a single point in time than through time. We'll see an example of this when we learn about credit and insurance in chapter 12.

Hayek's work changed the way we think about prices and the critical role that markets play in both developing and developed economies.

Roger W. Garrison and Israel Kirzner, "Friedrich August von Hayek," in *The New Palgrave: A Dictionary of Economics* (London: Macmillan, 1987), 609–14 (www.auburn.edu/~garriro/e4hayek.htm).

Friedrich A. von Hayek, "The Use of Knowledge in Society," *American Economic Review* 35 (September 1945):519–30 (www.econlib.org/library/Essays/hykKnw1.html).

out good access to markets, a poor household cannot market its produce, obtain inputs, sell labor, obtain credit, learn about or adopt new technologies, insure against risks, or obtain consumption goods at low prices. Equally important, it cannot use its scarce resources like land and labor efficiently. Its decision making is constrained.

### TRADABLES, NONTRADABLES, AND SHADOW PRICES

When an economy does not have access to outside markets for a good, the good is called a "nontradable" for that economy, and the economy is called a "closed economy" for that good. The economy in question could be of a country, village, or even a household. The price of a nontradable is determined by the intersection of demand and supply within the economy, as in an Econ 1 graph of market equilibrium; that is, it is *endogenous* to the economy.

When the economy is integrated with outside markets for a good, the good is said to be a "tradable," and the economy is called "open" for that good. The price of a tradable is determined outside the economy; that is, it is *exogenous*. At that price, if there is excess demand for the tradable, the difference is purchased in outside markets (imported). If there is excess supply, the surplus is sold in those markets (exported).

The notions of tradables, nontradables, and where prices come from apply to *any* economy—whether of a country, region, village, or household.

> *For a nation:* The minute a country opens up to international trade, world prices replace internal equilibrium prices for tradables. The world price is what people must pay for what they buy, or what they get for what they sell, on the world market.

> *For a village:* When a new road or communications network links a remote village up with a regional commercial center, goods that once were nontradable can become tradable. Village prices get replaced by prices determined in the outside market.

> *For a household:* A subsistence household—one that consumes what it produces and has to produce what it consumes—is a very small closed economy with respect to the subsistence good. The subsistence good has a price, which we call a "shadow price." You can think of it as being what the subsistence household would be willing to pay in order to have a little more of the subsistence good. We cannot see this price, because there is no market to show it to us, but it is there, and we can see its shadow (hence the name) and infer something

### Sidebar 11.3 Estimating the Shadow Price of Corn

You know what a shadow price is—you've surely "felt" one before. Imagine you're backpacking in a remote part of the Sierras and a bear gets your food. (That happened to one of us once, sad to say.) What you would pay for a freeze-dried pack of lasagna then! That's a shadow price. If you were standing in a backpacking shop, your shadow price would be the same as the price on the shelf. Hungry, isolated, and foodless in the mountains, *where there is no market,* you'd almost certainly be willing to pay more.

We can't see shadow prices, but sometimes we can estimate them. Consider a subsistence corn farmer in a remote village in southern Mexico. Assuming he follows basic economic precepts of optimizing behavior, he will produce at the point where the price just equals the marginal cost, as we saw in chapter 7. If we can estimate the marginal cost, then, we'll know what price the farmer is using to value his crop, whether it's for the market or for his family's own consumption.

A recent study used this approach to estimate the shadow price of maize for Mexican farmers. For commercial farmers, who are integrated with markets, the shadow price was found to be not significantly different from the market price. For subsistence farmers growing traditional maize varieties, though, it was significantly higher. The more remote the farmer was from markets, the higher his shadow price. Indigenous farmers were found to place a particularly high value on their traditional corn varieties.

This study showed how to estimate the shadow price of a subsistence crop, and it offered an explanation for why small farmers seem to produce corn at a loss: they put a higher value on their corn than the market does. Friedrich von Hayek would not be happy about that!

Aslihan Arslan and J. Edward Taylor, "Farmers' Subjective Valuation of Subsistence Crops: The Case of Traditional Maize in Mexico," *American Journal of Agricultural Economics* 91, no. 4 (2009):895–909.

about it if the right data are available (see sidebar 11.3). Keep this in mind as you read this chapter; it is fundamental to understanding trade and economic development. This shadow price gets replaced by an exogenous market price if the subsistence household becomes connected with village markets or markets outside the village.

Some goods by their very nature tend to be nontradables. Haircuts are an example: it's hard to buy them from somewhere else unless you travel to wherever the hairdresser is. (Ed "imported" a pretty good hair-cut from Paris last year, but that's because he happened to be there for a workshop.) Lodging and restaurant food are other examples of non-tradables. Sometimes, goods that are nontradable can become tradable. Highly perishable foods, like fish, are nontradables if they have to be carried by hand or on a donkey's back over long distances in the heat. They can become tradables if traders have trucks and ice boxes, public transport becomes available, or the fisherman gets a motorcycle.

When goods and services that *could* be tradable *are not,* two important questions arise. First, "Why not?" And second, "What are the consequences for economic welfare, particularly of the poor?"

## WHAT MAKES TRADABLES NONTRADABLES?

The explanations for why things that *could* be tradable are *not* tradable fall mostly into two categories: transaction costs and trade policies. High transaction costs can inhibit trade within as well as among countries. Trade policies almost always have to do with trade among countries; it is rare for a country to regulate trade within its own borders. In the rest of this chapter we will learn the essentials of understanding transaction costs and how they can limit or shut down markets within countries. In the next chapter we will learn about international trade and trade policies.

### Transaction Costs

Usually government policies do not limit trade within countries. However, *transaction costs* can turn tradables into nontradables within countries in much the same way that restrictive trade policies cut countries off from international markets.

The market price is what a buyer pays or a seller receives as a result of a transaction, like the ones that happen billions of times a day in marketplaces and stores around the globe. Transacting is not free, though. Buyers and sellers have to know where to find one another. Both have to know the specifics of what is being transacted, including its quality. When you sell something to me, property rights change hands. What was yours becomes mine. We both need to be convinced that you had the right to sell it and I have secure rights to the thing once I buy it. All of these things have to happen every time we buy or sell anything: a potato, a day's work, a piece of property, a loan, or an insurance policy.

Simply put, there are three kinds of transaction costs:

1. The costs of searching out buyers or sellers and discovering or signaling the quality of the good or service being bought or sold.
2. The costs of negotiating deals and setting up contracts.
3. The costs of enforcing contracts once the deal has been made.

For a potato, (2) and (3) would probably be too small to even think about, but (1) might be important. For property, credit, insurance, labor, and many other goods and services, all three are likely to be considerable. In developed countries, institutions (chapter 8) evolve to deal with these, but in poor economies, the institutions needed to lower these costs enough so that transactions actually occur are often weak or nonexistent. The result is market failure.

Many of the institutions we described in chapter 8 have big economic effects because they determine the transaction costs involved in these market transactions. For many transactions, like buying a lemon, transaction costs might be trivial. But what if the lemon is an old car?

*The Power of Information*

In 1970, UC Berkeley economist George Akerlof published a revolutionary paper called "The Market for 'Lemons.'"[1] The paper was so novel that it got rejected by three top economics journals before eventually winning Akerlof the Nobel Prize. It was about the power of information to make—or break—markets. Its argument goes something like this:

You want to sell your used car. After taking good care of it all these years, you know it's in top shape, and you want to get a good price for it. But what do the potential buyers know? Only what they can see. There is *asymmetric information:* you know more about your car's quality than they do. Unless you can persuade them otherwise, the most they'll be willing to pay will be the price of the average-quality car out there.

So what do you do? Unless you can figure out a way to resolve this information asymmetry, you either sell below what you know your car is worth, or else you pull your car off the market. If you decide not to offer your car for sale, the average quality of cars on the market falls. Over time, this lowers used car prices. Other people with high-quality used cars leave the market, quality and prices fall further, and before you know it, only low-quality cars are left. This is what Akerlof calls "The Market for Lemons."[2] In the extreme case, the market collapses.

When the *Journal of Political Economy* rejected this paper, the editor informed Akerlof that "if this paper was correct, economics would be different."

It was correct, and economics is different.

Today we understand that information is the lubricant that makes markets work. Yet information asymmetries abound, especially in poor countries. Because of them, markets can fail. Surrounded by market failures, poor people's prospects of escaping from poverty are grim.

Food export markets provide a classic example of information asymmetries that make markets fail—for small producers, at least. Diversifying into high-value export crops is critical if poor countries wish to increase their foreign exchange and raise farm incomes. Some African countries, such as Ethiopia, Kenya, and Uganda, are well positioned to supply crops year-round to developed countries, particularly in Europe. However, without the right information this trade cannot happen.

Take food safety, for example. High-income countries have stringent food safety standards. The United States inspects food imports to make sure they comply with food safety rules, even inspecting foreign food facilities.[3] The European Union, the world's biggest food importer, requires that all imported food meet the same level of food safety as food produced within the EU.[4]

Food safety concerns are understandable, of course. But even if a small African farmer can meet the EU's food safety requirements, how will she convince the EU that she has done so? The cost of many small producers complying with these requirements is likely to be significantly higher than the cost for a few big producers. Certifying food safety is a transaction cost of selling food to high-income countries, and it can impose high costs on poor countries (sidebar 11.4).

Another example involving certification is titling, which we discussed in chapter 8. A formal title provides security that the seller really owns the property being sold. Without it, a potential buyer would face risks that easily could kill the deal. Around the globe, governments keep public records of land and building titles and histories of sales, which permits "title searches." In the United States, you cannot get a loan to buy a house without a title search; this information creates the credit. That's why land titling has been a focus of development projects by international development banks.

Information is critical to making other markets work. Without the certification that a fruit or vegetable was organically grown, who would

### Sidebar 11.4 The High Cost of Saving Two in a Billion

If countries wish to export food to developed countries, they have to meet food safety standards concerning pesticide residues, harvesting and packing operations, and a means to trace back to their source any food safety problems that do arise. In 1997, the European Union set new, stringent limits on aflatoxins, which are toxic compounds that contaminate certain foods and can result in the production of acute liver carcinogens. The proposed limits were far below the limits that some individual EU countries had previously adopted. A number of food-exporting countries, including Bolivia, Brazil, Peru, India, Argentina, Canada, Mexico, Uruguay, Australia, and Pakistan, raised concerns that the new standards were unnecessary and overly restrictive.

What effect would this new food safety standard have on developing countries? Three World Bank economists estimated the impact on African food exports, using a gravity model (chapter 13). They found that the new standard would reduce health risk by approximately 1.4 deaths per billion a year, but it would cut African exports by 64%, or US$ 670 million, compared with existing international food safety standards. Their findings illustrate the trade-off between health risks and the high transaction costs rich-country food standards impose on poor-country producers.

Tsunehiro Otsuki, John S. Wilson, and Mirvat Sewadeh, "Saving Two in a Billion: Quantifying the Trade Effect of European Food Safety Standards on African Exports," *Food Policy* 26, no. 5 (2001):495–514.

pay the price to "buy organic"? Certification is the key to green, eco-friendly labeling. The same goes for any quality standard. The US Department of Agriculture enforces quality standards for agricultural products; no meat packing plant is without its USDA inspector and inspection stamps. These activities not only protect consumer health but also create information vital to making markets work.

In a striking example of the power of information and uncertainty, beef consumption in Japan fell 60% after the first case of mad cow disease was reported there in 2001. The vast majority of beef in Japan was free of the disease, of course, but without access to information about *which* meat was mad-cow free, the market reeled. The Japanese beef market recovered once the country began testing *all* of its cows.

## HOW MARKETS CAN LOWER TRANSACTION COSTS

What exactly is a market? When you think of a market you might conjure up images of a grocery store or a mall, or perhaps a marketplace like the one in Tigray, Ethiopia, to which we linked up earlier in this chapter. Markets do not have to be physical places, though. If you bought this book, there's a good chance you did it online, without going to a bookstore. More and more, commerce within and among countries is conducted online, thanks to the likes of Amazon, eBay, and many other companies. eBay is a prime example of a virtual marketplace. It brings buyers and sellers together without ever having them at the same location. People use it for one simple reason: it dramatically lowers transaction costs. Sellers can easily make their wares available for the whole world to see, and buyers can search these goods out effortlessly. The transaction can happen with the click of a mouse. What's someone else's becomes yours instantly. There are still transaction costs. Sellers have to make an effort to list their goods and describe them adequately so that prospective buyers can learn about them. Buyers have to sit down and search out what is available online. And information asymmetries have to be dealt with. Buyers need assurances that they will get what they think they are paying for, and sellers have to be sure that the buyer's money is good. Online marketplaces have solutions for these information problems. They track the reputation of buyers and sellers, facilitate the transaction by letting people pay with secure electronic wallets (like PayPal), and even provide quality guarantees and easy returns should a transaction not turn out right. These services are all about reducing transaction costs in online markets.

So what is a market, then? Here are some definitions taken from well-known dictionaries:

mar·ket \'märkət\
An open place or a covered building where buyers and sellers convene for the sale of goods. (Dictionary.com)

A meeting together of people for the purpose of trade . . . a public place where a market is held. *(Merriam-Webster)*[5]

A regular gathering of people for the purchase and sale of provisions, livestock, and other commodities. *(Oxford)*[6]

None of these captures what economists really mean when they talk about markets. Here's a more comprehensive definition, which encompasses virtual as well as physical markets:

A market is where

- buyers and sellers find one another and their wares,
- price discovery happens, and
- an infrastructure and set of institutions facilitate the transfer of property rights from one person to another.

The third function of markets above—facilitating the transfer of property rights—is fairly simple for a persimmon or laptop. However, it can be very complicated indeed for a loan or an insurance policy, which is why we have a special chapter in this book dedicated to credit and risk. The notion of information is central to all three aspects of our definition of markets. Buyers and sellers have to learn about each other and the true nature of the goods or services to be transacted. Prices have to convey information in order for the market to work properly, as we saw in sidebar 11.2. Buyers and sellers have to be reasonably sure of who holds the property rights before and after a transaction is made— and how these rights will be protected. If any bit of this information is missing, the transaction is likely to fall apart.

Information asymmetries can easily shut small farmers out of domestic as well as international markets. Consider a poor farmer who can produce high-quality berries at a low price. In town, exporters are willing to pay 20 cents a basket for berries like the ones he can grow. Poor roads and communications, however, cut the farmer off from information about buyers: where to sell, when to sell, how to ensure quality, and the price the farmer might get once he transports his berries to the market. This makes marketing a perishable crop too expensive and risky. So the farmer produces a few baskets for his family's and maybe a few neighbors' consumption, and he spends the rest of his time doing low-wage work, when available, on a nearby ranch. A basket of berries costs him 10 cents to produce (including the cost of his time). Implicitly, then, this is his decision price, or the price at which he is willing to produce berries. If he could become part of the export supply chain, his decision price would instantly rise to the market price. He could be more efficient, shifting some or all of his time from low-wage work to berry production, and he would have an incentive to invest in his farm. Most importantly, he could generate badly needed cash for his family.

We can illustrate the welfare loss from high transaction costs using the concepts of producer and consumer surplus. Let's begin by seeing what the producer and consumer surplus are without village-town trade, and then we'll see what trade does to them.

*Producer Surplus*

Without trade, village supply and demand determine the village equilibrium price and quantity of berries, as shown in figure 11.1. Following the basic rule for profit maximization, the quantity of berries supplied in the village is given by the point where $p_v$ = MC, that is, where the village price line hits the supply curve. You can see in figure 11.1 that, at the equilibrium price, the optimal output is $Q_v$. Producers make no profit on the last unit supplied (because its MC just equals the price). However, they *do* make a profit on all the other units ($Q < Q_v$), because on those units the price exceeds the MC. Total profits are given by the area of triangle B, which is the sum of the difference between price and MC for all of the units supplied, up to $Q_v$. (In calculus terms, in case that's how you like to think, it's the integral from zero to $Q_v$ of the function $p - MC(Q)$.)

This is the *producer surplus*. For all units from zero to $Q_v$, producers get a price higher than the minimum they would require in order to supply the goods. The producer surplus is our measure of producers' economic welfare.

*Consumer Surplus*

There is an analogue to the producer surplus for consumers. Not surprisingly, it is called the "consumer surplus." Have you ever paid less for something than you would have been willing to pay? Maybe picked up what you want on sale, surprised by how cheap it was, and then asked yourself what you'll do with all the money you saved? That difference between what you would have been willing to pay and what you did pay is your consumer surplus.

Look at the market demand curve in figure 11.1. It represents consumers' willingness to pay for each quantity of the good. The quantity demanded in the market is given by the point where the village price line hits this demand curve; in this figure it is $Q_v$. For all the quantities from zero to $Q_v$, consumers would have been willing to pay more than the village price. The sum of differences between consumers' willingness to pay and the village price, then, is the total consumer surplus in this market. It is shown as triangle A in the figure. It will be our measure of consumers' economic welfare.

Total economic welfare is the sum of producer surplus and consumer surplus. It is the sum of these two triangles.

Village Berry Market

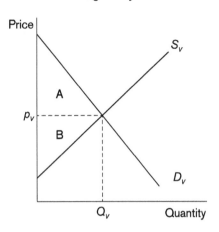

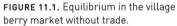

**FIGURE 11.1.** Equilibrium in the village berry market without trade.

*Trade and Economic Welfare*

What does village-town trade in berries do to villagers' economic welfare? Suppose that in town, our berry producer could sell his berries at a regional price equal to $p_r$. This price might be determined by supply and demand in the regional berry market, or it might even come from the world market, if town traders export the berries they buy from local farmers. The right side of figure 11.2 illustrates the case in which the price is determined by equilibrium in the regional berry market.

On the left side of figure 11.2 we see the village berry market again. The way we drew this figure, the regional price, $p_r$, is higher than the village equilibrium price, $p_v$. Naturally, given the choice, our berry farmer will choose to sell in the town, at the higher price. That's the price village consumers will have to pay the farmer if they want him to sell berries to them instead of to the town.

In this particular example, farmers gain from trade, but consumers lose. Consumer surplus falls by an amount equal to the trapezoidal area A in figure 11.2. That's the decrease in the size of the triangle underneath the demand curve when the price rises from $p_v$ to $p_r$. Producer surplus, however, increases by an amount equal to areas A plus B. The gain to farmers exceeds the loss to consumers, and total economic welfare increases. In theory, producers could fully compensate consumers and still have higher profits than without trade. (Whether they will or not is another question. It underlies controversies about free trade, which we will consider in chapter 12.)

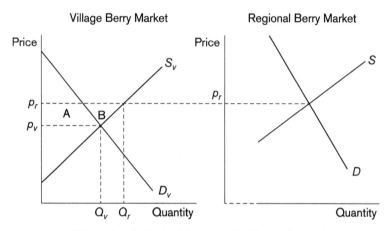

**FIGURE 11.2.** If the regional price is higher than the village price, trade increases the producer surplus more than it decreases the consumer surplus. Thus, the total economic surplus rises.

You might wonder what happens if the regional price is *lower* than the village price. We leave it as an exercise to show that the total economic surplus still increases from trade. If $p_r < p_v$, producer surplus decreases, but consumer surplus rises more than enough to compensate.

### How Transaction Costs Can Kill Trade

In order to sell in the regional market, though, the farmer will have to incur a transaction cost equivalent to $\$t$ per unit sold. You can imagine the high cost of transporting the berries over bad roads, and before that, whatever costs in money and time she has to incur to travel to town, find out about prices there, and arrange the sale (a cell phone might help). Then there's always a risk that, once she delivers the berries to the market, the buyer will change his mind and decide not to buy (an enforceable contract would help). Market uncertainty adds what economists call a "risk premium" to t. You can think of it as the amount the farmer would be willing to pay to insure against the possibility of the sale falling through. When you talk to farmers in poor villages, these are the sorts of things they mention when explaining why they do not sell in outside markets.

Given these transaction costs, the farmer's net price will be $(1 − t)p_r$. Figure 11.3 shows the case where the price the farmer gets by selling in town, net of transaction costs, is less than the village price. Faced by high transaction costs, the farmer is better off selling only in the village, at the village price $p_v$. In doing so, he produces less and loses profit

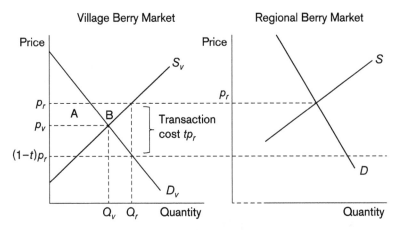

**FIGURE 11.3.** When transaction costs cut producers off from higher prices in outside markets, producer surplus falls (area A + B). Consumer surplus increases (area A), but not by enough to compensate for the fall in producer surplus.

(producer's surplus) equal to the areas A + B in figure 11.3. Consumers gain by being able to buy berries at the lower village price, but their gain (area A) is not enough to make up for the producer's loss.

In this age of the supermarket revolution, getting small farmers into the Walmart supply chain can be the key to raising agricultural incomes and reducing poverty. But transaction costs can make Walmart shut its doors to small farmers (see sidebar 11.5).

Microeconomics courses teach us that firms optimize by producing where their marginal cost (MC) equals the output price, or equivalently, where each input is used at the point where its marginal value product just equals its price. Consumers do something similar by demanding goods at the level where their marginal rate of substitution (MRS, the slope of the indifference curve or ratio of marginal utilities any two goods create) just equals the ratio of prices.

If everyone bases decisions on the same prices, things cannot be any more efficient. The MC will be the same for all producers (and equal to the output price). The marginal rate of substitution will be the same for all consumers (equal to the ratio of prices).

As you can see in figure 11.3, though, when there are high transaction costs, different producers (for example, near or far from markets) may face different prices and thus produce at different MCs. Recall that the supply curve *is* the marginal cost curve. The farmers who supply the regional market produce at an MC equal to $p_r$, whereas the village farmer produces at an MC equal to $p_v$. The same thing happens to consumers:

### Sidebar 11.5   Walmart in Nicaragua

Many people think of supermarkets as the rich world's place to shop, but the rapid rise of supermarkets is transforming agricultural supply chains in Africa, Asia, and Latin America. The supermarket explosion leaves development economists with big new questions. Can poor farmers make their way into the supply chains of Walmart and other major players in the supermarket space, given the exacting standards they face? Or will the supermarket revolution pass them by and possibly leave them more marginalized than before?

An economist at Columbia University's Earth Institute set out to answer these questions by asking what determines whether small farmers become suppliers of food to Walmart in Nicaragua. This is a tricky question, because as in program evaluation (chapter 2), unobservable variables may determine whether farmers participate in the Walmart supply chain, and they can easily confound estimates of how other things affect participation.

This study followed the same farmers over time. It found that only farmers with advantageous access to roads and water are likely to participate in the Walmart supply chain. The study is important because it identifies obstacles to small-farmer participation in the Walmart supply chain, including factors related to transaction costs.

Hope C. Michelson, "Small Farmers, NGOs, and a Walmart World: Welfare Effects of Supermarkets Operating in Nicaragua," *American Journal of Agricultural Economics* 95, no. 3 (2013).

they equate their marginal rates of substitution with the ratio of the prices they face, which may be very different from the prices others face.

When this happens, efficiency could be increased—dramatically, perhaps—by reducing or eliminating transaction costs, so that trade can equalize prices across markets. Remember this—it is the fundamental problem that high transaction costs create in poor economies: market failure occurs when economic actors are unable to get together to make efficiency-enhancing trades. Transaction costs resulting from imperfect information are a major reason why this happens. (Another is civil strife, as in the example from Tigray at the start of this chapter.) In fact, billions of people—particularly poor people—opt out of markets, apparently because the transaction costs of using markets are too high.

When transaction costs cause prices to vary across space, a cell phone can literally keep food from rotting on the vine—or fish from rotting on the beach (see sidebar 11.6).

### Sidebar 11.6 Saving Fish with Cell Phones

People need price information in order to trade efficiently. In Kerala, India, more than 1 million people fish. While at sea, fishermen can't observe prices at markets along the coast. Transportation costs are high, and fish are perishable. This keeps fishermen from moving from port to port looking for the best price once their boats are full. Thus, almost all fishermen sell their catch locally, and this can create a surplus of fish in some places—in fact, the price of fish can drop all the way to zero. When that happens, fish literally are left to rot. Meanwhile, just down the coast, people in other towns might be happy to pay a good price for this fish. If only the fishermen had known—they could have chosen to put in their boats down the coast, instead.

Between 1997 and 2001, mobile phone service was introduced in Kerala. Robert Jensen hypothesized that this could be very good for fishermen and consumers—not to mention the fish. He gathered data on the ups and downs of fish prices along the coast both before and after the introduction of cell phones. His analysis found that mobile phones dramatically reduced price variability and waste and raised fishermen's profits as well as consumers' welfare. Since improvements in market efficiency can benefit all market participants, even fishermen without cell phones were better off when some of their fellow fishermen started using them.

This study is a dramatic illustration of how the exchange of information via cell phones enabled fishermen to sell their catch where prices are high, leveling out price variability along the Kerala coast. Cell phones made the fish market work, and the market made people better off—while saving a whole lot of fish. And obviously, this effect is not unique to fish markets: development economists have found similar dramatic market effects due to the introduction of cell phones. Jenny Aker, for example, found that the arrival of mobile phones in Niger between 2001 and 2006 substantially reduced the variation in grain prices across rural markets, bringing big benefits to the hardest-to-reach markets.

Robert Jensen, "The Digital Provide: Information (Technology), Market Performance, and Welfare in the South Indian Fisheries Sector," *Quarterly Journal of Economics* 122, no. 3 (August 2007):879–924.

Jenny C. Aker, "Information from Markets Near and Far: Mobile Phones and Agricultural Markets in Niger," *American Economic Journal: Applied Economics* 2, no. 3 (July 2010):46–59.

## TRANSACTION COSTS IN INPUT MARKETS

So far we've focused on the effects of transaction costs in output markets. Asymmetric information and high transaction costs can also shut farmers out of input markets. When a farmer cannot get fertilizer or hire labor at the times needed, or cannot be sure of input quality, he may sow less land or not adopt more productive technologies, and his output may fall as a result. Efficiency is critical because even a small income gain can make a huge difference for an impoverished household—particularly if that gain can be sustained month after month, year after year.

### *Labor Markets*

Anyone who has taken microeconomics knows the textbook solution to the labor-hiring problem: employers should hire workers up to the point where their marginal value product (MVP) just equals the wage. The MVP is how much value (gross revenue) the last (marginal) worker will create. The wage is how much it will cost to hire him.

But how can we be sure that that last worker will really produce that MVP? Or the worker before him, for that matter? What if you hire him and he doesn't work hard, generating less revenue than the wage you have to pay him? This is called "shirking," and it is a form of moral hazard. Employers can deal with this problem by monitoring the workers they hire, just like a bank can monitor borrowers, but that's expensive.

There is also the possibility of adverse selection. Some workers are more productive than others. How do you know you'll end up with a "good" one—that is, a worker who produces an MVP higher than the wage? If the worker is a member of your own family, you'll have good information about him. If not, information may be asymmetric—the worker knows how good he is, but you do not. It might be possible to overcome adverse selection by offering a wage higher than the going market wage in order to attract more productive workers. But this, like monitoring, is costly.

The costs of monitoring and screening workers are transaction costs in labor markets. The true cost of hiring a worker is the wage plus these transaction costs. If the transaction costs are high enough, the labor market will fail: no workers will be hired. Then producers are forced to use their own labor. If you can hire workers, it doesn't matter how big your family's labor endowment is—you simply hire up to the point where the MVP equals the market wage. If you can't, then how much you produce depends on how much family labor you have.

In a labor-constrained household, the "family shadow wage," or opportunity cost of family time, is high. (The family shadow wage is the wage you would be willing to pay if you could hire workers.) In a labor-abundant household, the family wage is low; the market failure traps labor in the household. In that case, you would be willing to work for a relatively low wage, but no one will hire you because of the asymmetric information problem: employers are not sure how productive you'll be.

If my shadow wage is low and yours is high, we might both be better off if I worked for you. You'd pay a wage lower than your reservation wage, and I'd get a wage higher than my reservation wage. If transaction costs in the labor market are too high, though, the labor exchange won't take place.

There is a simple solution to the adverse selection and moral hazard problems in labor markets: pay workers a piece rate. It is common in both poor and rich countries to pay farmworkers a flat cash amount per unit harvested: box, kilo, bundle, and so forth. Harvest workers in Mexico often are paid a share of the corn crop. Fishermen often pay their crew a share of the catch. California farmers pay strawberry pickers a piece rate per twelve-pint tray during peak harvest periods.[7]

Piece rates have advantages and disadvantages. From the producer's point of view, they have the advantage of shifting all the risk associated with adverse selection and moral hazard onto the workers. Farmers know exactly how much it will cost to pick, say, a ton of peaches if they pay a piece rate, but not if they pay a wage. Piece rates have the disadvantage of encouraging workers to focus on quantity, not quality, for example, to pick as many peaches as possible but not worry about bruising them. Employers who pay piece rates thus have to be extra careful about monitoring quality, for example, by checking the fruit and docking workers for poor quality.

The piece-rate system ensures that workers get paid according to their productivity. Pick fast and your day's pay will be higher. Pick too slowly and you might not have enough food to eat. This is good news for highly productive workers, but it obviously is a disadvantage for less-productive ones. Less-productive workers may not be able to pick enough to cover their subsistence (or the minimum wage, if there is one). In California, farmers are required by law to pay all workers at least the minimum wage, even if they are not productive enough to "pick" the minimum wage. This shifts some of the risk associated with adverse selection and moral hazard back onto employers. While some kinds of work lend themselves to piece rates, others do not. It's easy to pay a piece rate to strawberry pickers, but what about workers in soil preparation, planting, or weeding?

*Other Inputs*

When people face transaction costs in input markets, the price they pay for their inputs includes the cost of making the transaction. Adverse selection and moral hazard are not so much problems in the case of purchased inputs; the quality of fertilizer usually is pretty much known by everyone, and fertilizer—unlike workers—does not have a mind of its own or need to be monitored.

Other problems can create transaction costs and make input markets fail, though. Foremost among them is timing. Not having an input at the time it is needed often is as bad as not having it at all. Seed, fertilizer, insecticides, and herbicides all must be applied at just the right time or the farmer will risk losing his crop. Input markets have to work efficiently to make sure this happens, yet often they do not.

Poorly functioning input markets can even keep people from adopting more productive technologies. The Green Revolution (high-yielding) seeds we encountered in chapter 9 were engineered to give high yields as long as complementary inputs, particularly fertilizer, are applied in a timely fashion. If a farmer is unsure that he'll be able to buy fertilizer at the moment it has to be applied, he may be better off not planting the high-yielding variety.

People could take measures to ensure that they have the inputs they need at the time they need them. For example, instead of investing their scarce cash in more productive activities, they could use it to stockpile fertilizer when they can get it, then let the fertilizer sit there until the time comes to apply it. Or they could invest time and money into searching out sources of inputs, from distant cities if needed. By taking steps like these, farmers could make sure they have the inputs they need at the time they are needed, but obviously these steps are costly. In the end, the effective price of fertilizer is the market price plus the transaction cost the farmer incurs to make sure he has the fertilizer when he needs it. That transaction cost may make all the difference (see sidebar 11.7).

## Sidebar 11.7 Nudging Poor Farmers to Use Fertilizer

Poor farmers in Africa do not use nearly enough fertilizer. For example, fertilizer use in sub-Saharan Africa was only 8 kg/ha in 2002, compared with 101 kg/ha in South Asia. Such massive disparities in fertilizer use between Africa and the rest of the world suggest that there are structural impediments limiting fertilizer availability and demand. It is very unlikely that African farmers are applying fertilizer at a level that equates its marginal value product with the world price. They act as though the price of fertilizer is much higher than the price in the market. Why the disparity?

One possibility is that poor farmers simply don't have the cash. Three economists offered a different explanation: timing. Even poor farmers who are willing to pay the market price for fertilizer cannot be sure they'll be able to get the fertilizer they need when they need it.

In a clever experimental study in Kenya, some farmers were offered free fertilizer delivery early in the season and others not, while still others were offered a fertilizer subsidy. The study found that offering delivery early was more effective at increasing fertilizer use than was a subsidy—not to mention cheaper.

Esther Duflo, Michael Kremer, and Jonathan Robinson, "Nudging Farmers to Use Fertilizer: Evidence from Kenya," *American Economic Review* 101, no. 6 (2011):2350–90.

### TRANSACTION COSTS AND SPATIAL MARKET INTEGRATION

So far, we have discussed participation in either output or input markets as a binary variable. That is, a given farm household either sells its maize in the local market or it does not; it either hires labor or it does not. As we've already explored, transaction costs can have a big influence on this decision, and the decision can, in turn, have a big effect on household efficiency and welfare. Because they affect these decisions, transaction costs can have a big impact on how markets in one location are related to other markets. This is what economists call "spatial market integration," which is often a key determinant of how and how well markets in developing countries function.

While potential buyers and sellers typically face a binary decision to participate in a market or not, spatial market integration is measured as a continuous variable. If a wheat market in Meknès, Morocco, is unintegrated with the other wheat markets in Morocco (much less international wheat markets), then wheat prices in Meknès will be completely determined by local supply and demand. In the case of drought, wheat prices will skyrocket. If instead the Meknès wheat market is fully integrated with the world wheat market, a local drought will not affect local prices because any local shortfall will be filled by the world wheat supply.

Most input and output markets in developing countries fall somewhere between these two market integration extremes. Whether a given market is poorly integrated or well integrated depends on many of the sources of transaction costs we have already encountered: information, transportation, contracts, tariffs and other barriers to trade, and so on. This degree of market integration can directly affect welfare outcomes.

In addition to subjecting households to greater price volatility—and, in the case of food markets, greater vulnerability to food insecurity—poor market integration can constrain local productivity by directly affecting production decisions. For example, a few years ago Travis was conducting focus group discussions with wheat farmers in Meknès. It was March, and it was shaping up to be a perfect rainfall year—the wheat looked beautiful. But the farmers were intentionally getting lower yields than they could have. Why? Because nearly all the farmers had decided not to use fertilizer once they realized how good the rainfall would be. This was especially perplexing to agronomists because fertilizer dramatically increases yields when rainfall is good. What then was holding back these farmers?

As the farmers explained (with impressive economic intuition), "We know fertilizer could really increase our yields this year because of the rainfall, but even without fertilizer everyone's yield will be high and wheat prices will collapse at harvest. With lower prices, we might not even cover the cost of the fertilizer!" This is what poorly integrated markets look like to poor farmers.

## THE ROLE OF GOVERNMENT

We conclude this chapter with some thoughts about the role of government in a world of asymmetric information and market failures.

Economists almost uniformly agree that markets are crucial to people's welfare. Free-market economists believe that the free functioning of markets, without government intervention, leads to the greatest common good, often citing Adam Smith's reference to "an invisible hand." This belief is an underpinning of free-trade agreements among nations and market reforms within them. The Fundamental Theorem of Welfare Economics states that competitive markets lead to a "first best" allocation of resources that is *Pareto efficient;* that is, nobody can be made better off without someone else being made worse off.

The fundamental theorem does not necessarily hold when markets are incomplete or information is imperfect—two common features of poor economies. We have seen that there are many cases in which there is no market, and we will see still others in the chapter on credit and risk. In such an environment, there is no first-best outcome, and a government hands-off or laissez-faire approach to markets is not likely to be optimal. As the Nobel laureate economist Joseph Stiglitz explained it, "The theories that said that markets work perfectly were all based on very simplistic models of perfect competition, perfect markets, and perfect information . . . The reason that the invisible hand often seemed invisible was that it wasn't there."[8]

The question today is no longer whether governments should be involved in markets, but how much—that is, finding the right balance between the market and government.

### Grounds for Government Intervention in Markets

One does not have to reject market economics to recognize situations in which governments should become involved in markets. One of these is the provision of information, which can lower transaction costs for everyone. Governments around the world have statistical bureaus that gather information and make it publicly available.

There are other instances in which a strong case can be made for government intervention in markets:

*Externalities:* The actions of an individual have bad (or good) impacts on others for which the individual doesn't pay (or get compensated). Externalities are crucial in environmental economics, from pollution to biodiversity. Markets, left to themselves, produce too much air and water pollution (which harms people who breathe the air or drink the water), too little research (which creates public benefits), too little education (my education can make other workers more productive), too few beehives (bees pollinate peach orchards), too much global warming (how much carbon did you put into the atmosphere today?), too little information (how do you turn a profit selling information in a poor village?), and too little biodiversity (sidebar 11.8). Yet another negative externality is trash, which sadly is a pervasive feature of developing-country landscapes.

*Public goods:* Roads, marketing infrastructure, communications, police, and firefighting are public goods that create benefits for society that are difficult for private investors to capture; thus, there are not likely to be enough of them unless governments get involved. A classic case is firefighting. If fire departments were private, I might pay for fire protection but my neighbor might not. Yet if her house catches fire, the firefighters will have to put it out in order to save my house—a classic free-rider problem.

*Market power:* The welfare gains from markets depend on competition. When someone gains too much market power, either as a seller or buyer, the fundamental theorem breaks down. This is the justification for antitrust legislation.

Resolving the information problems and providing the infrastructure needed to make markets function properly involves classic problems of increasing returns to scale and public goods. These are familiar to you from chapter 6, where we learned about the public goods nature of health and education investments. Let's review them here.

Creating an information system involves high (fixed) setup costs of gathering the information and making it available in a form that people can use. However, once an information system is in place, the cost of providing the information to an additional person is negligible or zero. Marginal cost pricing is not feasible, as in the case of a bridge. You can put information online and it can spread like wildfire. It's difficult to exclude people from having information once it is available. There's a natural free-rider problem here. Once new information gets out, no one can control where it goes, particularly in a world of online news, social media, and e-mail. Information creates important externalities, too. The positive spillovers from information were central to the endogenous growth model we learned about in chapter 7.

These characteristics of information have advantages and disadvantages. A big advantage is that once information gets out there, it can spread and create benefits widely. A disadvantage, though, is that there is little or no private incentive to invest in information systems, because it is hard for private investors to make money by producing something over which they have little control. These are problems similar to what we

### Sidebar 11.8   Which Seeds to Save?

Plant breeders have been remarkably successful at creating new high-yielding seeds to meet the growing global food demand. Green Revolution seed varieties were engineered from traditional varieties with the characteristics agronomists wish to breed into the new varieties. But what if the traditional varieties weren't there anymore?

To reap the benefits of high-yielding varieties, farmers have to plant them. But to create new seed varieties in the future, scientists need the genetic diversity found in traditional seed varieties. What if the new seeds are so superior that farmers stop growing traditional varieties altogether? What if other forces at work, like the spread of markets, lead farmers to stop growing traditional varieties, which then go extinct? How would scientists get the genetic resources they need to continue breeding new crop varieties—whether to increase yields or to breed in resistance to new diseases and pests?

There is not a market for biodiversity, so when farmers decide to stop growing traditional varieties, they do not take into account the costs to society of losing valuable crop genetic resources. Researchers have found evidence that traditional seed varieties are disappearing, a process called "genetic erosion."

Some research suggests that high transaction costs and marginal environments may slow crop genetic erosion. Studies of wheat in Turkey, potatoes in Peru, and maize in Mexico find that isolation from markets limits the spread of high-yielding varieties. When people face high transaction costs and must produce what they consume, they are much more likely to plant traditional varieties—because they taste better. Most high-yielding varieties were engineered to outperform traditional varieties, but only in high-quality environments with fertile, level land and access to water. Farmers are more likely to plant traditional seeds on marginal lands. Transaction costs and marginal environments, then, seem to be friends of crop genetic diversity.

This raises an important question: As rural markets become better integrated with national markets and new seeds are engineered to do well in marginal environments, how will we make sure that we have the genetic resources we need for agricultural research?

Stephen B. Brush and Erika Meng, "Farmers' Valuation and Conservation of Crop Genetic Resources," *Genetic Resources and Crop Evolution* 45, no. 2 (1998):139–50.

Stephen B. Brush, J. Edward Taylor, and Mauricio Bellon, "Technology Adoption and Biological Diversity in Andean Potato Agriculture," *Journal of Development Economics* 39, no. 2 (1992):365–87.

M. Van Dusen and J. E. Taylor, "Missing Markets and Crop Diversity: Evidence from Mexico," *Environment and Development Economics* 10, no. 4 (2005):513–31.

came across with regard to education and health investments. Left to their own devices, people will underinvest in information—and health and education, and roads and bridges. The same arguments apply to communications and marketing systems.

This is why Cornell economist Chris Barrett writes: "The institutional and physical infrastructure necessary to ensure broad-based, low-cost access to competitive, well-functioning markets" requires "significant investment, typically by the public sector, paid for out of tax revenues or aid flows. One has to get institutions and endowments, as well as prices, 'right' in order to induce market-based development" (p. 300).[9]

But, just because a market doesn't work well does not mean the government should fix it. There are many problems out there competing for scarce public funds. Is fixing a particular market failure the best use of scarce public resources? Picture a poor isolated village facing high transaction costs. The government could build a new road there and put in a cell phone tower, but the same money could be used to provide credit to poor farmers or schools or health care for their children. Policy makers, like poor people, often face cruel trade-offs.

### Markets and the "Knowledge Problem"

Understanding how markets work and where they work well can provide a yet deeper perspective on the role of governments in economic development. Hayek, who—as we learned at the beginning of this chapter—thought a lot about how markets work, was convinced that despite their potential flaws markets do something no individual, no committee, no team of experts, and no government agency could. Markets collect little bits of information from those choosing to transact in markets as well as from those choosing not to participate in markets. When they are able to adjust to changing conditions, prices convey extremely valuable information about the underlying conditions as experienced by individuals.

Hayek's insights about markets set the stage for what he called the "knowledge problem": we are quick to formulate big plans to directly improve society, but rarely possess the knowledge of current circumstances required to make these big plans succeed. No one person or committee possesses this knowledge because it "is not given to anyone in its totality" (p. 76).[10] But markets can aggregate this diffused knowledge—that is, if they function well enough.

As we have already seen throughout this book, this "knowledge problem" appears often in international development dilemmas. Big development plans and projects often fall far short of expectations because of this problem. According to Hayek, appreciating the nature of this knowledge problem and what it implies for program and policy design is fundamental to economics because it relates directly to markets: "The curious task of economics is to demonstrate to men [and women] how little they really know about what they imagine they can design" (p. 76).[11]

www.rebeltext.org/development/qr11.html
Learn more about information and markets by
exploring multimedia resources while you read.

### APPENDIX

*The Math of Lemons*

In his award-winning paper, George Akerlof gave a simple example to show how asymmetric information can lead to a market failure. Here's how it goes:

Everyone knows that used cars vary in quality. Imagine an index of quality such that the worst quality car gets a "0" and the best quality car gets a "1." We do not know how the quality of used cars out there is distributed across the [0,1] quality interval, so we'll assume it's even, or uniform. That means average quality equals ½.

Sellers and buyers both value cars based on their quality. Again, to make things simple, suppose sellers value cars identically to their quality, so that a car with quality equal to $q$ is worth $\$q$. This might sound strange, since $q$ is always between 0 and 1, but if you're thinking in, say, tens of thousands of dollars, a car worth $1/2 on the $q$ scale would cost $5,000, and so on.

To make this example interesting, buyers have to value cars differently than sellers. It makes sense to imagine that cars are worth more to buyers than sellers in terms of the utility or satisfaction an additional car would bring. Akerlof assumed that a car of quality $q$ is worth $\$3/2q$ to a buyer. (Actually, buyers routinely seem willing to spend more than sellers are willing to accept. Farmgate prices are far lower than what consumers pay for food at a grocery store, and anyone who buys something at auction has to pay a buyer's fee, which makes the price paid higher than the price received by the seller.)

In theory, then, it seems like the price for a used car will end up somewhere between $\$q$ and $\$3/2q$, depending on the bargaining power of the buyer and seller. Both buyer and seller would be better off if a transaction in this price range happened.

Now here's the catch: Only sellers know the quality of their car; in other words, information about car quality is asymmetric. The buyer's best guess is that a given car's quality is average—that is, $q$ = ½. If this is the case, the buyer won't be willing to pay $\$3/2q$; she'll only be willing to pay half that, or $½ \times 3/2\$q =$

3/4$q. But the seller won't sell a car of quality $q$ at a price less than $q. The market fails; the high-quality cars get pulled off the market, and only the worst cars ("lemons") are left.

The "market for lemons" problem can arise in any situation in which sellers have better information about the quality of a good or service than buyers do. The thing being traded (or not) could be a commodity. (Does your produce meet food safety standards? Is it organic?). As we'll see in the next chapter, it could also be a service. (Will you be a productive worker if I hire you? Will you pay me back if I loan you some money?)

**12**

# Credit and Insurance

By definition, economic development is a process that takes
time. Things that take time are risky because we don't know
what the future has in store for us. At the global or regional
level, we know something about these risks, which include
weather shocks and climate change, financial and commodity
market volatility, and sociopolitical instability. At the
household level, time and risk have very personal effects.
They determine a household's livelihood options, its level of
food security, and its ability to invest in its own future. We
have seen in prior chapters how time and risk can directly
shape development outcomes. In this chapter, we focus more
explicitly on these essentials of development economics
through the lens of credit and insurance—which, for poor
households, can take formal and informal forms.

**ESSENTIALS**

- Credit
- Market failures: asymmetric information
- Adverse selection and moral hazard
- Microfinance
- Risk and uncertainty
- Risk aversion
- Dynamics
- Insurance

There is a good chance that you bought this book with a credit card and
that you have a savings account, an ATM card, and maybe a student
loan. Yet well over half of the world's population does not participate
in financial markets at all. Nearly all of the world's financially unserved
adults live in Africa, Asia, or Latin America. In Kenya, Pakistan, and
Nicaragua, fewer than one in five people used financial services of any
kind, either as savers or borrowers, as of 2009.[1]

---

### Sidebar 12.1  Saving for a Rainless Day

In the West African semi-arid tropics, poor households engage in rainfed agriculture in a drought-prone environment. Most lack access to credit or insurance to see them through when the rains don't come. Without other alternatives, animals are both the bank and the insurance policy. In good years, households invest in animals, and in bad years they sell off animals in an effort to keep food on the table, like taking money out of the bank.

But a study by three development economists found that this is a far-from-perfect way of insuring against income shocks. The return to "livestock savings" is low if many people have to sell off animals at the same time to get through a drought. This study followed 631 Burkina Faso households over a period of four years that included a severe drought. It found that livestock sales play less of a consumption-smoothing role than expected. On average, sales of animals made up for 15%–30% of income shortfalls due to drought and other adverse shocks. Low prices from distress sales of livestock may make animals a poor way to save for a rainless day.

Marcel Fafchamps, Christopher Udry, and Katherine Czukas, "Drought and Saving in West Africa: Are Livestock a Buffer Stock?" *Journal of Development Economics* 55, no. 2 (April 1998):273–305.

---

Without access to financial markets, people can still save and insure themselves against adverse economic shocks, but they have to find ways to do it that don't involve banks, insurance companies, or other formal institutions. For example, instead of putting their savings into an account that will give them a sure return, they might just buy a goat (see sidebar 12.1).

Understanding the importance of credit and insurance, why credit and insurance markets fail, and what can be done about it is essential to development economics. These topics trace their roots to two of the deepest dimensions of the human experience: time and risk. Most of the big decisions we make in life directly involve both time and risk. While this is as true for you as it is for someone your age living in rural Pakistan, the welfare implications of risky decisions that play out over time are likely to be quite different in rural Pakistan. As evidence of how central these dimensions are to development economics, the World Bank's 2014 World Development Report is entitled "Risk and Opportunity: Managing Risk for Development."[2]

In several places throughout this book, we've seen how time and risk shape development outcomes, including vulnerability and poverty dynamics (chapter 4), educational investment decisions (chapter 6), capital investments over time (chapter 7), and agricultural technology adoption (chapter 9). In this chapter, we provide a distinctly microeconomic perspective on time and risk by learning about credit and insurance markets. As we shall see, the two are closely related. The same duo of problems, adverse selection and moral hazard, is likely to thwart both, particularly in poor and risky environments. These problems stem from the economics of information and market failures we learned about in chapter 11.

## CREDIT

As we will learn, credit fundamentally involves both time and risk dimensions. Before we turn to that topic, consider the three basic roles credit plays in modern economies.

First, it allows you to get ahead (credit for investment). Borrowing money enables people with good ideas, skills, and other assets who lack liquidity to make productive investments and raise income. Without credit, a farmer cannot purchase inputs ahead of the harvest (which she must do to get a good harvest) unless she has other sources of cash (like savings). A poor household usually cannot borrow money to set up a small business—even if all this means is buying a simple sewing machine.

Second, it prevents you from falling behind (credit for consumption). Borrowing allows households that experience a negative income shock to maintain their consumption levels and assets, preserving their ability to produce income in the future. If the crop fails or a breadwinner becomes sick or injured, there is cash to see the family through. Credit is insurance, as anyone who has lost his job and used his credit card to get through can attest.

Third, credit shifts risk from borrowers to lenders (credit as risk sharing). Default clauses and liability rules define the conditions under which a borrower does not have to repay a loan. Because default is an option, loans shift risks from borrowers to lenders. Defaulting on a loan doesn't sound very nice, but actually default and bankruptcy play an important role in modern economies. By shifting risk from borrowers to lenders, credit can induce people to take out loans and make high-return, but risky, investments that otherwise they would not make. Any investor knows that high-return investments entail risk, and the higher the return, the more risk there is likely to be. Without making risky investments, people are likely doomed to live in a low-return, low-income society.

Already you can see that credit and risk are related. In fact, in poor villages, it can be hard to tell where one ends and the other begins, as one development economist discovered in Nigeria (see sidebar 12.2).

Considering how important credit is, why don't more people have access to it? The answer to this question boils down to the information asymmetries we learned about in chapter 11. It's easy to buy a potato, but it's a lot harder to take out a loan. Credit is one of the most striking examples of how asymmetric information creates market failures.

### Why Credit Is Different from a Potato

When you buy a potato, the transaction is simultaneous: you pull the cash out of your purse or pocket, and the vender hands you the potato.[3] Usually, you and the seller agree on what you're getting. You can examine the potato and make sure it is fresh and firm. At the Davis farmers' market, summer peach vendors offer samples just to make sure we know how good their fruit is before we buy some.

Credit is not like that, for several different reasons. In a potato transaction, you pay and walk away with the potato, and after that, you and the vendor can forget about each other. Credit involves an *intertemporal* exchange. You loan me the money today; I pay it back to you (with interest) sometime in the future. You give up the use of the money in return for a promise to get the money back. I get the money today in return for a promise to pay you back the money tomorrow.

So, what's being transacted here? Promises, actually. The borrower is "selling" a promise that he will give the lender resources to use in the future. In return, he gets to use the resources today. The lender is "buying" this promise that the borrower will repay the loan in the future. In return, he gives up the use of the resources today.

If what's promised always happened, things would be simple and there would be a lot more credit in the world. In real life, though, repayment is uncertain. Borrowers face a variety of risks. Projects are risky: loans are used to create businesses that may or may not succeed or to plant crops that may fail if the rains don't come. A borrower might be unable to repay due to any number of adverse shocks. Bad weather, a

**Sidebar 12.2    Is It Credit or Insurance?**

If you considered only loans from banks, private companies, or projects, you'd conclude that the credit market is more or less nonexistent in the four villages in northern Nigeria that economist Christopher Udry studied. But Chris uncovered a thriving informal credit market. Most—65% of all households—in Chris's random sample of village households borrowed money from other households, mostly members of the same kinship group. Even more—75%—lent money out to other households. More surprisingly, most of the households in the sample were both borrowers and lenders: two-thirds of all of the households that lent money also borrowed money. Households with more wealth lent more, but they also borrowed more. Could households be "hedging their bets" by borrowing and lending at the same time?

You might think that if you borrow a *naira,* that's what you'll pay back, if you can. In the Nigerian villages, how much people paid back on their loans depended upon how big their harvest was. That makes sense; if things go badly people repay less; even in the formal sector, banks sometimes adjust people's loan terms when they are not able to make their payments. But Udry's study found that lenders' harvests affected loan repayments, too: the larger the harvest a lender got, the less his borrowers paid back. To put this in more familiar terms, this would be like Citibank telling its borrowers that they don't have to repay as much of their loan this year because its profits are good!

This is a vivid example of how lines can blur between credit and insurance. By lending, borrowing, and making repayment depend on how each party's harvest turned out, people in these villages insured one another against crop yield risk.

Christopher Udry, "Credit Markets in Northern Nigeria: Credit as Insurance in a Rural Economy," *World Bank Economic Review* 4, no. 3 (1990):251–69.

recession, illness, or an injury can keep him from turning the loan into the income he'll need in order to repay it.

These kinds of uncertainties pose challenges to credit transactions, but they don't necessarily kill the deal. If lenders can correctly evaluate the risk of each borrower, they can cover for this risk by charging higher interest rates. High-risk borrowers would pay a higher interest rate than low-risk ones. The credit market could work just fine; borrowers, on average, could make a profit off their loans.

*Credit and Asymmetric Information*

Unfortunately, evaluating credit risk is hard to do. Take you, for instance. There's a good chance you're reading this book because you're a student. Suppose you want to take out a student loan. You promise you'll pay it back once you're out of school and working. Should the bank say "here, take some money"?

Not so quick. From the bank's point of view, your repayment risk is unknown, because of things it cannot even see (maybe because you don't want it to!).

First, the risk depends on who you are, that is, your intrinsic characteristics. The bank can observe some of these. For example, it can verify that you're a student in good standing—a proof of enrollment and transcript will do. It can't see other things about you, though. How smart are you, really? And how driven to succeed? Making it to college is a good signal about your innate abilities, but how will that translate into labor market success, which is what you'll have to have in order to repay a student loan?

Strike 1 against getting a student loan.

Then there's the nature of the investment, itself. Your investment is in human capital. Is it a good investment? The bank would like to know that. It knows (from studies economists have done) that, on average, education translates into higher earnings for people in the workforce. (If you've ever taken an econometrics class, you may have estimated the economic returns to schooling, which usually come in at around a 7% earnings gain per year of additional schooling.)[4]

That's an average, though. Does it represent you? Maybe the field you decide to invest in won't be so marketable once you get out of school. In 2012, there was such a glut of lawyers that recent law graduates sued their law schools for fraudulently marketing the profession as a secure source of employment. (The New York Supreme Court ruled against the grads.)[5]

Strike 2 against getting your loan.

Then there's the question of whether you'll behave or not once you get the loan. The actions you take in life will determine the likelihood of paying back your loan. What choices will you make? Will you study hard and wisely use your loan to position yourself for labor-market success? Will you work hard once you are out of school? And if there is, indeed, a life after graduation, will you choose to repay the loan when you are able? These are definite concerns to lenders.

That's strike 3. You're out!

You're a lot like a poor farmer in this respect: who you are and what you do will shape your likelihood of repayment, and information about you is asymmetric. There are many intrinsic things about you that the bank *can't* see but you *can,* things that might well affect your ability to repay, positively or negatively. You probably know yourself pretty well, but the bank doesn't. You know more about your human capital investment project, too. And you can decide your own behavior, but the bank can't observe it until it might be too late.

Actually, the bank could get a lot of this information if it really wanted to. It could find out more about you and learn more about how your major and college are likely to affect your job prospects. It could even hire a private investigator to follow you around and make sure you study hard. Besides being kind of creepy, that would be expensive—so expensive that the bank would never do it. So the problem with asymmetric information is not that the bank can't get the information; it would simply cost a lot of money to get it. This is an example of a transaction cost: the cost of getting the information the bank requires before it will give you a loan. Transaction costs tend to be very high in credit markets (and even higher in insurance markets, as we'll see below).

If you've got a student loan, it's almost certainly government guaranteed. That means the government has agreed to repay your loan if you fail to. That's what the banks demand in order to take on an investment as risky as you! If you didn't know before why student loans are government backed, now you do.

Time, uncertainty, and information asymmetries imply that credit transactions require contracts—not necessarily written ones, as many villagers around the world know, but contracts nonetheless. You don't need a contract to buy a potato! Information flow is critical. So is legal enforcement of the contract. Without the ability to enforce the loan contract, the loan won't happen.

This means that *institutions* (chapter 8) play a *key* role in making credit markets work: the legal system, to enforce contracts; credit bureaus, to provide lenders with information about people's credit worthiness; and property registries, to verify that the owners of property purchased with (or used to secure) credit are who they say they are.

In 2001, three economists—George Akerlof (whom we met in chapter 11), Joseph Stiglitz, and Michael Spence—won the Nobel Prize for their roles in creating the field of information economics. They and others have given us a powerful framework for understanding imperfections and failures in many markets where contracts are critical. Their work centers around two notions: adverse selection and moral hazard. Both are intimately related to asymmetric information. They explain why credit markets (and often other markets) don't work for most people in poor countries, and also why insurance markets are almost nonexistent. To understand why credit markets fail to meet the needs of poor people, we need to understand these notions of adverse selection and moral hazard.

### Adverse Selection

Adverse selection occurs when "bad" outcomes happen because the seller knows more than the buyer about the product being sold—and exploits this advantage in some way. In Akerlof's market for lemons (chapter 11), the seller is the used-car owner, who knows more about the car's quality than any buyer could. I'm more likely to try to sell my car if I know it is crummy and unreliable, especially if these problems can be hidden under a coat of wax. (Buyer, beware!)

The same thing can happen with crummy promises. In credit markets, the seller is the borrower; she sells the promise of future repayment. This seller of promises knows more about her likelihood of default than the lender does. Since the quality of her promise depends on this default probability, she may try to make herself look more financially responsible than she knows herself to be.

This has a critical implication for credit availability. If the demand for potatoes exceeds the supply, the vender raises the price of the potato. If there really isn't enough credit in poor countries (i.e., demand for credit exceeds the supply), why don't banks raise the price of credit (the interest rate), and lend money until demand equals supply? Then, there would be equilibrium in the credit market, and the equilibrium "price of promises" would be the interest rate.

Adverse selection keeps banks from doing this. By increasing the interest rate, lenders may adversely affect the quality of their applicant pool, and this would lower their profits. Think about it: suppose you're totally credit worthy. You should be able to get a loan at a low interest rate because your promise is good (that is, your risk of default is low). You are willing to take out a loan at a low interest rate, but not at a high one—those high-interest loans are for high-risk people, not you.

So what happens if banks raise their interest rate? High-quality borrowers like you "select themselves" out of the market. You're the seller of promises. If you've got good ones to sell, then having to pay a high interest rate means you're selling your promises too cheaply. It's just like what happens in Akerlof's used-car market model. There, high-quality used cars leave the market when the price of used cars goes down. Because of asymmetric information, there is adverse selection; only low-quality cars (lemons) are left.

If the interest rate goes up high enough, only low-quality (high-risk) borrowers will be left in the credit market. You can see how the credit market, like the used-car market, can easily fail when there is adverse selection. You can find a numerical example that leads to this result in appendix 12.A.

*Moral Hazard*

The second big reason why credit markets fail is moral hazard, which is closely related to adverse selection: where adverse selection is about hidden information about quality, moral hazard is about hidden *actions* that affect quality (appendix 12.B).

In the market for lemons, if I plan to sell my car in the next few months, I might not bother to change the transmission fluid even if I was supposed to change it five thousand miles ago because it's unlikely the buyer will know. (That's why some people demand to see service records for the used cars they buy.)

In the world of credit, borrowers take actions that affect the quality of the promises they make, but the bank cannot see these actions. Credit shifts risk from borrowers to lenders. Consider this agricultural loan contract: "Repay if the harvest is successful and default (pay nothing) if the harvest fails."

This contract creates a disincentive for borrowers to take on "safe" projects, that is, ones with a high probability of success. A safe project might mean working hard and using seeds I'm pretty sure will give me a decent harvest, even if the weather is not great. An unsafe one might use a seed that *could* perform *really well* but only if the weather is perfect, which is unlikely in my village.

If my project fails, the worst that can happen to me is that I'll default on the loan, so I'll go for the unsafe project, knowing that if it does succeed I'll make a killing. The bank hopes a farmer who takes out a loan will buy seed, fertilizer, and other inputs that (weather permitting) will enable her to repay the loan after the harvest. But it knows the farmer *could* gamble on a risky seed. She could even use the money for something else, like playing the lottery. (You could do that with your student loan, too.)

The higher the interest rate, the more profit the borrower has to make in order to cover the loan and come out ahead, so the more likely he'll go for the high-risk, high-payoff investment. Thus, moral hazard, like adverse selection, can make lenders unwilling to raise interest rates and make loans even if there is excess demand for credit.

In short, when it comes to credit markets, adverse selection means that people who aren't credit worthy get the loan. Moral hazard means that once they get it, they don't do what they need to do in order to pay it back. Both happen because of asymmetric information: borrowers have greater information than lenders—information that affects the probability of involuntary as well as voluntary default. Borrowers know themselves, their projects, and the actions they take. If lenders raise the interest rate, they cause good types of borrowers to drop out of the market (adverse selection). They also can cause borrowers to take actions that the lender doesn't like, for example, choosing a risky technique (moral hazard). Lenders would have to charge a high interest rate in order to cover the risks of default caused by adverse selection and moral hazard, but if the interest rate is too high, the most credit worthy people leave and the market collapses.

In economics we're accustomed to thinking that the quantity of a product depends on its price. When it comes to credit, though, the quality of the customers and their actions depends on the price (the interest rate), too. When credit markets fail, profitable investments don't happen, and poor people stay poor. Research by development economists documents how big a difference credit can make (see sidebar 12.3).

### SOLVING ADVERSE SELECTION AND MORAL HAZARD IN CREDIT MARKETS

History provides frightening examples of illegitimate measures taken to overcome the problems of moral hazard and adverse selection, as anyone who has seen the Hollywood film *The Godfather* knows. (Even today, mafias and loan sharks have effective ways to make borrowers make good on their loans.)

There are two kinds of *legitimate* mechanisms that lenders can use to try to resolve the problems of adverse selection and moral hazard.[6] Indirect mechanisms involve the terms of contracts. Direct mechanisms are actions lenders can take that address information asymmetries.

## Sidebar 12.3   Credit and Productivity in Peru

Estimating how credit affects production is tricky because the kinds of people who get credit are different from the people who do not. For example, more productive farmers are probably more likely to succeed in getting credit. So if we find that farmers with credit are more productive, is it because of the credit or because productive farmers are the ones who get credit in the first place?

There are two main ways to get at this question using econometrics: first, control for the characteristics that determine whether farmers are credit constrained or not, and second, track the same farmers over time. Catherine Guirkinger and Steve Boucher did both, using what is called "switching regression" and data from a survey of farmers they carried out in northern Peru. Their analysis found that credit constraints lowered the value of agricultural output in the study area by 26%. This study was important because it documented the importance of credit for productivity while controlling for who gets credit and who doesn't.

Catherine Guirkinger and Stephen R. Boucher, "Credit Constraints and Productivity in Peruvian Agriculture," *Agricultural Economics* 39, no. 3 (November 2008):295–308.

*Indirect Mechanisms*

Credit contracts can include many different terms.

*The Interest Rate.* The most obvious term in loan contracts is the interest rate. We've already seen that if lenders set the interest rate too high they may lose quality borrowers and encourage borrowers to take riskier actions. By carefully adjusting the interest rate, a lender can partially control both adverse selection and moral hazard.

*Progressive Loan Size.* A second indirect mechanism involves the loan size. A lender could start out by offering a borrower a small loan. If it is repaid, he can offer the borrower larger and larger loans—like when the bank raises the limit on your credit card. This is called progressive lending. It addresses adverse selection by enabling the lender to cheaply identify really bad types (they default on the small loans). It addresses moral hazard because the promise of larger future loans gives the borrower an incentive to behave well (repay). An obvious problem here is that the larger the loan, the greater the incentive to misbehave (moral hazard). A bad guy could behave well, maximize his credit line, and then "cash out" by defaulting.

*The Threat of Termination.* If a borrower defaults, the bank denies future access to loans. This addresses moral hazard by providing incentives for borrowers to behave well or else risk termination. A problem with this mechanism is that you probably do not have access to information from other lenders who may have terminated someone who applies for a loan from you. That's why credit agencies were created: to provide lenders with credit information about you before they give you a loan. You won't find many of them in poor rural areas, though. Another problem is that default may be legitimate: even quality borrowers make investments that fail sometimes. That's what business bankruptcy laws were created for, but you will not find this institutional development in most parts of the world, either.

*Collateral.* Collateral requires borrowers to secure the loan with personal property like land or a house, which the lender can foreclose upon in the event of default. Collateral addresses adverse selection: risky types won't apply for a loan because the probability of losing their collateral will be too high. It addresses moral hazard: the threat of foreclosure creates incentives for borrowers to behave well so they can repay their loans and keep their house.

Collateral requirements create other problems, though, particularly in poor societies. Many people do not have the collateral required to secure a loan. The institutions described in chapter 8 can directly affect the feasibility and enforceability of collateral requirements. For example, as we described in that chapter, many small farmers do not have formal title to their land. For collateral to work, property rights must be well defined and easily transferable. Titled land, a house, a business, jewelry, machines, vehicles, or a standing crop (harvest) are good candidates for use as collateral. The value of the collateral must not be subject to moral hazard. (I could trash my house or run off with my jewels before the bank takes them.) The property must be immobile (like a house) or else really small, so that the lender can hold it (a diamond ring). By design, collateral also shifts some risk back onto the borrowers, which can create "risk rationing": people with good projects may not undertake them because collateral-based contracts force them to bear too much risk. I want to invest in a business, but I won't risk my house for it.

In short, collateral requirements are generally not a good way to get credit to poor people, who do not have many assets. The assets poor people have may be unacceptable to banks. The transaction costs of posting collateral are high. Even if they have some assets that banks accept, poor people may be unwilling to risk using them as collateral. Collateral requirements affect the demand for credit as well as the supply. A poor person may not have credit because she tried to get it but was denied (supply rationing), she was unwilling to pay the high interest rate (price rationing), or she didn't apply because she was unwilling to put her collateral at risk (risk [demand] rationing).

*Direct Mechanisms*

*Contractual terms* to deal with adverse selection and moral hazard are what we call "indirect mechanisms." They are indirect because they try to influence what kinds of people apply for loans (selection) and their behavior once they get a loan (moral hazard). Lenders can also try to deal with adverse selection and moral hazard *directly, by screening applicants ex-ante and monitoring them ex-post.* Direct mechanisms, like indirect ones, can take many forms.

*Ex-ante Actions.* Before a loan is made, loan officers can require would-be borrowers to fill out loan application forms, documenting their income and assets and providing other information critical to screening. They can require loan applicants to submit investment plans demonstrating that the project for which the loan will be used is viable. They can directly inspect applicants' farms, businesses, and assets to make sure they are good enough to use as collateral. A loan officer might interview family members and neighbors to learn about the applicant's integrity, work ethic, reliability, and other personal characteristics. If a credit bureau exists, the loan officer almost certainly will buy information about the applicant's credit history. This last step can be crucial because it provides information on the applicant's performance on loans from other lenders.

This all sounds like a lot of snooping around, and it is. But borrowers put up with this sort of thing all the time in order to get a loan. Lenders incur the costs of screening in order to get the best applicants.

These ex-ante measures deal mostly with the adverse selection problem. However, they also can address moral hazard, for example, by screening out the applicants who are most likely to shirk or misbehave once they have a loan.

*Ex-Post Actions.* After making a loan, lenders can take direct actions to increase the likelihood of repayment. They can visit borrowers and their farms or businesses to make sure the loan funds are being used properly and check on the progress of the project. Is the business being run efficiently? Are the fields being carefully tended? If the loan is for crop production, a loan officer might well show up just before the harvest—not a bad strategy given that the loan repayment is sitting out in the field! (Pretending your harvest is smaller than it is in order to avoid repayment is a great example of moral hazard.)

Direct and indirect measures like those outlined above can go a long way toward resolving the problems of adverse selection and moral hazard. However, they are costly; information is not free. The value of the time loan officers invest in screening applicants and monitoring borrowers can add considerably to the cost of loans. These are classic examples of transaction costs. They make the transaction more expensive, and if they are high enough, they keep the transaction from happening. Without them, though, information asymmetries may shut down the market altogether.

Given the high transaction costs of overcoming information problems in credit markets, it is little wonder that formal lenders do not serve poor people or, for that matter, farmers or entrepreneurs who are not poor but small. If you're a lender, and you have to incur these transaction costs no matter who you lend to, clearly you're better off making a few big loans than many little ones.

## THE MICROFINANCE REVOLUTION

That's where microfinance comes in. Microfinance, also called microcredit, is the provision of very small (micro) loans, typically less than US$100, by lending institutions. Microfinance institutions focus on people near or below the poverty line who have been excluded from the formal credit market (that is, banks). They also lend to micro-entrepreneurs, people with small-scale (typically informal) businesses. Micro-loans usually are made without collateral.

Wait a minute, you might say. Isn't this a setup for failure? Banks don't loan to poor people and small businesses because of the high transaction costs of overcoming adverse selection and moral hazard. Demanding collateral is a critical tool to ensure repayment. Why would a microfinance institution think it could pull off something that well-staffed banks—not to mention well-funded government credit programs—have failed miserably at?

Actually, making small loans to low-income people and microbusinesses is not new. Informal village moneylenders have been doing it profitably for centuries, usually at very high interest rates. What do they know that we don't?

Seeing local moneylenders thrive in villages that banks will not touch seems puzzling. But clearly there's a lesson here, and in the past couple of decades economists, microfinance institutions, and governments have begun to catch on. If banks won't make small loans to poor people, the transaction costs of doing so must be high for banks. If local moneylenders *do* make small loans to poor people, they must have figured out a way to overcome the problems of adverse selection and moral hazard, and at a low enough cost to turn a profit.

In 1976, the Bangladeshi economist Muhammad Yunus, third of nine children and son of a jeweler, began working with poor women who made bamboo furniture with usurious loans in the village of Jobra, near the university where he lectured. Three decades later, in 2006, he (together with the Grammeen Bank he founded) received the Nobel Peace Prize. The Nobel Committee declared: "Muhammad Yunus . . . managed to translate visions into practical action for the benefit of millions of people, not only in Bangladesh, but also in many other countries. Loans to poor people without any financial security had appeared to be an impossible idea. From modest beginnings three decades ago, Yunus has, first and foremost through Grameen Bank, developed micro-credit into an ever more important instrument in the struggle against poverty."[7]

Yunus figured out how to solve the asymmetric-information problem (see sidebar 12.4).

By 2010 the Grameen Bank had a total loan portfolio of $939 million—8.3 million active borrowers with an average loan of $113. The vast majority of its borrowers are women. Repayment rates are claimed to be 95%.

The Grameen Bank's methodology has been replicated and spread throughout the world, including the United States. Yunus became an international microfinance phenomenon, appearing on *The Daily Show with Jon Stewart* (2006), *The Oprah Winfrey Show* (2006), *The Colbert Report* (2008), and *The Simpsons* (2010). Texas named a holiday after him. The United Nations declared 2005 the "International Year of Microcredit."

### Sidebar 12.4   Muhammad Yunus and the Grameen Bank

The Bangladeshi economist Muhammad Yunus had an answer to the problems of adverse selection *and* moral hazard: design a system in which local information and monitoring could make loans viable. While visiting some of the poorest village households in India, he realized that very small loans could make a big difference. In the village of Jobra, women made bamboo furniture but had to pay usurious interest rates on loans to buy bamboo. Yunus's first loan, out of his own pocket in 1976, was for US$27, but it wasn't to a single individual; it was to forty-two women!

What was Yunus's secret to solving the moral hazard and adverse selection problems?

Informal groups of women apply for loans. They know each other. The group's members act as coguarantors of repayment. If one member fails to do what she needs to do to pay back her part of the loan, the rest of the group has to pay or else loses the chance to get loans in the future. The group, therefore, has a vested interest in seeing to it that every member of the group succeeds. That means monitoring and supporting one another—just what is needed to overcome moral hazard. What about adverse selection? Well, who would *you* choose to have in your group?

Yunus turned microfinance into a viable business model, which has spread around the world. That's why the Nobel Committee recognized his contribution to humanity by awarding him the Nobel Peace Prize in 2006.

Muhammad Yunus, *Banker to the Poor* (New Delhi: Penguin, 1998).

*Microfinance in Theory and Practice*

Grameen-style microfinance addresses asymmetric-information problems in two ways.

First, through self-selection into borrower groups. To take out a Grameen loan, people have to get together and form a borrower group. The loan goes to the borrower group, and then it is dispersed to individuals within the group. Loan repayments are made jointly by the group, and with high frequency. If one member does not repay, the entire group is denied access to loans in the future. This is called "joint liability." Thus, the group has to make sure each of its members pays back her loan—the rest of the group must cover for any members who do not repay.

Who, then, will you choose to have in your group? Clearly, you'll admit only good types of borrowers into your group. Since you live in the same village, you probably have pretty good information about who those people are; information asymmetries will be small. This addresses the adverse selection problem. Group monitoring to make sure each member repays addresses the moral hazard problem. Together, these make the group loan a low-risk investment for the microfinance institution, which thus can charge an interest rate low enough to keep the good types in the market. Microfinance solves the adverse selection and moral hazard problems by taking advantage of borrowers' information about each other, and also by designing contracts to give borrowers incentives to overcome the asymmetric information problems that banks cannot overcome.

As we've explored in several places in this book so far, however, development is not easy, and there are plenty of challenges and critiques when it comes to microfinance. Thus, some observers feel that the promise of microfinance is overblown.

First, it's hard to implement a successful microfinance scheme. For every Grameen-style success, there are ten failures! A lack of human capital, limited administrative expertise to build a microfinance institution, and corruption all are major obstacles to successful microfinance programs.

Second, microfinance may be better than loan sharks charging exorbitant interest rates, but it is still expensive by formal-sector standards. Average annual interest rates on microcredit loans are in the 30% to 40% range.

Third, most successful microfinance programs have had subsidies—sometimes large ones—to help them get started. The cost of these subsidies, which may be paid by governments or NGOs, often is not factored in when people guage the success of microfinance programs.

Fourth, microfinance programs are vulnerable to *covariate shocks*. When unexpected events like droughts or floods affect many people in a locality at the same time, the group can default. Large banks and insurance companies cover themselves for multivariate shocks by making loans over a large geographic area instead of focusing on individual locations. Even so, covariate risks can kill a deal even in rich economies, as anyone who's tried to get flood, earthquake, or hurricane insurance can attest.

Fifth, microfinance programs have a built-in problem of borrower "graduation." Good types of borrowers often don't need further micro-credit once they've succeeded in "getting ahead." This tends to drain credit groups of their lowest-risk members over time, which can make it hard for groups to remain viable and repay future loans.

Finally, as with any development project, microfinance raises the big question: Is this the *best* use of scarce development resources—not only money but also the effort and creative energy of international development agencies and local governments? Does it address the deeper, structural causes of poverty? Inequality, lack of infrastructure, poor educational systems, poor health-care systems—these are all critical issues that need to be addressed by development policies. Microfinance obviously is not a cure-all for these problems, but it has become an essential part of the development economist's tool kit.

### RISK AND RISK AVERSION

To understand the economics of insurance markets, you must first understand some essential details about risk and risk aversion. We've touched on related topics in many places in this book. In this section, we discuss risk and risk aversion as essentials in development economics and as prerequisites to understanding how insurance works in developing countries.

No matter who you are or where you live, risk and uncertainty are part of your daily routine—and the feelings they induce in you and in others are fundamental to the human experience. Great literature often offers compelling descriptions of characters confronting or taking great risks. *Les Misérables* epitomizes great literature of this sort and, through the confrontation of characters and circumstances, leads us to wonder how we would hold up in the face of such overwhelming risk and calamity.

While risk is part of life everywhere, some people in some places obviously face much greater and more consequential risks than others. In developed countries, most folks pay a premium to reduce their exposure to risk. Sometimes, people actually choose to literally pay a premium to avoid risk in the form of life, health, or property insurance. Other times, we choose to pay extra for safety features in cars or houses. Often, developed countries make public investments or require individuals to make investments to reduce risk in the workplace, in the environment, and at home. Entrepreneurs and others often willingly take great risks in the hopes of success, and indeed this willingness to take risks and try new things fuels much of the innovation machine we introduced in chapter 8. An individual is much more likely to take these kinds of commercial risks if she is protected from personal and property risks.

The average person living in Africa or India lives with a lot more risk in her life than does her counterpart in North America or Europe. This fact was immediately apparent to Travis's ten- and twelve-year-old kids during a recent sabbatical year in Ghana. They quickly noticed and commented on small risks like whether you have water or electricity, larger risks like traffic hazards and serious illnesses, and even (perhaps especially) the risks animals face when they are not coddled and pampered as pets.

*Measuring Risk Aversion*

While people in developing countries generally face greater risks, the impulse to avoid or reduce consequential risks where possible is an innate human survival instinct. But some people care more about risk— and are willing to do or spend more to reduce their exposure to risk— than others. Economists call such people "risk averse" and attribute these differences from one person to another to "risk preferences."

Because individuals' level of risk aversion can directly influence the decisions they make and can even shape market outcomes, risk preferences often play an important role in the theoretical models economists use to understand economic development processes. Since these preferences can really matter in practice, development economists have also developed experimental methods to measure individual risk aversion.

Suppose for a moment that you are a maize farmer in Malawi. If you are generally willing to take risks when potential returns are high, you will likely manage your farm differently than a more risk averse neighbor farmer. You may manage other dimensions of your household and livelihood activities differently as well. Because these differences can be important, any economist who comes to your village trying to better understand local development issues and opportunities will want to try to discern these differences in risk aversion.

The economist has three basic options for estimating your degree of risk aversion and that of your neighbors. First, she can ask you directly, "How willing are you to take risks?" Second, she can collect detailed information about you and your household and try to infer something about your risk preferences from this information. Third, she can create risk "games" and offer real money based on your performance in these "games." In the past decade, the third option, originally adapted from experimental psychology techniques, has emerged as a favorite tool of development economists.

Experimental economics has grown rapidly as a methodological tool for studying individual decision making. As mentioned in chapter 2, these methods are part of the recent experimental revolution in development economics. Development economists have made some important contributions to the field of experimental economics along the way. In the late 1970s, a development economist named Hans Binswanger was the first to take experimental economics out of university laboratories and classrooms and into the field—among Indian farmers no less.[8]

Binswanger wanted to understand how much risk aversion varied from farmer to farmer and how much it mattered to their adoption of high-yielding new seed varieties. He decided to create a risk experiment. Over the course of several visits to these farm households, he and his research team presented farmers with seventeen different risk "games." In each game, farmers would choose between essentially the following six payoff pairs (note that we've converted the original rupee payoffs into rough current dollar equivalents):

| Choice | Low payoff for "heads" | High payoff for "tails" |
| --- | --- | --- |
| O | $50 | $50 |
| A | $45 | $95 |
| B | $40 | $120 |
| C | $30 | $150 |
| D | $20 | $160 |
| E | $10 | $190 |
| F | $0 | $200 |

As you might have guessed from this list, after a farmer made his choice, the research team would flip a coin to determine which payoff the farmer would earn. You might also notice that these payoff pairs entail a basic risk-return trade-off: After choice "O," each pair is riskier than the one before it, but also provides a potentially higher payoff. Using this clever experiment, which is "incentive compatible" because there is real money on the table, Binswanger had a way of discerning the risk aversion of the farmers in his study. He found that roughly 75% of farmers were risk averse at moderate or intermediate levels and about 8% were severely or extremely risk averse.

Since Binswanger conducted this risk experiment in India, development economists have refined their use of experimental economics in the field. A more recent risk experiment used by Laura Schechter is even simpler than Binswanger's.[9] She gave farmers in Paraguay roughly $1.25 (two-thirds of the daily wage rate) and asked them how much they were willing to wager on the roll of a die where rolling a 1, 2, 3, 4, 5, or 6 multiplied the wager by 0 (losing the wager), 0.5, 1.0, 1.5, 2.0, or 2.5, respectively.

Development economists now have several experimental options for eliciting risky decisions from individuals, which can only be a good thing given how fundamentally these risk preferences shape individual and household decision making.

## Risk and Poverty

Risk really matters in development economics because it really matters to the poor and it can really shape development outcomes. We discussed how risk affects poverty in chapter 4 when we introduced vulnerability and poverty dynamics. There we used the "rolling marbles" profile to depict the dynamic forces that can expand or erode a household's assets over time. To distinguish between stable and unstable equilibria, we had you visualize what would happen to the marbles in the profile if we "bumped" the profile. Introducing risk into this kind of system is exactly like unpredictably bumping the profile.

Poor households routinely endure negative shocks to their assets. Sickness can sap individuals' strength and compromise their ability to work on the farm or work for wages. Storms can wash away land and crops. Drought can weaken and kill livestock. Theft or extortion can wipe out months of savings. But good things can unexpectedly happen, too. Bumper crops and high prices can provide extra income. A new road can bring new work opportunities. Better access to technology and information can improve productive decisions and increase profit margins. If the household is subject to anything like the dynamic forces described in figure 4.2, these positive and negative shocks ("bumps") can shape welfare outcomes for a long time to come and shift the household to a higher or lower equilibrium asset level.

Much of the work of economists on risk and poverty aims to understand the impact of shocks like these on poverty. Obviously, these shocks can be painful and, as we just described, they can have long-run implications if there are asset dynamics at work. But these shocks are not the only effect risk can have on poverty—indeed, they may not even be the most important effect. In many settings, the biggest impact risk has on poverty is much harder to see.

Consider the effect drought risk has on the maize farmer and his family in Ethiopia. How exactly does drought risk affect this household? First, if a drought happens to occur, the household clearly suffers. This is the obvious ex-post burden of drought. But a drought doesn't actually have to happen for drought risk to hurt the household. The threat of drought may be enough to hurt the household. Just as a sixth-grade bully causes some kids to change how they get to school and where they hang out at recess, so the threat of drought at the beginning of the maize season causes many households to make very conservative maize farming decisions. This is the *ex ante* effect of risk on poverty: it can make poor households exposed to risk so cautious and conservative that they miss out on better livelihood strategies.

### INSURANCE AND ASYMMETRIC INFORMATION

Output and credit markets illustrate how information problems can lead to market failure. Asymmetric information can also shut down insurance markets, and this can lead to efficiency losses that keep poor people poor.

### The Importance of Insurance

There is nothing more important to poor people than the security of putting food on the table—today, this week, and next month. Without any way to smooth consumption, income shocks would translate directly into consumption shocks. We illustrate this in figure 12.1 by graphing the hypothetical ups and downs of a family's income and consumption. You can see that the variation in income around its mean is high. In many years (six, to be exact), income is lower than the subsistence minimum needed for the family to survive. If consumption followed income exactly, this family would be in trouble.

How can a household decouple its consumption from its income enough to keep from falling below the subsistence minimum? Decoupling consumption from income is called "consumption smoothing." There are two ways to smooth consumption—ways that correspond to the two effects of risk we just described: ex-ante and ex-post.

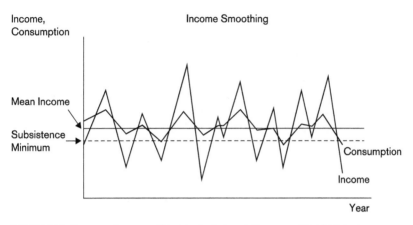

**FIGURE 12.1.** Consumption smoothing seeks to break the connection between consumption and income and keep households above their subsistence minimum even in bad years.

*Ex-ante,* a household can take steps to smooth out its income. For example, instead of specializing in a single source of income (say, a single cash crop), it can diversify its activities. It can put some land in cash crops, some in staples; some labor in crop production, some in wage work or migration. Ex-ante risk coping tries to compress the income profile in this figure, pulling the troughs up, but in the process almost certainly pushing the spikes downward (see sidebar 12.5).

*Ex-post,* households can try to smooth their consumption given income swings like the ones shown in the figure. If households had access to formal insurance, this would be easy. They'd pay a premium (the price one pays to buy an insurance contract), which would bring down their income in good years. However, in bad years the policy would pay out, providing cash for consumption. Formal income insurance is virtually nonexistent in poor societies, though, for reasons we'll look at below.

How else can you smooth your consumption when income is so volatile? You might use your credit card, but that isn't an option for a poor household in rural Malawi for the reasons described above. Poor people could save in good years and dis-save in bad ones, but that's easier said than done when there is no access to savings institutions.

In ancient times there were no banks, and people kept their savings for a rainy day in silver and gold coins, hidden away in a metal box. This was called "hoarding." Today ancient coin hoards are still found from time to time around the Mediterranean Sea. Behind every one of

---

**Sidebar 12.5   Why Poor People Pay a High Price for (Ex-Ante) Insurance**

A study of rural Indian households by Mark Rosenzweig and Hans Binswanger found that in order to protect themselves against income uncertainty, poor households diversify their activities more than rich households. That way, for example, if the rains don't come and the crop fails, they'll have other activities to fall back upon. The authors found that in places with high climate risk, poor households diversify more.

By diversifying, though, poor households forfeit the income gains from specializing in what they do best. The authors concluded that access to insurance could bring substantial economic benefits to rural households, especially the poor. A crop insurance policy guarantees that poor families will have food on their table even if the rains don't come, and this should make them more willing to plant crops, if that's what they do best.

Mark Rosenzweig and Hans Binswanger, "Wealth, Weather Risk, and the Consumption and Profitability of Agricultural Investments," *Economic Journal* 103 (1994):56–78.

---

these uncovered hoards is a story, long lost, that no doubt would illustrate why hoarding is not a very good insurance strategy.

Without markets, households could use their money in good times to buy things they can sell off in hard times. Many poor people in rural areas use livestock as a bank. Distress sales of animals are a common feature of people trying to make it through an adverse shock, for example, a severe drought.

There are problems with selling off assets, though. One is the price: if you're selling because of a drought, there's a good chance other people are, too, so the price is likely to be low at just the wrong time. In a poor economy facing high transaction costs, cut off from outside markets, there's the question of whom to sell your assets to. The biggest problem is that once you sell off your assets you've lost the chance to use them to recover from the shock. Knowing that makes it hard to sell off that last animal (see sidebar 12.6).

Credit and insurance often come up in the same breath when we talk about risk. The possibility of using credit or savings ("borrowing from yourself") to get through hard times makes credit and insurance close relatives when it comes to survival in poor societies.

### Sidebar 12.6 Holding On to the Last Cow (or Two)

When a covariate shock (for example, drought) or an idiosyncratic one (illness) strikes, one way to pull through is to sell off some assets—say, your animals—to keep up your consumption. We saw in sidebar 12.1 that economists used data from Burkina Faso to show that on average households only offset 15%–30% of the income shortfall due to drought with livestock sales. This seems like very little consumption smoothing, but there's more to the story.

As is often the case, it is useful to look beneath this "average" response. What does this limited consumption smoothing response on average imply about how different kinds of households responded to drought? Exploring this question sheds new light on consumption smoothing.

Using the same panel data from Burkina Faso as described in sidebar 12.1, Travis and Michael Carter discovered that the average response is composed of two very different types of households: a small group that completely smooth their consumption by selling livestock and a large group that don't sell livestock at all. The small group of consumption smoothers have much bigger herds than the large group of "asset smoothers" who resist selling livestock. By holding on to their last few animals, poor households cling to the chance of being able to recover from the drought instead of falling into an "asset poverty trap" they might not be able to get out of. Remember the "rolling marbles" profile in chapter 4? Asset smoothers have small herds that are close to the unstable equilibrium on top of the middle hill: the slightest bump—in this case selling off an extra animal to smooth consumption in the short run—can cause the marble to roll down the hill to the left and into the poverty trap.

But there's a big catch. If holding onto those last few animals means your family doesn't have enough food to eat, you are effectively drawing down your future human capital (the bodies and brains of your children, who cannot develop properly without food and thus may be less productive in the future) in order to avoid drawing down your tiny herd and ending up in the likely poverty trap that comes with it. A lack of insurance to protect assets leaves poor households with this cruel intertemporal choice.

Michael R. Carter and J. Travis Lybbert, "Consumption versus Asset Smoothing: Testing the Implications of Poverty Trap Theory in Burkina Faso," *Journal of Development Economics* 99, no. 2 (2012):255–64.

## IDIOSYNCRATIC VERSUS COVARIATE SHOCKS

Broadly speaking, people face two kinds of shocks in life: idiosyncratic and covariate.

> *Idiosyncratic shocks* affect specific individuals but not others around them. If a farmer has an accident in his field and is injured, for example, he has experienced an idiosyncratic shock. The kinds of policies that are widely available to people in high-income countries primarily insure against idiosyncratic shocks: fire, theft, death, and so on.

> *Covariate shocks* affect many people at once. If the rains don't come to your farm, they won't come to your neighbors' farms, either. Examples of covariate shocks are weather, earthquakes, and epidemics. The fine print in insurance policies frequently contains exclusions associated with covariate shocks, like floods and earthquakes in homeowners' insurance policies.

Within an economy, it is easier to insure against idiosyncratic shocks than against covariate shocks. If I become ill, my fellow villagers might be able to help me out (informal insurance). If I have insurance from a private company, it can pay me if I suffer an idiosyncratic shock covered by the policy, knowing that it can cover this loss with premiums paid by others around me.

A private company will be loath to issue protection against covariate shocks, like a storm or earthquake, knowing that if such a shock hits it will have to pay out on many claims simultaneously. After the 1994 earthquake centered in Northridge, California, insurance companies stopped issuing policies covering earthquake damages. The state of California had to step in and create its own earthquake insurance for homeowners.

Insuring against covariate shocks usually requires having access to resources outside the economy in which the shocks might occur. Insurance companies recognize this. They buy insurance policies from other insurers—that is, outside their own companies—to protect themselves in the event many claims hit at the same time. Some global "reinsurance" companies specialize in insuring insurers.

## WHY INSURANCE MARKETS FAIL

The same problems of adverse selection and moral hazard that constrain credit markets virtually prevent the formation of insurance markets in poor areas.

*Adverse Selection*

When a person takes out life or crop insurance, he buys a promise from the insurance company to "pay off" if he dies or the crop fails. He pays the insurance company the price of the policy (the policy premium) in return for this promise. The insurance company sells him the policy if his risk of death (or crop failure) is low enough that, on average, the company will make a profit. The higher the risk of death (or crop failure), the higher the premiums the insurance company will have to charge.

That's where adverse selection and moral hazard come in. People with a high risk of death or crop failure have more of an incentive to get insurance than people with a low risk. Often, the high-risk people know who they are, but the insurer does not. If I have a terminal disease, I will want life insurance. If I farm in a risky environment, I will want crop insurance. There's no reason to buy earthquake insurance on your house if you live in Kansas, but a big reason to if you live in San Francisco. In short, the kinds of people with the greatest incentive to get insurance are the worst bets for the insurance company. This drives the price of insurance upward. But as the insurance premium rises, low-risk people no longer find it advantageous to buy insurance. Only the high-risk types stay in the market.

Adverse selection is a big reason why insurance markets function the way they do. It also explains why insurance companies test people and look at their medical records before selling them a life insurance policy, why "Obamacare" requires everyone to have health insurance, and why private health insurance is hard to get and often has exclusion clauses for "preexisting conditions" (a practice not permitted under the new US health reform law).

*Moral Hazard*

Once a person gets insurance, the moral hazard problem of hidden action comes in. Knowing the insurer will pay off in the case of my crop failure, what incentive do I have to work hard in my field? Armed with a good life and health insurance policy, am I more inclined to take on risky behavior, like smoking or flying over the Himalayas in a hot-air balloon? With a good theft policy, I could sell my bike, declare it stolen, collect on insurance, and double my money (and hope no one catches me!).

As in the case of credit, insurers could invest in screening (getting information about how risky I am) and monitoring (making sure I work hard on my land); however, this is expensive. Screening and monitoring are part of the transaction cost of insurance. The rarity of insurance suggests that this cost is simply too high for formal insurance markets to form in most parts of the world.

In short, when it comes to insurance markets, adverse selection means that high-risk people get insured. Moral hazard means that once they get insured, they engage in risky behavior. Sometimes the line between these two concepts can be a bit thin. For example, Travis is a risk taker. That's a characteristic that the insurance company can't see. Once he gets his life insurance policy, he starts taking hot-air balloon rides over the Himalayas, knowing his family's needs will be covered if he goes down. Anyone who really knows him wouldn't be surprised, but the insurance company doesn't know Travis.

Here, as in the case of credit markets, both adverse selection and moral hazard happen because of asymmetric information: those seeking insurance have greater information than the insurers do—information that affects the probability of an insurance policy having to pay out. If insurers raise their premiums to cover these risks, they drive the good risk types out of the market (adverse selection). They also cause the insured to take actions that the insurer doesn't like, for example, going for a risky investment (or taking hot-air balloon rides over the Himalayas). That is moral hazard. If premiums are too high, the "best-bet" people leave the insurance market, and the market collapses.

### INDEX INSURANCE

There is, in theory, a simple solution to both adverse selection and moral hazard in insurance: design the insurance policy so that its payout is completely independent of who demands insurance and how he behaves. That's what *index insurance* does. An index insurance policy pays out if some trigger goes off that has nothing to do with what the insured people do.

An example of an index trigger is a drop in the average yield for a whole region, the water level in a reservoir, or rainfall measured at a local weather station. Even if you choose a risky action or fail to work hard, you won't affect any of these indexes, so your riskiness to the insurance company will not depend on who you are or what you do. If your yields tend to move up and down with the yields of others around you, though, index insurance can be valuable to you. It can also be profitable for an insurance company: knowing what the probability of

**Sidebar 12.7    Insuring with Satellites**

A big challenge in index insurance is how to come up with a good index. If there is no irrigation, you can't draw a line on the side of the irrigation reservoir. You could base the index on local rainfall data, but crop yields depend on when the rains come as well as how much rain there is. Ideally, the index would be based on whether overall yields, say, in a valley, drop enough to trigger an index insurance payout. But that would require annual yield surveys in the valley, which would be costly.

That's where satellites can help.

Satellite pictures provide a way to measure vegetation density, using the Normalized Difference Vegetation Index (NDVI). Every ten days NDVI is measured and freely available on the Family Early Warning System Network website, at a resolution of 8 × 8 kilometers. Rachid Laajaj and Michael Carter showed that the NDVI can be used to make an effective insurance index. In the region they studied in Burkina Faso, they showed that a satellite-based index captured 89% of the variance of village yields—much better than an index based on rainfall.

Rachid Laajaj and Michael Carter, "Using Satellite Imagery as the Basis for Index Insurance Contracts in West Africa" (draft, 2009; www. agriskmanagementforum.org/doc/using-satellite-imagery-basis-index-insurance-contracts-west-africa).

the trigger event is, the company can price its product to make a profit, on average.

Access to index insurance might enable farmers to get bank credit and achieve higher crop yields. Imagine two farmers soliciting a loan, both farmers identical except that one has index insurance and the other does not. Which one would you give the loan to if you were the bank?

The big drawback to index insurance is that it cannot insure people against risks associated with idiosyncratic shocks, or with covariate shocks that are not related to the index. If a farmer has an accident and is injured, or if a disease sweeps through everyone's herds, the water level in the local reservoir obviously is not affected, so an index policy linked to the water level will not pay out. Nevertheless, if the index chosen is both easily measured and highly correlated with a key income source, like farming, index insurance has the potential to contribute toward reducing—though not eliminating—income risk.

A trick is coming up with a good index. Satellites can help (see sidebar 12.7).

## GOVERNMENT, CREDIT, AND RISK

In light of the problems of adverse selection and moral hazard that we have looked at in this chapter, it is little wonder that governments have had a poor record of solving credit market failures. India gives us a striking example: in 2008, the finance ministry had to forgive government loans to 40 million small and marginal farmers, at a cost of over US$15 billion. What went wrong? Asymmetric information. The government did not know the people it was lending to. This resulted in both moral hazard and adverse selection. In trying to address a credit market failure, India ended up with a big-time policy failure on its hands.

That doesn't mean there isn't anything governments can do to address credit and insurance market failures. We have seen the importance of public goods to the functioning of credit markets, including titling of collateral, legal institutions to enforce credit contracts, and credit market information. These are likely to fall into the domain of the public sector. So is investment in public education to increase "financial human capital," including poor people's awareness of, and ability to use, financial institutions.

There may also be a role for subsidies to give poor people better access to financial institutions, particularly in rural areas. In Mexico, a relatively high income developing country, 74% of all counties *(municipios)* had no bank branches in them at all in 2007. Not surprisingly, these are mostly rural counties in which the transaction costs of offering banking services tend to be high. It might make sense to have government subsidies that encourage banks to locate branches in these rural counties by partly offsetting these transaction costs. Alternatively, governments could attack the transaction costs at their roots by investing in new rural infrastructure.

Public provision of weather and other geographic information system (GIS) information, not to mention satellite imagery, is critical to the functioning of index insurance schemes. Providing critical public goods can have positive repercussions that go well beyond credit and insurance markets.

Whatever policies are considered to provide credit and income security to poor people, it is important to keep in mind that the same problems that make markets fail in the first place are likely to hamper government efforts to correct market failures.

www.rebeltext.org/development/qr12.html
Learn more about credit and insurance by
exploring multimedia resources while you read.

### APPENDIX 12.A

*Adverse Selection: A Tale of Two Types*

You're a loan officer. A man walks in the door and says: "I'm Honest Abe. I've got a 'sure thing' that will yield a 50% rate of return. I need $1,000 to finance it."

You know there are two *types* of borrowers in the world:

"Honest Abe" always repays the loan.

"Slick Willy" takes the money and runs (defaults).

Suppose you also know that the population is equally split between these two types. That is, if you randomly pick someone from the population, there's a 50% chance you'll get an Abe and a 50% chance you'll get a Willy. Your problem is that you can't observe a borrower's true type. Slick Willy may pretend to be Honest Abe.

To set up our problem, let's define the following variables:

$i$ = the interest rate (.05 → 5% interest rate)

$R$ = the loan repayment (this is the lender's revenue)

$L$ = the loan principal; assume it is $1,000 (this is the lender's cost)

$\pi$ = the lender's profit

Our first objective is to find the interest rate, $i$, that allows the lender to earn zero *expected* profit. That is what we would expect the lender to get in a competitive credit market, in which the interest rate is the normal rate of return on loans. The lender's profit is $\pi = R - L$. $R$ is the amount he gets repaid, or his revenue. $L$ is the opportunity cost of the money he lent out, or simply his cost.

$\pi$ is a random variable. When the creditor loans out the money, he doesn't know if he will get the money back. The value of repayment, $R$, is a random variable, and this makes $\pi$ a random variable, too. The expected value of $\pi$, $E(\pi)$, equals expected revenue, $E(R)$, minus the cost of the loan, $L$. So we need to figure out what $E(R)$ is.

$$E(R) = Pr(\text{Borrower is Abe}) * (\text{Repayment if Abe}) + Pr(\text{Borrower is Willy}) * (\text{Repayment if Willy})$$

... where $Pr(\cdot)$ means "the probability that what is in the parentheses happens." There's a 50-50 chance the borrower is an Honest Abe, in which case the lender gets back the $1,000 with interest. However, there's also a 50-50 chance he's a Slick Willie, in which case he gets nothing back at all. In math:

$$E(R) = (\tfrac{1}{2}) * [(1 + i) * 1,000] + (\tfrac{1}{2}) * \$0$$
$$E(R) = (\tfrac{1}{2}) * [(1 + i) * 1,000]$$

This makes sense: expected revenue is the total amount repaid when the borrower is an "Abe" times the probability that the borrower is an "Abe." Since $L = 1,000$, the lender's expected profit is:

$$E(\pi) = E(R) - L = (\tfrac{1}{2}) * [(1 + i) * 1,000] - 1,000$$

When does this expected profit just equal zero? When

$$E(\pi) = (\tfrac{1}{2}) * [(1 + i) * 1,000] - 1,000 = 0$$

Let's solve this for $i$ to find out what the equilibrium interest rate must be in this world of Slick Willies and Honest Abes:

$$0 = (\tfrac{1}{2}) * [(1 + i) * 1,000] - 1,000$$
$$500 * (1 + i) = 1,000$$
$$1 + i = 2$$
$$i = 1$$

Thus, the interest rate must be 100% in order for the lender to break even on average. That's a problem: Abe's rate of return on the investment is only 50%. It would not make sense for him to pay 100% interest on a loan to make an investment that yields only 50%.

Abe won't take this loan.

Willy will, though! The lender will be left with only "Slick Willy" types in the market. The only way to get Abe back is to lower the interest rate.

#### APPENDIX 12.B

*Moral Hazard: A Tale of Two Actions*

Again, you're a loan officer. Suppose there's only one type of borrower: Farmer Jimmy. But now there are two possible *actions* that Jimmy can take: he can choose either of two techniques.

*Technique 1:* Grow safe *regular peanuts* (RP). Jimmy invests $1,000 and gets $1,200 in revenues with certainty. His profit is $\pi = 1,200 - 1,000 = \$200$.

*Technique 2:* Grow risky *salted peanuts* (SP). Again, Jimmy invests $1,000, but with this technique, 20% of the time he is successful, earning $2,000 in revenues. The other 80% of the time he fails, with $0 revenues.

The loan contract requires Jimmy to repay the loan if the harvest is successful, but if the harvest fails, Jimmy defaults (pays nothing). As a loan officer, you think: "If I charge $i$, what will Jimmy do?"

What *does* Jimmy do? Jimmy compares his expected profit under the two techniques.
Recall that, in general, *E(Profit)* is given by the following equation:

$$E(\text{Profit}) = Pr(\text{Success}) * (\text{Profit if success}) + Pr(\text{Fail}) * (\text{Profit if fail})$$

His expected profit given that he chooses regular peanuts (RP), which we call $E(\text{Profit}|RP)$, is

$$E(\text{Profit}|RP) = 1,200 - (1 + i) * 1,000 = 200 - 1,000i$$

If he chooses salted peanuts (SP) his expected profit is

$$E(\text{Profit}|SP) = .2 * [2,000 - (1 + i) * 1,000] + .8 * 0 = 400 - (1 + i) * 200 = 200 - 200i$$

The expected profit growing the riskier salted peanuts, $200 - 200i$, clearly is greater than the expected profit growing regular peanuts, $200 - 1,000i$. So Jimmy will always choose SP!

Now, the lender is smart, so he knows that Jimmy will choose SP. What does he do, then? Let's see what the lender's profit looks like given that Jimmy plants SP:

$$E(\pi|SP) = E(\text{Repayment}|SP) - 1,000$$
$$E(\pi|SP) = .2 * (1 + i) * 1,000 + .8 * 0 - 1,000$$
$$E(\pi|SP) = 200 * (1 + i) - 1,000$$

We can set this equal to zero and see what interest rate the lender must charge to break even:

$$200 * (1 + i) - 1,000 = 0$$
$$1 + i = 5$$
$$i = 4$$

Knowing Jimmy will plant SP, the lender must charge 400% to break even. Would Jimmy want this loan? Let's see what his expected profit growing SP would be if he had to pay a 400% interest rate:

$$E(\text{Profit}|SP) = .2 * [2,000 - (1 + 4) * 1,000] = -600$$

At $i = 4$, Jimmy's expected profit growing SP is negative. That's a problem. Jimmy would never agree to take such a loan. The loan market collapses.

# 13

# International Trade and Globalization

The efficiency gains a country can reap from specializing and trading with other countries can be huge. It is no wonder, then, that the most spectacular episodes of economic growth in recent decades have happened as countries traded more and more internationally. Yet, it is often politically difficult to open one's borders to international trade. Separating efficiency from equity is especially hard when it comes to trade because the distribution of gains and losses straddles international borders: some groups in some countries appear to gain in the short run while other groups in other countries appear to lose. This chapter provides an overview of the role of international trade in economic development. We begin with trade in goods, services, and factors of production—including foreign direct investment and international migration—and we conclude by asking whether international aid—a particular type of "free trade"—is good or bad for development.

## ESSENTIALS

- Inseparability of efficiency and equity
- Import substitution and export promotion
- Specialization and diversification
- Comparative advantage
- Neoclassical trade theory
- Gravity trade models
- New trade theory
- Globalization and free-trade agreements
- Migration
- Social welfare analysis

Massive protests rocked the streets outside the Washington State Convention and Trade Center in November 1999. It was the largest demonstration ever in US history against an organization dedicated to free trade. It came to be known as the "Battle of Seattle." Afterward, the Seattle police chief said the protesters had won, and he resigned.

In the fall of 2013, Ukraine president Viktor Yanukovych refused to sign a free-trade agreement with the European Union, and massive protests *in favor of* trade integration shook the nation's capital, Kiev.

Why is international trade so contentious? Does free trade promote or hinder economic development? Understanding international trade is essential to development economics. Some developing countries see international trade as a major threat; others see it as an unparalleled opportunity to boost their economies. Several—most recently, China— have tapped this opportunity with spectacular success.

Trade is a big topic, the subject of whole courses, PhD theses, and dedicated journals. Our goal is to cover the basics of how development economists think about the role of trade in economic development, building upon what we learned about markets in chapter 11. As we shall see, there are strong similarities between how trade within and among countries affects people's welfare.

## THE THEORY OF COMPARATIVE ADVANTAGE

Ed's wife, Peri, is a great cook—way better than Ed. She's also faster at cleaning the kitchen. You might think she ought to do both, then. But that isn't what Ed and Peri do. Peri cooks; Ed cleans up. Both agree they are better off that way.

Peri and Ed are just following David Ricardo's Theory of Comparative Advantage, laid out in his classic 1817 book *The Principles of Political Economy and Taxation.*[1] Ricardo presented a remarkably simple model with only two countries and two goods. Here's how it works:

Take two countries—country A and country B. (In Ricardo's famous example, country A was England and country B was Portugal.) Table 13.1 gives each country's cost of producing one unit of cloth and wine. As you can see, country B is better at producing both. Country A would love to get cloth *and* wine at the cost of producing them in country B, but why would country B ever want to trade with country A?

You might think trade isn't going to happen, but Ricardo says it will. Country A will specialize in producing only cloth and country B only wine. Then they will trade.

Here's the logic: suppose wine and cloth have the same price, so one unit (say, a bolt) of cloth trades for one unit (a case) of wine.[2] If country

TABLE 13.1  DAVID RICARDO'S
ILLUSTRATION OF COMPARATIVE
ADVANTAGE

| | Unit Labor Costs | |
| --- | --- | --- |
| Country | *Cloth* | *Wine* |
| A | 100 | 110 |
| B | 90 | 80 |

SOURCE: David Ricardo, *On the Principles of
Political Economy and Taxation* (reprint, 1965;
London: J.M. Dent and Son, 1817).

A produces only cloth, then each unit of cloth it makes will cost it 100. By trading with country B, it can buy one unit of wine with one unit of cloth. So through trade it can get a unit of wine for 100 (the cost of producing the cloth to export). If it produced the wine at home it would cost 110. Thus, country A is better off specializing in cloth and trading for wine. (Besides, who would doubt that Portuguese wine is better than British wine?)

What about country B? After all, it takes two to tango. If country B produces the thing it makes comparatively efficiently—wine—and then trades for cloth, it can get a unit of cloth at a cost of 80. Producing cloth at home would cost 90. So country B is better off specializing in wine and trading for cloth.

Ricardo's genius was in recognizing that country B doesn't really pay country A its cost of producing cloth (100). Instead, it produces wine (at 80) then exchanges the wine for cloth, which it would have to pay 90 to make itself. Trade lets it do that.

Both countries, then, are better off because of trade. A country might not have an *absolute* advantage in *anything,* but *all countries have a comparative advantage in something.* Ricardo's advice is to follow your comparative advantage, specialize, and trade. Everyone will be better off because of it.

By exploiting comparative advantage, trade can offer huge advantages by letting people specialize. This is true for nations as well as for individuals, households, villages, and regions. But as the "Battle of Seattle" attests, moving from a conceptual appreciation of comparative advantage to actually trading stuff between countries can be controversial. This is because in practice international trade can be simultaneously good for some people and bad for others—at least in the short run.

*International Trade Can Be Good*

International trade opens up potentially vast markets for the goods countries produce and consume. Without it, a country would have to satisfy all of its own demand for goods and services. When a country can export and import, the whole world becomes its market! It can follow Ricardo's advice and specialize in what it produces best. Then it can import a diversity of goods that simply would not available if all the country's demand had to be met by its own producers. International trade can make countries more food secure, too. If a drought strikes, a bad harvest can raise food costs and even lead to famines, but food prices will not rise at all if the country can import food at world prices. Bad weather in any one country is unlikely to have much—if any— impact on world food prices, so trade can provide food security—if countries let it.

By producing for the world market, poor countries can put large numbers of low-skilled workers to work earning wages that, although low by rich-country standards, are typically much higher than what workers would earn without trade. As the demand for labor in export production expands, eventually wages rise. We see this in China, where the average wage for a factory worker nearly quadrupled in real terms, from US$67 to $312 per month, between 1996 and 2008 (see figure 7.9 in chapter 7). Rising wages and employment can have a big impact on reducing poverty—including in the poor villages from which many factory workers migrate and to which they send remittances, as we saw in chapter 10.

Opening up to global capital markets can give countries access to investment funds far beyond what domestic savings could provide, enabling them to invest in capital. Trade gives countries access to new technologies and ideas as well as goods and services. Imported technologies and ideas can make domestic firms more productive and raise people's incomes. In chapter 7 we saw how important both capital and ideas are to promoting economic growth.

*International Trade Can Raise Concerns*

The case against free trade rests largely on how the benefits of trade are distributed, worries about whether poor countries can compete in global markets, and fears of becoming vulnerable to global economic shocks.

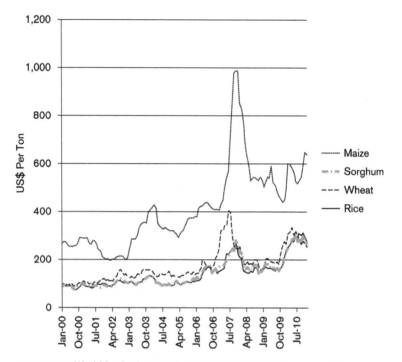

**FIGURE 13.1.** World food prices are increasing and becoming more volatile. Source: UN FAOSTAT (http://faostat.fao.org/).

Small open economies are vulnerable to global trade shocks. It might feel unsettling to think that at any moment world prices might change and prices on your country's store shelves will follow. When the prices of commodities like iron ore, copper, rare-earth metals, or other raw materials are booming in the world market, a country that exports those commodities (like many African countries do) can prosper. If global commodity prices suddenly plunge, though, the negative impacts can reverberate through the whole domestic economy. Many poor countries depend on food grain imports. The prices of grains have become increasingly volatile as the world's population and income have risen and as competition over the use of grain for food, feed, and fuel has intensified (figure 13.1).

Countries worry about having to compete with other countries' producers, who might undercut them in the global marketplace. If a country opens its borders to trade, not everyone in it will be able to compete. Look at Ricardo's example (table 13.1) again. If country A specializes in cloth, its cloth producers will be happy, but its wine production will evaporate. Conversely, country B's wine producers will be toasting to their own success, but its cloth industry will fold. That's under the best of circumstances.

Technology can flip countries' comparative advantage. Most Mexican farmers grow corn, often with labor-intensive ox-and-plow technology. Iowa grows corn with the most capital-intensive technology in the world. It is way cheaper to grow corn in Iowa than in Mexico.

Economic crises can spread fast, like a contagion, when countries are connected through trade. The collapse of several major US banks in September 2008 triggered an economic crisis that almost instantly went global, thanks to world capital markets. Free trade in capital means that investors can buy stocks in foreign companies, banks in capital-rich countries make loans to private individuals or governments in poor countries, and multinational corporations build factories around the globe (and repatriate their profits wherever they wish). Countries that borrowed heavily on global capital markets—like Greece—were particularly hard hit by the 2008 crisis. The idea that bad home loans in the US could spark a severe global recession testifies to how quickly things—bad and good—can spread across an interconnected world, and how vulnerable everyone is to market shocks.

Political economy—that is, how political forces affect the choice of economic policies—always plays a central role in free-trade discussions. Even if the overall gains from trade are positive, the losers may block a free-trade agreement unless they can be convinced that there is something in it for them.

## MODELING THE GAINS FROM TRADE: NEOCLASSICAL TRADE THEORY

In chapter 11 we saw how a household or village can increase its welfare by trading on markets within a country. The measure of welfare we used there was the economic surplus. We saw in figure 11.2 that when berry producers got access to an outside market with high berry prices instead of having to sell all their berries in the village, their producer surplus (profit) went up. Consumer surplus fell, but the gain in producer surplus increased more than the drop in consumer surplus. Producers could easily compensate consumers, and everybody could be better off with trade. If the outside market price had been lower than the village price, consumers would have gained more than enough to compensate producers for lower profits.

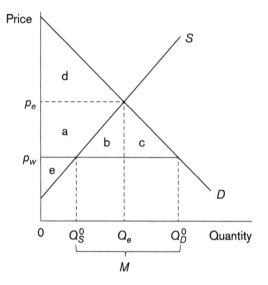

**FIGURE 13.2.** With trade, the consumer surplus equals the sum of areas a + b + c + d. The producer surplus is area e.

This same basic argument applies to free trade among countries. Figure 13.2 illustrates a country's supply and demand for some good, say, rice. If the country could not trade with the rest of the world, its equilibrium price and quantity of rice would be given by the intersection of the supply and demand curves: the country would consume an amount $Q_e$ of rice at a domestic price equal to $p_e$. We can call this domestic price without trade the "autarkic" price. ("Autarky" means economic independence or self-sufficiency—in this case, for a country.) Without the possibility for trade, rice would be a nontradable.

Rice is a globally traded commodity, so if the country's policies permit it, there most certainly will be trade. When there is trade, the world price, $p_w$, replaces the equilibrium price, $p_e$. The world price could be higher or lower than $p_e$, depending on whether the country is an efficient or inefficient rice producer (the position of its supply curve) and whether it is a large or small demander of rice (the position of the demand curve). If $p_w > p_e$ the country will supply more rice than it produces and export the difference; if $p_w < p_e$ (as in this diagram) it will do the opposite. The country in our figure imports an amount $M$ of rice from the rest of the world.

Trade in this case makes consumers happy: they can pay the lower world price for rice. The country's rice producers are not so happy, though. They have to sell at the low world price; if they charge the higher equilibrium price, no one will buy from them. Given that there are winners and losers from international trade, how do we know whether opening up to trade is good or bad for a country? We need a way to measure countries' total welfare.

In chapter 11 we learned about consumer and producer surplus, the basic tools of economic welfare analysis. We can use those same tools to demonstrate that economic welfare is higher with trade than without it, as well as to show how restrictionist trade policies reduce economic efficiency as well as welfare.

*Trade and Welfare*

To understand how trade affects economic welfare, we have to start by agreeing on what we mean by "economic welfare." Economic welfare is the sum of producer and consumer surplus. Figure 13.2 shows the consumer and producer surplus with trade. The consumer surplus is given by the triangle under the demand curve and above the world price, which has an area equal to a + b + c + d in the figure. The producer surplus is the triangle below the world price and above the supply curve, which has an area equal to e. Total economic surplus with trade, then, equals the sum of all these areas.

You can do exactly the same thing as in chapter 11 to demonstrate that the economic welfare with trade is larger than the economic welfare without trade. Without trade, at an equilibrium price higher than the world price, as in figure 13.2, the producer surplus will increase, but the consumer surplus will fall by a greater amount. If we had drawn the same figure but with the world price above the equilibrium price, the reverse would happen: without trade, the consumer surplus would increase, but the producer surplus would fall by more. In either case, total economic surplus is lower without trade.

In short, if a country opens up to trade, its economic pie will be larger, and the winners (consumers, in figure 13.2) could compensate the losers (producers). Whether compensation actually happens depends on the political process in the country and on the influence producers and consumers have over policy and trade agreements. To complicate matters, the same people may win and lose from trade. A farmer might gain, by being able to buy cheap imported fertilizer, and lose, because the world price for his crop is lower than the domestic price. Households might gain, as consumers of goods that are cheaply imported, but lose with respect to other goods, or maybe even with respect to income if workers in the household find themselves competing with workers in low-wage countries.

The power of the theory, though, is that in any market, total economic surplus is higher with trade than without it (or at least never lower), regardless of who benefits. The worst that can happen is no change in economic surplus, and that only occurs if the world price happens to be the same as the equilibrium price without trade.

### What Restrictive Trade Policies Do to Economic Welfare

Based on what we have just learned, you might imagine that trade restrictions lower economic welfare. Many countries impose taxes (tariffs) on the goods they import and/or export. The main justification for import tariffs is to protect domestic producers from foreign competition. A justification for both import and export tariffs is to collect tax revenue, which is easy for the government to do at the port. (Collecting sales tax from thousands of businesses or income tax from millions of households is much harder.) Both of these policies create what economists call a "deadweight" welfare loss to the country because they divert the economy away from what it does best.

An import tariff distorts trade by protecting domestic producers from foreign competition. In the process, it creates winners and losers while reducing overall economic welfare. By imposing an import tariff, a country hurts consumers, but producers of the protected good will thank the government all the way to the bank. That's what rice farmers do in Japan, where the price of rice is often seven times the world price because of trade policies! But if you add up the economic welfare of producers and consumers, it will be lower than without the tariff. That's because import tariffs, like other distortionary trade policies, create what is called a "deadweight loss."

### Import Tariffs and Deadweight Loss

Import tariffs raise the price people in the country have to pay for imports by the per-unit amount of the tariff. That is, instead of paying $p_w$ per ton of imported rice, consumers have to pay $p_w(1 + t_{im})$, where $t_{im}$ is the per-ton tariff. Export taxes lower the price the country's producers get for selling their goods abroad; instead of $p_w$ they get paid $p_w(1 - t_{ex})$, where $t_{ex}$ is the export tariff per ton.

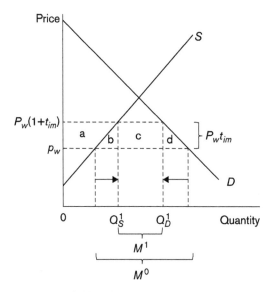

**FIGURE 13.3.** With an import tariff, consumers lose a + b + c + d, government gains c, producers gain a, and there is a deadweight loss of b + d.

The case of an import tariff is illustrated in figure 13.3.

With an import tariff of $t$ per unit of the good, the relevant price (everyone's *decision price*) is now $p_w(1 + t)$, as shown in figure 13.3. Before the tariff, the country's consumers demanded $Q_D^0$, and producers supplied $Q_S^0$. The country imported the difference, $M^0 = Q_D^0 - Q_S^0$ (see figure 13.2). After the tariff is imposed, the country imports a smaller amount because consumers demand less and producers supply more. The new level of imports, shown in figure 13.3, is $M^1 = Q_D^1 - Q_S^1$.

Let's see what this does to economic welfare. First, it raises the producer surplus by an amount equal to the area of the trapezoid with area a in the figure. Producers now sell at the higher price, so they make more profits than before. Producers' welfare goes up as a result of the tariff. Second, it generates tax revenue for the government. The government's tax gain is given by the area of the rectangle c. It is the tariff, $t$, times the level of imports after the tariff is in place, $Q_D^1 - Q_S^1$. The government, like producers, is better off with the tariff than without it.

What happens to consumer surplus? Consumers have to pay a higher price than before, so their surplus falls. Remember that the consumer surplus is the difference between the price line and the demand curve.

Thus, the fall in consumer surplus is given by the area (a + b + c + d). That's how much the economic welfare of consumers falls when the tariff is imposed.

Let's take stock of what happened here. Producer surplus went up by a. Government revenue went up by c. But consumer surplus *fell* by a + b + c + d. That's b + d more than the gains to producers and government. Where did that consumer loss go? Whose gain did it become?

The answer is: nobody's. The tariff distorted the economy and led to an efficiency loss equal to the areas of the two triangles, b + d. That's what economists call a *deadweight loss*. Avoiding deadweight losses is the core of the argument for free trade. Eliminating the tariff makes total economic welfare increase because the economic pie becomes bigger. If a tariff is eliminated, producers and government lose, but consumers gain more. In short, everyone could be made better off if the government didn't charge the tariff and then taxed consumers and handed some of the proceeds to producers.

Of course, this means the government must have the administrative capacity to efficiently collect taxes from consumers and make transfers to producers. Some taxes are easier to collect than others. Import tariffs are easy to levy at the port. Income taxes are notoriously difficult to levy because they require having information on incomes of large numbers of people. Sales taxes and value-added taxes are levied on businesses and are easier to collect than income taxes but more difficult than import tariffs. In countries lacking the administrative expertise to levy taxes efficiently, there may be large deadweight losses from tax collection.

Tariffs create a wedge between the import and export price. If the tariffs are large enough, it becomes too expensive for the country to import or export rice. In figure 13.4, the import price (including tariff) is above the autarkic (equilibrium) price, and the export price is below it. (Assuming there's no export tariff, the export price is the world price.) If you want to buy rice, you are better off paying the autarkic price $p_e$ than the import price plus tariff. If you are selling, you'll get a better price selling to local consumers, at the autarkic price, than exporting at the world price. (All the more if there is an export tariff, too!) Thus, in our example, consumers will buy from domestic producers, and producers will sell to domestic consumers. There will be no trade. The country will be self-sufficient in rice. This self-sufficiency will come at a cost, though. Producers will be happy, gaining a surplus equal to area a in the figure, but consumers will lose more—areas a + b + c. That means total economic surplus will fall by areas b + c, which represent

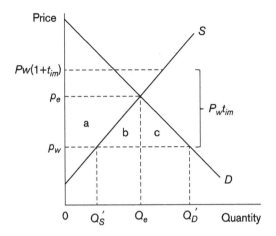

**FIGURE 13.4.** A very high tariff can drive an economy into self-sufficiency, producing a deadweight loss of b + c.

the deadweight loss in this case. (The government gets no benefit from a policy that drives the country into self-sufficiency.)

This example illustrates how you can use trade policy to take a tradable and turn it into a nontradable—that is, force the economy to become self-sufficient, or autarkic, with respect to a particular good. A more direct way is simply to restrict imports by imposing a *trade quota*. There is bound to be a welfare loss, though. That makes sense: if someone else can make something more cheaply than I can, I should buy it instead of making it myself. That's what we do every time we go to a farmers' market or grocery store. Countries, it seems, should do the same.

### STRATEGIES FOR TRADE-BASED GROWTH

There is no conclusive experiment to help us determine whether and how much free trade promotes economic growth. Over the years, different countries have followed different trade strategies, but not randomly. Countries decide which trade strategies to follow concurrently with many other decisions that, along with trade, shape economic development outcomes. Other policies influence the impacts of trade on income growth. For example, a country that opens up to trade and also invests heavily in public education, roads, ports, and communications is likely to see different outcomes from those of a country that opens to trade without making the investments required to be competitive. Institutions affect policy choices as well as growth outcomes. In countries with inclusive institutions (chapter 8), we might expect to find greater and more broad-based benefits from trade than in countries with extractive institutions. When economists try to figure out how free trade affects economic development, they are haunted by questions like, "Is it trade, or is it institutions, that led to the outcomes we see?" Things can get pretty complex.

That said, history gives us the opportunity to compare the development records of countries that did and did not open themselves up to trade. Trade strategies fall broadly into two categories: import-substitution industrialization and export-led growth. Let's see what these strategies entail and then compare the records of countries that followed each one.

### Import-Substitution Industrialization

In chapter 1 we briefly met Raúl Prebisch and Hans Singer, who argued that developing countries should shift from producing primary goods, like crops and raw materials, to manufactured goods. They based their argument on a simple observation: as people's and countries' incomes rise, the share of income spent on manufactured goods increases. This puts upward pressure on the prices of manufactured goods compared to primary goods. In other words, the prices of primary goods relative to manufactured goods—what economists call the "terms of trade for primary goods"—decrease as incomes rise around the world. Thus, if a poor country specializes in producing, say, food crops, it will find itself paying ever higher prices for the imported manufactured goods its consumers and industries demand.

Wouldn't a poor country be better off developing its own capacity to produce manufactured goods, for its own population or, better yet, exports? Doing so would require, among other measures, imposing high tariffs or even limits (quotas) on imported manufactured goods to ensure that domestic "infant industries" are profitable until they are able to stand on their own feet. Such measures are part of what is called "import-substitution industrialization."

Prebisch and Singer found support from others in political science and economics who argued that poor countries lose by virtue of the way in which they are integrated into the "world system."[3] Proponents of dependency theory claimed that, through trade, a "core" of rich countries extract resources from a "periphery" of weaker, poor countries. Thus, trade results in the economic exploitation of poor countries and the transfer of economic surplus (production beyond subsistence) from poor to rich countries. The idea that poor countries (the periphery) have to sell what they produce at low prices while buying from rich countries (the center) at relatively high prices is central to dependency theory.

Dependency theory influenced trade policies in many countries. A major dependency theorist, Fernando Henrique Cardoso, was president of Brazil from 1995 to 2002. Singer was an Argentine economist who worked for the United Nations Economic Commission on Latin America. Both argued that developing countries needed to impose at least some protective trade policies if they wished to achieve self-sustaining economic growth. In a number of Latin American countries, including Argentina, Brazil, and Mexico, arguments against free trade were reinforced by a strong sense of nationalism and political sovereignty. Some dependency theorists, inspired by Marxist theory, believed that socialist revolution would be required in order to eliminate economic disparities in the world system.

Countries that followed Prebisch and Singer's advice used a number of different policy levers to promote import-substitution industrialization, including the following:

- Protective trade policies: Tariffs or quotas on imports of manufactured goods that might compete with local industries.

- Exchange-rate policies: Artificial overvaluation of the country's currency made imported inputs and technology needed by infant industries cheaper. It also made imported food cheaper—a way to keep food prices and thus wages low in order to make new industries more profitable.

- Sectoral policies: Governments combined these trade policies with subsidies, preferential credit, and investments in infrastructure (electricity, transportation, communications) targeting infant industries.

- Parastatals: The creation of government-controlled companies was the most extreme measure countries took to create new industries.

It is important to bear in mind that all of these policies, by making industrial production more profitable, also made agriculture and other primary-goods production relatively less profitable. Thus, they discriminated against some sectors in order to encourage the movement of labor, capital, and other resources into the protected industries.

Although these distortions in the economy were strategic, they nonetheless created deadweight loss, as in the case of the trade barriers described above.

### Export Promotion: Learning from Tigers

In contrast to the countries that followed import-substitution industrialization, exports were the centerpiece of economic development strategies in some Asian countries, like the Asian Tiger economies (Hong Kong, Singapore, South Korea, and Taiwan) and more recently, China. They based their development model largely on "export-led growth."

Proponents of export-led growth point to a number of problems with import-substitution industrialization. Corruption (chapter 8) is one. Control over the economy, particularly through the creation of parastatals, concentrates economic power in the hands of government officials, who are not subject to the same controls that market competition places on private companies' behavior. Once measures are in place to protect and subsidize favored industries, those industries tend to become politically powerful, and this makes it difficult to eventually wean them off of subsidies and force them to compete in a global marketplace. Better, say the Asian Tigers, to make domestic industries compete with foreign industries from the get-go.

Companies that have to compete in world markets have an incentive to be efficient, to innovate, and to produce high-quality products. Subsidies to infant industries are expensive and divert scarce public resources from other uses, including the sorts of poverty programs we learned about in chapters 2, 4, and 6. This becomes even more of a concern once countries find themselves saddled with inefficient industries exerting political power to maintain their preferential treatment.

Exchange-rate policies that make imported technology and inputs cheaper also make exports more expensive to the rest of the world. This can lead to ongoing trade imbalances. Protected industries and governments easily can get into trouble by borrowing heavily from foreign banks to finance inefficient industries that might never become competitive enough to generate the income and foreign exchange (from exports) to pay back their loans. If an economic crisis hits, companies and governments may default on foreign loans.

When countries lack the political will to move beyond import substitution, history shows that major economic crises often are required before governments choose—or else are forced by international devel-

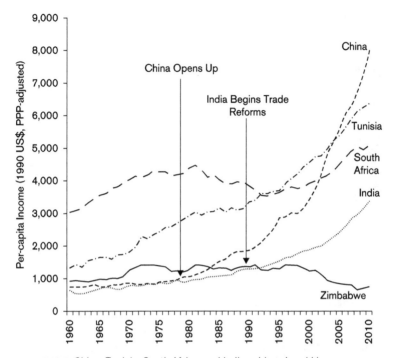

**FIGURE 13.5.** China, Tunisia, South Africa, and India achieved rapid income growth after opening up to trade. Zimbabwe, which followed import-substitution policies, saw its per capita income decline. (This figure and fig. 13.6 use Geary-Khamis dollars, which are real values in 1990 US dollars adjusted for purchasing power parity throughout the time-series range.) Source: Maddison Project (www.ggdc.net/maddison/maddison-project/home.htm).

opment agencies like the International Monetary Fund (IMF)—to dismantle their costly import-substitution policies.[4]

Overall, countries that followed export-led growth policies fared better than countries that adhered to import-substitution industrialization policies. There are plenty of examples of this—most clearly the Asian Tigers, but there are others (see figure 13.5). China's economic growth skyrocketed—and poverty there plummeted—after the country opened up to trade and enacted internal market reforms, led by Deng Xiaoping in 1978. India broke out of economic stagnation and began to grow once it started opening up to trade in 1990; its per capita income nearly tripled between 1990 and 2010. Outsourcing of tech jobs to India played an important role in this growth. In Africa, Zimbabwe has followed import-substitution industrialization, and it is one of the worst performers on

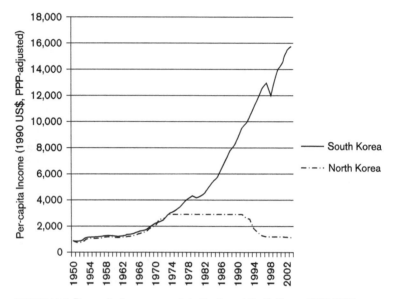

**FIGURE 13.6.** Per capita income growth in South and North Korea, 1950–2002.
Source: Maddison Project (www.ggdc.net/maddison/maddison-project/home.htm).

that continent. South Africa and Tunisia, on the other hand, emphasized more export-led growth, and their performance has been impressive.

The two Koreas provide us with an interesting experiment. In 1953, after the armistice that ended the Korean War, North and South Korea had similar per capita incomes, populations, and resource endowments. From that point onward, South Korea followed an export-led development strategy, while North Korea isolated itself from world markets and pursued an import-substitution strategy. Today, South Korea is the sixth largest exporter and the seventh largest importer in the world. North Korea describes itself as a *Juche* (self-reliant) state, which sounds a lot like autarky. It ranks 111th and 132nd among countries in exports and imports, respectively (most of the trade it has is with China).[5] South Korea's average per capita income exploded after 1974, while North Korea's fell (see figure 13.6). Today, South Korea's per capita income is US$39,950. That's twenty-two times North Korea's per capita income, which to the best of our ability to measure it is around $1,800, lower than that of Bangladesh. The disparities between these two countries show up in other measures as well. For example, average life expectancy at birth is sixty in North Korea and eighty-one in South Korea.

Does the huge difference in economic growth and development between South and North Korea prove that export-led growth is superior? Not exactly. We could debate how other policies and institutions shaped these two countries' growth performance, but one thing is clear: South Korea could not have accomplished what it did *without* trade.

There is more general evidence that trade promotes growth. In chapter 7 we met the empirical growth economist Xavier Sala-i-Martin, who conducted a systematic analysis of what determines economic growth. You might recall that Sala-i-Martin found a positive and statistically significant association between countries' outward orientation and their rates of income growth.

In short, empirical evidence suggests that trade is beneficial for economic growth and development. It does not tell us much about why, though. For that, we need some more theory.

### WHERE DOES COMPARATIVE ADVANTAGE COME FROM? THE HECKSCHER-OHLIN MODEL

Ricardo doesn't tell us where a country's comparative advantage comes from. In 1931, two Swedish economists, Eli Heckscher and his student, Bertil Ohlin, gave an answer: factor endowments. Some countries are labor rich and capital poor; others are the opposite. Factors produce output. It makes sense, then, that countries rich in labor would have a comparative advantage in producing labor-intensive goods. Those rich in capital (including human capital) have a comparative advantage in producing more capital-intensive goods. Logically, then, labor-rich countries should trade with capital-rich countries.

Factors are not limited to labor and physical capital. Natural resources can be considered a factor of production. A country rich in oil (Saudi Arabia) naturally has a comparative advantage in oil, one rich in gorgeous beaches (Tahiti) or historical sites (Italy) has a comparative advantage in tourism, and so forth. In today's world, the most important factor shaping economic growth is human capital. Countries rich in human capital (like the United States) have a comparative advantage in creating new technologies and exporting them around the globe.

The Heckscher-Ohlin model builds upon Ricardo's model in a simple way, with two countries, two goods, and two factors (labor and capital). Its insights can be generalized to situations involving more countries, goods, and factors, though.

This view of trade has important implications for world income inequality. If a labor-rich country follows its comparative advantage and produces more and more labor-intensive goods, what will happen to wages? Paul Samuelson, who won the Nobel Prize in 1970, proved that, under general conditions, trade causes factor prices to equalize across countries. This theoretical finding was considered so important that it became a theorem in economics: the Factor Price Equalization Theorem (FPET). As labor-abundant countries rev up their production of labor-intensive goods, they demand more labor, and their wages converge toward wages in labor-scarce countries. According to the FPET, low-skilled workers' wages should rise in China and Mexico—and they may fall in the United States—as these countries trade with each other and jobs for low-skilled workers shift across borders. The FPET predicts that trade will equalize the prices of other factors over time, including the rental rate on capital, in other words, the profit rate.

## PUTTING RICARDO AND HECKSCHER-OHLIN TO THE TEST

Ricardo and Heckscher-Ohlin give us to two clear predictions. First, countries should specialize in goods whose production is intensive in the factors they possess in greatest abundance. Second, we would expect to find that most of the world's trade is between countries with different factor endowments. Samuelson's FPET adds another hypothesis: that wages and other factor prices equalize across countries over time as a result of trade in commodities.

It is relatively easy to come up with examples of countries that export goods in which they have a comparative advantage. Guatemala exports handpicked berries and tropical fruits to the United States, while the United States exports high-tech products to Guatemala. China exports labor-intensive manufactured goods to everyone. Saudi Arabia exports oil. Tourism is the main source of foreign exchange in Tahiti—in effect, Tahiti "exports" its beaches by letting us go there and lie on them.

But the prediction that most trade is between countries with different factor endowments just doesn't hold up. Most of the trade we see is between countries with similar factor endowments. Take the United Kingdom, for example (table 13.2). With one exception—China—all of the UK's top trading partners are other high-income countries, arguably with similar kinds of factor endowments: lots of capital and human capital, not much labor. If we exclude China from the list, 60% of the UK's exports go to high-income, capital-rich countries, and 54% of its imports come from such countries. China is the one clear example that seems to fit the Heckscher-Ohlin predictions. Having become the workshop of the world, it features highly on pretty much every country's import list.

TABLE 13.2  THE LARGEST TRADING PARTNERS OF THE UNITED
KINGDOM (2011)

| | Exports | | Imports | |
|---|---|---|---|---|
| Rank | *Country* | *%* | *Country* | *%* |
| 1 | United States | 13 | Germany | 12.6 |
| 2 | Germany | 11.3 | United States | 7.7 |
| 3 | France | 7.8 | China | 7.6 |
| 4 | Netherlands | 7.7 | Netherlands | 7.1 |
| 5 | Irish Republic | 5.8 | Norway | 6.1 |
| 6 | Belgium | 5.3 | France | 5.9 |
| 7 | Italy | 3.4 | Belgium | 4.8 |
| 8 | Spain | 3.3 | Italy | 3.6 |
| 9 | China | 2.9 | Irish Republic | 3.2 |
| 10 | Sweden | 2.1 | Spain | 2.8 |
| TOTAL | | 62.6 | | 61.4 |

SOURCE: HM Revenue and Customs, Overseas Trade Statistics (www.uktradeinfo.com
/Statistics/Pages/Statistics.aspx).

What if we look at a poor country? Table 13.3 shows Zambia's top ten trading partners. Most of its major trading partners are its neighbors, with two big exceptions: China is Zambia's largest supplier of imports, and Switzerland and China are its largest markets for exports (75% of which are copper or copper related). Almost all of its other top ten trading partners are African countries.

Uganda's top trading partners for exports and imports are, respectively, Sudan and Kenya; Bolivia's are Brazil and Chile; Paraguay's are Uruguay and Argentina on the export side and China and Brazil on the import side. South African Customs Union countries are Zimbabwe's major partners on both the import and export sides. Some high-income countries appear on these top-ten lists; the farther north we go in Africa, the more western European countries feature in African countries' lists of top trading partners, and the US appears on the lists of many Latin American countries. China seems to be on everyone's list of top import suppliers, and it is a major buyer of raw material exports from many countries. Nevertheless, what we see does not seem to support the hypothesis that most trade happens between countries with vastly different factor endowments.

What about the factor price equalization theorem's prediction that wages and profit rates equalize between countries that trade with each other? We have seen that low-skilled workers' wages increased sharply in

TABLE 13.3   ZAMBIA'S MAJOR TRADING PARTNERS

| | Exports | | Imports | |
|---|---|---|---|---|
| Rank | *Country* | % | *Country* | % |
| 1 | Switzerland | 37.3 | China | 18.6 |
| 2 | China | 30.9 | Nigeria | 11.1 |
| 3 | So. African Customs Union | 5.6 | Uganda | 7.2 |
| 4 | Korea, Rep. | 3.6 | Cameroon | 6.8 |
| 5 | Congo, Dem. Rep. | 3.4 | Kenya | 6.3 |
| 6 | Saudi Arabia | 2.5 | Tanzania | 6.1 |
| 7 | Zimbabwe | 2.3 | Zambia | 5.2 |
| 8 | Egypt | 2.1 | So. African Customs Union | 5.2 |
| 9 | United Arab Emirates | 1.8 | Netherlands | 4.9 |
| 10 | Malawi | 1.2 | Germany | 4.8 |
| TOTAL | | 62.6 | | 61.4 |

SOURCE: Massachusetts Institute of Technology, *The Observatory of Economic Complexity* (http://atlas.media.mit.edu/).

China between 1996 and 2008. A recent study found that real wages for high school graduates in the US fell more than 10% between 1965 and 2013.[6] China-US trade may have closed the wage gap for workers without a college education; however, the wage gap between rich and poor countries is enormous, despite a tremendous expansion in global trade.

### What Do the Econometric Models Show?

Applied trade economists routinely crunch through gigabytes of data on international trade flows. In fact, there is an extensive literature in empirical trade modeling alongside the theoretical trade models. It probably won't surprise you to learn that their findings generally do not support the hypothesis that trade takes place mostly between countries with contrasting factor endowments, and studies do not find consistent evidence in support of the FPET hypothesis that wages and returns to capital converge as countries at different levels of development trade with each other.

There is one model that gives pretty good results when predicting trade between countries, but it looks nothing like the neoclassical trade models we've been learning about. In fact, it's straight out of astrophysics! The gravity trade model posits that trade between any two countries—call them country *i* and country *j*—depends on how big the two countries' economies are (that is, their economic masses) and on the distance between them. This is the same kind of model used to calculate the gravitational attraction between celestial bodies. Big celestial bodies have a lot of attraction—that is, unless they are very far away from each other. Smaller bodies, like the earth and moon, can attract each other a lot if they are close to each other. When it comes to trade, economies seem to be connected in the same way that gravity connects stars, planets, and moons.

The main difference between the way applied trade economists think of trade and the way physicists think about gravity is that to an economist's mind, "distance" is a fairly abstract concept. It is only partly about space. Two countries can be far apart yet easily accessible to one another by sea (like China and the United States). They can have special agreements that make trade easier—or not. Historical (colonial, cultural, language) ties also can facilitate trade. All of these things figure in what economists think of as "distance," which really is more like "trade friction."

Gravity models overwhelmingly find that larger countries trade with each other. Consumers in high-income countries buy a huge diversity of goods from other high-income countries. A lot of this trade is in what seem to be similar products. Germans buy Volvos from Sweden, and Swedes buy BMWs from Germany. Gravity models are pretty good at predicting how much trade happens between countries, but not so good at predicting trade in BMWs versus Volvos.

Proximity matters, too, though not as much as size. The United States's first and third largest trading partners are Canada and Mexico (China is number two). Malawi and Lesotho's top trading partner is South Africa. Some gravity models find that history matters. Reflecting colonial history, Morocco's major trading partner is France, while Ghana trades more with the UK. Free-trade agreements reduce trade frictions and stimulate trade among members of the agreement. For example, Mexico's imports to and exports from the United States increased sharply after NAFTA took effect (figure 13.7).

Theoretical trade economists have criticized the gravity model because it does not seem to have much connection with the theory of comparative advantage. It almost seems to have just dropped out of the sky! In many ways, what happened with trade is similar to what happened with growth (chapter 7). In both cases, empirical models failed to confirm key predictions from theoretical models. Theorists had to go back to the drawing board.

That's what the theoretical trade economist Paul Krugman did, and the New Trade Theory was born.

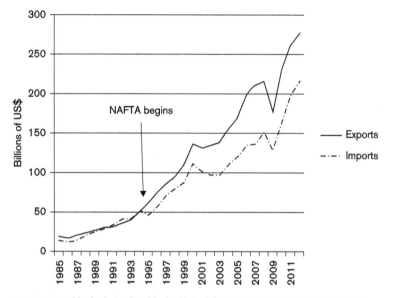

**FIGURE 13.7.** Mexico's trade with the United States increased after NAFTA took effect on January 1, 1994. Source: US Department of Commerce, Bureau of Census, Foreign Trade (www.census.gov/foreign-trade/balance/).

## THE NEW TRADE THEORY

Back in chapter 7 we learned about the new (endogenous) growth model. Increasing returns to scale take center stage in that model. As economies grow, they not only invest in capital but also become more productive because of technological change, which in turn stimulates more growth. Basically, the faster an economy grows, the more productive it becomes. The cost of production falls as production rises. Double all inputs and output more than doubles, because the production function itself changes.

Paul Krugman argued that something similar happens when countries engage in trade.

Over the years, Germans have gotten very good at making BMWs, as well as a lot of other finely engineered machinery. The United States became dominant in computer technology, then the Internet, and now social networking. In fact, it seems like the more a country does of something, the better it gets at doing it and the more dominant it becomes in global markets. That sounds a lot like increasing returns to scale.

Thanks to trade, countries build up a comparative advantage that feeds on itself. They become globally dominant. There are few limits to how dominant a country can become in a particular production sector, as long as the world is its market.

Increasing returns to scale reshape comparative advantage. Once a country begins to grow a sector, like automobile production, the economy changes in ways that actually reduce production costs, making the country ever more competitive in international trade.

An often-cited example is the enormously successful automobile industry in Japan. After World War II, Japan experienced record economic growth, which included the birth of a globally dominant auto industry. What raw materials did it take to make automobiles? Oil and coal for energy, iron ore, and other metals. Japan had none of those—it had to import them. But it more than paid for these imports by exporting manufactured goods, and it built the most productive auto industry in the world.

Japan wasn't only about cars. When Ed was little, "Made in Japan" meant about the same thing that "Made in China" means today. Almost all of Ed's wind-up toys were made in Japan! Japan started out by using its abundant labor to export cheap manufactured goods. Then it began innovating. On his sixth birthday Ed got a monkey that clashed two cymbals together, like a musician in an orchestra, and you didn't even have to wind it up! Japan had created the first battery-powered toys. You can think of Ed's monkey as a crude robot. Pretty soon Japan was making much better robots, and robots were making cars. As Japan's exports became more diverse and expanded, its industries innovated and became more productive, and they became increasingly dominant in global trade. The population benefited: Japan's per capita income more than quadrupled between 1955 and 1973. The country's transformation through trade was dubbed "the Japanese economic miracle."

When most people think of the Japanese miracle, they think "export-led growth." In reality, though, the key to Japan's success was more complicated than simply following an export-promotion development strategy. It was a mixed model. Japan succeeded through close cooperation between government, on one hand, and manufacturers, suppliers, distributors, and banks, joined in closely knit groups called *keiretsu*. Japanese companies were given preferential access to foreign exchange and other government support to import needed foreign inputs and technologies, but they were required by law to produce 90% of their parts domestically within a short period of time. Meanwhile, protectionist measures limited consumers' access to foreign-produced goods like cars. Basically, Japanese consumers had to buy Japanese. That doesn't sound exactly like free trade. Japan's development strategy included *both* import-substitution industrialization *and* export promotion.

It worked, though. Households in Japan benefited as their incomes rose dramatically during the miracle years. As consumers, they suffered in the short run by not being able to purchase cheaper and higher quality goods from abroad, but in the long run they thrived. Of course, today Japan's consumers, like those in California and South Africa, can buy vehicles and other goods made in Japan that are among the most economical and high quality in the world. Japan illustrates how a combination of export promotion with strategic deviations from free trade ended up creating world-dominant industries and stimulated tremendous economic growth in the process.

The New Trade Theory offers an explanation for the findings from gravity models that large economies trade with each other. Increasing returns to scale (IRS), superimposed upon comparative advantage, enable countries to become increasingly globally dominant in particular production niches over time. Dominance in international trade makes countries rich. Rich consumers demand diversity, which they import from other dominant players—Ed has a Volvo, his wife has an Audi, and his neighbor has a Mitsubishi.

IRS also explains the failure of international trade to diminish income inequality over time. Global dominance means there's a lot of money to be made. Factors—labor, land, capital, human capital—create income. Increasing returns to scale plus free trade enable factors in a given country and sector to produce income at an increasing—and sometimes astonishing—rate. Samuelson's theoretical prediction that trade causes factor prices to converge across countries over time does not necessarily hold in a world where increasing returns to scale permit a country to increase its global dominance in product areas over time. The more productive you are, the more productive you become in the future. Comparative advantage is not a given. It changes over time, and carefully crafted trade policies may be able to help countries attain a comparative advantage in new product areas.

## THE NEW TRADE THEORY AND DEVELOPMENT PRACTICE

We saw that, historically, countries that followed an export-promotion strategy grew faster than countries that followed an import-substitution strategy. New trade theory suggests that there might be a reason to revisit import substitution industrialization—or perhaps combine export promotion and import substitution in new and strategic ways. If a country can protect an infant industry by limiting import competition, if it can make sure the industry "grows up" to become internationally competitive, and if increasing returns to scale eventually take hold to make the growth self-perpetuating, there might be a case for including an element of import-substitution industrialization in a country's development strategy. Those are a lot of "ifs," but there is no question that the New Trade Theory adds a new dynamic dimension to the way we think about comparative advantage in international trade.

Cambridge University economist Ha-Joon Chang argues that rich countries, including Britain and the United States, historically used heavy government subsidies, import tariffs, and weak (or no) respect for others' intellectual property to help promote their economic development. By urging poor countries to embrace free trade, he claims, "rich countries are trying to kick away the ladder that allowed them to climb where they are."[7] The implications of this argument for poor countries are clear. In Chang's words, when it comes to trade and other development policies, "there can be no 'best practice' policies that everyone should use."

Today, most developing countries in the world appear to be convinced that international trade and trade policy are an important component of successful development strategies. This requires forming trade agreements that give member countries access to one another's markets. Making trade agreements and enforcing them once they are in effect is not easy, though. Where does a country begin? If it enters into a free-trade agreement, but then its trade partners employ unfair trade practices like giving export firms an unfair advantage through subsidies and other means, what redress does it have? Countries face high transaction costs when it comes to making international trade agreements and enforcing their provisions.

Enter the World Trade Organization, or WTO.

The WTO is a place where governments can get together to negotiate trade agreements and settle trade disputes, where member governments try to sort out the trade problems they face with each other. In effect, it tries to lower the transaction costs of making and enforcing international trade agreements. While its motto is "free trade," it does not impose trade agreements upon unwilling parties. Countries have to choose to be members of the WTO. This is how the WTO describes what it does: "The *rules* of the WTO system are agreements resulting from negotiations among member governments, the rules are *ratified* by

TABLE 13.4 MAJOR FREE-TRADE AGREEMENTS BY YEAR

| Agreement | Year Established |
|---|---|
| Greater Arab Free Trade Area (GAFTA) | 1957 |
| European Economic Community (EEC) | 1957 |
| Asia-Pacific Trade Agreement (APTA) | 1975 |
| Gulf Cooperation Council (GCC) | 1981 |
| Southern Common Market (MERCOSUR) | 1991 |
| ASEAN Free Trade Area (AFTA) | 1992 |
| Southern African Development Community (SADC) | 1992 |
| Central American Integration System (SICA) | 1993 |
| Common Market for Eastern and Southern Africa (COMESA) | 1994 |
| G-3 Free Trade Agreement (G-3) | 1995 |
| North American Free Trade Agreement (NAFTA) | 1994 |
| South Asian Free Trade Area (SAFTA) | 2004 |
| Trans-Pacific Partnership (TPP) | 2005 (proposed) |
| Central European Free Trade Agreement (CEFTA) | 1992 |
| Central American Free-Trade Agreement (CAFTA) | 2004 |

members' parliaments, and *decisions* taken in the WTO are virtually all made by consensus among all members. In other words, decisions taken in the WTO are negotiated, accountable and democratic."[8]

Members can bring trade disputes before the WTO's Dispute Settlement Body (which consists of all country members); this body determines whether a country has broken a trade accord of which it is part. If so, it has to change what it does in order to conform to the accord.

Even with the WTO's help, attempts to craft global free-trade agreements have faltered. Instead, most of the success in recent decades has been in creating *regional* trading blocks, many of which include less-developed countries. The European Economic Community was a pioneer in this area; it combined European countries into a common market beginning in 1958. The North American Free Trade Agreement (NAFTA, 1995) was unusual in bringing together countries at very different levels of per capita income and development (Canada and the United States, on one side, and Mexico, on the other). It was extended southward into Central America and the Caribbean through the Central American Free-Trade Agreement (CAFTA, 2006). Table 13.4 lists major regional trade agreements around the world.

Regional trading blocks are somewhat of a mixed bag from the point of view of people advocating free trade. On one hand, they have proven good at stimulating trade between members of the blocks. On the other hand, they tend to divert trade away from the rest of the world, shifting it inside the block (that is, discouraging trade between the block and the rest of the world). In the long run, though, one might see regional trade blocks as a step along the way toward global free trade. It might well be easier for a few blocks to enter into a global trade agreement than for many diverse countries to do so. That, someday, could make the WTO's job easier.

The great challenge for poor countries and those assisting them is how to harness new trade opportunities while designing economic development programs and policies. As one group of international development agencies wrote in its joint report: "[Trade] has created many new opportunities, but also new questions regarding the roles, functions and core capacities of the various key players. Deep-rooted principles and paradigms have been cut down in a short period. It is sometimes like mixing an Italian basketball team with Nigerian soccer players, and trying to play in a volleyball tournament. The new situation raises many questions about how the game is played, and who are the winners and losers."[9]

## TRADE IN CAPITAL, PEOPLE, AND BRAINS

Goods aren't the only things that flow between nations. Factors—capital, people, and brains (human capital)—do, too. Capital, people, and brains are pretty different from goods and services. Yet many of the lessons we learned from models of trade in goods and services are relevant here, as well. For example, there are deadweight losses associated with restrictions on trade in factors, much like what we see with restrictions on trade in goods and services.

### Trade in Capital

Foreign direct investment is a capital flow. Instead of producing a capital-intensive good in a capital-rich country, someone can invest in a factory to produce the good in a capital-poor (but labor-rich) country. In fact, there is a basic economic incentive to do that, because where capital is scarce, the economic returns to capital (rents) often are high, just as where labor is scarce, wages are high.

Global capital markets make it possible for poor countries to invest more in new capital than would be possible from domestic savings alone.

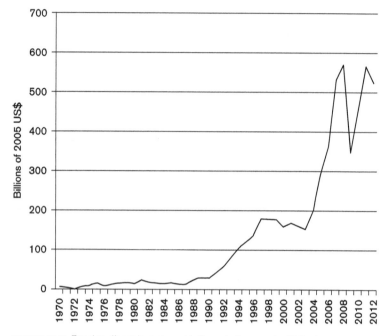

**FIGURE 13.8.** Foreign direct investment inflows to low- and middle-income countries have increased sharply in the new millennium. Source: World Bank (http://data.worldbank.org/indicator/BX.KLT.DINV.CD.WD).

Each year, vast amounts of capital flow from rich to poor countries in the form of foreign direct investment (FDI), often bringing new technologies along with it (see figure 13.8). Jobs shift from high- to low-wage countries, a process called "offshoring" or "outsourcing." Offshoring can include highly skilled work, like computer programming, as well as low-skilled work, like garment and other "sweatshop" production.

Enormous advances in shipping and communications allow large firms to fragment their operations, moving more unskilled, labor-intensive stages of production to countries where unskilled wages are low. Sweatshops employ millions of workers in poor countries to produce goods that are immediately exported to rich countries. The wages these workers earn are low by the standards of high-income countries, yet they are clearly high enough to lure workers to the factory floor.

Labor standards, including worker safety, as well as their enforcement, also tend to be more lax in poor countries. Ensuring safe and comfortable working conditions costs money; not doing so can enhance an industry's international advantage when it comes to producing labor-intensive goods. The results can be tragic. In 2012, a fire and collapse of clothing factories killed more than 1,100 workers in Bangladesh. Growing consumer awareness in rich countries puts pressure on global companies to certify that the factories to which they outsource follow acceptable labor standards.

How can they be sure? You'll recognize an asymmetric information problem here, similar to what we learned about in chapter 11. The Fair Labor Association, a nonprofit consortium of universities, civil service organizations, and private companies, certifies that its member companies and their suppliers comply with national and international labor laws.[10] Its monitoring includes independent and unannounced audits of factories abroad. Its efforts are not without controversy, but without independent monitoring and certification, the information needed to create a "market for fair labor practices" would not exist.

*Trade in Labor*

In addition to capital flowing across the globe to where the workers are, workers can move to where the capital is. Trade in labor across international borders is called "labor migration," and the payment countries receive for "exporting workers" is called "migrant remittances."

There is no question that international migration is increasing, and so are remittances—to the point of being a major source of both income and foreign exchange for many countries. In some countries, migrant remittances exceed the value of all merchandise exports combined. In those countries, it can be said that people are the major export, in terms of the income they provide.

In 2013, the United Nations estimates that more than 231.5 million people in the world were immigrants, that is, people living outside their country of birth.[11] That was 51% more than in 1990. The world's total population grew by 33% over that same period (from 5.3 to 7 billion). In other words, international migration is growing faster than world population. If one could take all of these people and bring them together into a single country, that nation of immigrants would be the sixth largest on earth, with a population about the size of Indonesia's.

Migrant remittances are rising more rapidly than the number of migrants (figure 13.9). Globally, the World Bank's data show that

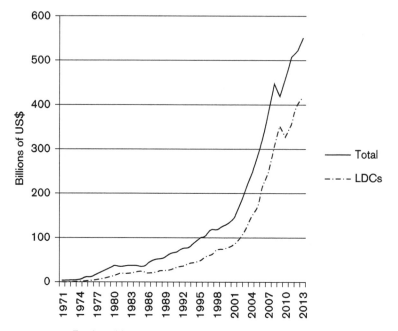

**FIGURE 13.9.** Total world remittance receipts have increased sharply since 1970. Source: World Bank (http://go.worldbank.org/092X1CHHD0).

remittances to less-developed countries surpassed $400 billion in 2013. That's a whopping thirteen times higher than the estimate for 1990. To put remittances into perspective, we could compare them to international aid as a source of support for less-developed countries. If we added up all of the development assistance provided by all of the countries in the world, migrant remittances would be 3¼ times greater.

Remittances have captured the imagination of international development agencies, including the United Nations and the World Bank, for several reasons. First, they are big. Second, unlike aid, they happen without using rich countries' taxpayer money. Third, much of this money flows to relatively low-income households, including households in poor rural areas. In short, migrant remittances could be an important resource to help countries develop.

They also have costs, though. In order to get remittances, a country has to sacrifice workers. In the process, it may lose skills and other human capital, like enterprising spirit, to other countries. Poor countries bear the cost of educating children who grow up and migrate abroad, taking their human capital with them. The human capital, then, is put to work creating value-added for the foreign country. The loss of human capital to migration is called the "brain drain."

The remittances migrants send home might compensate for the loss of human capital, but this won't necessarily be the case. It depends, in part, on how much value the migrant would contribute to the economy by not migrating abroad. Here you'll immediately notice that we have a selection problem, like the ones we studied in chapter 2. Once an individual migrates, we can see the remittances she sends home, but we cannot see how much income she would have created by not migrating. Conversely, we see income produced at home only for the people who do not migrate. This selection problem arises regardless of whether it is countries, households, or individuals we are looking at. With countries, since people tend to emigrate from (and send remittances to) poor countries, it might look like remittances increase poverty, even if poor countries would be poorer without them.

Suppose we wish to evaluate the impacts of migration and remittances on a poor migrant-sending economy. Think of the households with migrants as a treatment group—they get the "migration treatment" by sending family members abroad and receiving remittances. The households without migrants, then, are the control group. If migration were a random process, we could simply compare outcomes like poverty or crop productivity between these two groups.

But migration is not random, you might say. It is selective, and as we saw in the case of internal migration (chapter 10), it may select people with high levels of human capital. The kinds of people who migrate are different from the kinds of people who don't.

You'd be absolutely right—unless, maybe, you are in Tonga (see sidebar 13.1).

Tonga might not be representative of other migrant-sending countries, but to our knowledge, there is no other case in the world in which international migration can be treated as being random (or more accurately, nearly random, because people chose whether or not to apply for the Tonga migration lottery to begin with). That leaves us with two other alternatives to evaluate migration's impacts on development outcomes: natural experiments and econometrics. We can also use simulation methods to explore how migration impacts local economies.

In chapter 2 we met Dean Yang, a development economist at the University of Michigan who spotted a natural experiment opportunity to study the impacts of migration on poverty and investment in the Philippines (sidebar 2.5). He found strong evidence that migration and

### Sidebar 13.1    A Migration Lottery

What would be the ideal experiment to test the impacts of international migration on migrant-sending households? Randomly plucking migrants out of some households but not others, sending those migrants abroad, then after some time elapses going back and comparing development outcomes in the households with and without migrants? Sounds unrealistic, doesn't it?

Not in the case of migration from the Tonga Islands, a poor country, to New Zealand, a rich country. Each year, New Zealand runs a lottery allowing up to 250 Tongan Islanders the chance to immigrate as permanent residents. Three economists spotted a research opportunity here. Think of a treatment group consisting of households with a member lucky enough to win the lottery and emigrate to New Zealand. Those households get the "migration treatment" of losing a member to New Zealand but gaining remittance income. The control group is households with members who were in the lottery but not chosen. The only thing separating these two groups is the "luck of the draw," making this migration treatment almost as good as random.

The researchers found that the households whose members won the lottery ended up *worse off* than those that lost. The remittances their migrants sent home did not make up for the migrants' lost earnings in the Tonga Islands; thus, per capita incomes in their households fell—even though household size (the denominator in per capita income) was smaller without the migrants. The study also found evidence of less food intake among the family members left behind.

David McKenzie, Steven Stillman, and John Gibson, "How Important Is Selection? Experimental vs Non-Experimental Measures of the Income Gains from Migration," *Journal of the European Economic Association* 8, no. 4 (2010):913-45.

remittances have favorable development impacts in Philippine households, increasing investments and children's schooling.

Two economists from the University of California, San Diego, used an econometric approach to study the impacts of Mexico-to-US migration on business investments in Mexico.[12] They had to come up with a convincing instrument to deal with a selection problem resulting from the fact that entrepreneurial people might be more likely to migrate as well as to have businesses in Mexico. That is, they needed a variable correlated with migration but not with business investments, except through migration. History gave them one (see sidebar 13.2).

**Sidebar 13.2 Migrants on Rails**

Before Mexico had a road system, railroads were the main way to get migrants from Mexico to the United States. The authors of one study found that the location of railroads in the early 1900s is closely associated with migration today. They used states' distance to the nearest stop on a north-south railroad line in the early 1900s as their instrument for migration. This strategy allowed them to estimate the impacts of migration on microenterprise investments while dealing with the selection problem. The authors found evidence that migration increases investments and capital-output ratios in Mexico's microenterprises. They also found higher levels of profits and sales by microenterprises in states with strong migration networks with the United States. These findings suggest that Mexico-US migration may be an important source of knowledge and funds for microenterprise investments in Mexico.

C. Woodruff and R. Zenteno, "Migration Networks and Microenterprises in Mexico," *Journal of Development Economics* 82, no. 2 (2007):509–28.

The pessimistic findings from Tonga (sidebar 13.1) seem to contrast with those from Mexico (sidebar 13.2). An explanation for this might lie in the differences between the two countries' economies. The Mexican economy is far larger and more diverse than that of Tonga. In fact, migrant remittances were equivalent to 12.6% of Tonga's GDP in 2012, compared with 2% of Mexico's.[13] A large, complex economy might have more possibilities to substitute for emigrants' labor. Remittances flowing into such an economy might be better able to stimulate income growth by loosening liquidity constraints on production activities and raising the local demand for goods and services produced within the country. Not surprisingly, Tonga relies heavily on imports to meet local demands; its imports are equivalent to 63% of GDP, while Mexico's are equivalent to only 34%.[14]

*Trade in Brains (Human Capital)*

When a person migrates, she takes her human capital with her. The "brain drain" is poor countries' biggest worry when it comes to international migration. Home countries invest in educating their youth, but when educated people emigrate, they take this schooling with them. The destination-country economy benefits when highly skilled and motivated immigrants arrive on their shores. The history of the United States—a nation of immigrants—clearly attests to this.

Data on poor countries' loss of highly skilled workers to emigration highlight the brain drain problem. For example, here are some striking examples from news reports:

- Ghana's official statistics institute reported that between 1999 and 2004, 448 doctors, or 54% of those trained in the period, left to work abroad.[15]
- Over 80% of Jamaicans with higher education live abroad.[16]
- Ethiopia, according to one study, lost 75% of its skilled professionals over ten years.[17]

Of course, many of these skilled emigrants send home remittances, which may exceed the income they would earn by staying home. In fact, some countries actively train people to emigrate in the expectation that the remittances they send home will exceed the cost of training them. The Philippines is an example of this. At the end of 2012, over 10 million Filipinos were living overseas.[18] Nevertheless, human capital that emigrates cannot be put to work for development at home.

Not all economists agree that the brain drain is a serious problem for poor countries as a whole, though. The concept of the brain drain has a major limitation: it is static. If a country has a fixed amount of human capital in it, and emigration takes it away, logically there is less human capital than before in the migrant-sending country.

The dynamics of real life can turn this static picture on its head. Human capital is the result of investments people make. Economist Oded Stark and coauthors posited that skilled emigration actually may increase the amount of human capital in migrant-sending countries.[19] People in poor countries can see the benefits of education followed by migration. This creates an incentive for them to invest in their own and their children's schooling. Schooling investments increase human capital. If not all of the increase in human capital emigrates, there is a possibility that a static brain drain creates a dynamic brain gain.

Something similar, it seems, happens with baseball (see sidebar 13.3).

In theory, whether emigration results in a brain drain or a brain gain depends on two key questions. First, does the possibility of migrating to work abroad create incentives for people to invest in schooling? Second,

### Sidebar 13.3   Bat Drain or Bat Gain?

The Dominican Republic is the biggest exporter of major league base-ball players in the world. The baseball commissioner's office reports that 28.1% of all US major league baseball players in 2013 were born outside the United States. Of those, 37% were *dominicanos*.

While Ed was in the Dominican Republic doing research a few years back, he hired a taxi to drive him around the island. Every time they passed through a town the driver proudly listed off the names of people from the town who had become major league baseball players in the United States. It sounded a lot like a bat drain.

"All those baseball players leaving your country—isn't that really bad for baseball here?" Ed asked.

"No, it's the best thing that could happen," the driver responded.

"But you're losing a lot of players," Ed protested.

"You don't understand," said the driver. "Every kid in my country dreams of playing big league baseball. Many become great, but only a few get to play in the United States. The rest play here. We've got the best baseball in Latin America."

But what would happen if the Dominican Republic actually played a baseball game against the United States? That happened in 2013 at the World Baseball Classic—baseball's equivalent of soccer's World Cup—held in San Francisco, California. The US team had a major league all-star in every position. The Dominican Republic won, 3 to 1. It went on to become the first team ever to win the Classic without losing a single game.

It seems that the taxi driver's "bat gain" hypothesis had won the day.

"2013 Major League Baseball Racial and Gender Report Card," *Sports Business News*, May 15, 2013 (www.sportsbusinessnews.com /content/2013-major-league-baseball-racial-and-gender-report-card).

do enough of the people who get schooling in the hopes of someday emigrating end up staying at home?

The answer to the first question seems to be "yes" for children in India who want to grow up to be computer engineers in California's Silicon Valley, but probably "no" for kids in rural Mexico expecting someday to take low-skilled jobs as unauthorized immigrant farm-workers in California's Central Valley.

The answer to the second question depends on a number of things, including immigration policies in migrant-destination countries, migration costs, and probably most importantly, what kind of future educated people see for themselves in their home countries.

At the very least, it is safe to say that the question of whether the emigration of educated people leaves poor countries less educated than before does not have a clear answer. In the best of cases, as economists Oded Stark and Yong Wang argue, the hope of someday emigrating could be a catalyst for poor people to invest in schooling. In this way, it could help solve the problem we learned about in chapter 6 that left to their own devices, people tend to underinvest in education.[20] Then there is the possibility that people who emigrate eventually return home, bringing new skills with them.

Empirical economists have put the brain gain hypothesis to the test by comparing educational attainment in countries with and without high levels of emigration. One study found that average education levels were higher in countries from which large numbers of educated people emigrated.[21] That seems to suggest a brain gain. But looking at it from a different angle, you also could say that more educated people leave countries with high average schooling levels. That sounds more like a brain drain. There is a classic reflection problem here. Average schooling and emigration of educated people seem to move up or down together, and it is not clear which causes which. There is no way to run an experiment that plucks educated people randomly out of some countries but not others and then compares schooling investments. Using instrumental variables, this study found evidence that high-skilled emigration does promote schooling investment back home.

This does not mean that countries shouldn't worry about the brain drain. Perhaps a more nuanced and proactive view is in order: that countries need to invest in education and reap the benefits of remittances from highly skilled emigrants, while at the same time creating incentives for skilled workers to stay home—and for emigrants to return once they've gotten new skills abroad. After all, most people seem to be home—97% of the people in the world live in the country in which they were born.

*Interconnections among Trade and Migration*

If you're thinking that trade in goods and services, capital, and people are not unrelated, you are right. In the new global economy they are interconnected in ways that can have far-reaching ramifications for economic development.

Mexico's President Salinas, while negotiating the North American Free Trade Agreement (NAFTA) in the early 1990s, came up with a now-famous quote: "We want NAFTA because we want to export goods, not people."[22] Salinas, a Harvard-trained economist, knew about trade models. His quote comes straight out of the Factor Price Equalization Theorem. Salinas knew that without trade, Mexico, a labor-abundant country, would continue having low wages, but with free trade, the price of the abundant factor eventually will rise. That means NAFTA will increase wages in Mexico. Econometric models show that people migrate from low- to high-wage economies. In short, rather than migrating to pick tomatoes in California, Mexican workers can pick tomatoes in Mexico, and then Mexico can export the tomatoes to the United States. Their children can go to school and get jobs in factories that are financed by foreign capital and export automobiles to showrooms in the United States. Without trade, this would not be possible, and migration pressures would be higher.

United Nations secretary-general Kofi Annan sees linkages among migration, capital flows, and trade that go beyond any trade model we've considered in this chapter:

> Today's international migrants are, more than ever before, a dynamic human link between cultures, economies and societies . . . just a few seconds are needed for the global financial system to transmit their earnings to remote corners of the developing world, where they buy food, clothing, shelter, pay for education or health care, and can relieve debt . . . The skills and knowhow they accumulate are also instrumental in transferring technology and institutional knowledge. They inspire new ways of thinking, both socially and politically. India's software industry has emerged, in large part, from the intensive networking among expatriates, returning migrants and Indian entrepreneurs at home and abroad. After working in Greece, Albanians bring home new agricultural skills that enable them to increase production . . . It should be no surprise that countries once associated exclusively with emigration, including Ireland, the Republic of Korea, Spain and many others, now boast thriving economies, which themselves attract large numbers of migrants.[23]

#### "FREE TRADE" AND INTERNATIONAL AID

As we described in the introduction to this chapter, international trade can be very contentious. While planet Earth would almost certainly be richer if it were integrated through international trade into a single giant market, the distribution of these gains would just as certainly be uneven. In the short run, some people would win big; others would lose. Perhaps the most common "national interest" concern about international trade is that it pushes down the price of some goods and factors of production. Even though consumers may be better off, for those producing and selling these goods or earning a living from these factors of production (e.g., their own labor), lower prices hurt. Lower prices are simultaneously a boon to consumers and a bane to producers. What do you think might happen, then, if trade pushed prices for some goods all the way to zero in some places? In addition to who is helped and who is hurt, how do you think free goods and services would impact an economy?

These might seem like purely rhetorical questions since competitive markets normally do not push prices lower than marginal cost (firms that incur costs to produce something must charge a price that at least covers their cost of producing the good). International aid, however, makes these questions very real—particularly from the perspective of recipient countries. International aid effectively pushes the price of some goods at specific times and places to zero. To the ultimate recipients, aid can look like free trade of a literal sort: rich countries sending free stuff to poor countries. Throughout this book we have touched on aid and on the ongoing debate about whether it works or not. We conclude this chapter by looking at international aid through the lens of international trade.

While private investment in and trade with developing countries now far outstrip international aid to these countries, aid continues to play an important role—for better or for worse—in many countries. International aid can take many forms. It can be "official development assistance" (ODA)[24] that is provided from one government directly to another (bilateral) or from a coalition of governments to a particular government through an international organization (multilateral). Some of this ODA aims explicitly to induce greater private investment and trade by providing subsidized loans and insurance for businesses to engage with firms and markets in developing countries. For example, the US government's development finance arm, the Overseas Private Investment Corporation (OPIC), has mobilized over $200 billion in private capital to "help U.S. businesses gain footholds in emerging markets, catalyzing revenues, job and growth opportunities both at home and abroad."[25]

Aid can also come from private foundations or nongovernmental organizations (NGOs). While such "private" aid has been around a long time, the Bill and Melinda Gates Foundation has recently put this form of aid on par with many ODA donors. Whatever its form, aid is typically earmarked for a particular use, such as specific projects or interventions (e.g., building schools and roads, supporting health programs), technical assistance, training and capacity building (e.g., agricultural research, medical training), subsidized loans (e.g., for building dams or power plants), or emergency and humanitarian response (e.g., relief from famine, natural disaster, or conflict). A goal, explicit or implicit, of many current public and private aid projects is to enable poor people and nations to engage with local and global markets more effectively. The International Fund for Agricultural Development (IFAD) calls for "a new approach . . . that is both market-oriented and sustainable." Its president writes: "It is time to look at poor smallholder farmers and rural entrepreneurs in a completely new way—not as charity cases but as people whose innovation, dynamism and hard work will bring prosperity to their communities and greater food security to the world in the decades ahead."[26]

Not surprisingly, international aid is not as free as it may appear. Obviously, the goods and services transferred from a rich country to a poor one cost something, and someone must ultimately pay this bill. Those paying these bills may be concerned purely with the well-being of the poor and the future prosperity of poor countries, but they are also likely to have ulterior motives related to political or military support or their own economic interests. Such motives are apparent not only in bilateral aid but also in the pressure rich countries often exert on the multilateral organizations to which they contribute. While the goods and services transferred as aid are clearly not free from the perspective of the donor, they are typically not free from the perspective of the recipient, either, because they often come with strings attached. In addition to the political support that the recipient must provide to keep bilateral ODA flowing from the US, for example, US funds earmarked for constructing a new road may stipulate that the work be done by an American construction company. Since 2000, China has become a major player in Africa using a distinct and rather opaque version of this model of international aid (see sidebar 13.4). Overall, then, we can understand the flows of ODA from rich to poor countries around the world as simply a manifestation of familiar concepts of comparative advantage—albeit broadened to include political and strategic elements.

*Food Aid*

From the perspective of both donor and recipient governments, international aid is not as free as it may appear, but at some point in the deliv-

### Sidebar 13.4 "The Dragon's Gift," "The New Scramble for Africa," and "Aid 2.0"

For a development economist, conversations with taxi drivers do not normally qualify as "data collection," but they can be insightful and interesting (e.g., see sidebar 13.3). For several years now, one of Travis's favorite topics to raise with taxi drivers in Africa is the role China plays in their country. This is a natural taxi topic because China has been investing heavily in African infrastructure: roads, bridges, and especially oil pipelines.

Reactions from taxi drivers to this Chinese aid generally fall into two quite different categories. Many complain about Chinese reliance on Chinese companies and workers, the quality of the work, and a perceived disregard for environmental impacts of the work (especially in mining). Others praise the Chinese for focusing primarily on what Africa needs most: infrastructure. A similar range of opinions appear almost daily in African newspapers and have spurred a flurry of books and international media coverage on the topic.

Many claim that China's generosity to African countries is driven by its appetite for natural resources: oil from Sudan and Angola and copper from Zambia and the Democratic Republic of Congo, for example. Others see this as a strategic "soft power" "charm offensive" with a broader geopolitical agenda and, as evidence, cite China's widespread investment in Chinese culture and language centers and in sports stadiums throughout the continent. China does not condition its aid on human rights performance or governance outcomes, and it seems to pay less attention to labor and environmental standards than traditional donor countries do, which is often cited as a potential threat to conventional ODA. As *Foreign Policy* editor-in-chief Moisés Naím wrote in 2007, China is "effectively pricing responsible and well-meaning aid organizations out of the market in the very places where they are needed the most. If they continue to succeed in pushing their alternative development model, they will succeed in underwriting a world that is more corrupt, chaotic, and authoritarian" (www .foreignpolicy.com/articles/2007/02/14/rogue_aid).

Investigating any of these claims has been difficult, because Chinese aid flows are opaque, even secretive (which naturally raises popular suspicions). Recently, a team of economists from William and Mary College compiled a database of Chinese aid to Africa using media reports. This new database provides some interesting insights.

China committed roughly $75 billion to Africa between 2000 and 2011. (US aid to Africa was $90 billion during this same period.) Of this Chinese aid, $20 billion went to two countries that didn't appear in the top-ten list of recipients of US aid: Ghana and Nigeria. The vast majority of these aid commitments indeed target oil pipelines, mining, energy, and roads. Chinese aid also looks different from aid from traditional donors because the heavy involvement of state-owned enterprises makes it difficult to distinguish between official assistance and private investment flows, and often it raises additional suspicions during the bidding process for new construction and mining projects.

Other emerging powers, including India and Brazil, are ramping up their international aid programs. In 2011, the *Economist* magazine described this shift as "Aid 2.0" and called it encouraging: "Like trade, aid benefits from specialization and comparative advantage. Emerging countries, with recent experience to draw from, might do a better job of infrastructure spending" (www.economist.com/node /21525899).

Deborah Brautigam, *The Dragon's Gift: The Real Story of China in Africa* (Oxford: Oxford University Press, 2009).

Padraig Carmody, *The New Scramble for Africa* (Cambridge: Polity Press, 2011).

Andy Sumner and Richard Mallett, *The Future of Foreign Aid: Development Cooperation and the New Geography of Global Poverty* (Basingstoke, UK: Palgrave Macmillan, 2012).

ery process these transfers effectively become free stuff. And at this point, the questions we asked at the beginning of this section become quite important. To answer these questions, consider first what is arguably the highest profile and most tangible form of ODA: food aid.

The largest food aid donor in the world is the US, which launched its food aid program in 1954. Over its sixty-year history, it is estimated that US food aid has benefited over 3 million people around the world.[27] While the political and strategic goals of US food aid—both domestic and international—have changed over the years, the basic model has remained essentially the same: the US government buys food commodities from US farmers and pays to ship the food to countries in crisis or with chronic food shortages. Chris Barrett, a development economist at Cornell University, is a leading expert on US food aid—and a vocal critic of this model.[28] Among its flaws, two stand out as especially disturbing. First, it is extremely inefficient, with more than half of each food aid dollar going to transportation and overhead. Second, flooding local markets with free food can hurt local producers and discourage investments in productivity.

Notice that this second flaw of US food aid is a manifestation of essentially the same concerns that international trade triggers when it lowers the price received by producers in a given country—albeit a more extreme version in which local producers compete against imported goods that are not just cheap but free.[29] To illustrate this point, imagine how Starbucks would have felt about the "Battle in Seattle" if the WTO negotiations included distributing free coffee outside all its coffee shops. It might well have joined the demonstration!

Of course, Sudan is not Seattle. During times of emergency response—in the wake of an earthquake, hurricane, or tsunami that destroys or disrupts local food supply chains—there may be few local food alternatives, and food delivery could be well justified. But much of US food aid is delivered into markets where local farmers and traders have food to sell. The arrival of US food in such a market not only reduces local food purchases but also can directly suppress local food prices because much of this food is "monetized" (sold) by governments to raise money they can allocate to local needs as they see fit. Local farmers and local food supply chains risk being severely undercut precisely during years when market prices would normally be high, and this can discourage investments in productivity, storage, and transportation technologies. Development practitioners know that administering emergency food relief is not as hard as figuring out what to do afterward.

After decades of pressure from economists like Chris Barrett, NGOs, and even other governments to change this system—to untie food aid from food—there are finally signs of hope. The 2008 US Farm Bill authorized pilot programs to purchase food aid on local and regional markets, something most other countries started doing a long time ago. The 2014 farm bill allows USAID to spend just over 5% of its food aid budget on these local food purchases, much less than the 40% the Obama administration wanted but seemingly a move in the right direction.

### Other Kinds of Aid and "Free" Trade

What about international aid that delivers free or heavily subsidized malaria or tuberculosis treatments to poor countries? Or what about Doctors without Borders offering free medical services in such countries? Even though such transfers are akin to free food flooding a local market, there is an obvious and important difference: many of these countries lack the capacity to procure, much less produce, such pharmaceutical products or lack qualified medical technicians to provide these services. Although the local market effects of "free" trade of this sort are therefore negligible—especially compared to the urgency of pressing health threats—such transfers can impose a longer term dynamic opportunity cost that is not unlike some of the concerns that make international trade contentious. In short, chronic dependence on free medical supplies and services imported from abroad may in the long run discourage the creation of local medical capacity and competency.

To appreciate this dynamic opportunity cost, consider what might have happened to that shirt you recently gave to Goodwill, the Salvation Army, or other charity. If you are anything like us, you may have felt a bit of "warm glow" after donating a box of old clothes or shoes to charity and imagining that someone needy will benefit from your generosity. Many of these clothing donations end up in giant bails that are shipped to Africa and eventually make their way to fascinating and chaotic "second-hand" clothing markets. While a flood of cheap used clothes can drive down prices in local markets (good for consumers), this would seem to pose no real threat to local producers because without much of an apparel industry most African countries would seem to have no or few producers to be hurt. But this ignores the dynamic opportunity cost that cheap clothes impose on these economies, namely, that a thriving textile and apparel industry may never emerge because the steady flow of cheap, donated used clothes keeps prices low and thereby discourages entrepreneurs from being the first to start such a factory.[30]

www.rebeltext.org/development/qr13.html
Learn more about international trade and globalization by exploring multimedia resources while you read.

# 14

# Choose Your Own Epilogue

In chapter 1 we wrote that the goal of this book is to cover "the fundamental things that distinguish rich and poor countries and the methods we use to analyze critical development economic issues." Identifying the essentials is not an easy thing; one of the biggest challenges in writing *Essentials of Development Economics* was deciding what to put in the book and what to leave out. At every step of the way, we had to ask ourselves what the *essentials* of development economics are, as opposed to topics—however important—whose study requires fluency with the essentials. Along the way, we have touched on many different topics— in fact, nearly all of the topics in a conventional textbook can be found somewhere on these pages. Mostly we have emphasized microeconomic development, because we believe that's the logical place to start; it is where most of the cutting-edge work in development economics today is happening, and it reflects our own areas of expertise.

In addition to distilling the essentials of development economics, we've aimed to highlight in this book what development economists actually do and how they do it. Now obviously, everyone cannot grow up to be a development economist. Although we can't understand why everyone wouldn't *aspire* to become one, even Ed and Peri's kids do not harbor this aspiration (sigh; on the other hand, there may still be hope for Travis and Heather's). We are convinced, however, that no matter what kind of future you envision for yourself, appreciating the essentials of development economics can enrich your career as well as your life more broadly. In true economist form, this conviction has an empirical basis. Combined, we have taught these essentials to thousands of students over many, many years. On the basis of interactions with friends, colleagues, and students (many of whom keep in touch for years after taking the final exam), we are convinced that some of the essentials we have covered can have a significant effect on your view of the world and perhaps even shape your career choices.

The conviction that there is truly something for everyone in the study of development economics has shaped our parting words in this epilogue. Some of you may have read (or at least heard of people reading in the 1980s and 1990s) *Choose Your Own Adventure* books. We've opted for a similar structure here and have written three separate epilogues—one for budding development economists, a second for aspiring "internationalists," and a third that showcases deep truths that are relevant for everybody. And don't worry: you can read all three epilogues without spoiling the ending.

## EPILOGUE FOR BUDDING DEVELOPMENT ECONOMISTS

Development economists have always been more likely to do fieldwork than other kinds of economists (many of whom experience spectacular professional success without leaving their offices). Many students end up in graduate programs in development economics precisely because they want to experience—and perhaps change—the wider world. This is perhaps truer now than it ever has been because of the push for rigorous empirical methods in development economics.

As we've described along the way, one of the biggest recent developments in development economics is that researchers are collaborating closely with practitioners from a wide range of fields. This creates some fascinating and sometimes challenging fieldwork opportunities. Over the past three years Ed has found himself designing and analyzing the evaluation component of social cash transfer programs set up by UNICEF specialists in child protection and health, in conjunction with African social welfare ministries, and he has advised the president of Mexico on rural development options. Travis has collaborated closely to design and evaluate the impact of agricultural projects in Haiti, Kenya, and India and of nutrition interventions in Ghana, Burkina Faso, and Malawi. Partners in these projects range from small NGOs to large multilateral development organizations and from private companies to large foundations and government ministries. In many of these projects, it is hard to draw a line between research and practice because the two are so closely intertwined.

In the best of circumstances, the evaluations development economists carry out as part of these projects involve a randomized treatment to deal with the selection problem. However, the analytical tools economists use run the gamut presented in chapter 2, from straightforward randomized controlled trials to econometric models to impact simulations. They include ways to measure economic outcomes like income, poverty, inequality, and human development (chapters 3–7). They have to grapple with challenging institutional environments (chapter 8). The diversity of the development economist's tool kit reflects the programs, contexts, and outcomes of development projects, which are becoming more varied over time.

Development practitioners usually want to know not only whether a program has an impact, but why. Understanding why is crucial in order to design and carry out effective development interventions. This requires having a firm grounding in theories of how economic actors behave, how markets work (and don't work), and how to design interventions that address the challenges of working in places where the basic assumptions of the economic theories we're accustomed to break down. Chapters 8–13 provide some of the theoretical foundations needed to make impact evaluations make sense. In recent years, many research economists—worried that simple experiments are displacing economic theory—have pushed for greater theoretical rigor. As RCTs did over the past decade, this push is now shaping development economics. Economics is defined by a set of disciplinary tools, and development economists must know how to use multiple tools in order to make contributions as economists.

Finally, measuring and having impact are two entirely different things in development economics. Having an impact requires asking the right questions, doing a convincing analysis, and conveying findings to people for whom they can make a difference. "Conveying findings" means getting people's ears (and eyes) *and* crafting presentations so that the findings resonate with those we wish to reach—many or most of whom probably are not economists. Our theories, models, and empirical findings together give us a compelling story to tell. Effectively packaged in narratives and PowerPoint images, they can empower development economists to have an impact on development practice and policies. Sadly, we often do not make the effort required to have an impact beyond the journals in which we publish. The institutional environment (chapter 8) in which we work all too often does not reward it.

Few students ever take a course on how to make economic findings come to life in a PowerPoint presentation or a policy briefing flyer. In the end, though, we know who our main clients are—they are the poor—and having an impact on them is the reason we do development economics.

## EPILOGUE FOR ASPIRING "INTERNATIONALISTS"

If you envision yourself in an international career more broadly, the insights and essentials of development economics may help you appreciate the complexity of the world in new and useful ways. As you develop and deepen your expertise along your chosen path, we believe these insights will also enable you to engage with projects and people more effectively.

In several chapters, we encountered important intersections between development economics and other disciplines. These interdisciplinary boundaries are often the most important and rewarding places for researchers to explore and decision makers to understand. Regardless of your plans for an international career, you are likely to share a broad frontier with economics that is worth appreciating, and you're almost certain to encounter development economists with whom you'll have to communicate along the way. Here are a few examples—there are many more—that illustrate how development economics interfaces with other fields of study.

### Climate Change, Natural Resources, and Environmental Sustainability

Are you a globally focused environmentalist, ecologist, or climatologist? Environmental economics is all about market failures of the sorts covered in this book. Households and firms extract natural resources and pollute the environment without considering the costs this creates for society. Poor farmers take down forests to plant crops without considering the impact on climate change and biodiversity. They decide which seeds to plant without thinking about the importance of conserving crop genetic resources for future agricultural research. Environmental externalities create a classic justification for public action to internalize the externality—that is, make individual actors take into account the social impacts of their actions.

Climate change takes environmental externalities to a whole new, global, level. Ultimately, though, it all boils down to the decisions of firms and households. Firms "use up" clean air and water when they pollute. Households extract and consume firewood and other natural resources, much as they produce and consume crops, but without considering the impacts on carbon loads in the atmosphere, erosion, or other adverse social consequences of their actions.

Resource extraction and other activities are connected with each other in complex ways. A rich and rapidly growing literature in economics, environmental studies, and development journals examines resource extraction and environmental impacts from the perspective of agricultural households in imperfect-market environments, and development economists are commonly brought in to help evaluate environmental programs in poor countries. Much of this work involves development economists teaming up with environmental scientists. The skills and concepts in this book are a prerequisite for studying development-environment interactions.

### Nutrition and Public Health

Is international health or nutrition your thing? Collaborations among nutritionists, agronomists, and development economists have become commonplace as foundations and development agencies spearhead large-scale interventions to enable farmers to grow more nutritious crops and to make nutritional supplements available to poor and malnourished children. Nutritionists have come up with ways to provide a developing child with all the essential nutrients she needs in small, low-cost packets.[1] Yet, to provide a sustainable solution, there needs to be an effective demand for these food supplements and crops among poor households. Is there? Methods in this book are instrumental in providing answers to questions like this, as well offering insights into how nutritional programs raise productivity, educational attainment, and other outcomes needed to enable people to escape from poverty over time.

### Migration

Ed has done more work on migration and development than perhaps any other topic. He was the lone economist on a team of demographers and sociologists that wrote the 1999 book *Worlds in Motion*—the most cited thing he ever did.[2] It should come as no surprise, then, that Ed drafted a chapter on migration. We decided not to put it in this book, because it is more of a topic than an essential of development economics. Without a doubt, migration and development is one of the most important topics in development economics. It is poised to become even more important in the future as people continue moving off the farm and across borders. To understand it, we need the essential skill and idea sets in this book as well as insights from population studies. We need trade, because migration and remittances involve trade in labor, as we learned in chapter 13. We need agricultural household modeling, because migrants come from households, and households are where the immediate impacts of migration and remittances are evident. We also need to understand markets, because the impacts of migration and remittances are different in an environment with missing markets for goods, factors, insurance, and credit, and migration decisions are partly a response to market failures. And we need the tools of impact evaluation to understand migration's impacts and how to harness them for development.

*Population and Fertility*

Are you a population scientist? We also drafted a chapter on population and economic development but in the end decided that it was more of a topic than an essential. Population growth is the outcome of fertility, mortality, and migration. These are the basic components of the field of demography, and all three involve decisions by households—to have children, to invest in health, and to emigrate or not. Parents make fertility decisions without taking into account the implications for society at large; in other words, fertility generates externalities. This is the rationale for government actions to curb fertility in poor countries, the most extreme of which was China's famous one-child-per-couple policy. We saw in chapter 6 that health and life expectancy are affected in complex ways by household and public investments, and they involve externalities, public goods, and scale economies that commonly lead to a divergence of the private from the public good.

*Psychology*

Psychology—say what? Actually, some of the most interesting and important advances in thinking about development have come when psychologists team up with economists and even brain physiologists to study poverty. The "Hope" sidebar in chapter 2 is an example in which a development program might have changed the way people think about their futures.

Economists Sendhil Mullainathan, Eldar Shafir, and others have brought together new methods in psychology and behavioral economics to test basic propositions about people's behavior, including the behavior of the poor. One explanation for why people are trapped in poverty might be that the very condition of being poor keeps people from "thinking" their way out of poverty. As the title of one article states, "poverty impedes cognitive function."[3] People under economic stress have little mental room to think about the optimal strategy to get out of poverty, like investing in schooling or a new crop technology. If this is true, then cash transfers and other programs that reduce the mental as well as physical stress of poverty might have the added benefit of making strategies to become more productive "top of mind," instead of being buried deep below the immediacy of where the next meal will come from. Many development projects try to change people's behavior, for example, getting them to send their kids to school and spend more of their scarce income on nutritious foods and health care. We cannot assume that the underlying parameters shaping people's decisions are given, yet in almost every undergraduate economics class—not to mention most of our economic models—we do precisely that! Instead, behavior and cognition may be endogenous, influenced by, as well as influencing, development outcomes.

### Business Management

Thinking of business? It is easy to slip into a mind-set that confounds international development with international aid. Most of the real development gains the world has witnessed in the past fifty years are attributable to the functioning of markets and private-sector firms. Small-scale entrepreneurs create value and tap opportunities at a local level. Small and medium enterprises are engines of job growth in cities around the world. Even large multinational corporations, which are popular targets for protests of all sorts, contribute in important ways to local economies. Development economists have studied these impacts, but so have business consultants. Many business schools have programs devoted to international business, and many of these relate to doing business with the poor—so called Bottom of the Pyramid strategies. Social impact investing that often aims at a "triple bottom line" (economic, environmental, and social impact) has similarly expanded rapidly in the past decade. Development economists are currently using the tools we described in this book to evaluate these impacts in collaboration with social impact investing firms.

*Politics and International Relations*

There's a reasonably good chance you have a background in international relations or political science—many of the students who take our courses do. What in this book *doesn't* relate in some way to politics and international relations? Development policy, poverty, inequality, human development, institutions, corruption, crime, globalization, aid. It is difficult for a foreign relations expert to do anything without thinking about development economics, just as it is unrealistic for a development economist to ignore politics and institutional environments. If you walk the halls of the United Nations, the Organization for Economic Cooperation and Development (OECD), the Carnegie Endowment for International Peace, or any other organization with a focus on global politics, as we often do, you are guaranteed to find a potpourri of experts with development economists mixed in—all of whom will be interacting and collaborating with one another, trying to make their distinct disciplines merge and make sense to one another.

## EPILOGUE FOR EVERYBODY: DEEP TRUTHS FROM DEVELOPMENT ECONOMICS

This epilogue really is intended for everybody. You may have no desire to even visit Africa, Asia, or Latin America, much less work there, but there are nevertheless deep truths we draw from development economics that might just enrich your life and expand your worldview. These deep truths stem from several of the essentials we have discussed in this book. Four such deep truths stand out in our minds.

*Deep Truth One: "What is, is for a reason"*

If there is any single lesson that emerges from this book, it's that context matters. Economists, like any scientists, seek to identify patterns amidst the complexity of the world. While there are many patterns to be found in development economics—otherwise there would be no "essentials"—universal truths are highly elusive in social science research. When we are new to a place, it is easy to wonder why on earth people do the things they do; it is easy to see perplexing behaviors as fundamentally irrational or inefficient. Often, this is because the context creates constraints that we don't fully understand or appreciate—because the people we are observing understand the richness of their economic environment better than we do as outsiders. These contextual constraints may or may not serve a clear social or cultural purpose and may have emerged simply by accident, but they often impose real constraints on the behavior of individuals and households. This implies that humility beats hubris when it comes to achieving real impact. The knowledge problem implies that we often know less than we think we know, which can undermine our best-laid plans.

*Deep Truth Two: "True development expands freedom"*

Money buys a lot of things, but anytime money becomes the end rather than a means to an end we get in trouble—at both personal and societal levels. Development economists have focused increasingly on broader measures of human development in developing countries to reflect this fact. But the objective of expanding human agency and freedom is relevant for every country. For rich or for poor, true development enriches lives by building agency and enabling individuals to be and do what they want to be and do. True development expands freedom and opportunities—opportunities that come from having a healthy body and brain, an education and intellectual stimulation for cognitive development, and access to markets to secure a livelihood and contribute to society in the process. Freedom is not just about having more choices, but must also build accountability, because when accountability breaks down—whether it is the elite abusing their power or common individuals being denied the fruits of their labor—having more choices means very little.

*Deep Truth Three: "Markets that work are powerful, but they are not free"*

When markets work well, they can dramatically improve individual lives and social outcomes. They not only allow individuals to enjoy the greater freedoms that true development brings but can also harness enhanced choice and accountability for the broader social good. In order to work well, though, markets require a basic infrastructure of political, social, and cultural institutions—norms, rules, and processes that govern our interactions with others. While it is true in rich and poor countries alike that governments rarely improve things by tinkering directly with markets, this does not mean that governments don't have a role to play. Markets that function well—that adjust freely as underlying conditions change—do not come free. They require major public investments and targeted government action. They also require deeply rooted supporting institutions that, whether they emerge from the bottom up or are imposed from the top down, are shaped importantly by government action.

### *Deep Truth Four: "Be self-seeking and fellow-feeling"*

Adam Smith's insight that an invisible hand leads people, through market interactions, to outcomes that were not part of their intention is one of the most important ideas in modern social thought.[4] In these pages, we have repeatedly seen how critically markets and the efficiency gains they bring can shape economic development. The invisible hand that makes markets so powerful works through a basic human instinct to promote one's own well-being and interests—through our "self-seeking" nature. We've also seen that conditions in developing countries often make it important to consider efficiency and equity at the same time. In a similar vein, Adam Smith insisted that markets could improve society most when market interactions between people reflect their instincts to be both self-seeking and fellow-feeling. This fellow-feeling impulse—a sense of sympathy for others' circumstances—provides the most basic motivation for doing development economics. The way we address fundamental questions of human development and social welfare as economists, the way we seek to harness markets to achieve both efficiency and equity objectives, and indeed, the way we each try to fill our lives with meaning and purpose must take both instincts into account: be self-seeking as well as fellow-feeling.

www.rebeltext.org/development/qr14.html
Explore multimedia resources while you read this
epilogue.

# Notes

1. The true cost of living is difficult to compare across countries. Here we use the purchasing power parity method. Even income can be hard to measure in a country where most crop production is for home consumption. These issues will be addressed later in this book.

2. A least-developed country, according to the United Nations, is a country that has the lowest indicators of socioeconomic development and the lowest Human Development Index (HDI; see chapter 6) levels of all countries in the world. We'll learn about country-development typologies in more detail at the end of chapter 2.

3. Mateusz Filipski and J. Edward Taylor, "A Simulation Impact Evaluation of Rural Income Transfers in Malawi and Ghana," *Journal of Development Effectiveness* 4, no. 1 (2012):109–29.

4. Chewe Nkonde, Nicole M. Mason, Nicholas J. Sitko, and T. S. Jayne, "Who Gained and Who Lost from Zambia's 2010 Maize Marketing Policies?" (working paper no. 49, Food Security Rresearch Project, Lusaka, Zambia, January 2011; www.aec.msu.edu/fs2/zambia/wp49.pdf).

5. http://web.worldbank.org/wbsite/external/countries/africaext/malawiextn /0,,contentMDK:21575335~pagePK:141137~piPK:141127~theSitePK: 355870,00.html.

6. You can read about some of these programs at the Transfer Project website, housed at the University of North Carolina, Chapel Hill (www.cpc .unc.edu/projects/transfer).

7. Economist William Easterly provocatively argues that the real origins of development economics trace further back, to the 1920s and 1930s, and that the "technocratic" approach to development that continues to shape high-level discussions and plans about development was born of a general disregard for

the rights of the poor as individuals during these early decades. See William Easterly, *The Tyranny of Experts: Economists, Dictators, and the Forgotten Rights of the Poor* (New York: Basic Books, 2014).

8. Walter W. Rostow, *The Stages of Economic Growth: A Non-Communist Manifesto* (Cambridge: Cambridge University Press, 1960).

9. Roy F. Harrod, "An Essay in Dynamic Theory," *Economic Journal* 49 (1939):14–33; Evsey Domar, "Capital Expansion, Rate of Growth, and Employment," *Econometrica* 14, no. 2 (1946):137–47.

10. W. Arthur Lewis, "Economic Development with Unlimited Supplies of Labor," *Manchester School of Economic and Social Studies* 22 (1954): 139–91.

11. Gustav Ranis and John C. Fei, "A Theory of Economic Development," *American Economic Review* 51 (September 1961):533–58.

12. Theodore W. Schultz, *Transforming Traditional Agriculture* (New Haven: Yale University Press, 1964).

13. Raúl Prebisch, "Commercial Policy in the Underdeveloped Countries," *American Economic Review* 49 (May 1959):251–73; Hans Singer, "The Distributions of Gains between Investing and Borrowing Countries," *American Economic Review: Papers and Proceedings* 40 (1950):473–85.

14. A. Hirschman, "A Generalized Linkage Approach to Development with Special Reference to Staples," *Economic Development and Cultural Change* 25 (1977):67–98.

15. John W. Mellor, *The New Economics of Growth: A Strategy for India and the Developing World* (Ithaca, NY: Cornell University Press, 1976).

16. United Nations, *Encyclopedia of the Nations* (www.nationsencyclopedia .com/United-Nations/Economic-and-Social-Development-first-un-development-decade.html).

17. Simon Kuznets, "Economic Growth and Income Inequality," *American Economic Review* 45 (March 1955):1–28.

18. H. B. Chenery, M. S. Ahluwalia, C. L. G. Bell, J. H. Duloy, and R. Jolly, *Redistribution with Growth* (London: Oxford University Press, 1974).

19. I. Adelman and C. T. Morris, *Economic Growth and Social Equity in Developing Countries* (Stanford, CA: Stanford University Press, 1973).

20. World Bank archives (http://web.worldbank.org/wbsite/external/extaboutus /extarchives/0,,contentMDK:20502974~pagePK:36726~piPK:437378~theSit ePK:29506,00.html).

21. See www.un.org/millenniumgoals/bkgd.shtml.

22. Later in this book we will encounter one of the lead detractors of the MDGs, economist William Easterly, and explore his arguments.

CHAPTER 2

1. This is the amount reported by the twenty-four members of the Organization for Economic Cooperation and Development's (OECD) Development Assistance Committee for 2011 (http://stats.oecd.org/Index.aspx?DatasetCode = ODA_DONOR). About 80%–85% of developmental aid comes from government sources as official development assistance (ODA). The remaining 15%–

20% comes from private organizations such as nongovernmental organizations (NGOs), foundations, and other development charities (e.g., Oxfam).

2. Opportunity NYC, an experimental CCT, was launched in New York City with support from the Rockefeller Foundation, the Robin Hood Foundation, the Open Society Institute, the Starr Foundation, AIG, and Mayor Bloomberg's personal foundation. It ended on August 31, 2010.

3. J. Angrist and S. Pischke, *Mostly Harmless Econometrics: An Empiricists' Companion* (Princeton: Princeton University Press, 2008).

4. Now called the Abdul Latif Jameel Poverty Action Lab (J-PAL).

5. www.povertyactionlab.org/news/randomized-evaluations-interventions-social-science-delivery.

6. Poverty Action Lab, "What Is Randomization?" (www.povertyactionlab .org/methodology/what-randomization).

7. For an excellent discussion see Benjamin Davis, Marie Gaarder, Sudhanshu Handa, and Jenn Yablonski, "Evaluating the Impact of Cash Transfer Programmes in Sub-Saharan Africa: An Introduction to the Special Issue," *Journal of Development Effectiveness* 4, no. 1 (2012):1–8.

8. Dean Karlan and Jonathan Zinman, "Expanding Credit Access: Using Randomized Supply Decisions to Estimate the Impacts," *Review of Financial Studies* 23, no. 1 (2010): 433–64, doi:10.1093/rfs/hhp092.

9. Suresh de Mel, David McKenzie, and Christopher Woodruff, "Returns to Capital in Microenterprises: Evidence from a Field Experiment," *Quarterly Journal of Economics* 123, no. 4 (2008): 1329–72.

10. Sarah A. Janzen and Michael R. Carter, "After the Shock: The Impact of Microinsurance on Consumption Smoothing and Asset Protection" (Working paper no. 19702, National Bureau of Economic Research, Washington, DC, 2013).

11. Rachid Laajaj, "Closing the Eyes on a Gloomy Future: Psychological Causes and Economic Consequences" (working paper, University of Wisconsin, Madison, and Paris School of Economics, December 7, 2011; http://agecon .ucdavis.edu/research/seminars/files/laajaj-closing-the-eyes-on-a-gloomy-future .pdf).

12. Measuring impact and putting a value on it are often two different things. For example, measuring the impact of a literacy program on literacy test outcomes is straightforward, but valuing these literacy gains can be very difficult. In such cases, a good alternative to cost-benefit analysis is cost-effectiveness analysis, which measures how costly it is to achieve a specific impact (e.g., an increase in literacy of one standard deviation).

13. For more discussion, see http://marcfbellemare.com/wordpress/2013/11 /impact-evaluation-and-nimby-comments-and-discussion/.

14. An excellent discussion appears in Christopher B. Barrett and Michael R. Carter, "The Power and Pitfalls of Experiments in Development Economics: Some Non-random Reflections," *Applied Economic Perspectives and Policy* 32, no. 4 (2010):515–48.

15. A next-best strategy might be to use the same farmers prior to the subsidy as a control group, provided that before-and-after data are available. This effectively is what Sadoulet, de Janvry, and Davis did in their fixed-effects analysis of

the income effects of Mexico's PROCAMPO crop subsidy program. This strategy can be confounded by the inability to adequately control for time-varying variables, however. For example, changes in the economy at large might coincide with the timing of the transfers and affect the outcomes of interest. See E. Sadoulet, A. de Janvry, and B. Davis, "Cash Transfer Programs with Income Multipliers: PROCAMPO in Mexico," *World Development* 29, no. 6 (2001):1043–56.

16. In Keynesian economics, government spending can increase income by more than the amount of the spending. This is the idea behind economic stimulus programs in the US and other countries in response to the economic crisis beginning in 2007–2008.

17. Poverty Action Lab, "What Is Randomization?" (www.povertyaction lab.org/methodology/what-randomization).

18. www.millenniumvillages.org/uploads/ReportPaper/MP-2010-Annual-Report---Complete---FINAL.pdf.

19. His experiment and results are presented in Hans Binswanger, "Attitudes toward Risk: Experimental Measurement in Rural India," *American Journal of Agricultural Economics* 62, no. 3 (1980):395–407.

20. Christopher B. Barrett and Michael R. Carter, "The Power and Pitfalls of Experiments in Development Economics: Some Non-random Reflections, *Applied Economic Perspectives and Policy* 32, no. 4 (2010):515–48.

21. Angus S. Deaton, "Instruments of Development: Randomization in the Tropics, and the Search for the Elusive Keys to Economic Development" (working paper, no. 14690, National Bureau of Economic Research, January 2009; www.nber.org/papers/w14690).

22. Esther Duflo, Michael Kremer, and Jonathan Robinson, "Nudging Farmers to Use Fertilizer: Evidence from Kenya," *American Economic Review* 101, no. 6 (2011):2350–90.

23. Development banks often evaluate the costs and benefits of a new project over a fifteen- to twenty-year period, depending on the nature of the project. They also tend to use conservative (that is, high) discount rates—typically on the order of 10% or higher. Risk plays a role here: The riskier you think the future is, the sooner you'll want your money back and the higher the discount rate you'll use in your CBA.

24. Dwayne Benjamin, "Household Composition, Labor Markets and Labor Demand: Testing for Separation in Agricultural Household Models," *Econometrica* 60, no. 2 (March 1992):287–322; H. Jacoby, "Shadow Wages and Peasant Family Labor Supply: An Econometric Application to the Peruvian Sierra," *Review of Economic Studies* 60 (1993): 903–21; A. de Janvry, M. Fafchamps, and E. Sadoulet, "Peasant Household Behavior with Missing Markets: Some Paradoxes Explained," *Economic Journal* 101 (1991):1400–1417.

25. E. Sadoulet, A. de Janvry, and B. Davis, "Cash Transfer Programs with Income Multipliers: PROCAMPO in Mexico," *World Development* 29, no. 6 (2001):1043–56.

26. M. Angelucci and G. De Giorgi, "Indirect Effects of an Aid Program: How Do Cash Transfers Affect Ineligibles' Consumption?" *American Economic Review* 99(2009):486–508.

CHAPTER 3

1. Center for the Continuing Study of the California Economy, "California Poised to Move up in World Economy Rankings in 2013," *Numbers in the News* (July 2013; www.ccsce.com/PDF/Numbers-July-2013-CA-Economy-Rankings-2012.pdf).

2. Melvin Backman, "Britain, Italy Add Drugs and Sex to GDP," *CNN Money*, May 30, 2014, http://money.cnn.com/2014/05/29/news/economy/uk-italy-prostitution-gdp/.

3. http://siteresources.worldbank.org/datastatistics/Resources/gnipc.pdf.

4. R. Repetto, W. Magrath, M. Wells, C. Beer, and F. Rossini, *Wasting Assets: Natural Resources in the National Accounts* (Washington, DC: World Resources Institute, 1989).

5. www.who.int/mediacentre/factsheets/fs311/en/.

6. You can see all the countries' PPP-adjusted GDPs at the World Bank website, http://data.worldbank.org/indicator/NY.GDP.PCAP.PP.CD.

7. Paul Leroy-Beaulieu, *De la colonisation chez les peuples modernes* (Paris, 1874). See also the discussion in chapter 2 of G. Rist, *The History of Development: From Western Origins to Global Faith* (London: Zed Books, 2002).

8. Interestingly, some WTO agreements also grant privileges to "developing countries" (e.g., the original Agreement on Trade Related Intellectual Property Rights) without clearly defining which countries can qualify by this definition. In such cases, member countries of the WTO designate themselves as developing countries, but there are obvious bounds on which countries can get away with this self-designation!

9. Source: World Bank. For a complete listing, see http://data.worldbank .org/about/country-classifications/country-and-lending-groups#Low_income.

10. http://povertydata.worldbank.org/poverty/home/. Unless otherwise specified, you can assume that per capita incomes mentioned in this chapter are PPP adjusted.

11. World Bank, *2011 World Development Report* (http://web.worldbank .org/wbsite/external/extdec/extresearch/extwdrs/0,,contentMDK:23256432~pa gePK:478093~piPK:477627~theSitePK:477624,00.html).

12. *United Nations Human Development Report* (2011; http://hdr.undp .org/en/statistics/hdi/).

CHAPTER 4

1. See www.who.int/nutrition/topics/nutrecomm/en/index.html.

2. Some nutrients are easier to get from cheap foods than others. The most costly essential nutrients would have a relatively large impact on the cost of this poverty food basket.

3. The Development Research Group at the World Bank established the LSMS in order "to facilitate the use of household survey data for evidence-based policy-making." See http://go.worldbank.org/IPLXWMCNJ0.

4. This is the approach proposed by Joel Greer and Erik Thorbecke, "Food Poverty Profile Applied to Kenyan Smallholders," *Economic Development and Cultural Change* 35 (1986):115-41.

5. World Bank, "Poverty Overview" (www.worldbank.org/en/topic/poverty /overview).

6. This figure is for the forty-eight contiguous states plus the District of Columbia. The poverty lines are higher in Alaska and Hawaii.

7. See www.bbc.co.uk/news/magazine-17312819.

8. J. Foster, J. Greer, and E. Thorbecke, "A Class of Decomposable Poverty Measures," *Econometrica* 52, no. 3 (1984):761–66.

9. The seminal article on poverty and asset dynamics is Travis J. Lybbert, Christopher B. Barrett, Solomon Desta, and D. Layne Coppock, "Stochastic Wealth Dynamics and Risk Management among a Poor Population," *Economic Journal* 114 (October 2002):750–77. A more recent article directly addresses the dilemma described here: Michael Carter and Travis J. Lybbert, "Consumption versus Asset Smoothing: Testing the Implications of Poverty Trap Theory in Burkina Faso," *Journal of Development Economics* 99 (2012): 255–64.

10. Travis J. Lybbert, Christopher B. Barrett, Solomon Desta, and D. Layne Coppock, "Stochastic Wealth Dynamics and Risk Management among a Poor Population," *Economic Journal* 114 (October 2002):750–77.

11. In much of East Africa, the herder relies as much or more on the blood of the cattle as he does their milk.

12. Paul Rosenstein-Rodan first outlined this model in 1943. Paul Rosenstein-Rodan, "Problems of Industrialization of Eastern and South-Eastern Europe," *Economic Journal* 53, no. 210/211 (1943):202–11.

CHAPTER 5

1. The frequency distribution for Mexico was constructed from data in Gerardo Esquivel, "The Dynamics of Income Inequality in Mexico since NAFTA" (El Colegio de México, December 2008; www.cid.harvard.edu/Economia /GEsquivel.pdf). Swedish disposable income data are from Statistics Sweden (www.scb.se/Pages/TableAndChart___226030.aspx).

2. H. Shalit and S. Yitzhaki, "The Mean-Gini Efficient Portfolio Frontier," *Journal of Financial Research* 28, no. 1 (2005):59–75.

3. If you aren't statistically inclined, don't worry: Excel will take the covariance for you. Just pick a cell and insert "= covar(array1, array2)" where array1 is the data in the second column and array2 is the data in the third column.

4. Postscript to Bob Sutcliffe, "World Inequality and Globalization," *Oxford Review of Economic Policy* (Spring 2004; http://siteresources.worldbank.org /INTDECINEQ/Resources/PSBSutcliffe.pdf).

5. Some of the fastest-growing countries in recent decades have been poor countries with very large populations, especially China and India. While this has dramatically raised the average income of nearly 40% of the world's population, these two countries account for barely 1% of all the countries in the world. Therefore, the effect on the global Gini is much greater than on the disparities between countries.

6. This social welfare function was proposed by Shlomo Yitzhaki, "Stochastic Dominance, Mean Variance and Gini's Mean Difference," *American Economic Review* 72 (1982):178–85.

7. In calculus terms, the derivative of $W$ with respect to income is positive (since $G < 1$), and the derivative with respect to $G$ is negative.

8. Esther Duflo, "Gender Equality in Development" (BREAD policy paper no. 011, December 2005; http://siteresources.worldbank.org/INTAFRREG TOPGENDER/Resources/EstherDufloGenderEqualityinDevelopment. pdf; Amartya Sen, "More Than 100 Million Women Are Missing," *New York Review of Books* 37, no. 20, 1999 (www.nybooks.com/articles/archives/1990/dec/20/more-than-100-million-women-are-missing/).

9. It is a property of covariances that $\text{Cov}(x + y, z) = \text{Cov}(x, z) + \text{Cov}(y, z)$.

CHAPTER 6

1. Mahbub ul Haq, *Reflections on Human Development* (New York: Oxford University Press, 1995).

2. You can learn more about the IHDI at the UNDP website, http://hdr .undp.org/en/statistics/ihdi.

3. Choosing between the average and geometric mean might seem technical, but really it's about what we care about in development. Should a country that does well on one dimension but poorly on another have the same HDI as a country that does reasonably well on both? If all three indexes are the same (say, ½), you can easily verify that the average and geometric mean will be the same:

$$\sqrt[3]{(1/2)^3} = 1/2$$

$$(1/2+1/2+1/2)/3 = 1/2$$

Otherwise, they will be different: for example if the indexes are ¼, ½, and ¾, the average is still ½, but the geometric mean is only 0.45. Suppose two countries have the same education level, but one has moderate income and moderate life expectancy, while the other has high income and low life expectancy. Even if the average of the three indexes is the same for the two countries, the second one will have a lower HDI according to the geometric mean. The geometric mean penalizes countries that do well on one component but poorly on another.

4. You can read about the Global Peace Index at www.visionofhumanity .org/gpi-data/#/2011/conf/.

5. We are grateful to the United Nations Children's Fund (UNICEF Lesotho) and the Food and Agricultural Organization (FAO) for allowing us to use these data to illustrate the costs and benefits of going to school.

6. You can find real interest rates for different countries at the World Bank's data website: http://data.worldbank.org/indicator/FR.INR.RINR.

7. These percentages are for children twelve to nineteen years of age.

8. Centers for Disease Control and Prevention, "State-Specific Healthy Life Expectancy at Age 65 Years—United States, 2007–2009," *Morbidity and*

*Mortality Weekly Report* 62, no. 28 (July 19, 2013):561–66 (www.cdc.gov/ mmwr/preview/mmwrhtml/mm6228a1.htm).

9. These statistics are from the United Nations, "UNAIDS Report on the Global AIDS Epidemic" (2010; www.unaids.org/documents/20101123_Global Report_em.pdf) and "World AIDS Day Report 2011" (www.unaids.org/en/ media/unaids/contentassets/documents/unaidspublication/2011/jc2216_ worldaidsday_report_2011_en.pdf).

10. C. Bell, S. Devarajan, and H. Gersbach (2003) (PDF). *The Long-run Economic Costs of AIDS: Theory and an Application to South Africa* (working paper no. 3152, World Bank; http://siteresources.worldbank.org/INTPRH/Resources /Longrun_economic_costs_of_AIDS.pdf).

11. These estimates come from John Strauss and Duncan Thomas, "Health, Nutrition, and Economic Development," *Journal of Economic Literature* 36, no. 2 (1998):766–817.

12. Ibid.

13. Xiao Ye and J. Edward Taylor, "The Impact of Income Growth on Farm Household Nutrient Intake: A Case Study of a Prosperous Rural Area in Northern China," *Economic Development and Cultural Change* 43, no. 4 (1995): 805–19.

14. Lant Pritchett and Lawrence H. Summers, "Wealthier Is Healthier," *Journal of Human Resources* 31, no. 4 (1996):841–68.

15. Jean Dreze and Amartya Sen, *India: Economic Development and Social Opportunity* (Oxford: Clarendon Press, 1999).

16. Amartya Sen, *Development as Freedom* (New York: Anchor Books, 1999), pp. 3–4.

CHAPTER 7

1. Robert Lucas, "On the Mechanics of Economic Development," *Journal of Monetary Economics* 22 (1988):5–42.

2. Marcelo Mello, "Decomposing the International Variation in Capital per Worker," *Economics Letters* 113 (2011): 189–91.

3. The data for life expectancy are from the Department of Health and Human Services, National Center for Health Statistics, *National Vital Statistics Reports* 54, no. 19 (June 28, 2006; www.dhhs.gov; http://americandigest.org /mt-archives/american_studies/america_in_1900.php); Richard H. Steckel, *A History of the Standard of Living in the United States* (http://eh.net/?s=A+Hist ory+of+the+Standard+of+Living+in+the+United+States). The data for US GDP in 1900 were compiled by GAPMINDER (www.gapminder.org/data/documen tation/gd001/#.U--qoGMY6EA), using estimates from Angus Maddison, *The World Economy: Historical Statistics* (www.ggdc.net/maddison/maddison-project/data.htm), and converting them to 2002 dollars.

4. George E. P. Box and Norman R. Draper, *Empirical Model-Building and Response Surfaces* (New York: Wiley, 1987).

5. For a discussion of this adjustment and why it may matter, see "Global Economic Inequality: More or Less Equal?" *Economist* (March 2004; www .economist.com/node/2498851).

6. Paul M. Romer, "The Origins of Endogenous Growth," *Journal of Economic Perspectives* 8, no. 1 (Winter 1994):3–22.

7. Paul M. Romer, "Idea Gaps and Object Gaps in Economic Development," *Journal of Monetary Economics* 32, no. 3 (1993): 543–73.

8. See the Millennium Villages Project website: www.unmillenniumproject .org/.

9. William Easterly, *The Elusive Quest for Growth* (Cambridge, MA: MIT Press, 2002).

10. See "Economics Focus: The Big Push Back," *Economist* (December 3, 2011; www.economist.com/node/21541001).

11. William Easterly, *The Tyranny of Experts: Economists, Dictators, and the Forgotten Rights of the Poor* (New York: Basic Books, 2014).

CHAPTER 8

1. Raymond Fisman and Edward Miguel, "Corruption, Norms, and Legal Enforcement: Evidence from Diplomatic Parking Tickets," *Journal of Political Economy* 115, no. 6 (December (2007):1020–48.

2. Yasmine Saleh, "Egypt Diplomats Worst Traffic Offenders, Says London Paper," *Daily News Egypt* (2008; http://emiguel.econ.berkeley.edu/assets /miguel_media/60/ParkingTicket_DNE20081210.pdf).

3. "Foreign Diplomats Owe Huge Parking Fine Debt," *The Local: Sweden's News in English* (August 17, 2012; www.thelocal.se/20120817/42678).

4. Emily Wyman and Hannes Rakoczy, "Social Conventions, Institutions, and Human Uniqueness: Lessons from Children and Chimpanzees," in *Interdisciplinary Anthropology* (Berlin, Heidelberg: Springer, 2011), 131–56.

5. R. Fisman and Edward Miguel, *Economic Gangsters: Corruption, Violence, and the Poverty of Nations* (Princeton: Princeton University Press, 2008).

6. One person who witnessed one of Sutton's robberies said that it was like being at the movies, except the usher had a gun.

7. The Corruption Perceptions Index data can be found at Transparency International's website: http://cpi.transparency.org/cpi2012/results/.

8. In ancient Greek mythology, Sisyphus was a cruel king condemned to spend eternity rolling a huge stone up a hill in Hades, only to have it roll back down as he neared the top.

9. D. Acemoglu and J. Robinson, *Why Nations Fail: The Origins of Power, Prosperity, and Poverty* (New York: Random House Digital, 2012).

10. For more of this institutional view of domestic violence and economic development, see D. C. North, J. J. Wallis, S. B. Webb, and B. R. Weingast, eds., *In the Shadow of Violence: Politics, Economics and the Problems of Development* (Cambridge: Cambridge University Press, 2012).

11. J. Sachs, "Review Essay: Government, Geography and Growth—The True Drivers of Economic Development," *Foreign Affairs* 91, no. 5 (2012): 142–50.

12. William Easterly, "Institutions: Top Down or Bottom Up?" *American Economic Review* 98, no. 2 (2008):95–99.

13. Peter J. Boettke and Christopher J. Coyne, "Entrepreneurship and Development: Cause or Consequence?" *Advances in Austrian Economics* 6 (2003):67–87.

CHAPTER 9

1. The full lecture is available at www.nobelprize.org/nobel_prizes /economic-sciences/laureates/1979/schultz-lecture.html.

2. This point was made by Peter Timmer in his paper, "The Agricultural Transformation," published as chapter 8 in the *Handbook of Development Economics,* vol. 1, edited by H. Chenery and T.N. Srinivasan (Amsterdam: Elsevier Science, 1988), 275–331.

3. Christopher B. Barrett, "Smallholder Market Participation: Concepts and Evidence from Eastern and Southern Africa," *Food Policy* 33 (2008):299–317.

4. Gregg Easterbrook, "Forgotten Benefactor of Humanity," *Atlantic,* January 1997 (www.theatlantic.com/magazine/archive/1997/01/forgotten-benefactor-of-humanity/306101/).

5. United Nations Food and Agricultural Organization (FAO).

6. Again, the full text of this lecture is available here: www.nobelprize.org /nobel_prizes/economic-sciences/laureates/1979/schultz-lecture.html.

7. Adam Smith, *An Inquiry into the Nature and Causes of the Wealth of Nations,* edited by Edwin Cannan (reprint, 1904; London: Methuen, 1776). The quotation is the title of book 1, sec. 3.

8. www.oxfam.org/en/emergencies/east-africa-food-crisis/famine-somalia-what-needs-be-done.

CHAPTER 10

1. www.fao.org/about/en/.

2. The terms "rural" and "urban" are problematic. At what population does a village become a town? (Many governments, including the US Bureau of the Census, use 2,500 as the cutoff.) As expanding roads, communications, and markets integrate town and country, the distinction becomes ever more blurred.

3. "Transition day," as this day has become known, is largely symbolic. The date was estimated from the UN's prediction that the world would be 51.3% urban by 2010. Researchers at North Carolina State University and the University of Georgia interpolated the transition date by using the average daily rural and urban population increases from 2005 to 2010.

4. E. Jonasson, M. Filipski, J. Brooks, and J.E. Taylor, "Modeling the Welfare Implications of Agricultural Policies in Developing Countries," *Journal of Policy Modeling* 36, no. 1 (2014):63–82.

5. Aslihan Arslan and J. Edward Taylor, "Transforming Rural Economies: Migration, Income Generation and Inequality in Rural Mexico," *Journal of Development Studies* 48, no. 8 (2011):1156–76.

6. US Department of Labor, National Agricultural Worker Survey (NAWS) (www.doleta.gov/agworker/naws.cfm).

7. Francisco and his family are a composite constructed from field surveys carried out by researchers at UC Davis and the Colegio de México in Mexico City.

8. W. Arthur Lewis, "Economic Development with Unlimited Supplies of Labour," *Manchester School* 22, no. 2 (1954):139–91.

9. Gustav Ranis and John C. H. Fei, "A Theory of Economic Development," *American Economic Review* 60 (September 1961):533–65.

10. In a subsistence household, on the other hand, raising productivity can free up family time for other activities, including wage work.

11. C. Peter Timmer, "The Agricultural Transformation," chapter 8 in *Handbook of Development Economics,* vol. 1, edited by H. Chenery and T. N. Srinivasan (Amsterdam: Elsevier Science, 1988).

12. J. Mellor, *The New Economics of Growth* (Ithaca, NY: Cornell University Press, 1976).

13. Jan Nijman, "A Study of Space in Mumbai's Slums," *Tijdschrift voor economische en sociale geografie* 101, no. 1 (February 2010):4–17.

14. United Nations Human Settlements Programme, *The Challenge of Slums: Global Report on Human Settlements 2003* (London and Sterling, VA: Earthscan, 2003).

15. The World Bank has a dedicated website on urban development: www. worldbank.org/en/topic/urbandevelopment.

16. John R. Harris and Michael P. Todaro, "Migration, Unemployment, and Development: A Two-Sector Analysis," *American Economic Review* 60 (1970):126–42.

17. The best introduction to building CGE models is Mary Burfischer, *Introduction to Computable General Equilibrium Models* (Cambridge: Cambridge University Press, 2011).

### CHAPTER 11

1. George A. Akerlof, "The Market for 'Lemons': Quality Uncertainty and the Market Mechanism," *Quarterly Journal of Economics* 84, no. 3 (1970):488–500.

2. George A. Akerlof, "Writing the 'The Market for "Lemons"'": A Personal and Interpretive Essay" (www.nobelprize.org/nobel_prizes/economics/laureates /2001/akerlof-article.htm).

3. United States Food and Drug Administration (www.fda.gov/Food/Inter nationalInteragencyCoordination/default.htm).

4. European Commission, "Health and Consumers" (http://ec.europa.eu /food/food/chemicalsafety/residues/third_countries_en.htm).

5. www2.merriam-webster.com/cgi-bin/mwthesadu?book=Dictionary&va= market.

6. www.oxforddictionaries.com/us/definition/american_english/market.

7. "Labor: U.S. Fruits and Vegetables," *Rural Migration News* 17, no. 1 (January 2011) (http://migration.ucdavis.edu/rmn/more.php?id = 1596_0_5_0).

8. Joseph E. Stiglitz, "Smith's 'Invisible Hand' a Myth?" Address to the Commonwealth Club of San Francisco (February 22, 2010; www.youtube. com/watch?v=9qjvwQrZmpk).

9. Christopher B. Barrett, "Smallholder Market Participation: Concepts and Evidence from Eastern and Southern Africa," *Food Policy* 33, no. 4 (2008): 299–317.

10. Friedrich August Hayek, *The Fatal Conceit: The Errors of Socialism* (Chicago: University of Chicago Press, 2011).

11. Ibid.

CHAPTER 12

1. Alberto Chaia, Aparna Dalal, Tony Goland, Maria Jose Gonzalez, Jonathan Morduch, and Robert Schiff, "Half the World Is Unbanked" (Financial Access Initiative Framing Note, October 2009; http://financialaccess.org /sites/default/files/110109%20HalfUnbanked_0.pdf).

2. See http://go.worldbank.org/OSAT4FHFP0.

3. We are indebted to Steve Boucher for coming up with this intriguing comparison.

4. You can see a cool example in *RebelText: Essentials of Econometrics,* chapter 7 (rebeltext.org).

5. "Glut Leads Lawyers to (Surprise) Sue Law Schools," *Businessweek,* March 23, 2012 (www.businessweek.com/articles/2012-03-23/glut-leads-lawyers-to-surprise-sue-law-schools).

6. Karla Hoff and Joseph E. Stiglitz, "Introduction. Imperfect Information and Rural Credit Markets: Puzzles and Policy Perspectives," *World Bank Economic Review* 4, no. 3 (1990):235–50.

7. www.nobelprize.org/nobel_prizes/peace/laureates/2006/presentation-speech .html.

8. Hans P. Binswanger, "Attitudes toward Risk: Experimental Measurement in Rural India," *American Journal of Agricultural Economics* 62, no. 3 (August 1980):395–407.

9. Laura Schechter, "Risk Aversion and Expected-Utility Theory: A Calibration Exercise," *Journal of Risk and Uncertainty* 35, no. 1 (2007):67–76.

CHAPTER 13

1. David Ricardo, *The Principles of Political Economy and Taxation* (reprint, 1965; London: J. M. Dent and Son, 1817).

2. You can pretty much always make two things have the same price by redefining their units—like pricing beer in six-packs instead of bottles or chocolate in ounces instead of pounds.

3. Some of the major dependency texts include Paul A. Baran, "On the Political Economy of Backwardness," *Manchester School* 20, no. 1 (1952):66–84; Andre Gunder Frank, *The Development of Underdevelopment* (Boston: New England Free Press, 1966); Immanuel M. Wallerstein, *World-Systems Analysis: An Introduction* (Durham, NC: Duke University Press, 2004).

4. The IMF makes loans to bail out countries that cannot make good on their foreign debts, and it will not do this unless countries agree to enact policy changes that the IMF thinks are needed to make them more solvent.

5. The World Trade Organization, International Trade Statistics (www.wto .org/english/news_e/pres12_e/pr658_e.htm).

6. Pew Research Center, "The Rising Cost of Not Going to College" (February 2014; www.pewsocialtrends.org/2014/02/11/the-rising-cost-of-not-going-to-college/).

7. Ha-Joon Chang, "Kicking Away the Ladder," *Post-Autistic Economics Review* 15 (September 4, 2002) (www.paecon.net/PAEtexts/Chang1.htm).

8. World Trade Organization, "Understanding the WTO: Basics: What Is the World Trade Organization?" (www.wto.org/english/thewto_e/whatis_e /tif_e/fact1_e.htm).

9. The Royal Tropical Institute (KIT), Faida MaLi, the International Institute for Rural Reconstruction (IIRR), and L. Peppelenbos, eds., *Chain Empowerment: Supporting African Farmers to Develop Markets* (Amsterdam: KIT, 2006; www.kit.nl/kit/Publication?item=1952).

10. The Fair Labor Association's website is www.fairlabor.org/.

11. It is difficult to separate labor migration from migration for other motives, for example, accompanying a spouse or parents abroad.

12. C. Woodruff and R. Zenteno, "Migration Networks and Microenterprises in Mexico," *Journal of Development Economics* 82, no. 2 (2007): 509–28.

13. World Bank, data, personal remittances received (% of GDP) (http:// data.worldbank.org/indicator/BX.TRF.PWKR.DT.GD.ZS).

14. World Bank, data, imports of goods and services (% of GDP) (http:// data.worldbank.org/indicator/NE.IMP.GNFS.ZS).

15. Stuart Price, "Reversing the Brain Drain," *All Business.com* (November 1, 2004; http://archive.is/5orQF).

16. Onlineuniversities.com, "10 Countries Facing the Biggest Brain Drain" (www.onlineuniversities.com/blog/2011/07/10-countries-facing-the-biggest-brain-drain/).

17. Ibid.

18. Commission on Filipinos Overseas, "Stock Estimate of Overseas Filipinos as of Dec. 2012" (www.cfo.gov.ph/index.php?option=com_content&view =article&id=1340:stock-estimate-of-overseas-filipinos&catid=134).

19. Oded Stark, Christian Helmenstein, and Alexia Prskawetz, "A Brain Gain with a Brain Drain," *Economics Letters* 55, no. 2 (1997):227–34.

20. Oded Stark and Yong Wang, "Inducing Human Capital Formation: Migration as a Substitute for Subsidies," *Journal of Public Economics* 86 (2002):29–46.

21. Michel Beine, Frédéric Docquier, and Hillel Rapoport, "Brain Drain and Economic Growth: Theory and Evidence," *Journal of Development Economics* 64, no. 1 (2001):275–89.

22. http://archive.fortune.com/magazines/fortune/fortune_archive/1992/12 /28/77310/index.htm.

23. *International Migration and Development—Report of the Secretary-General* (United Nations General Assembly, Sixtieth Session, May 18, 2006; www.unhcr.org/44d711a82.html).

24. For simplicity, we refer to international aid from governments as ODA, but in practice there are other official aid flows that are classified separately.

25. See www.opic.gov/.

26. International Fund for Agricultural Development, *Rural Poverty Report 2011* (www.ifad.org/RPR2011/index_full.htm).

27. http://foodaid.org/resources/the-history-of-food-aid/.

28. See Christopher B. Barrett and Daniel G. Maxwell, *Food Aid after Fifty Years: Recasting Its Role* (London: Routledge, 2005); Christopher Barrett, "How to Get Food Aid Right," *CNN World* (http://globalpublicsquare.blogs.cnn.com/2013/05/06/how-to-get-food-aid-right/).

29. As economists like to point out, there is no free lunch. This conventional wisdom often applies even to food aid recipients. Long lines at distribution depots and other features that impose opportunity costs on recipients are often used in an attempt to ensure that those with the greatest need receive the food.

30. See G. Frazer, "Used-Clothing Donations and Apparel Production in Africa," *Economic Journal* 118, no. 532 (2008):1764–84. As you might expect, good data on used clothing donations and imports are tough to come by, and any rigorous analysis is fraught with potential data problems; see A. Brooks and D. Simon, "Unraveling the Relationships between Used-Clothing Imports and the Decline of African Clothing Industries," *Development and Change* 43, no. 6 (2012):1262–90.

### CHAPTER 14

1. For example, see Pat Bailey, "Tiny Packets of Hope: UC Davis Leads Efforts against Malnutrition with a $16 Million Gates Foundation Grant," *UCDAVIS Magazine Online* 27, no. 2 (Winter 2010) (http://ucdavismagazine.ucdavis.edu/issues/win10/tiny_packets_of_hope.html).

2. Douglas S. Massey, Joaquin Arango, Graeme Hugo, Ali Kouaouci, Adela Pellegrino, and J. Edward Taylor, *Worlds in Motion: Understanding International Migration at the End of the Millennium* (Oxford: Oxford University Press, 1999).

3. A. Mani, S. Mullainathan, E. Shafir, and J. Zhao, "Poverty Impedes Cognitive Function," *Science* 341, no. 6149 (2013):976–80.

4. Adam Smith, *An Inquiry into the Nature and Causes of the Wealth of Nations*, edited by Edwin Cannan (reprint, 1904; London: Methuen, 1776); E. L. Khalil, "Beyond Natural Selection and Divine Intervention: The Lamarckian Implication of Adam Smith's Invisible Hand," *Journal of Evolutionary Economics* 10, no. 4 (2000):373–93.

# Index

Tables, figures, and sidebars are indicated by *t*, *f*, and *b* after the page number, respectively.

CPSIA information can be obtained
at www.ICGtesting.com
Printed in the USA
LVHW03*1237200618
581130LV00003B/44/P